New Frontiers in Forensic Linguistics

Themes and Perspectives in Language and Law in Africa and beyond

EDITORS
Monwabisi K. Ralarala
Russell H. Kaschula
Georgina Heydon

New Frontiers in Forensic Linguistics:
Themes and Perspectives in Language and Law in Africa and beyond

Published by AFRICAN SUN MeDIA under the SUN PReSS imprint

All rights reserved

Copyright © 2019 AFRICAN SUN MeDIA and the editors

This publication was subjected to an independent double-blind peer evaluation by the publisher.

The editors and the publisher have made every effort to obtain permission for and acknowledge the use of copyrighted material. Refer all enquiries to the publisher.

No part of this book may be reproduced or transmitted in any form or by any electronic, photographic or mechanical means, including photocopying and recording on record, tape or laser disk, on microfilm, via the Internet, by e-mail, or by any other information storage and retrieval system, without prior written permission by the publisher.

Views reflected in this publication are not necessarily those of the publisher.

First edition 2019

ISBN 978-1-928480-16-7
ISBN 978-1-928480-17-4 (e-book)
https://doi.org/10.18820/9781928480174

Set in Warnock Pro Light 10/14.5
Cover design, typesetting and production by AFRICAN SUN MeDIA

SUN PReSS is a licensed imprint of AFRICAN SUN MeDIA. Scholarly, professional and reference works are published under this imprint in print and electronic format.

This publication can be ordered directly from:
www.sun-e-shop.co.za
www.africansunmedia.store.it.si (e-books)
www.africansunmedia.co.za

CONTENTS

Dedication vii

Acknowledgements ix

About the editors xi

Foreword xiii

Introduction 1

Part 1 | Police investigative interviewing

1   Incarcerated, incriminated or vindicated? An investigation into
    socio-pragmatic elements of police interviewing 15
    Monwabisi K. Ralarala & Theo Rodrigues

2   Tell us the story in your Portuguese, we can understand you:
    The Mozambican justice system's dilemma in enforcement of the
    sole official language policy 33
    Eliseu Mabasso

Part 2 | Language practice in the legal process

3   "Like giving a wheelchair to someone who should be walking":
    Interpreter access and the problematisation of linguistic diversity
    in the justice system 51
    Joseph MacFarlane, Ceyhan Sirma Kurt, Georgina Heydon & Andy Roh

4   Monolingual language of record: A critique of South Africa's new
    policy directive 71
    Zakeera Docrat & Russell H. Kaschula

5   Multilingualism in the South African legal system:
    Attorneys' experiences 89
    Annelise de Vries & Zakeera Docrat

6   Justice in the mother tongue: The task of court interpreters in
    Ghanaian law courts 113
    Mercy Akrofi Ansah & Prince Ofei Darko

7   Language and the right of access to procedural justice
    in South Africa 147
    Noleen Leach

Part 3 | Language as evidence

8   Judges as language referees for Caribbean English
    vernacular speakers: How do they score? 149
    Celia Brown-Blake

9   A Zimbabwean perspective on the effect of interpreter-initiated turns:
    Interactional dynamics in the adversarial courtroom 175
    Paul Svongoro & Kim Wallmach

10 Conflicts emanating from the translation and interpretation of
    the term "domicile": For consumers in the South African context 219
    Stanley Madonsela

11 Interpreters' renditions in Zimbabwean courtrooms: A corpus-based
    analysis from frequency profiles to key semantic domains 199
    Paul Svongoro & Patson Kufakunesu

Part 4 | Forensic linguistic evidence

12 Road markers for reliability in authorship identification evidence 241
    Lirieka Meintjes-van der Walt

13 The act of threatening: Applying Speech Act Theory to threat texts 255
    Karien van den Berg & Michelle Surmon

    Appendix: Text of Unabomber's Letter received by the *New York Times*
    26 April 1995 278

14 Sign language and hate speech: The potential pitfalls of iconic signs 279
    Terrence R. Carney

15 A case of crying wolf? A linguistic approach to evaluating
    hate speech allegations as linguistic acts of violence 301
    Karien van den Berg

About the contributors 327

LIST OF FIGURES

Figure 2.1	The PEACE Model	37
Figure 5.1	Legal practitioners' language attitudes and experiences of multilingualism in the legal profession	102
Figure 5.2	Legal practitioners' language attitudes and experiences regarding translation and interpretation	103
Figure 5.3	Legal practitioners' language attitudes and experiences regarding the interests of their clients	104
Figure 5.4	Legal practitioners' language attitudes and experiences concerning transformation in the legal profession	105
Figure 9.1	Relative occurrence of interpreter-initiated turns	184
Figure 10.1	The partitions of private law	204
Figure 11.1	Proportion of content vs grammatical words in the Shona-only corpus	223
Figure 11.2	Key word cloud for the English-only corpus compared to the BNC sampler (spoken)	228
Figure 11.3	Key word cloud for the Shona-only corpus compared to the BNC sampler (spoken)	228
Figure 11.4	Key domain cloud of the English-only corpus compared to the BNC sampler (spoken)	229
Figure 11.5	Comparative occurrence of "but"/"so" prefaced questions	232
Figure 13.1	The developmental stages of written textual threats	258
Figure 14.1	*Know* in South African Sign Language	283
Figure 14.2	*Name* in South African Sign Language	284
Figure 14.3	Transparent iconic signs in South African Sign Language	285
Figure 14.4	Non-transparent iconic signs in South African Sign Language	285
Figure 14.5	*Person(s) with disability* in British Sign Language	287
Figure 14.6	*Jew* in Afrikaans and Flemish Sign Language	288
Figure 14.7	*Native American* in Flemish Sign Sign Language	289

LIST OF TABLES

Table 1.1	Transcription symbols	23
Table 2.1	Profile of main languages of Mozambique	34
Table 4.1	National language demographics of South Africa	78
Table 4.2	Legal Aid South Africa: 2016 survey on the primary spoken language in criminal matters	78
Table 4.3	Legal Aid South Africa: 2016 survey on the primary spoken language in civil matters	79
Table 4.4	Legal Aid South Africa: 2016 language survey on English proficiency in criminal cases	79
Table 4.5	Legal Aid South Africa: 2016 language survey on English proficiency in civil cases	80
Table 5.1	Clients' English proficiency from the perspective of the legal practitioner	98
Table 5.2	Summary of clients' English proficiency from the perspective of the legal practitioner	98
Table 5.3	Legal Aid South Africa's 2016 survey on English skills in criminal and civil cases	99
Table 5.4	Results of questionnaire on attorneys' language attitudes, needs and choices	100
Table 5.5	Summary of the Lickert scale data from the questionnaire	105
Table 5.6	Average scores for multilingualism per province	106
Table 5.7	Statistical relation between attorneys' language preference and multilingualism: Most used at home	107
Table 5.8	Statistical relation between attorneys' language preference and multilingualism: Most used in social circles	107
Table 5.9	Statistical relation between attorneys' language preference and multilingualism: Most used in oral communication	107
Table 5.10	Statistical relation between attorneys' language preference and multilingualism: Most used in communicating with colleagues	107

Table 5.11	Statistical relation between attorneys' language preference and multilingualism: Most used in written communication	108
Table 5.12	Statistical relation between language proficiency and multilingualism: Attorneys' English reading and writing skills	108
Table 5.13	Statistical relation between language proficiency and multilingualism: Attorneys' English-speaking skills	108
Table 5.14	Statistical relation between language proficiency and multilingualism: Clients' English reading and writing skills	109
Table 5.15	Statistical relation between language proficiency and multilingualism: Clients' English-speaking skills	109
Table 6.1	Professional background of interpreters in Ghanaian courts	120
Table 6.2	Language backgrounds of judge and magistrates	122
Table 9.1	Elements of transcription notation used in the Extracts	182
Table 9.2	Types of interpreter-initiated turns and frequency of occurrence	184
Table 11.1	A word-frequency list showing types on the left and tokens on the right	217
Table 11.2	Sample concordances for "pants" from the study's corpus of rape trials	218
Table 11.3	AKWIC display of the concordances retrieved for the search pattern "complainant"	219
Table 11.4	Shona-only corpus showing the distribution and frequency of the top 10 words	223
Table 11.5	Six of the 26 occurrences of the search term "rape" in the English corpus	224
Table 11.6	Six of the 20 occurrences of the search term *chibharo* (rape) in the Shona corpus	224
Table 11.7	Five of the 556 occurrences of the pronoun "you" in the English corpus	225
Table 11.8	Top 5 of the 31 occurrences in the Shona corpus of the pronoun *iwe* ("you" singular)	225

Table 11.9   Top 2 of the 33 occurrences in the Shona corpus of the
             pronoun *imimi* ("you" in the emphatic form) 226

Table 11.10 Top 7 of the 187 occurrences of the pronoun "she"
             in the English corpus 226

Table 11.11 Top 5 of the 44 occurrences of the pronoun *iye*
             ("he/she" or sometimes "now" in English) 226

Table 11.12 The use of "then"– prefaced questions 233

DEDICATION
to Nandipha Bruella Gila

We wish to dedicate this special volume to Ms Nandipha Bruella Gila, whose tragic and untimely death in November 2018 left us devastated. Nandi, a PhD student of Professor Ralarala, was on the cusp of completing her doctoral degree; and her research topic, "Codeswitching discourse in police investigative interviewing in the Eastern Cape" (registered with the University of Fort Hare), belongs in our growing field of forensic linguistics/language and the law in South Africa. She was the first candidate we have encountered who was working in the niche area of police interviewing in South Africa, following Professor Ralarala. Her passing is a great loss to her family, to the Dutywa community, to South Africa, and to the entire academic community. We sincerely hope that recognising and dedicating this volume to her will partly assist the family in their healing process and help to bring some part of their loss to closure. May her soul rest in peace.

ACKNOWLEDGEMENTS

We started thinking about this book while attending a conference in Portugal at the University of Porto. The idea was finally consolidated at a subsequent conference held at the Lagoon Beach Hotel in Cape Town, South Africa. This was the First Southern African Regional Conference of the International Association of Forensic Linguists, held in April 2018.

Primarily, we would like to acknowledge the contributing authors and co-authors who have ensured that the project did not remain merely an idea, but became reality, as planned. We are indebted to each one of you.

Peer review is the lifeblood of academic scholarship. The editors of this book would like to express their genuine gratitude to thirty-four anonymous peer reviewers – drawn from international and local universities – who took the time to engage profoundly and meticulously with the review process. All the chapters in this book have been subjected to the rigorous process of anonymous peer review.

Working with Ms Denise February (Fundani CHED) in the initial stage of this project was a rewarding experience. Her project administration skills and willingness to go the extra mile brought us the success that we are witnessing in as far as this project is concerned. Ms Onele Tshaka, too, deserves our gratitude for being both our right and left hand in the administration of our work throughout the project.

We would also like to thank our friends and colleagues from our respective Centres, Departments and Schools for their moral support and fascinating discussions on a series of topics that inspired our debates on forensic linguistics/language and the law.

The National Heritage Council also deserves our sincere gratitude for their generous funding of our project. The project would not have flourished without their support.

We are also indebted to the Cape Peninsula University of Technology's Fundani Centre for Higher Education Development, as well as to the Senate Language Committee under the Chairmanship of Professor Anthony Staak, for supporting the hosting of the conference, as well as providing recommendations on funding for the publication of this book.

We wish to express our appreciation to Dr Jenny Wright who served as a critical reader for this volume. Her thorough grounding in editing has served the project well in ensuring additional quality control for this work.

We are also grateful to our publisher, Emily Vosloo from AFRICAN SUN MeDIA, for her patience, enthusiasm and willingness to work with us in meeting the deadlines of this project.

ABOUT THE EDITORS

Monwabisi K. Ralarala, is Director of the Fundani Centre for Higher Education Development at the Cape Peninsula University of Technology. He is an Associate Professor, an NRF-rated researcher (C2), and Chairperson of the African Language Association of South Africa. Previous positions include: Director: Language Centre, University of Fort Hare; Chairperson, Western Cape Language Committee; Director of Research and Policy Development, Commission for the Promotion and Protection of the Rights of Cultural, Religious and Linguistic Communities; and Lecturer, Department of African Languages, University of Stellenbosch. He is a Canon Collins Educational and Legal Assistance Trust Alumnus; the 2017 recipient of the Neville Alexander Award for the Promotion of Multilingualism; and holds two PhDs (Universities of Stellenbosch and Free State respectively) on persuasion in African Languages and in Language Practice, with emphasis on forensic linguistics. His diverse research interests follow three lines: language rights and multilingualism in higher education; forensic linguistics; and translation studies. He has held positions of visiting scholar, both national and international. He has also published in journals and books, mainly in forensic linguistics, and translation studies. He is co-editor of *African language and language practice research in the 21st century: Interdisciplinary themes and perspectives* (CASAS, 2017).

Russell H. Kaschula is Professor of African Language Studies at Rhodes University, where he has been awarded both Vice Chancellor's Distinguished Senior Teaching and Vice Chancellor's Distinguished Senior Research awards. He holds the NRF SARChI Chair in the Intellectualisation of African Languages, Multilingualism and Education. He has published widely in the field of applied language studies and literature, and is an award-winning creative writer. He has a particular interest in language and law; his interest in forensic linguistics stems from his background in law and African languages. He is the 2019 Mellon Global South Senior Fellow at the American University in Cairo, Egypt.

Georgina Heydon is an Associate Professor of Criminology and Justice Studies at the Royal Melbourne Institute of Technology, and President of the International Association of Forensic Linguists. Her work focuses on the discourse and conversational structures of police interviews and other forms of crime reporting. She is an internationally recognised expert in the field of forensic linguistics and investigative interviewing. She has published numerous academic papers and a book, *The language of police interviewing: A critical analysis* (Palgrave Macmillan, 2005), on the topic of interviewing and information. As a forensic linguist, she provides expert evidence on authorship attribution, threat identification and in commercial trademark cases. She has delivered interviewing training and advice to police and legal professionals in Australia, Sweden, Belgium, Indonesia, Mozambique and Canada, and to members of Australian judicial colleges and tribunals, as well as to lawyers and corporate clients.

FOREWORD

Africa has extreme linguistic richness, diversity and complexity. Furthermore, it has a varied, if troubled, colonial history, which led to the introduction of European language legal systems. This means Africa is of great potential interest for forensic linguistics. Yet this is poorly recognised outside Africa.

One problem is the poor communication between the Francophone, Anglophone and Lusophone academic communities (not to mention work published in other languages such as Swahili and Arabic). This poor recognition comes from both sides – the introduction to this collection mentions that many African scholars are unaware of the rapidly expanding body of forensic linguistic work elsewhere. This collection of papers will go some way to address this unfortunate situation.

There has been significant African publication on forensic linguistic issues, particularly by lawyers in South Africa, see for example Müller & Newman (1997), and recent work by Ralarala (Ralarala & Kaschula, 2004; Ralarala, 2014; 2016 and 2017). There is also well known and widely referenced work such as Moeketsi (1999) and Moeketsi and Mollema (2006) on courtroom interpreting. In this collection, it is also interesting to see Brown-Blake's paper from the African diaspora.

The richness of this collection can be seen in the way it addresses many important themes in Forensic Linguistics. There are several chapters on two forensic linguistic issues in multilingual societies – police interviewing and legal interpreting. Other chapters address linguistic minorities in the courtroom, the language of record in courts, language attitudes amongst lawyers, legal literacy, language as evidence, and hate speech. Many of these themes can be tied to social justice in the legal system, and equality before the law, particularly for those for whom the language of the legal system is opaque.

This means that this collection is a timely and significant contribution to the field of Forensic Linguistics in general, but more importantly it fosters greater social justice before the law in Africa.

John Gibbons
(Adjunct Professor, Monash University, Australia)

References

Moeketsi, R.H. 1999. *Discourse in a multilingual and multicultural courtroom: A court interpreter's guide*. Pretoria: Van Schaik.

Moeketsi, R.H. & Mollema, N. 2006. Towards a perfect practice in South African court interpreting: A quality assurance and quality management model. *International Journal for Speech Language and the Law*, 13(1):76-88.

Müller, K. & Newman, S. (eds.). 1997. *Language in court*. Port Elizabeth: Vista University.

Kaschula, R.H. & Ralarala, M.K. 2004. Language rights, intercultural communication and the law in South Africa. *South African Journal of African Languages*, 24(4):252-261.

Ralarala, M.K. 2014. Transpreters' translation of complainants' narratives as evidence: Whose version goes to court? *The Translator*, 20(3):377-395.

Ralarala, M.K. 2016. An analysis of critical "voices" and "styles" in *transpreters*' translations of complainants' narratives. *Translation and Translanguaging in Multilingual Contexts*, 2(1):142-166. https://doi.org/10.1075/ttmc.2.1.08ral.

Ralarala, M.K. 2017. Language and law: Cultural translation' of narratives into sworn statements. In *Multilingualism and intercultural communication: A South African perspective*, R.H. Kaschula, P. Maseko & E. Wolff, pp. 211-222. Johannesburg: Wits University Press.

INTRODUCTION

Developments on the New Frontiers of Forensic Linguistics

*Monwabisi K. Ralarala, Russell H. Kaschula
& Georgina Heydon*

Background

In July 2017, a group of sociolinguists, aspiring forensic linguists, and language practice specialists from Southern Africa met in Portugal at the 13th Biennial Conference of the International Association of Forensic Linguists at the University of Porto. At the conference, it became apparent that there was a need to host a similar professional meeting in Southern Africa in the following year. The group undertook to host the First Southern African Regional Conference of the International Association of Forensic Linguists in South Africa in April 2018, led by the Cape Peninsula University of Technology (CPUT) in affiliation with Rhodes University (NRF SARChI Chair in African Languages), the University of South Africa (UNISA) and University Eduardo Mondlane (UEM). This volume was born out of a collection of papers presented at the conference.

Although the literature of forensic linguistics – broadly known as the interface of language and the law – is fairly well known to scholars in the United States of America, the United Kingdom and Australia, it is often (in our experience) virtually unknown to African scholars, and as a matter of fact the field is in its infancy in Southern Africa in particular, with a handful of universities introducing the field as an academic programme offered within the respective domains of applied language studies, language practice, paralegal studies and applied linguistics, to mention but a few.

A central purpose of this book is to bring together significant scholarly contributions to knowledge that collectively affirms fundamental issues of an applied nature and which have a direct bearing on legal practice – not only in terms of legal recognition of cross-cultural communication, but also addressing serious considerations of language as evidence; language in the legal process; and the promotion and protection of previously marginalised (minority) languages within the criminal justice system.

The novelty of this book is not only in its grounding in interdisciplinary studies, but in its dominant share of contributions hailing from Africa (Ghana, Mozambique, Zimbabwe and largely South Africa): a deliberate strategy primarily meant to address the scanty research and gaps of knowledge in language and the law in the region. Views originating from the other sides of the oceans (Australia and the Caribbean) bring another fresh perspective to the debate and to this book.

Developments on the new frontiers of Forensic Linguistics

More than simply expanding the geographical reach of forensic linguistics, this volume is representative of the new spheres of influence of forensic linguistic research. Traditionally, the topics addressed within the field of forensic linguistics have been of interest to linguists and, to a lesser degree, lawyers. Even within linguistics, there has been surprisingly little uptake of research frameworks or innovations emerging from the forensic linguistic literature.

William Labov's highly cited contributions to forensic linguistics, regarding the use of African-American varieties of English in New York schools (Labov, 1972), was followed by a considerable volume of published research in forensic linguistic topics. Despite this, in the intervening years, linguistics and applied linguistics associations and conferences, and also producers of textbooks, have been slow to embrace research that addresses questions concerning language and the law. It has been a long road towards mainstream acceptance of forensic linguistic research as a suitable pursuit for linguists but, in 2018, forensic linguistics was given its own stream amongst the parallel sessions at the annual conference of the American Association for Applied Linguistics (AAAL) in Chicago. Notably too, the AAAL Inaugural Distinguished Public Service Award went to a judge, the Honourable Ida K. Chen and the Interpreter Program Administrator of her court, Mr Osvaldo Aviles.

From 2016, the Australian Linguistics Society and the Applied Linguistics Association of Australia have included a forensic linguistics session in their combined annual conference, with strong support from the organisers. Beyond the academic fraternity in linguistics and applied linguistics, Australian legal practitioners, notably the judiciary, have also been at the forefront of engagement in language issues. The Australian Northern Territory Supreme Court hosted a "Language and the Law" conference involving judges, lawyers, interpreters, linguists, police and paralegal agencies. This remarkable event was the first of its kind in Australia – and perhaps the world. Part academic conference, part professional development workshop, and part policy summit, the event will be held for a third time as this book goes to press, this time in the central Australian town of Alice Springs.

As mentioned, legal scholars have always maintained an interest in language, and the International Association of Forensic Linguists (IAFL) has welcomed legal practitioners as members from its earliest days. There are also societies and conferences on legal rhetoric and the semiotics of law. These topics intersect with those of interest to forensic linguists, but while lawyers are interested in the interpretation of texts to resolve legal problems, linguists will always be more focused on systematic analysis of the language according to theories of language structure and use. This has led to a certain degree of distance between these two seemingly cognate disciplines: closing the gap between legal scholars of language and linguistic scholars of the law is an important step towards broader recognition of the contribution to be made by forensic linguists.

Turning from the disciplines of linguistics and law towards research into crime and justice, more recent developments in this field warrant closer attention by the forensic linguistics community. A significant amount of work now being published on police interview training and practices reflects collaboration between linguists, psychologists and scholars of policing (see for instance Oxburgh, Myklebust, Grant & Milne, 2016). The analysis of naturally occurring language data, especially the institutional discourse structures of a police interview, is well suited to linguistic research. Additionally, in a multilingual society, the engagement of interpreters has been a critically important step towards equality before the law for all people. Linguists who understand legal or justice discourse processes as well as theories of language acquisition are well-placed to work alongside scholars of interpreting and translation to improve outcomes in the justice system. Finally, a more recent expansion of forensic linguistics has been in criminological research. With the advent of online text-based communications, there has been an explosion in the availability of vast quantities of language data which is influencing the nature of social science research generally, and criminological research in particular. Researchers are analysing justice outcomes or patterns of victimisation using blogs, social media posts, and even more traditional legal data, such as judges' decisions, published online in massive, publicly available corpora; and these data sets require linguistic tools to facilitate systematic analysis.

This volume represents collaboration across all the aforementioned disciplines, and thus it is pushing forward towards "new frontiers" – not only in forensic linguistics, but in law, policing, justice and criminology as well.

A further notable feature of both this volume and the conference in Cape Town in 2018, which has emerged since that event, is the collaboration between two continents: Africa and Australia. Although the link between forensic linguists in both continents is narrowly concentrated on a few individuals at present, there is clear evidence that a wide array of collaborative projects can flourish with further and deeper engagement. Perhaps it is the sheer level of diversity of the Australian linguistic landscape that encourages innovative responses, or perhaps it is the vast distances and challenges of life in a society characterised by remoteness, but there are relevant parallels between Australia and Africa that are worth exploring. Many of the themes addressed by African scholars in the following chapters are similarly of interest to Australian scholars. The multitude of Aboriginal languages in the north of Australia and the effects of colonisation on those language communities produce a crisis of communication in the courts very similar to that being experienced in South Africa and Mozambique, for example. However, the responses of each of these three countries to their linguistically diverse communities has been quite distinct. In South Africa, the massive social and political shift following the election of the African National Congress (ANC) in 1994 led to the recognition of eleven official languages and as a consequence, the South African justice system has been at the leading edge of language reform from the top down, with linguists and scholars in cognate disciplines scrambling to address the many complex communication issues that arise as a result. This contrasts strongly with the situation in most countries, including other African nations, where linguists work for many decades to achieve even modest changes to the justice system in terms of language recognition.

Nonetheless, whether working from the ground up to effect change, as in Australia and the many other colonised nations represented in the following chapters; or working to address changes brought by shifts in government policy, as in South Africa: linguists are still grappling with many of the same problems and utilising many of the same analytical frameworks as they work. Most importantly, as this collection is intended to demonstrate, there is opportunity for members of the dispersed community of forensic linguists in Africa, Australia and the Caribbean to share their experiences, and create new communities of practice, in research that addresses issues at the intersection of language and the law.

Outline and summary of chapters

The book encompasses four interconnected themes: Police investigative interviewing; Language practice in the legal process; Language as evidence; and Forensic linguistic evidence.

Part 1

The first part, comprising two chapters, deals with police investigative interviewing. It begins with a chapter by Monwabisi K. Ralarala and Theo Rodrigues entitled *Incarcerated, Incriminated or Vindicated? An investigation into socio-pragmatic elements of police interviewing*. Employment of a socio-pragmatic approach makes use of actual co-construction of record or sworn statements within a police station precinct, which are presented for evidential purposes and analysed. This research seeks to create an understanding of how selected interactional patterns and devices, meant to seek and obtain information during pre-statement sessions, contribute to incarceration, incrimination or vindication of the alleged perpetrator.

Chapter 2, authored by Eliseu Mabasso, is titled *Tell us the story in your Portuguese, we can understand you: The Mozambican justice system's dilemma in enforcement of the sole official language policy.* Mabasso points out that neither the country's Constitution, nor the various legal tools adopted in the country, clearly indicate how to communicate with Mozambican nationals who do not speak Portuguese, or who are not sufficiently competent in the language to communicate clearly when they appear at a police station or in a court of law. Data recorded in a police station and in the courtroom is used to highlight communicative challenges.

Part 2

This section of the book explores language practice in the legal process, and comprises five chapters.

Chapter 3 is innovatively titled *"Like giving a wheelchair to someone who should be walking": Interpreter access and the problematisation of linguistic diversity in the justice system.* In this chapter, authors Joseph MacFarlane, Ceyhan Sirma Kurt, Georgina Heydon and Andy Roh argue that while Australian society claims to celebrate and value cultural diversity, the same cannot always be said about the country's approach to non-English languages. With over 300 languages spoken, including more than 100 Indigenous languages, public institutions are faced with the challenge of recognising and catering for linguistic diversity in practice. A key approach in addressing this is the enhanced provision of interpreters. While improvements have been made in many government services, a notable exception is the justice system where, in legal settings, the provision of interpreters remains inadequate, both in terms of quantity and quality. Furthermore, the discretionary use of interpreters means that, even where qualified interpreters are available, they can still be underused in practice. Both problems are indicative of an ideology which privileges English monolingualism and suppresses the language practices and preferences of minority language speakers. This chapter addresses the practical concerns that this ideological position gives rise to and looks to promote an orientation which views linguistic diversity as a resource to be harnessed, rather than a "problem" to be overcome by imposing the normative standards of English monolingualism.

In Chapter 4, Zakeera Docrat and Russell H. Kaschula explore the challenges of language usage in South African courts, under the title *Monolingual language of record: A critique of South Africa's new policy directive.* They set out to interrogate and contextualise the contentious English-only "language of record" policy directive for South African courts, issued by the Chief Justice as the result of a decision made behind closed doors in 2017. The authors summarise the history of language usage in South African courts against the backdrop of colonialism and apartheid. The constitutional and legislative framework is also analysed to give appropriate context to the chapter. Furthermore, the authors provide the most recent language statistics related to participants in the law courts. The languages spoken by litigants are presented and critiqued in relation to the demographics of the nine South African provinces. Finally, recommendations are made and a way forward is proposed.

Annelise de Vries and Zakeera Docrat, in Chapter 5, present *Multilingualism in the South African legal system: Attorneys' experiences.* In 2017, the authors distributed a language survey amongst attorneys, accessed via four specific law societies, in an endeavour to gather data about the language attitudes and experiences of attorneys across all nine provinces in South Africa. The survey returned data for approximately 2 500 registered attorneys in South Africa. A primary purpose of this survey was to gauge whether attorneys felt obliged to communicate in English with their clients and colleagues, regardless of their mother tongue. The survey was conducted in light of the Chief Justice's policy directive in 2017 on the language of record, intended to make English the sole official language of record in South African high courts. After describing their findings, the authors conclude with recommendations on how to ensure transformation in the attitudes of legal practitioners towards language as a tool to enhance access to justice.

Mercy Akrofi Ansah and Prince Ofei Darko, in Chapter 6, present their study of *Justice in the mother tongue: The task of court interpreters in Ghanaian law courts.* Their research was conducted in relation to the 1992 Constitution (Republic of Ghana 1992) and the Interpreter's Oath under the Oaths Act (Ghana Legal 1972), and covered practices in five magistrate courts and two high courts in Accra. Interviews and discussions were conducted with court interpreters, magistrates, judges and lawyers. Observation notes of court proceedings are presented in this chapter. The authors argue that court interpreters who lack the necessary skills of interpretation impede the smooth running of court proceedings and could affect the outcome of a trial. The study therefore recommends rigorous professional training for court interpreters and substantial remuneration.

Noleen Leach, in Chapter 7, discusses *Language and the right of access to procedural justice in South Africa.* She explores the notion of literacy and legal literacy, and how it enables individuals and communities to obtain information, and to develop the knowledge and acquire the capability to access and navigate the various domains of social interaction, legal and otherwise, without having to rely completely on legal assistance. Knowledge of the law is a cornerstone of a true democracy. It is therefore argued in this chapter that it is essential for a functioning member of contemporary, highly regulated South African society to have a rudimentary understanding of the law in order to claim protection of the law, and even to obey it. However, barriers to access to justice, such as poverty and low levels of education, cement the legal isolation of the poor, and distort the power relations in legal disputes; this may result in violation of a person's right to a fair trial. Furthermore, the guarantee of protection, afforded by Section 35(3)(k) of the Constitution, seems to have been called into question by the controversial decision of the heads of courts to declare English the sole language of proceedings in the courts. The chapter explores how access to procedural justice in South Africa is measured, and examines how the courts interpret language and the right to a fair trial, and identifies emerging principles and practices around these concerns.

Part 3

The focus of the four chapters in this section is to examine and debate the notion of language as evidence.

Chapter 8, by Celia Brown-Blake, is titled *Judges as language referees for Caribbean English vernacular speakers: How do they score?* The author is concerned with the process of evaluation used by judicial officers in determining the linguistic proficiency of speakers of Caribbean English vernaculars, specifically Jamaican and Guyanese. These creole languages historically emerged from language contact situations between Africans and Europeans (predominantly English), within Caribbean slave plantation societies. The chapter furthermore examines three court cases arising from different jurisdictions – Jamaica (where Jamaican is widely spoken as the first language of the majority of the population); the United States of America (US); and Canada. The latter two jurisdictions are leading emigration and visitor destinations for many nationals of Caribbean countries. In Jamaica and the US, English is the official language of the judicial system. In Canada, English is also an official language of the court system. Using judgments, court memoranda and orders and other documentation issued by or filed in the relevant courts, the author analyses the judicial approaches to language proficiency evaluation of Caribbean English vernacular speakers against the background of sociolinguistic knowledge about the vernaculars and their speakers.

Paul Svongoro and Kim Wallmach, in Chapter 9, title their work *A Zimbabwean perspective on the effect of interpreter-initiated turns: Interactional dynamics in the adversarial courtroom.* The authors investigate how court officials' power to regulate turn-taking, ask questions and manipulate question forms by means of various rhetorical devices may be diminished if the meanings of questions are not reproduced in the interpreted version. This primary objective is achieved by analysing the frequent occurrence and use of specific conversational phenomena (turn-taking and questioning, for example) by the different court players, as well as how these phenomena were rendered by interpreters during court proceedings. The chapter draws on authentic courtroom data from Zimbabwean courtrooms, and illustrates how the court interpreter may exercise greater control over the discourse in the courtroom by initiating turns with the speaker(s), even though other bilingual court interlocutors may usurp the court interpreter's role. This capacity by court interpreters to exercise greater control over courtroom interactions reveals that, contrary to the court interpreter code of ethics, which generally requires interpreters to adhere to interpreting and to refrain from clarifying ambiguous situations with witnesses and accused persons, it is commonplace for interpreters to depart from this ethical code. The chapter discusses the impact of such control and the implications for interpreter training in Zimbabwe.

Stanley Madonsela, in Chapter 10, discusses *Conflicts emanating from the translation and interpretation of the term "domicile" for consumers in the South African context.* Madonsela argues in this chapter that when translating a legal text, the legal system in which the source text is grounded should be considered as it is structured in a manner that suits the culture concerned, and this is reflected in the legal language used. Similarly, it is assumed that the target text will be read by a person who is familiar with the legal system corresponding to the jurisdiction for which the target text is prepared. Since the term and concept of "domicile" constitutes an important connecting factor in issues pertaining to private-law status in South Africa, this chapter seeks to disinter the factors that bring about conflict emanating from the translation and interpretation of this concept in the South African legal system. The chapter also amplifies the legal and practical implications stemming from the inappropriate translation and interpretation of this particular legal concept for consumers, whose rights to be granted credit are compromised in this way. Consumers find their right to apply for credit in terms of Section 60 of South Africa's National Credit Act (NCA) being repudiated due to their having been listed with credit bureaus because they have not received any notice of the intention to list them. This chapter further argues that translation of "domicile" typically does not provide for a full understanding of the concept.

In Chapter 11, Paul Svongoro and Patson Kufakunesu present *Interpreters' renditions in Zimbabwean courtrooms: A corpus-based analysis from frequency profiles to key semantic domains.* This corpus-based research into interpreting in Zimbabwean criminal courtrooms analyses the frequency and use of different lexico-grammatical and syntactic features by different court players, and how these were rendered by court interpreters during court proceedings. They include, for instance, lexical items; pronouns and other forms of address; and question forms, such as tag questions, "yes/no" questions, "who" questions and "but –/so –" prefaced questions. The corpus for the study totalled nearly 89 000 words and was derived from transcripts of consecutively interpreted rape trials heard in two regional magistrates' courts in Zimbabwe. The findings reported in this chapter illustrate the various ways in which lexico-grammatical and syntactic features are used by courtroom players, and how these are rendered by interpreters in the course of a trial. The chapter illustrates that, through the use of various lexical items and question forms, for instance, the power of a participant, and thus his or her control over a triadic exchange, is realised not only in the role(s) he or she is capable of playing, but also through the participant roles of the co-present court actors. The chapter shows that the interpreter, working with bilingual court officials and interpreting for bilingual lay people, sees his or her power considerably reduced by other bilinguals (the magistrate and the public prosecutor, on the one hand, and the witness(es) and accused, on the other): these assume not only the roles of speakers (questioners) and addressees of witnesses' interpreted evidence, but also as hearers of the witnesses' answers and able to assess the accuracy of the interpretation.

Part 4

This part of the book presents a discussion on forensic linguistic evidence, and comprises the remaining four chapters.

In Chapter 12, Lirieka Meintjies-van der Walt presents *Road markers for reliability in authorship identification evidence*. She discusses authorship attribution from a legal perspective and attempts to provide linguists working in this field, particularly those who proffer expert evidence in a court of law, with guidelines that will ensure reliability and validity of their evidence. She defines authorship attribution and explains the nature of opinion evidence which, in Anglo-American jurisdictions such as South Africa, demands that such evidence must be relevant and useful to the court. With regard to reliability, the chapter interrogates the importance of the landmark 1993 case, *Daubert v Merrell Dow*, which ruled that opinion evidence should be tested, peer-reviewed and published; that the error rate should be indicated; and that cognisance should be taken of the general acceptance of the theory on which the evidence is based. The author explains the implications for technical evidence of the reports of the US National Academy of Science and the President's Council of Advisors on Science and Technology, which concluded that all traditional forensic disciplines, with the exception of DNA identification evidence, are not necessarily scientifically reliable because work in these areas has traditionally lacked scientific rigour. While the *Daubert v Merrell Dow* rules for determining the reliability of opinion evidence are not mandatory in South Africa, the author points out that these criteria could greatly assist presiding officers in deciding what weight should be attached to the expert opinion evidence proffered in court. To assist linguists in research design and in giving evidence in court, a number of typical and likely cross-examination questions with regard to factors such as testability, peer-review and publication, error rate and personal proficiency, general acceptance and bias are provided. The chapter refers to the guidelines recommended by the linguist, Chaski (2013), to ensure judicially acceptable and scientifically sound authorship attribution evidence, and concludes with a number of "road markers" extracted from relevant case law.

Chapter 13, *The act of threatening: Applying Speech Act Theory to threat texts*, is authored by Karien van den Berg and Michelle Surmon. Here, the authors offer a linguistic characterisation of a *threat*, drawing on pragmatic Speech Act Theory to contribute to a more comprehensive understanding of what a speaker does when threatening. Specifically, the authors address the question: How may the pragmatic theory of speech acts contribute to a more comprehensive understanding of the language used in textual threats? In so doing, the authors offer a point of reference that may then be further interpreted in view of authenticating threats, evaluating the urgency of a threat, and assigning authorship.

Terrence R. Carney, in Chapter 14, discusses *Sign language and hate speech: The potential pitfalls of iconic signs*. This chapter explores the ways in which some identity signifiers in sign language may be seen as examples of hate speech. The issue is considered by posing three questions: To what extent do iconic signs qualify as hate speech? In what way do iconic signs qualify as hate speech when observed by hearing nonsigners? How sufficient are the definitions in current legislation to address hate speech transgressions in sign language? Before these questions are dealt with individually, an overview of the lexis for sign language explains what iconic signs are and how some are considered politically incorrect. This is followed by an outline of the criteria for hate speech in both the Equality Act and the Hate Speech Bill. The conclusion is that sign language, like any other language, falls within the ambit of the law. The existing legislative definitions and terminology include communication of a visual nature, placing signing deaf people on par with everyone else.

In Chapter 15, *A case of crying wolf? A linguistic approach to evaluating hate speech allegations as linguistic acts of violence*, Karien van den Berg explores the notion of hate speech, and presents a taxonomy of hate speech as a linguistic act of violence. In this, she draws on linguistic theory, since law is intrinsically a linguistic entity. This chapter therefore offers a starting point for addressing the need for an objective yardstick of hate speech, based on a comprehensive scientific approach, to combat the problem of hate speech as a linguistic act of violence. It is argued that hate speech cannot be evaluated fairly without consideration of the context in which the utterance was produced. As such, the speaker's intent becomes a central determiner – rather than the impact of the utterance on the hearer alone – in investigations of speech crimes. The author relates the linguistic notion of intent to the legal interpretation of intent, and, in so doing establishes a working definition of hate speech. She demonstrates how linguistic theory can be applied to realise a working definition of hate speech, with reference to a South African case study (*AfriForum and Another vs Julius Sello Malema and Others*, 2010). It is argued that linguistic theoretical tools are valuable in exploring characteristics of linguistic crimes with violent intent and, in so doing, can aid legal enquiry to address such offences fairly and objectively.

Conclusion

The research presented in this book consolidates the viewpoint that Forensic Linguistics is now an integral part of Applied Language Studies and the broad discipline of Sociolinguistics. If one is to research the relationship between language and society, then discipline-related studies such as those concerned with language and law become part of the broader sociolinguistic debate. Indeed, forensic linguistics as presented in the chapters of this book, can bring to life, and bring into contention, linguistic evidence which has previously been ignored in courts of law.

Challenges presented through the interpretation of courtroom discourse in multilingual societies, as well as the challenges of monolingual languages policies within multilingual settings, bring to the fore the inextricable link between Forensic Linguistics, Language Planning and Applied Language Studies. Language policy planning is related to implementation at a broader political and societal level, thus policy-makers should take cognisance of forensic linguistics data, both on the ground and within the courtroom scenario.

Finally, this book brings together a range of authors from across Africa, Australia and the Caribbean, and interrogates forensic linguistic issues by providing practical and innovative examples from these regions, it provides comparative work that fills an academic lacuna in the body of knowledge pertaining to global studies in the subject.

References

Labov, W. 1972. *Language in the inner city: Studies in the Black English vernacular*. Philadelphia PA: University of Pennsylvania Press.

Oxburgh, G.; Myklebust, T.; Grant, T. & Milne, R. (eds.). 2016. *Communication in investigative and legal contexts: Integrated approaches from forensic psychology, linguistics and law enforcement*. Chichester: John Wiley & Sons.

PART 1
Police investigative interviewing

INCARCERATED, INCRIMINATED OR VINDICATED?

An investigation into socio-pragmatic elements of police interviewing

Monwabisi K. Ralarala & Theo Rodrigues

> *Probably the most distinctive and most widespread linguistic feature of legal talk is the question ...*
> Holt and Johnson (2013:21)

Introduction

This chapter seeks to create an understanding of how selected interactional patterns and devices in police interviews, intended to seek and obtain information during pre-statement sessions, contribute to incarceration, incrimination or vindication of an alleged perpetrator. We closely examine influencing factors, such as relative interviewing competence or questioning techniques, interactional dominance, and lack of translation ethics, as these are considered to drive the establishment of evidential discourse in police interviewing. The data in this chapter are derived from a narrative analysis of a subset of data collected for a research project that was conducted in the Western Cape. From a theoretical perspective, we draw on the socio-pragmatic model. The rationale for using this model is to provide a lens to examine selected interactional patterns and devices (Holt & Johnson, 2013) that tend to be prevalent in pre-statement sessions, as well as in sworn statements, during the process of police record construction.

South African police officers (henceforth "transpreters"[1]) are constantly at the forefront of facilitating the construction of records by interviewing and taking statements of complainants or perpetrators (for detailed accounts see Ralarala, 2014; and Harding &

---

[1] Ralarala first used this term in his article in *Stellenbosch Papers in Linguistics*, 41 (2012): 56, explaining that his "coining and using the term "transpreters" to refer to the designated police officers is informed by the type of dual dramatic competence and performance required – on the job – in order to render the cognitive and social service of message production and reception within the framework of both translation and interpreting of sworn statements".

Ralarala, 2017). Within the linguistically diverse society that is South Africa, most resident citizens, particularly international citizens in the Western Cape, are assisted by transpreters who speak a language different to theirs. This situation is further exacerbated when one considers that the differences in the proficiencies of these role players in terms of ability to communicate, linguistic skills, relative literacy, and fluency are different. One could appreciate that these role players, being second and third language speakers of English, would be challenged to communicate effectively in English, the current language of record. This linguistic situation tends to perpetuate notions of linguistic incarceration and incrimination, which is a concern of this chapter, in respect of the language events of complainants who are differently literate in English (Rodrigues, 2017).

In the legal processes of our everyday South African context, a formal sanction is normally imposed when a crime is reported by a complainant. This is followed by the apprehension of the alleged perpetrator by the transpreter; and the perpetrator is subsequently charged and then prosecuted. Conviction and punishment depend mainly on the evidence obtained through written or verbal testimonies presented during police interviewing. According to the National Research Council (2014:133), the "first step in the process – reporting the crime – is critical". This common source of evidence is often erroneous in the judicial process and ultimately leads to courts not being able to fulfil their duty to uncover the truth because the "statement of facts or criminal responsibility [are] based on incorrect testimonies" (Elek, 2016:121). Elek highlights questioning techniques, amongst others, as influential factors that contribute to these erroneous testimonies.

The police interviewing process is characterised by the posing of questions as a means of obtaining and seeking information and to ascertain the veracity and gravity of that information. This process, however, is challenged by questions that carry implicit assumptions and presumptions over which the respective role players have no control (Lempp, 2002). During this process, the transference and the co-construction of the complainant's narrative may be manipulated; and, when the complainant's testimony is given, may lead to one or more of these:

- incarceration, when police officers facilitate the interviewing process by formulating questions outside the scope of the intended visit;
- incrimination, when complainants divulge or present extra information owing to the manner in which transpreters engage with them, like a state prosecutor during record construction; or,
- vindication, as a result of how police officers advise them, for example, on evidential issues, as if they are functioning as their legal counsel.

In this chapter, we will examine three cases regarding the notions of linguistic incarceration, linguistic incrimination and vindication, with specific reference to complainants and transpreters' co-construction of legal records or sworn statements. As much as we refer to legal terminology, we approach these conditions primarily from a linguistic perspective. In so doing, we take a closer look at selected interactional patterns and devices (in the terms proposed by Holt & Johnson, 2013) with a view to determining textual traces that emerge from pre-statement sessions and which culminate in evidential discourse (and which could potentially lead to incarceration, incrimination or vindication). From a theoretical base, it remains apparent that a socio-pragmatic approach provides a thorough grounding for seeking and obtaining information for legal and evidential purposes.

Theoretical framework

The socio-pragmatic model is a sub-field of pragmatics. However, before we embark on elucidating the socio-pragmatic model, a brief overview of pragmatics is important. Although no concise definition of pragmatics can be agreed upon (Crystal, 2003; Leech, 1983; Mey, 2001), the scope of pragmatic study is narrowly confined to "a study of utterance meaning as intended by the speaker, effects of non-literal and indirect communication strategies, context and appropriation of utterances, speech acts, politeness principles and situational constraints on interlocutors" (Agbara & Omole, 2014:173). In other words, pragmatics is a study that deals with how a "speaker conveys peculiar meaning as distinct from sentence meaning and how listeners are able to decipher speaker meaning from sentence meaning" (Agbara & Omole, 2014:173).

Crystal (2003) and Mey (2001) attest that pragmatics also deals with language options of interlocutors and the consequences it has on respective listeners. The way speakers use their language amidst constraints in any communication situation may result in misinterpretation by listeners – such as transpreters in a police interviewing context (Ralarala, 2014). Pragmatics distinguishes between these two concepts, i.e. speaker meaning and sentence meaning. The former refers to the intention or peculiar information of the interlocutor; the latter refers to the literal meaning of a sentence. Understanding the difference between these concepts in a communication situation is referred to as "pragmatic competence".

Compared to the sole aim of pragmatics, which is to analyse the meaning-making process between a speaker and a listener, socio-pragmatics describes the ways in which pragmatic meanings reveal "specific local conditions of language use" (Leech, 1983:10); and this makes the model relevant for analysis of the respective data sets used for this chapter. However, the socio-pragmatic model is different from general pragmatics, which seeks either to indicate how theory is illustrated by data, or how occurring data develop theory. In this regard, LoCastro (2012) highlights the relationship between context and utterances by questioning whether contexts are created through utterances, or whether a speaker's way of presenting themselves is inhibited by the context. Following this discussion, she argues that context is likely to determine how language will be used by rendering that "variables [such] as gender, age, social class, and race" are vital parts of any discourse (LoCastro, 2012). This coincides with her notion that "meaning, structure and the use of language are socially and culturally relative" (LoCastro, 2012:69), and "contextual features are without exception significant in any instance of language use" (LoCastro, 2012:185). This attests that the socio-pragmatic model concerns itself with the "social rules of speaking, those expectations about interactional discourse held by members of a speech community as appropriate and "normal" behaviour" (LoCastro, 2012:159).

Against these statements, it is clear that this model views communication as social action and interaction; and that it follows various schools of thought, i.e. conversation analysis (Sacks 1992), discourse analysis (Schiffrin, 1994), dialogue theory (Linell, 1998), language use theory (Clark, 1996; Levinson, 1993), speech act theory (Austin, 1962; Searle, 1969), communication action theory (Habermas, 1984), symbolic interaction (Strauss, 1993), linguistic anthropology (Duranti, 1997) and social semiotics (Halliday, 1994). One of these frameworks, speech act theory, plays an important role in understanding how speakers perform in a communication setting. Similar to the socio-pragmatic model, speech act theory also regards speech as an action.

Speech act theory distinguishes three basic acts of speech: the locutionary act, the illocutionary act and the perlocutionary act. The locutionary act refers to the act where the locutor makes meaningful utterances to the receiver. The illocutionary act relates to what the locutor does when delivering the utterance (asking clarifying questions, reporting, making a request or a promise, etc.). The perlocutionary act refers to the consequence(s) of the utterance for the receiver (who is persuaded, informed, incriminated, incarcerated, influenced, etc.).

Searle (1979) further classified the illocutionary acts into five classes: representatives, directives, commissives, expressives and declaratives. "Representatives" refer to the utterances that clearly state a current situation and which the locutor views and commits to as the expressed truth during a communication event (reporting, explaining, illustrating, etc.). "Directives" are utterances that motivate a receiver's response and are based on the wishes of the locutor expressed during the communication event (requests, orders, suggestions, etc.). "Commissives" are utterances that obligate the locutor to carry out the expression made during the communication event (swearing an oath, pledging, vowing, etc.). "Expressives" refer to utterances that articulate the psychological mindset of the locutor (regret, worry, concern, etc.). "Declarations" refer to utterances which effect change in the current situation (giving the verdict in a trial, pronouncing a couple united in marriage, christening a ship, etc.).

Any one of these speech acts, however, can only be successful when it conforms to certain conditions, i.e. the propositional content condition, the preparatory condition, the sincerity condition, and the essential (intentionality) condition (Searle, 1969:57, 64). In this regard, Searle (1969) amplifies the importance of a trusting relationship between speakers and listeners by stressing that speakers' speech should be sincere in the communication event to enable listeners to hear and understand their language. In response to these conditions, Habermas (1984:38) introduced the concept of a validity claim as an "equivalent to the assertion that the conditions for the validity of an utterance are fulfilled". He distinguishes four claims, namely, truth, normative rightness, sincerity and comprehensibility.

Searle (1969:178) also highlights the importance of syntactic and formal features of questioning when he introduces the notion of an "indirect speech act" where certain sentences do not coincide with the sentence function. These indirect speech acts are basically formed by "primary" and "secondary" illocutionary acts. According to Searle (1969), the former act refers to an indirect act where the meaning created by the speaker is not performed literally. The latter act, however, refers to the direct form which agrees with the customary sentence function and performance of the speaker.

Notwithstanding the focus of the socio-pragmatic model on speech as an action, it also considers silence as a speech act. Two main types of silence are identified: unintentional and intentional. The former refers to a silence where the speaker responds with silence as a result of personal inhibitions, perhaps motivated by psychological shortcomings. The latter is the result of a deliberate action on the part of the speaker to be uncooperative during a communication event. This response coincides with the right of the person to remain silent within a legal context. This choice of remaining silent also provides meaning (Kurzon, 1995). Brunea (1973) distinguishes between three types of silence: psychological silence, where the speaker attempts to help the receiver understand the message often exhibited by hesitations; interactive silence, where speakers intentionally suspend their utterances consenting to receivers' making unfounded suppositions; and socio-cultural silence, which refers to silences based on specific cultural codes, for example, where, as a sign of respect, indigenous African people in South Africa refrain from responding verbally.

Within the context of linguistic analysis, silence is viewed as another feature of spoken discourse. Sacks et al. (1974) highlight silence as an instrument whereby one may distinguish that there has been a breakdown in the communication event. These breakdowns are often seen in a question-answer scenario in a legal adversary interview where the addressee has an inability to answer a particular question. In this regard, a person's silence could be construed as suspicious.

To turn the proverbial tables during an interview session, the interviewer may reframe questions by using polar interrogatives (yes-no questions) to obtain the required answer (Bülow-Møller, 1991; Stubbs, 1983). Stubbs attests that these questioning techniques may lead to the asking of leading questions. Interrogating techniques may also shift guilt and implications thereof onto addressees (Kurzon, 1995). These questioning techniques lead to an asymmetrical power relationship between the addressee and interviewer. The choice of any person to remain silent, therefore, creates a different power dimension between the addressee and interviewer. Exercising their right of silence ultimately breaks the interviewer's power over them (Kurzon, 1992). In essence, it increases distance between the parties in the communication event.

Analytical constructs

In attempting to ascertain the notions of linguistic incarceration, linguistic incrimination, and vindication, it is proper and insightful to outline and define these conditions before forging ahead with the analysis:

Incarceration

Prinsloo, Alberts and Mollema (2015:135) define the notion of incarceration as "the confinement, detainment, jailing or imprisonment of an individual". The *Merriam Webster Dictionary* articulates that this lemma refers to the act of imprisoning someone or as a state of being imprisoned. These definitions coincide with its original Medieval Latin form *'incarcerare'*, meaning to imprison or confined to an enclosed space. If we consider that the type of question during the [police interviewing process results in a specific response (Rodgers, 2000:48), one can propose the notion that an alleged perpetrator could be linguistically "incarcerated" in the process of police record construction. In a very subtle way, the police officer could create a power imbalance through questioning techniques that could have an impact on, or eventually contribute to, the incarceration of that person who is suspected to have been embroiled in a criminal activity.

Incrimination

Prinsloo et al. (2015:137) describe incrimination succinctly when suggesting that it means "Accusation of the commission of a crime". They go further to define an incriminating statement, pointing out that such a statement is meant to "connect the accused with crime" (Prinsloo et al., 137). According to the *Cambridge Essential English Dictionary*, "incrimination means to create a situation where a person appears guilty of a crime". Drawing on the definition provided by *Black's Law Dictionary*, 2014 this concept refers to charging someone with a crime; exposing someone to an accusation or charge of crime; involving oneself or others in a criminal prosecution or the danger thereof, especially when the rule that a witness is not bound to give testimony that would tend to incriminate him or her is disregarded. The questioning techniques would provide unnecessary stress on the complainant, placing him or her in a compromised position when required to divulge information that presents the original knowledge in a different light, and which, thus, could incriminate the alleged perpetrator.

Vindication

According to the *Cambridge Essential English Dictionary*, vindication refers to proving the truthfulness of someone's testimony after other people have disputed it. It also refers to proving someone's innocence, or that the person is blameless, after others have blamed him or her. According to *The Free Dictionary*, vindication includes the concepts of absolution, accounting for, acquitting, clearing, declaring innocent, discharging, dismissing, exculpating, excusing, exonerating, giving good reasons for, justifying, pardoning, probating, pronouncing not guilty, purging, releasing, relieving of burden, reprieving, setting free. From a private law perspective, however, Baker (2017) asserts that there are various legal meanings for the concept of vindication. According to her, the idea is multilayered and highlights the notions of protection, enforcement and declaration of private rights which are informed by private and public validations. Drawing on definitions in dictionaries and on how the term is discussed in a law context, the reader becomes aware that vindication is clearly not exclusively a phenomenon in law. What one could derive from this definition is that vindication, in all spheres, emphasises the notion of human rights.

Data

The data used in this chapter were drawn from a narrative analysis of a subset of data collected for a research project that was conducted in the Western Cape in 2013. The data sources consist of the transcripts of audio-recordings of 18 interviews (I1-I18) in isiXhosa with corresponding written statements (S1-S18) translated into English by the transpreter responsible for conducting the interview (see Ralarala, 2014). It is important to note that the construction of the record, as well as the compilation of the sworn statement, is drafted by hand during the interview and placed onto a template for the complainant to affirm his or her understanding of the contents of the dossier upon reading the English version. More importantly, once the reading process is over and the interview complete (see Harding & Ralarala, 2017), the complainant is bound to append his or her signature on the dossier, thus not only committing to the comprehension of the statements but also confirming that the legal text is fully constituted by his or her verbatim statement (see Ralarala, 2017). In the event that the complainant is not in a position to read the translated version, the transpreter assumes responsibility for reading the statement aloud to the complainant. In some cases, the transpreter will conduct sight-translation from English back into isiXhosa (Harding and Ralarala, 2017, offer a detailed account).

For the purpose of this analysis, we refer to extracts drawn from three cases (5, 16 and 18), all of which were not previously subjected to any form of analysis. The English translations in brackets that appear alongside each turn-taking utterance are those of a professional and sworn translator.

Synopsis of cases

Case 1 (5)

On a certain date (stated in full in the original text) in 2013, the complainant (***-year-old male, name stated in full in the original text) suffered a break-in, theft and arson. He reported his ex-girlfriend (name stated in full in the original text) for allegedly breaking into his apartment, stealing and starting a fire. The police opened a case of theft and arson against the ex-girlfriend. Owing to claims made by the complainant that she was abusive and violent towards him, he was advised to hold on to a Protection Order previously endorsed against her.

Case 2 (16)

On a certain date (stated in full in the original text) in 2013, the complainant (***-year-old female, name stated in full in the original text) suffered bodily injuries from being stabbed. She reported a crime of assault against a man whom she claimed allegedly wanted to rape her daughter. The police opened a case of theft and assault with grievous bodily harm (GBH).

Case 3 (18)

On a certain date (stated in full in the original text) in 2013, the complainant (***-year-old male, name stated in full in the original text) suffered theft at the hands of an alleged perpetrator, a panel beater. The complainant reported a crime of theft against the alleged perpetrator for allegedly stealing one of his car lights. The police opened a case of theft.

Analysis

Possibilities of incrimination and incarceration from
Cases 2 (16) and 3 (18)

Interactional dominance and control are a hallmark of police interviewing and record construction (for a detailed account, see Adelsward, Aronsson, Jonsson and Linell, 1987; and Ralarala, 2012 and 2017). In evidential discourse, this form of behaviour can easily facilitate incrimination and thus incarceration. Facilitating these conditions is the reshaping and reformulation of the complainant's talk through interactional dominance and control. Table 1.1 lays down some conventions used in the transcriptions, based on the outline of Eades (2010), Heydon (2004), and Rock (2001).

TABLE 1.1 Transcription symbols

Symbol	Description
::	The sound is lengthened by one syllable for each colon
(.)	Micro-pause of less than 0.2 seconds
...	Omitted words
(1.35)	Silence measured in seconds
(( ))	Transcriber's remarks, including comments made on voice quality or non-verbal sounds
H	Audible out breath

Extract 1 from Case 2 (16) illustrates the interactional dominance of the transpreter, as indicated by the italicised words (line 144). The italicised words not only suggest leading questions (line 142, italics) but demonstrate a degree of implicit imposition by the transpreter to obtain affirmation from the complainant in respect of the estimated age of the perpetrator (line 143 is a case in point). Shepherd and Milner (1999:130) view this line of questioning as belonging to a "counter-productive questions" category and, as such, this kind of questioning carries the potential "to shape the responses of witnesses." Such questions should be avoided as they "trigger short, frequently affirmative, answers and thus involve less concentrated retrieval" (Shepherd & Milner, 1999:129). Quintessentially, the locutionary speech acts of the complainant that encapsulate meaningful and unambiguous statements could become compromised, in that she provides coerced utterances. In these respects, the narrative does not conform to the conditions of validity (see Searle, 1969; Habermas, 1984).

EXTRACT 1 From Case 2 (16)

Turn & speaker	Utterance	English gloss
142-T	(.) *Xa umjongileyo nje inoba ukwi 80s or 70s?*	When you look at him, can he be in the 80s or 70s?
143-C	(0.3) *Inoba' upha ko 70s.*	He may be in the 70s.
144-T	*70s nhe?*	70s neh?
145-C	(0.2) Bendiqal' umbona mna andimazi.	I was seeing him for the first time, I don't know him.

In our case, the transpreter through this assertion possibly hoped to achieve an impression, an addition which is not explicit in the pre-statement, that reflects a vast difference in terms of age between the perpetrator (who was said to have had intentions to commit a sexual offence) and the complainant (whose 12-year-old daughter was to be subjected to the crime of rape). In this part of the narrative it becomes clear how the perlocutionary speech acts of the transpreter impact the illocutionary acts of the complainant. By asking leading questions or suggesting certain descriptors, the transpreter directs the complainant in responding in a particular way. As is clear from this evidential discourse, the cited features of dominance and control do, to some extent, contribute to the possibility of incarceration and incrimination.

EXTRACT 2 From Case 3 (18)

Turn & speaker	Utterance	English gloss
150-T	(0.11) Uthi yimalini ivalue yaso?	How much did you say is its value?
151-C	(.) Yho! *inoba ipha koma two thousand randi.*	...! It may be around two thousand rand.
152-T	(.) *Ndingabhala' u two thousan qha? (0.2) Okanye two point something?*	So, can I write two thousands only? Or two point something?
154-C	(0.3) *Inoba ipha koma two point seven.*	It may be around two point seven.
155-T	*So ndibhale two point seven?*	So I should write two point seven?
156-C	*Mh::*	Mh::

The implicit imposition to obtain affirmation from the complainant is not only common – as part of the interactional discourse and control – but rather seems purposeful with a view ultimately to obtain a conviction, hence incrimination and incarceration. (Reference is made to lines 150, 151, 152, 153, 154, 155 and 156.) This notion of controlling the outcome coincides with the illocutionary acts of persuading the speaker to commit to the proposition expressed in the original untainted narrative. This in turn affects the perlocutionary speech acts when the actual narrative captured by the transpreter provides a different tale – one that has been rewritten to serve a particular purpose. In this interactional pattern, apart from obtaining the critical information for purposes of evidence, the transpreter tends not only to impose but to create, through inferences, some idea towards determining the value of the stolen item (see particularly lines 152 and 155, italicised) which would not have been as precise if it was not because of her influence in the established evidential discourse. Adelsward et al. (1987:320-321) reiterate what is reflected in our data when pointing out the following: "In many asymmetrical situations, the dominant party takes or is given the right to make interpretations of what the subordinate party says or does, and these interpretations are commonly treated as the correct, as it were, ratified". As can be seen, the assertion is not only embraced by the less powerful interlocutor (complainant) (see line 156, italicised), but it is given the status of truthfulness, as it is bound to find its way into the actual sworn statement as per the interpretation and compilation of the formal evidence by the transpreter who holds the position of a dominant interlocutor in the presentation of this evidential discourse. The extract drawn from the actual statement with the transpreter's determined value of the stolen item illustrates this.

Another important dimension that facilitates incarceration and incrimination relates to the application of translation ethics in police interviewing and record construction. Our analysis of the data reveals that the police officer herself is not the best listener that one would expect in someone taking a statement that is to be submitted for further investigation. The complainant stated that he asked a boy next door; but the statement says he asked the neighbours. In this regard, the perlocutionary speech act of the transpreter is characterised by misinterpretations and declaratives that could change the outcome of the judicial process. Furthermore, the conditions of validity (Seale, 1969; Habermas, 1984) are grossly negated, especially when we consider that the interviewing process concerns itself with capturing the truth. This is apparent from line 23, italicised, when compared to a selected portion of the actual statement below the interaction ("I then asked my neighbours"). These different versions that emerge from the same interview are not just an anomaly which can be attributed to inter-lingual translation and intra-lingual translation (see Harding & Ralarala, 2017 for a detailed account): they carry serious implications for incrimination and incarceration. Firstly, the capturing of inaccurate information is dismissive of the conception that sworn statements are verbatim accounts of complainants or witness. Heaton-Amstrong (1995:138) puts it succinctly: "The fiction that witness statements are verbatim accounts should, however, now be more difficult to sustain." Secondly, this notion brings into question the competence of the transpreters as accurate and competent translators, as well the extent to which they act ethically in dealing with the specialised translation practice in respect of legal texts. Arising from this challenge, a similar observation has been made in a study conducted by Ralarala (2014) in which some of the statements appeared not to be a true reflection of the original narratives as presented by the complainant. The point made was this:

> This dangerous inconsistency and lack of accuracy affects not only the content layer but also the intentional layer, in that it officially modifies a charge of Common Assault into a possible Attempted Murder in the eyes of the future readership or audience, who solely rely on this official record for their legal decision-making process.
>
> (Ralarala, 2014:392)

As can be seen in a number of cases, as a result of translation incompetence and a lack of translation ethics by transpreters in police interviewing and sworn statement-taking, such anomalies could easily contribute to purposeful incarceration and incrimination, if not vindication. Further analysis is advanced to demonstrate possibilities of incrimination and incarceration.

EXTRACT 3 Pre-statement and sworn statement from Case 18

Turn & speaker	Utterance	English gloss
	Pre-statement	
23-C	Ha-a *ndiy' buzile le ntwana yaseneksdo* straight apho bekuwe khona iingceba ze:: zelantika ze:: nantsika zesbane (.) so khang' abone nto.	I *did ask this young man* from next door straight where the bits of:: whatsname of:: whatsname, of the light (.) so he did not see anything.
Sworn statement selection, reflecting the construction based on the Pre-statement		
	I noticed that my back light was stolen and some small pieces of the light were still hanging on the vehicle. *I then asked my neighbours* if they did not see anyone breaking my car, so no one saw anyone. The value of missing back light is R2 700.	

Possibilities of vindication from Case 1 (5)

In an attempt to co-construct, recreate and transform the narrative into evidential discourse, the transpreter could go to some extent in bungling the interviewing or record construction process. It is not known whether this is a deliberate act or not. The point to note is that it could lead to vindication of the alleged perpetrator if not subjecting the same to severe sentencing which otherwise would have been less or vice versa. Based on our observation and, as the analysis will show, the record that follows not only reflects possibilities of both vindication and incarceration, but also poor abilities of both the transpreter and complainant in respect of relaying the narrative and taking the statement.

EXTRACT 3 From Case 1

Turn & speaker	Utterance	English gloss
108-T	(0.2) Ubuphi wena?	Where were you?
109-C	Bendiphaya kuNikelo.	I was at Nikelo's place.
110-T	(.) *Ngubani uNikelo*?	Who is Nikelo?
111-C	Ngulo bhuti bendize ndihamba naye izolo.	He is the one I came with yesterday.
112-T	Yitshomi le yakho?	The one who is your friend?
118-T	(0.10) *Ngubani igama likaNikelo?* ((confused))	What is Nikelo's name?
119-C	NguNikelo.	It is Nikelo.
120-T	(0.2) *Ngubani igama lakhe?*	What is his name?
121-C	Lilo (.) nguNikelo ((forcefully)).	That is it.

For example, on the one hand, the complainant is very long-winded and it is not very easy to follow his reporting. The transpreter, on the other hand, is not a very attentive listener. For instance, her repetition and seeking the same detail becomes problematic and thus constitutes an anomaly in questioning. Shepherd and Mortimer (1999:271) relate to this position when asserting "other oblique verbal constructions can avoid or obscure identification of a key individuals". As evidence of this, we refer to Extract 3, lines 110, 118 and 120 (italicised) which reveal transpreter's failure to listen to the complainant's narration and that she had forgotten what the complainant said earlier when responding to the same question, more than one Apparently, this failure to pay attention to detail could result in an omission, if not a distortion, of the facts; and eventually, if the matter is brought before the court with insufficient or misplaced evidence from the record, vindication of the perpetrator could prevail.

EXTRACT 4 From Case 1

Turn & speaker	Utterance	English gloss
521-T	(0.7) *Uright apha entloko usisi wakho?*	Is your lady normal mentally?
522-C	Andiva?	I beg your pardon?
523-T	(0.2) *Ndiyabuza ubhadlile na?*	I'm asking, is she normal mentally?

A striking omission in her summary of the statement made is the real source of the lady's fury against the alleged perpetrator. The complainant was in love with the lady, Nikelwa, but because of her unbecoming behaviour, he suggested to the lady that they stop or end the relationship. This turned out to be an extreme, unbearable scorn for the lady. In her comments during the pre-statement session, the transpreter, strangely, expresses doubt about the lady's mental state. (Reference is made to Extract 4, lines 521 and 523, italicised.) One can easily sense that the course of the case will focus more on the criminal aspect and less, if at all, on its psychological aspects. Although the transpreter probes the complainant for further information, her (the transpreter's) speech acts are characterised by declaratives which alludes to changing the current situation or attempting to steer the narrative in a different direction. The complainant's locution in the samples below is the direct result of the illocutionary acts of the transpreter.

That said, it brings into question the role and responsibilities of the transpreter in respect of generating an evidential discourse, as well as the extent to which his or her voice can influence the final sworn statement that can be used as evidence in court. Ralarala (2016:149) emphasise this critical point: "The actual statement – as reconstructed by the transpreters – remains the only official and acceptable record, and thus the only audible voice in the dossier." The same sentiments about the mental state of the suspect, as uttered by the transpreter, also bring into question the goal of a sworn statement, its evidential purpose and the extent to which it can constitute a meaningful statement. In the final analysis, if such sentiments find their way into the final record, probabilities of vindication cannot be ruled out.

The latitude given to transpreters when seeking information for purposes of evidence remains fundamental, particularly when information is sought from complainants. Maintaining an empathetic relationship is bound to facilitate and elicit critical detail needed and meant to constitute relevant and desirable evidence. Conversely, the creation of a relationship of unequals ("superior-subordinate", in Shepherd and Milne's 1999 terms) between the transpreter and the complainant, as displayed in the interview, is problematic (also see Kurzon, 1995, in this regard). This interview behaviour inclines towards an undesirable line of questioning which resembles interrogation. In fact, this approach is arguably typical of a cross-examination rather than for the purpose of obtaining information for evidential purposes. In the following passage, in Extract 5, lines 292, 294, 296 and 298 (italicised), reference is made to this line of questioning which could lead to the vindication of the perpetrator as it influences a shift of focus from the perpetrator to the complainant, as if he is fabricating the statement. In the context of the transpreter-complainant interaction, this pattern is not only risky but dangerous; and the danger associated with this approach is not only counterproductive, but holds potential threats on the part of the complainant to volunteer information freely and engage meaningfully in evidential discourse that could assist in the process of an arrest. Shepherd & Milne (1999:130) echo this view: closed confirmatory questions are risky because they notionally reduce the witness's response options to a "yes" or "no". Hence vindication of the perpetrator remains a probability in this instance.

EXTRACT 5 From Case 1

Turn & speaker	Utterance	English gloss
292-T	(0.2) *Kulo::myalezo uyatsho ukuba ndizakutshisa?*	In this message, does she say that she is going to burn things?
293-C	(0.3) Akatsho ukuba uza kutshisa.	She does not say that she is going to burn things.
294-T	(.) *Uyatsho ukuba uzakophula ifestile?*	Does she say that she is going to break the window?
295-C	(0.2) Hayi.	No.
296-T	(.) *Akatsho?*	Does she not say so?
297-C	Ewe.	Yes.
298-T	(.) *Uthini lo myalezo wakhe?*	What does this message of hers say?

Discussion

This study set out to examine three cases in respect of the notions of incarceration, incrimination, and vindication with specific reference to complainants and transpreters' co-construction of pre-statements, as well as sworn statements, during the course of record construction. In this chapter, we have considered selected interactional patterns and devices with a view to determining textual traces that emerge from pre-statement sessions, and sworn statements that culminate in evidential discourse. Identifiable interactional patterns and devices such as (i) questioning techniques (Holt & Johnson, 2013; Shepherd & Milne, 1999), (ii) interactional dominance (Adelsward et al., 1987; Ralarala, 2012) and (iii) translation ethics (Harding & Ralarala, 2017) are some of the critical issues that have formed the ground for discussion. Essentially, a point of emphasis remains their analytical and conceptual contribution in police record co-construction and sworn statements, and thus linguistic incarceration, linguistic incrimination, and vindication of the alleged perpetrator.

Throughout this chapter, evidence has been provided that the three conditions used as the basis for our study provide a clear characterisation of dominance and control between the complainant and transpreter. These instances of dominance and control are masked by, amongst others, the questioning techniques used in the course of record construction, which oftentimes results in a subjective legal text (sworn statement) towards the transpreter's inclination to control and dominate the interaction. Arguably, these questioning techniques, with their associated anomalies such as declarative, imposing and leading questions, tend to compromise the validity and veracity of the complainant's original narrative, as pointed out by Komter (2002:168): "These statements are supposed to be written down as far as possible in the suspect's own words, but they are in fact the police officer's written versions of what was said in the interrogation room". Although Komter addresses the issue from the perspective of suspect interrogation, similar observations and findings are revealed through our data analysis in respect of complainant-transpreter interactions.

Another important observation of a phenomenon which permeates the language dynamics in police interviewing and record construction relates to inter-lingual and intra-lingual translations. The context of our diverse linguistics profile and infrastructure demands that sworn statements in the language of the complainant must first be dictated and drafted by hand with pen and paper and then be translated into the language of record, which is predominantly English. It is through this peculiar reformulation of the complainant's narrative and meaning-making for future readership that a somewhat differing version of the same story is generated. Based on our analysis, our findings demonstrate that some of the anomalies associated with this process (such as misrepresentations and distortions, and even manipulation, potentially leading to incrimination and incarceration) could be attributed to various factors which may include, but are not limited to, linguistic incompetence of transpreters, and thus poor interviewing techniques. Harding and Ralarala (2017:159) remark on the seriousness of the situation: "The English and literacy proficiencies of these officers are, in some cases, exceedingly low, which makes them ill-equipped to meet these demands." For this reason, Harding and Ralarala's argument suggests the following:

> The labour of simultaneous inter-lingual translation for an officer already struggling with low-level literacy and English proficiency serves only to increase the difficulty of the task. It benefits nobody but the English-speaking court and so, at this stage, should be eliminated.   (Harding & Ralarala, 2017:170)

Comparatively few, if any, studies have interrogated complainant-transpreter interaction with a view to establishing the possibilities of incrimination, incarceration and vindication. These are most probable in the context of accused-police interrogations (see Coulthard, 2002). Be that as it may, apart from drawing data on victims of crime (complainants), our analysis sheds some light on the significance of the description of the relevant interaction patterns and devices and also draws some inferences regarding the notions of incrimination, incarceration and vindication.

Conclusion

Various problems during the interview process – language, translation, interpreting and effectively taking statements (Ntuli & Bruce, 2001) – were identified in this chapter. Drawing on the speech acts of both the complainant and transpreter, we have highlighted how interactional patterns and devices could impact inversely on the three conditions outlined in this chapter. By accentuating the subjective interpretation and consequential erroneous translation of the complainant's narrative into English by transpreters, we account for the current reality where these practices at police stations result in the misrepresentation of the truth. In essence, the transpreter contributes to perpetuate the status quo – to marginalise citizens who are not proficient in the language of record, and to continue the asymmetrical power relations between the complainant and the transpreter.

To transcend these injustices of linguistic human rights, one should consider a client centre where language services could be offered to parallel (same linguistic or literacy group) and non-parallel (different language and literacy groups) communities to allow client voices to be heard during the interview process. A client centre modelled on the community interpreting practices is used in countries like Australia, where the language of record is different to the language of the complainant. This could be a step in the right direction. Using paralegals or other individuals who are trained in judicial matters could also provide support to limit the possible misinterpretation of complainants' statements by police officers, or by assisting complainants to avoid misrepresenting themselves.

References

Adelsward, V.; Aronsson, K.; Jonsson, L. & Linell, P. 1987. The unequal distribution of interactional space: Dominance and control in courtroom interaction. *An Interdisciplinary Journal for the Study of Discourse*, 7(4):313-346.

Agbara, C.U.B. & Omole, K. 2014. A pragmatic analysis of speech acts strata in Nigeria legislative discourse. *International Journal of Research in Arts and Social Sciences*, 7(2):172-180.

Austin, J.L. 1962. *How to do things with words: The William James lectures delivered at Harvard University in 1955*. Cambridge MA: Harvard University Press.

Barker, K. 2017. Private and public: The mixed concept of vindication in torts and private law. In: S.G.A. Pitel, J.W. Neyers & E. Chamberlain (eds.), *Tort law: Challenging orthodoxy*. Oxford: Hart. p. 59.

Black's law dictionary. 2014. 10th Edition. St Paul MN: Thomson Reuters Legal.

Bruneau, T.J. 1973. Communicative silences: Forms and functions. *Journal of Communication*, 23(1):17-46.

Bülow-Møller, A.M. 1991. Trial Evidence: Overt and Covert Communication in Court. *International Journal of Applied Linguistics*, 1(1):38-60. https://doi.org/10.1111/j.1473-4192.1991.tb00004.x

Cambridge essential English dictionary. 2011. 2nd Edition. Cambridge: Cambridge University Press.

Clark, H.H. 1996. *Using language*. Cambridge: Cambridge University Press.

Coulthard, M. 2002. Whose Voice Is It? Invented and Concealed Dialogue in Written Records of Verbal Evidence Produced by Police. In: J. Cotterill (ed.), *Language in the legal process*. New York: Palgrave Macmillan. pp. 19-34.

Crystal, D. 2003. *A dictionary of linguistics and phonetics*. 5th Edition. Oxford: Blackwell Publishing.

Duranti, A. 1997. *Linguistic anthropology*. Cambridge: Cambridge University Press.

Eades, D. 2010. *Sociolinguistics and the legal process*. Bristol: Multilingual Matters.

Elek, B. 2016. To the recommendation of using "linguistic fingerprints" in the criminal procedure. *Comparative Legilinguistics*, 28:119-136. http://dx.doi.org/10.14746/cl.2016.28.6

Habermas, J. 1984. *The theory of communicative action, Vol. 1: Reason and the rationalization of society*, reprint edition, translated by T. McCarthy. Boston MA: Beacon Press.

Halliday, M.A.K. 1994. *An introduction to functional grammar*. 2nd Edition. London: Edward Arnold.

Harding, S. & Ralarala, M.K. 2017. "Tell me the story is and do not leave out anything." Social responsibility and ethical practices in the translation of complainants' narratives: The potential for change. *The Translator*, 23(2):158-176. https://doi.org/10.1080/13556509.2017.1327792

Hart, J. 1996. Why expert testimony on the meaning of language has no place in libel suits. *Communications Lawyer*, 14:8-11.

Heaton-Armstrong, A.; Shepherd, E. & Wolchover, D (eds.). 1999. *Analysing witness testimony: A guide for legal practitioners and other professionals*. London: Blackstone Press.

Heydon, G. 2004. Establishing the structure of police evidentiary interview with suspects. *Speech, Language and the Law*, 11(1):27-49.

Holt, E. & Johnson, A. 2013. Socio-pragmatics aspects of legal talk: Police interviews and trial discourse. In: M. Coulthard & A. Johnson (eds.), *The Routledge handbook of forensic linguistics*. New York: Routledge. pp. 21-36.

Komter, M. 2002. The suspect's own words: The treatment of written statements in Dutch courtrooms. *International Journal of Speech, Language and the Law*, 9(2):168-187.

Kurzon, D. 1992. When silence may mean power. *Journal of Pragmatics*, 18(1):92-95.

Kurzon, D. 1995. The right of silence: A socio-pragmatic model of interpretation. *Journal of Pragmatics*, 23:55-69.

Lawson, G.S. 1995. Linguistics legal epistemology: Why the law pays less attention to linguists than it should. *Washington University Quarterly*, 73:995-999.

Leech, G.N. 1983. *Principles of pragmatics*. London: Longman.

Lempp, J.H. 2002. The method of appropriate questioning. *Psychotherapy*, pp. 397-406.

Levinson, S.C. 1983. *Pragmatics*. Cambridge: Cambridge University Press.

Linell, P. 1998. *Approaching dialogue: Talk, interaction and contexts in dialogical perspectives*. Amsterdam: John Benjamins.

LoCastro, V. 2012. *Pragmatics for language educators: A sociolinguistic perspective*. Abingdon: Routledge. https://academic.oup.com/eltj/article-abstract/68/2/208/383146 [Retrieved 7 March 2019].

Mey, J.L. 2001. *Pragmatics: An introduction*. Oxford: Wiley-Blackwell.

National Research Council. 2014. *The growth of incarceration in the United States: Exploring causes and consequences*. Washington DC: The National Academies Press. https://doi.org/10.17226/18613

Ntuli, S. & Bruce, D. 2001. *Witnesses in the criminal justice system: A report on focus groups with detectives and prosecutors at Moroka Police Station and Protea Magistrates Court in Soweto*. Research report written for the Centre for the Study of Violence and Reconciliation, 2001. http://www.csvr.org.za/docs/policing/witnessinthecriminal.pdf [Retrieved 19 March 2019].

Prinsloo, M.; Alberts, M. & Mollema, N. 2015. *Legal terminology: Criminal law, procedure and evidence*. Cape Town: Juta.

Ralarala, M.K. 2012. A compromise of rights, rights of language and right to a language in Eugene Terre'Blanche's (ET) trial within a trial: Evidence lost in translation. *Stellenbosch Papers in Linguistics,* 41:55-70. https://doi.org/10.5774/41-0-43

Ralarala, M.K. 2014. Transpreters' translations of complainants' narratives as evidence: Whose version goes to court? *The Translator*, 20(3):377-395.

Ralarala, M.K. 2016. An analysis of critical "voices" and "style" in transpreters' translations of complainants' narratives. *Translation and Translanguaging in Multilingual Contexts,* 2(1):142-166. https://doi.org/10.1075/ttmc.2.1.08ral

Ralarala, M.K. 2017. Language and law: "cultural translation" of narratives into sworn statements. In: R.H. Kaschula, P. Maseko & H.E. Wolff (eds.), *Multilingualism and intercultural communication: A South African perspective*. Johannesburg, South Africa: Wits University Press. pp. 211-222.

Rock, F. 2001. The genesis of a witness statement. *Forensic Linguistics*, 8(2):44-72.

Rodgers, J. 2000. *Befolyásolási képesség* [*Influencing abilities*]. Translated by A. Borbás, Budapest: Scolar.

Rodrigues, T.R. 2017. Transcending solely print-based texts through blogging – a multimodal approach. *Alternation*, 24(2):167-190.

Sacks, H. 1992. *Lectures on conversation*, Vols. I & II. Oxford: Blackwell.

Sacks, H.; Schegloff, E.A. & Jefferson, G. 1974. A simplest systematics for the organization of turn-taking for conversation. *Language*, 50:696-735.

Schiffrin, D. 1994. *Approaches to discourse*. Oxford: Blackwell.

Searle, J.R. 1969. *Speech acts: An essay in the philosophy of language*. Cambridge: Cambridge University Press. https://doi.org/10.1017/CBO9781139173438

Searle, J.R. 1979. *Expression and meaning: Studies in the theory of speech acts*. Cambridge: Cambridge University Press.

Shepherd, E. & Milne, R. 1999. Full and faithful: Ensuring quality practice and integrity of outcome in witness interviews. In: A. Heaton-Armstrong, E. Shepherd & D. Wolchover (eds.), *Analysing witness testimony: A guide for legal practitioners and other professionals*. London: Blackstone Press. pp. 125-145.

Shepherd, E. & Mortimer A. 1999. Identifying anomaly in evidential text. In: A. Heaton-Armstrong, E. Shepherd & D. Wolchover, *Analysing witness testimony: A guide for legal practitioners and other professionals*. London: Blackstone Press. pp. 267-287.

Strauss, A. 1993. *Continual permutations of action*. New York: Aldine de Gruyter.

The Free Dictionary. http://www.thefreedictionary.com [Retrieved 20 August 2018].

TELL US THE STORY IN YOUR PORTUGUESE, WE CAN UNDERSTAND YOU

The Mozambican justice system's dilemma in enforcement of the sole official language policy

Eliseu Mabasso

Introduction

In multilingual Mozambique, where around 22 African languages are spoken as citizens' first language, the ex-colonial language, Portuguese, is the only official language and it is also the language of the justice system. According to available data (Ngunga & Bavo, 2011), only about 10% of the population speak Portuguese as their first language. Neither the country's Constitution, nor the various legal tools adopted in the country, clearly indicate how to communicate with Mozambican nationals who do not speak Portuguese at all, or who are not sufficiently competent in the language to communicate clearly when they appear at a police station or in a court of law. Using an example recorded in a police station and in a courtroom case as data for this research, this study aims to bring to light one of the major language challenges facing the main stakeholders of the legal system when interviewing and trying suspects or defendants who are not at all, or only partially, proficient in Portuguese.

This chapter adopts a descriptive research methodology and attempts to discuss the negative impact caused by the government's non-inclusive language policy, which hinders the delivery of free and fair justice in the country while also likely embarrassing stakeholders of the justice system in enacting their role. It is hypothesised that, in an effort to comply with the law, police officers and judges conducting interviews and cross-examining suspects and defendants with poor Portuguese proficiency occasionally "persuade" them not to speak their African mother tongue to tell their side of the story, but to do so in the only language of the justice system, despite the negative consequences for justice for the suspects and defendants.

The findings of this study demonstrate that the adoption of a language policy in which Portuguese is the only official language (and therefore the only language of the justice system) negatively affects both police officers and judges who have to comply with legal provisions that prohibit them from using any language other than Portuguese. Occasionally, however, they could end up interacting with suspects or defendants who can understand the official language; although the latter often do not want to cooperate in a language which is alien to them.

The problems arising out of the exclusive use of Portuguese in forensic settings have been a source of major concern in countries with speakers of minority languages, such as in Mozambique. However, to date, there have been few reports on the matter and, as a result, speakers of minority languages are likely to be in trouble when they appear at a police station or in court. Despite this being an issue of major concern in sub-Saharan Africa, particularly in Mozambique (see Heydon & Mabasso, 2018), it has also been reported in Brazil, as reported by Vitorelli (2014). Glougie (2015) argues that speakers of minority a language who are required to speak an official language (L2, second language) should be protected against discrimination on the basis of the level of their L2 proficiency. This chapter examines the negative impact caused by the non-inclusive language policy adopted by the Mozambican government which, on the one hand, hinders the delivery of free and fair justice for citizens of the country and, on the other, is likely to embarrass the stakeholders of the justice system in fulfilling their role.

As mentioned in several studies on forensic linguistics and language and the law, police officers operate at the primary stage within the legal system of most countries, as they are the first to deal with offences before they are taken to a court of law (Gibbons, 2001; Heydon, 2005, 2012; Linfoot, 2008). On the other hand, courtroom judges are the key players when cases are forwarded from police stations, as they have the power vested in them to decide a case. In countries like Mozambique – whose numerous challenges include, amongst others extreme poverty and very low living standards – the population experiences several types of crimes, ranging from minor offences to severe physical and psychological ones. It should be noted that, overall, police officers receive no specific training, neither on language diversity issues nor on investigative interviewing as a whole; and these omissions likely impact on the quality and fairness of a court's "verdict" (which is most often decided at the level of police rather than by a court of law). Likewise, judges are likely to be challenged by communication difficulties caused by language matters in multilingual Mozambique.

TABLE 2.1 Profile of main languages of Mozambique

No.	Language	First-language speakers	%	Provinces
1	Emakhuwa	3 097 788	26.1	Cabo Delgado, Nampula, Niassa, Sofala, Zambézia
2	Portuguese	1 693 024	10.8	All country provinces
3	Shangaan	1 660 319	10.5	Gaza, Maputo, Maputo Cidade, Inhambane, Niassa

INE 2010, National Statistical System from www.ine.gov.mz, cited by Ngunga and Bavo, 2011

Table 2.1 profiles the three largest groups of some 22 languages[1] in multilingual and multicultural Mozambique. These figures[2] demonstrate the low percentage of mother-tongue Portuguese speakers in Mozambique, figures that are far below those for Emakhuwa, the largest group of African language speakers in the country. The quoted figures and percentages must have increased after almost eight years, bearing in mind that the country's life expectancy also increased from 45 years in 2000 to 54 years in 2013, and then to 57.6 years in 2017. These figures are likely to have risen in the 2017 census report, which was due to be released in 2018.[3] Nevertheless, in my view, the figures for both Portuguese mother-tongue speakers and L2 speakers are unlikely to rise even as high as around 12% and 45% respectively.

This situation identifies Mozambique as a country with a mid to high linguistic diversity, if one considers the linguistic diversity suggested by Robinson (1993:52-55). He defines "high linguistic diversity" as "a situation where no more than fifty per cent of the population speak the same language." Despite Portuguese being the only official language enshrined since the country's first Constitution of 1975 (Republic of Mozambique 1975[4]), about 90% of Mozambicans speak one of a number of African languages in the "Bantu" language group; and of this majority, only an estimated 40% speak the official language, either as bilinguals – alongside a local language – or as their mother tongue (about 10%). Portuguese is, however, the sole language used for all official settings, including those of the justice administration system. The negative impact of this single-language policy on suspects and defendants with limited or no mastery of Portuguese has already been discussed elsewhere (Heydon & Mabasso, 2018; Mabasso, 2013, 2014, 2015; Timbane, 2016). The discussion in this chapter focuses on the impact of Mozambique's language policy on delivery of justice in the judicial administration system, particularly in the way police officers and judges deal with language diversity in the fulfilment of their tasks.

Because training is critical for law providers to ensure quality and fair delivery of their work, both police officers and judges are required to fulfil this requirement. A university degree and additional training at a judicial training college is essential for the judges. In Mozambique, the only judicial training college available in the country is located in Matola, a neighbouring city to the capital city, Maputo. Here law graduates are trained to become

---

[1] A more comprehensive list of Mozambican languages can be found at https://www.worldatlas.com/articles/what-languages-are-spoken-in-mozambique.html

[2] According to a recent government announcement, the latest and official figures for the 2017 census were to be announced by the end of October 2018: https://clubofmozambique.com/news/census-reaches-99-per-cent-of-projection-ine/. Results were not available at the time of going to press in 2019. The slightly significant changes that may have occurred over time since the last census should be borne in mind.

[3] See https://www.pambazuka.org/pt/human-security/mo%C3%A7ambique-expectativa-de-vida-aumentou-para-576-anos-de-idade-ainda-longe-da-m%C3%A9dia [Retrieved 5 June 2018].

[4] cedis.fd.unl.pt/wp-content/uploads/2016/02/CONST-MOC-75.pdf [Retrieved 12 December 2018].

either magistrates or judges. They are then employed in the various levels of prosecution and courts across the country. A recent study by Heydon and Mabasso (2018:84-106), which also analysed data collected at the judicial training college, has revealed the need for trainees to be provided with training to "recognise the obstacles to justice caused by language in Maputo and elsewhere in Mozambique".

Basic requirements for police force applicants

According to Decree No. 24/99 of 24 May 1999, which passed the Police Statute, the requirements for Mozambican citizens to apply and qualify for basic police positions are as follows: (i) a minimum education the level of Standard 10; (ii) a minimal age of 19 and a maximum age of 30; (iii) candidates should have successfully served in the army; (iv) candidates should have a pass mark in the basic police course (six months); and (v) candidates should have successfully served for at least two years as probationers.[5]

Overall, any Mozambican citizen would be eligible for membership in the Mozambican police force. However, because of increasing suspicion over alleged cooperation of most police officers with most wanted criminals and, more recently, evidence of police directly participating in crimes of kidnapping with huge ransom demands, particularly of wealthy citizens, there have been widespread attempts to improve the selection process. Local populations where potential candidates reside are called upon to gather and clear those candidates of any link to people suspected of misconduct and misbehaviour within the communities concerned. This process occurs in the presence of senior police officers and the local traditional leadership. Only after community "approval" can candidates expect to become members of the police force, once they have undergone the police course. Despite this, crime has increased a great deal over the past couple of decades; and, apparently, low wages and poor working conditions within the police force are the main causes of this phenomenon.

As soon as shortlisted candidates are known, they are taken to a police training camp called "Centro de Formação Policial de Matalane" (Matalane Police Training Centre). Here they undergo a six-month training programme in very basic police skills. It should be noted that even the newly established "Serviço Nacional de Investigação Criminal" (SERNIC (National Forensic Police Service)) undertakes the same course; and they usually receive no additional specific training, such as investigative interviewing and guidance in dealing with language related crimes. At the higher education level, there is a police academy called "Academia de Ciências Policiais" (ACIPOL (Police Training College)) which trains police officers at the undergraduate and postgraduate levels. The first Master's curriculum in

---

[5] http://bit.ly/2WAOCjq [Retrieved 12 December 2018].

Criminal Investigation to be developed has been approved and is now offered to post-graduate trainees in various related fields. In addition, a module on forensic linguistics is now being offered (I taught the module for the 2018 student intake).

In my view, one of the major challenges facing the master's course in criminal investigation is the establishment of a proper code of practice and a model, or technique, that would guide police officers in their daily work. Despite the fact that ACIPOL has been training police officers for about a decade, it was clear, based on accounts from master's course students gathered by myself through a module evaluation form, that investigative interviewing techniques and other critical police skills are not given the required attention, so students do not learn to handle criminal offences of several kinds. Nevertheless, the new master's course seems to bring new hope for the development of modern practices for police interviewing in Mozambique. There are two well-known major models that have been developed which could form the basis for police training: the PEACE Model and the Reid Technique (Mulayim, 2015). The former, designed as a guideline for all types of interviews about any case, is illustrated in Figure 2.1.

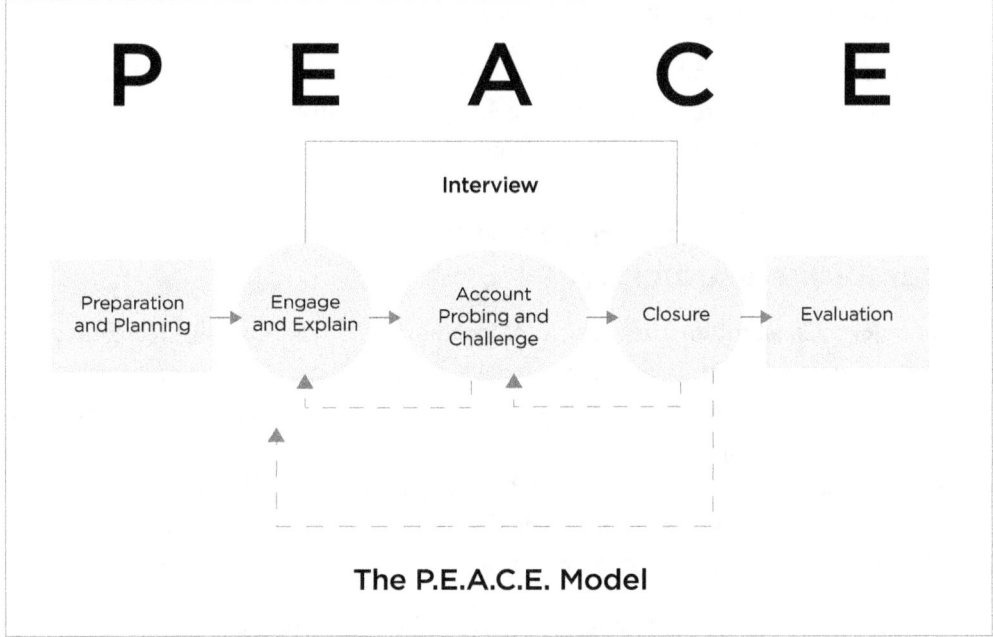

FIGURE 2.1 The PEACE Model
Mulayim et al., 2015

This model seems by far to be the best option for the interviewing process in countries like Mozambique. According to Mulayim et al. (2015), the model originated in the 1990s as a result of a number of miscarriages of justice in the United Kingdom. It was a response to a series of cases in which the police would begin an interview on the assumption that the suspect was guilty and then proceed to ask intimidatory, threatening and rather biased questions so as to incriminate the suspect (Mulayim et al., 2015). As demonstrated in Figure 2.1, the PEACE Model takes the interview process through the five stages of (i) planning and preparation, followed by repetition of the next three phases in circular (ii) engagement and explanation, (iii) probing of the account, (iv) and closure, until there is sufficient evidence for reasonable (v) evaluation.

The Reid Technique (Mulayim et al., 2015), another well-known framework, has some features similar to the PEACE Model. This technique was developed in the United States and is mostly aimed at training police with skills to persuade suspects to confess a crime (Mulayim et al., 2015). The technique is characterised by two main approaches during the interviewing and interrogation process, namely maximisation – which includes intimidation, presentation of false evidence and exaggeration of the seriousness of the crime or charge; and minimisation – which includes downplaying the seriousness of the crime, with a view to persuading a suspect to confess a crime. Because of its intimidatory and oppressive approach, there have some criticisms of the technique. Nonetheless, it still enjoys popularity and support by the US judicial authorities.

As mentioned, notwithstanding the absence of a code of practice in Mozambique's police force, the strategies adopted in the Reid Technique are probably closer to the strategies currently adopted by the police in Mozambique.

Customary law and written law practices in Mozambique's judiciary

Mozambique's Constitution (Republic of Mozambique, 1975) formally recognises the country as a state where the rule of law prevails, and the Romano-German law system is (or, at least, should be) the only legal system enforced in courts of law and, by implication, in police stations (Mabasso, 2013). As a logical corollary, various legal provisions in force within the country's justice system need to be strictly fulfilled. On the language front, this includes the measure that Portuguese, being the country's sole official language, is the only language that can be used in courtroom sessions and also in police interviews.

On the contrary, for reasons including historic and cultural factors, the so-called "customary law" system, based on traditional methods for finding someone guilty or innocent, is widely used for punishing offenders; particularly – but not only – in the rural areas of Mozambique. Historically, application of the so-called "written law" in Mozambican society was implemented only after the commencement of Portuguese settlement in the 15th century AD. Long-existing traditional techniques to punish the criminal had already been in force since the earliest indigenous communities arrived in the territory. These remain in force even today, as most communities, particularly in rural areas, rely predominantly on traditional methods based on common sense to ensure that "justice" and order prevail in their communities. Furthermore, in their interactions, both traditional leadership and the respondents/claimants emphasise narratives as the basic genre for suspects to give account of a criminal event or offence (see also Mabasso, 2012, 2013).

One remarkable feature of investigations in numerous police stations in Mozambique is the use by both suspects and complainants of family members or friends who join them during the interviewing process. They usually act as if they are witnesses summoned by the police. In the so-called "summary" crimes, for instance, their role ranges from pressuring the police to release their family member(s) based on positive personal characteristics that make their family member not guilty of the charge concerned, to persuading the police to drop the case (Mabasso, 2013). This is a typical occurrence in the customary law system, where relatives and community members play a critical role in the reaching of a "verdict" for the case (compare Gluckman, 1966). Given that police officers usually share the same cultural values as the suspects, they end up "tolerating" the presence of suspects' relatives and friends, who often play a major role in the way the process will be addressed. This would probably not occur in other societies, such as Western societies where the written law is strictly enforced.

In courtroom sessions, there is also a timid attempt to incorporate a few aspects of the customary law system. In Mozambique's judicial system, so-called "community judges" at a court trial are usually a couple of people (usually a male and a female) selected from the community to represent community inclusiveness in the process of the jury's decision-making. These people, who are expected to be "ideal" adults, could be compared to jurors in the common law system (see Gibbons, 2017) and are not trained legal practitioners. In addition, in most cases, they do not necessarily understand the various components of individual legal proceedings, despite being allowed to take part in first instance judgements that lead to decisions in a case.[6] Their ultimate role is to represent community sensitivity over a case, which could also be controversial to some extent, as their word would never actually alter a judge's decision.

The method, the field and the data

As pointed out previously, the findings in this chapter result from a case involving an audio-recorded police interview and a hearing in a court on the outskirts of Mozambique's capital city, Maputo. The target population was a police officer interviewing two male suspects, and a female defendant being questioned by a judge in a courtroom.

---

[6] http://www.jornalnoticias.co.mz/index.php/politica/50809-juizes-eleitos-ar-analisa-candidaturas.html [Retrieved 2 June 2018].

For the case study, I adopted a descriptive research design with aspects of an ethnographic approach (Saville-Troike, 1989). This approach was adopted to account for variables such as suspects' education, mother tongue, language proficiency, age, etc., which are critical for describing the accused. I collected the data (recording with a smartphone at the aforementioned police station and in a courtroom) from the questions, some focused, but mostly open-ended, posed to two suspects by a police officer; and to a defendant by a judge. After making transcripts, I analysed them by identifying fragments where the language issues occurred, and these fragments themselves played a superordinate role (Mabasso, 2013). As the researcher, I did not interfere in the interview processes, except to collect personal details of the suspects. Aspects such as hesitations, interjections, stuttering, silence and even poor quality of audio recording were taken into account in the verbatim transcripts (Gibbons, 1996). This is because, in the case of hesitation and silence, for instance, several different interpretations could emerge as a result of the interviewing process (Goldflam, 1995; Mabasso, 2013).

The transcriptions of the audio recordings were grouped into short sets of selected interactions and conversation turns between the suspects and the defendant and the police officer and the judge in each case. Through analysing these transcripts, I will attempt to demonstrate the potential for miscarriages of justice present in both the police interviews and in the courtroom hearings, due to the linguistic diversity of suspects and their lack of proficiency in Portuguese; bearing in mind that a participant's lack of proficiency in the state's official language (and language of their judicial system) can prevent a suspect or defendant's access to justice (Gibbons, 2003).

It should be noticed that the recording of police interviews and of courtroom sessions in Mozambique (verbatim transcripts) is not a common practice and, therefore, not yet encouraged by the judicial authorities, even for research purposes. Because of suspicion by the police officer and the judge in both cases, I had to present credentials provided by Eduardo Mondlane University to the local police authorities; but, even then, collaboration was far from reasonable. This was probably due to the existing record of media and public criticisms over alleged unfair delivery of justice and corruption in the judiciary in Mozambican society[7]. I had to negotiate skilfully to convince the authorities that the aim of my research was merely for academic purposes, that the identity of the stakeholders would be protected, and that the handling of "sensitive" issues related to both cases would not be released to the general public, particularly at police station level.

---

[7] http://www.verdade.co.mz/destaques/democracia/44564-corrupcao-ainda-e-um-obstaculo-a-justica-em-mocambique [Retrieved 13 December 2018].

Data analysis

The following extracts were taken from a police interview conducted at one of the major police stations located on the outskirts of Mozambique's capital city, Maputo. The police station serves a range of neighbourhoods well known for high crime rates. The case involved two suspects accused of stealing a mobile phone and both suspects were apparently seen nearby the crime scene by the complainant.

No.	Utterance	English gloss
	Police: Senhor X, pode contar bem o que aconteceu?	**Police**: Mr X, can you tell us what happened?
1	**Suspect (1)**: eu e o meu *brada* estivemos a tomar uns copos naquela barraca amarela. Eu pedi o meu *brada* para controlar o meu copo porque … porque … eu queria ir fazer xixi [urinar]. Depois aquele ali,… aquele senhor mulato falou que eu, eu, eu … eu e esse senhor aqui *roubou* celular dele e foi esconder nas casa de banho, eu yhu!!! *Anitivi telefone, mina* [não tenho conhecimento de nenhum telefone, eu]! *Eu não levou* celular de ninguém nem nada, eu! *A malta estamos* a bater copos e *a malta não vimos* telefone de ninguém. Eu, eu, eu … eu *não rouba* de ninguém, eu!! *Eu não sabe* de nada, eu! *Anitekanga xa munhu mina* [eu não retirei nada alheio]!	**Suspect (1)**: my friend and I were having a few drinks at that yellow take away. I asked my friend to look after my glass because … because … I wanted to piss. Then that coloured man said that I, I … I stole his mobile phone and hided it in the toilet and, I said "yhu"!!! I know nothing about your mobile! I did not rob anyone's mobile or anything alike! We are having a few drinks and we have not seen anyone's mobile. I, I, I … don't steal people's things!!! I did not take anyone's things.
2	**Police**: e depois …	**Police**: and then …
	Suspect (1): e depois aquele senhor disse que vamos *queixar o problema no esquadra* [delegacia]. É por causa disso ai que *a malta viemos* para aqui. *Eu não roubou* nada eu! *Eu não sabe* de nada de telefone de ninguém, eu!	**Suspect (1)**: then that man said we should forward the case to the police. That is why we came here. I did not steal anything. I know nothing about anyone's mobile phone!

No.	Utterance	English gloss
	Police: e o senhor é o Y? Conta o que se passou.	**Police**: and are you Mr Y? Tell us what happened.
3	**Suspect (2)**: Senhor Agente, fiquei estupefato ao ser acusado de ter roubado um telemóvel. É a pior aberração que alguma vez me ocorreu na vida. Este senhor aqui [o ofendido] cismou com a minha pessoa pelo desespero de ter ficado sem o telemóvel dele. Ora fui eu, ora foi este jovem aqui. Em minha casa não me falta o mínimo, sr. Agente. O que faria eu com a venda de um S3 [Samsung Galaxy Smartphone 3]? Olha bem para mim, senhor [referindo-se ao ofendido]. Enxerga-me bem e repare em ti [referindo-se à comparação do traje dois dois]!	**Suspect (2)**: Yo sir, I was stunned when I found myself as a suspect of stealing a mobile phone. This is the weirdest thing that could happen to me. This man [pointing towards the complainant] is insisting that I am the one who stole his mobile phone because he is desperate to find it back. Sometimes he says it was me and at other times he says it was this young man. I have everything I need in my house, sir. What can I do with the money from selling an S3? Look carefully at me [turning to the complainant]. Have a look at me and then look at you [comparing the clothing both were wearing].
4	**Police**: Está bem. Sr. Y, fica dispensado, por enquanto. Nós temos os seu dados pessoais. Logo que for necessário será contactado. Vamos fazer a diligência com com este jovem aqui, por enquanto. Está compreendido? Mas isso não significa que seja inocente, que fique bem claro isso! Nós vamos fazer o nosso trabalho de investigar o caso. A qualquer momento podemos chamar.	**Police**: Alright Mr Y, you may go for now. We have recorded your personal details. We will contact you when deemed necessary. The diligence will be over for this man, in the meantime. Do you understand that? But that does not mean you are cleared and that should be crystal clear! We are going to pursue our investigation over the case. You may be called back at any time.

As mentioned, this is a case about a stolen mobile phone, a device which, in today's Mozambican society, may be stolen by people regardless of their social background; and, given the market value that mobile phones and other related devices hold, anyone could, within reasonable expectations, be a perpetrator of such a robbery in public areas and even on private premises. It is, indeed, a device that could easily be stolen and sold.

Suspect X in the transcript is a 25-year-old man who speaks Shangaan as his mother tongue. He has reportedly completed primary education to Standard 4. Not surprisingly, he is unemployed and he survives as a hawker. Suspect Y, on the other hand, is said to be 29 years of age and has a technical diploma in Chemistry. He works for a well-known local company in Maputo. His mother tongue is Portuguese and he lives in one of the more affluent Maputo City neighbourhoods.

As far the language proficiency of X is concerned, his Portuguese proficiency is relatively poor, or at least it does not meet average standards for L2 speakers in Maputo. For example, he uses an English loan word which means "brother" in the source language; but, in the case of the Portuguese slang in Maputo, this word has undergone a restrictive semantic process and the only meaning is "friend" (see Lopes et al., 2013). Overall, this word is used by young people from both Maputo City and its outskirts. However, if its use in informal settings is easily accepted, this is not the case in formal settings, such as in police stations or courtrooms, as the use of this word could be interpreted as a pointer to a speaker's lack of education or even of some delinquency.

Another issue with suspect X's language proficiency is over-elaboration, as seen in his exaggeration of the personal pronoun *eu* (I). Unlike English, in Portuguese, which is also a language of the SVO (subject, verb and object) typology, the use of a subject marker is not necessarily mandatory once it has been announced. This is because, in Portuguese, the subject marker can be found in the verb inflection itself, which differs from one personal pronoun to another. Amongst speakers of Portuguese in Mozambique, over-elaboration can be viewed as lack of basic knowledge of the standard Portuguese grammar rules. In line with this, in fragments (3) and (4), the suspect has demonstrated a poor command of verbal inflection and poor command in number, which is very important in Portuguese: for example (in the italicised phrases), he uses *a malta estamos* ("we are" – instead of the correct form *a malta está*); *a malta não vimos* ("we did not see" – instead of *a malta não viu*); *eu não roubou* ("I did not steal" – instead of *eu não roubei*). There was also codeswitching between Portuguese and Shangaan (the second major African language in Mozambique following Emakhuwa).

It is true that, from a communication viewpoint, the aforesaid phenomena alone could not prevent the police officer from understanding the suspect's message. However, the stereotypes that have already been constructed over time about people who speak "broken" Portuguese with similar features might have played a role in the officer's decision on who to incriminate. These features of "broken" and undereducated Portuguese would have favoured suspect Y instead of suspect X. The former has a better command of the Portuguese language as noted by his making better grammatical and vocabulary choices. Another key factor that is critical and can be an advantage for a suspect when interviewed is their accent. It is true that dialectal features of suspects are beyond the scope of this study, but the fact that suspect Y's accent was closely near native Portuguese was certainly something to be taken into account. In her study, Glougie (2015) has demonstrated how accent can be a critical issue for second language speakers if they are not protected by a legal tool, as in a case in British Columbia. As she puts it "minority language speakers who are required to operate in a majority language, which is their L2, ought to be protected against discrimination on the basis of their proficiency in that L2" (Glougie, 2015:1). Despite accent not being the focus of this study, it needs to be mentioned that it plays a key role in assigning people to a particular social status. From ordinary people's daily experience, it seems that the closer an accent is to the native Portuguese accent, the more likely it is for that person to be assigned to a middle or even higher social class status; and the opposite (that is, when someone's accent is more "Africanised") also seems to hold true. In addition to this, suspect Y was dressed in better clothing and was very quiet. These details are critical when one is being interviewed by the police in Mozambique. Unfortunately, such factors are never ignored by the justice administration stakeholders, including police officers and judges. Suspect X's poor proficiency seems to be the only ground used by the police to incriminate him, because this kind of crime tends to be committed by people who have not been to school and, therefore, have little or no command of Portuguese. People who live in neighbourhoods known for their poverty have limited access to jobs. Bearing in mind the commonly held view of the general population, they could be innocent, but their living conditions, with very low or no income, means that they are more likely to be driven to commit criminal offences.

Trials of cases involving mobile phone theft are rare in the Mozambican context and, in most cases, complainants either end up withdrawing the case and accepting the loss, or police's coercive measures lead to disclosure of the "truth". The use of coercive measures by Mozambique's police force to obtain confessions from suspects has been a widespread practice, despite efforts by civil society organisations acting as government watchdogs. As mentioned earlier, neither the PEACE Model nor the Reid Technique is formally adopted by the Mozambique police force when interviewing suspects (see Mulayim et al., 2015). Nonetheless, based on practical evidence from previous studies (Mabasso, 2012), maximisation as a valid tactic is often used by the police to intimidate, present false evidence and exaggerate the seriousness of a crime and charges, on the one hand; while minimisation, on the other hand, is less likely to be adopted. The final outcome of the case under analysis is unknown; but, if one looks at the way the case was dealt with at the outset, investigation carried out with the young man with very low proficiency and a "bad" accent in Portuguese (see also Glougie, 2015) makes it very likely that, as in many other similar cases (including those studied elsewhere by Benneworth-Gray, 2014; and Newbury and Johnson, 2006), this case was not escalated to court and the police might have adopted oppressive measures to find the "truth".

The case that follows concerns a lady who appeared before the court as a defendant after being sued by her partner for refusing to have sexual intercourse with him. It was recorded at a local court called the Tribunal Judicial do Distrito Municipal KaMaxakene (the Ka-Maxakene Municipality District Court). Although an English gloss has been provided for each extract to assist the reader in understanding the dialogue, it should be noted that cross-language aspects of the defendant's Portuguese, such as code mixing and grammar issues, cannot be understood from the English gloss.

No.	Utterance	English gloss
5	**Judge:** *Senhora X, não foi a senhora quem negou de continuar a manter relações com o senhor Y?*	**Judge:** Mrs X, wasn't it you who refused to keep your relationship with Mr Y?
	Defendant: *Não, a timhaka i kuvutisa svaku kasi i mhaka muni, só! Se ahitwanani!*	**Defendant:** [speaking in Shangaan] No, the problem is just because I only asked him what the problem was! So, we did not understand each other.
6	**Judge:** *Quando é que surge essa casa, antes ou agora que há problemas entre vocês os dois?*	**Judge:** When did this house come up in your lives? Was it before or now that you are both in trouble?
	Defendant: *Hi svosvi hingani mapurubulema.*	**Defendant:** [in Shangaan] It was now that we're in trouble.
7	**Community judge:** *No meio do vosso casamento há filhos?*	**Community judge:** In your marriage, did you have any children?
	Defendant: *Nada, anipsvalanga na yena.*	**Defendant:** No, [in Shangaan] we don't have any children together.
8	**Judge:** *Senhora X, pode sentar-se, por favor. Sinta-se à vontade! Pode dizer o que está a acontecer?*	**Judge:** Mrs X, you may sit please. Feel free! Can you tell us what the matter is?
	Defendant: *Eu vai falar em changana. Anixitivi xilungu mina! Eu não estudou.*	**Defendant:** I will speak in Shangaan. [in Shangaan] I don't speak any Portuguese. I did not go to school.
9	**Judge:** *Diga-nos o que aconteceu em Português, nós conseguimos entender!*	**Judge:** Tell us your story in Portuguese, we can understand you!
	Defendant: *Anixitivi xilungu mina!*	**Defendant:** [in Shangaan] I don't speak any Portuguese!

Fragments 5 and 6 above could be pointers to the defendant's poor language proficiency: she refuses to speak Portuguese when questioned by the judge. Additionally, in fragments 8 and 9, she attempts to convince the judge that she cannot defend herself in Portuguese; but, after hearing a few words in a sentence in which she codeswitches sentences and commits grammar errors, the judge goes on by reaffirming that she should tell her story in Portuguese because they (he) could understand her. A recent study by Heydon and Mabasso (2018) has revealed how linguistic perception, particularly by judges, should be addressed as a priority, as they seem to regard issues such as language diversity from a different perspective. In other words, it seems to be strongly believed by most lawyers and judges that their clients and plaintiffs or defendants do not need to understand various aspects of the legal proceedings. All clients need, they argue, is to hear what their legal representatives will tell them about their case (Heydon & Mabasso, 2018). In this case, the judge can clearly understand the defendant's language but is aware that he should not speak any language other than Portuguese (Art. 10 of Mozambique's Constitution[8] and Art. 139

---

[8] http://www.portaldogoverno.gov.mz/index.php/por/Governo/Legislacao/Constituicao-da-Republica-de-Mocambique [Retrieved 13 December 2018].

of Civil Proceedings Code (Issa et al., 2010)). Article 98 of the Criminal Procedure Code (2014) requires courts to appoint an interpreter for non-Portuguese speaking defendants, and states that a court case can be suspended if the defendant does not speak the language of the court or is not proficient enough and cannot be assisted by a qualified interpreter. Strikingly but not surprisingly, the judge is also "breaching" the law by allowing the defendant to present her side of the story in a language that is "forbidden" by the law. This is a widespread dilemma faced by both the police and judges as a result of the coexistence of the aforesaid two legal frameworks that can sometimes be contradictory.

It should be recalled that Mozambique is one of the former Portuguese colonies where indigenous languages were neglected and even undermined by the ruling colonial regime; and that all legal tools are written in Portuguese. Furthermore, over the years, there have been attempts to "kill" these indigenous languages in favour of the language of the "civilised" people, the Portuguese. The case of the languages of indigenous people in Brazil, another former Portuguese colony, could fall into the same category as those of people in Mozambique. Vitorelli (2014) describes the discrimination faced by native people of Brazil in which indigenous people are strictly forbidden to speak their native languages when they appear in court, despite various bills passed to protect their civil rights in that country.

Judges in Mozambique are supported by so-called "community judges" as representatives of the communities in the legal process; these are people taken from the communities and are said to be reliable and in good community standing, but in most cases they end up not adding value in terms of filling the gap created by the defendants and plaintiffs' poor language proficiency, owing to the aforesaid legal barriers. Indeed, in most cases the community judges may not even speak the language of either of the parties involved.

Conclusion

This study points to the fact that, in Mozambique as a whole and particularly in the justice system, language issues still need to be addressed if people's human rights are to be respected. On the one hand, both police officers and judges are aware of the barriers created by the need to comply with the legal provisions of language; but, on the other hand, they also are aware of the complexities surrounding the need to comply with the law and reach a verdict for individual cases. Justice cannot be served if communication is not established between the participants. Thus, a more inclusive language policy should be approved in Mozambique to ensure than neither party is pushed to breach the law. A revised law would allow people who come before a police station or a court of law to present their account of an issue in the language they know best.

Police officers and judges need to be provided with robust training to enable them to handle cases involving vulnerable people, such as speakers of languages other than Portuguese, or those with poor or low proficiency in Portuguese. The PEACE Model seems to be the most appropriate tool and a pathway towards a more structured interviewing framework for policing in Mozambique, despite the Reid Technique being much closer to the actual practices in Mozambican policing. Likewise, it is recommended that judges are provided with regular language training so as to raise their awareness of the matter; and the training and engagement of bilingual courtroom judges should also be considered. Finally, full-time and qualified police-station and courtroom interpreters would have to be trained and engaged by the government, to assist speakers of languages other than Portuguese to communicate without risking self-incrimination. This would also go some way to preventing police officers and lawyers from demonstrating stereotypical bias based on defendants and plaintiffs' relative Portuguese language proficiency.

References

Benneworth-Gray, K. 2014. "Are you going to tell me the truth today?" Invoking obligations of honesty in police-suspect interviews. *The International Journal of Speech, Language and the Law*, 21(2):251-277.

Gibbons, J. 1996. Distortion of police interviews process revealed by video-tape. *Forensic Linguistics*, 3(2):288-298.

Gibbons, J. 2001. Revising the language of New South Wales Police Procedures: Applied Linguistics in action. *Applied Linguistics*, 22(4):439-470.

Gibbons, J. 2003. *Forensic linguistics. An introduction to language in the justice system*. Oxford: Blackwell Publishing.

Gibbons, J. 2017. Towards clearer jury instructions. *Language and Law/Linguagem e Direito*, 4(1):142-160.

Glougie, J. 2015. Linguistic proficiency and human rights: The case for accent as a protected ground. *Language and Law/Linguagem e Direito*, 2(1):76-89.

Gluckman, M. 1966. *Ideas and procedures in African customary law*. Oxford: Oxford University Press.

Goldflam, R. 1995. Silence in court! Problems and prospects in Aboriginal legal interpreting. In: D. Eades (ed.), *Language in evidence: Issues confronting aboriginal and multicultural Australia*, Sydney: University of South Wales Press. pp. 28-54.

Heydon, G. 2005. *The language of police interviewing: A critical analysis*. London: Palgrave Macmillan.

Heydon, G. 2012. Helping the police with their enquiries: Enhancing the investigative interview with linguistic research. *The Police Journal*, 85:101-122.

Heydon, G. & Mabasso, E. 2018. The impact of multilingualism on reporting domestic violence. *Language Matters*, 49(1):84-106.

Issá, A.C.M.; Garcia, I.; Jeque, N. & Timbane T. 2010. *Código de Processo Penal (com as Alterações Introduzidas)*. Maputo: Unidade Técnica de Reforma Legal.

Linfoot, K. 2008. Forensic linguistics, first-contact police interviews, and basic training. (Abstract of PhD thesis). *International Journal of Speech Language and the Law*, 15(2):267-270.

Lopes, A.J.; Sitoe, S. & Nhamuende, P. 2013. *Moçambicanisos: Para Um Léxico do Português Moçambicano*. Luanda: Editora das Letras [original publication 2002, Maputo: Livraria Universitária].

Mabasso, E. 2012. Língua oficial, direito positivo e direito costumeiro nas esquadras de Moçambique: Um caso para a linguística forense. *Revista Científica da Universidade Eduardo Mondlane*, 1:40-61.

Mabasso, E. 2013. *Official language, written and customary laws in Mozambican police stations*. Paper presented at the 11th Biennial Conference of the International Association of Forensic Linguists on Forensic Linguistics/Language and Law, Universidade Autónoma do México, Mexico City, 24-27 June.

Mabasso, E. 2015. Justiça Justa ou não Justiça Justa: Eis a Questão Linguística na Administração da Justiça em Moçambique. *Savana*, 20 February. pp. 14-15.

Mulayim, S.; Lai, M. & Norma, C. 2015. *Police interviews and interpreting: Context, challenges, and strategies*. London: CRC Press.

Newbury, P. & Johnson, A. 2006. Suspects' resistance to constraining and coercive questioning strategies in the police interview. *The International Journal of Speech, Language and the Law,* 13(2):213-240.

Ngunga, A. & Bavo, N. 2011. *Práticas linguística em Moçambique: Avaliação de vitalidade linguística em seis distritos*. Maputo: Centro dos Estudos Africanos.

República de Moçambique. 2014. *Código de Processo Penal de Moçambique e Legislação Complementar de Moçambique*. 2nd edition. Maputo: Colecção Universitária.

Robinson, C.D. 1993. Where linguistic minorities are in the majority: Language dynamics amidst high linguistic diversity. *AILA Review*, 10:52-70.

Saville-Troike, M. 1989. *The Ethnography of Communication*. Oxford: Blackwell.

Timbane, A.A. 2016. A justiça moçambicana e questões de interpretação forense: Um longo percurso a percorrer. *Language and Law/Linguagem e Direito*, 3(2):78-97.

Vitorelli, E. 2014. Linguistic minorities in court: The exclusion of indigenous peoples in Brazil. *Language and Law/Linguagem e Direito*, 1(1):159-173.

PART 2
Language practice in the legal process

"LIKE GIVING A WHEELCHAIR TO SOMEONE WHO SHOULD BE WALKING"

Interpreter access and the problematisation of linguistic diversity in the justice system

Joseph MacFarlane, Ceyhan Sirma Kurt, Georgina Heydon & Andy Roh

Introduction

While Australian society claims to celebrate and value cultural diversity, the same cannot always be said about the country's approach to non-English languages. With over 300 languages spoken, including more than 100 indigenous languages, public institutions are faced with the challenge of recognising and catering for linguistic diversity in practice. A key approach for addressing this is the enhanced provision of interpreters. While improvements have been made for many government services, a notable exception is in the justice system where, in legal settings, the provision of interpreters remains inadequate, both in terms of quantity and quality. Furthermore, the discretionary use of interpreters means that, even where qualified interpreters are available, they can still be underused in practice. Both problems are indicative of an ideology which both privileges English monolingualism and suppresses the language practices and preferences of minority language speakers. In this chapter, we address the practical concerns that this ideological position gives rise to, with the aim of promoting an orientation that views linguistic diversity as a resource to be harnessed, rather than a "problem" to be overcome by imposing the normative standards of English monolingualism.

National diversity

Australia is seeing an increase in its linguistic diversity, with over 300 languages spoken, and 21% of the population primarily speaking a language other than English at home. Since 2011, the proportion of English monolingual speakers has decreased from 77% to 73%, indicating that multilingualism has also become an increasing part of Australian society, according to the Australian Bureau of Statistics (ABS, 2016a). Further to this, over 450 000 people between the ages of 15 and 69 who speak a language other than English have also reported speaking English either not well or not at all (ABS, 2016b). While this represents only a small percentage of the population, it remains important to recognise that, for many, English is not always the preferred language through which to communicate. According to the second National Indigenous Languages Survey in 2014, 120 indigenous languages were still being spoken in Australia, a number which has decreased from 145 in 2005; and prior to the British invasion, over 250 traditional indigenous languages were spoken (Marmion, Obata & Troy, 2018). The National Aboriginal and Torres Strait Islander Social Survey has also found that around 38% of Aboriginal and Torres Strait Islander people over the age of 15 speak an indigenous language, with 11% speaking an indigenous language at home (ABS, 2016b). Over 70% of Aboriginal and Torres Strait Islander people living in remote communities speak an indigenous language (ABS, 2016b). While this is only a brief snapshot, it indicates that linguistic diversity remains a significant aspect of Australian society.

The increasing diversity of Australian society has been accompanied by political rhetoric that often claims to celebrate this diversity. This is exemplified in Australia's Multicultural Statement which depicts the country as a united, egalitarian society which "flourishes in part thanks to our cultural diversity" (2017:7). However, while cultural differences might be celebrated, linguistic diversity is a less welcome presence. The Statement makes a point of stressing that "English is and will remain our national language and is a critical tool for migrant integration" (2017:13), implying that not to speak English is not to integrate into Australian life. Furthermore, while the statement recognises that Australia has historically been a highly multilingual society, with over 250 indigenous languages and hundreds more dialects spoken before colonisation began in 1788, it also states that "modern" Australia was realised through British and Irish settlement (2017:7), which brought with it the introduction and imposition of English as the de facto national language (Marmion et al., 2014; Lo Bianco, 1987). Indeed, the deliberate suppression of indigenous languages has been well documented, with speakers sometimes facing physical punishment for using them (Human Rights and Equal Opportunity Commission, 1997; Lo Bianco, 1987). While Lo Bianco (1987) claims that Australia has sought to reverse its trend towards English monolingualism, its contemporary multicultural statement largely depicts English as the language of modernity, progress, opportunity and national unity. Furthermore, public spaces and major institutions are frequently built on an ideal of English monolingualism that renders them inaccessible to many (Piller, 2016). The high value afforded English in Australia is further reflected in an ongoing push to implement tougher English-language testing for newly arrived migrants in order for them to gain citizenship. As such, while the country might claim to tolerate limited amounts of linguistic diversity in private circles, efforts to enforce linguistic unification through English remain structurally embedded, especially in public domains.

Access to language services

Given the hegemonic status of English in Australia, access to language services has become a necessity to mitigate the disadvantage that this creates for speakers of minority languages. This has typically come via the growth of interpreter services and accreditation bodies, for example, the National Translating and Interpreting Service (TIS National), initially established in 1973 and renamed the Emergency Telephone Interpreter Service; the 1977 founding of the National Accreditation Authority for Translators and Interpreters (NAATI); and the introduction of two government-funded indigenous interpreting services – the Northern Territory Aboriginal Interpreter Service, in 2000, and Western Australia's Kimberley Interpreting Service (also established in 2000 and now named Aboriginal Interpreting WA). Given this expansion, many clients from a Non-English Speaking Background (NESB), or who speak English as an additional language (EAL speakers), have been given greater access to interpreting services to the point where they are often available by request in many public service encounters. This trend in state and federal policies is further reflected in annual reports released by the Access and Equity committee and NAATI (Access and Equity Inquiry Panel, 2012; NAATI, 2016), in which the former mainly stresses increasing "responsiveness" of public services, while the latter presents a statistical increase in demand for accredited language professionals each year.

Exclusion and inadequate services in the justice system

However, a notable exception to the availability and effective use of interpreters is in the justice system. This has long been recognised as a concern with the 1992 report of the Australian Law Reform Commission (ALRC), *Multiculturalism and the Law*, indicating that the justice system suffered from an underuse and under-availability of on-site legal interpreters for people whose first language was not English. While this report focused specifically on Culturally and Linguistically Diverse (CALD) communities in Australia, multiple reviews have also found that the inadequate number of interpreter services for often excludes Aboriginal and Torres Strait Islander people who primarily speak an indigenous language. Illustrative of this is that a year prior to the ALRC review, the 1991 Royal Commission into Aboriginal Deaths in Custody (RCIADIC) had found that indigenous language speakers were being denied legitimate participation in legal matters that affected them because of the absence of interpreters. Almost 30 years later, and the ALRC's (2017) *Pathways to Justice* report echoed the criticisms of the RCIADIC by suggesting that a shortage of properly trained indigenous interpreters was contributing to the stark overrepresentation of Aboriginal and Torres Strait Islander people being held in custody. This is largely because the absence of interpreters can prolong a person's stay in custody if their hearing cannot be fairly conducted in English. Ultimately, this means that, in one of Australia's major institutions, the imposition of a dominant language, combined with the inadequate use and provision of interpreters, continues to marginalise people who predominantly speak a minority language, and devalues their linguistic repertoires. The repeated failure to provide legally-trained, high quality interpreter services for indigenous language speakers, as well as non-indigenous non-English speakers, continues to exclude many from any kind of meaningful participation in the legal process.

It is especially important to recognise that the underuse and under-provision of indigenous language interpreters is especially critical in the justice system. Whereas Aboriginal and Torres Strait Islander people constitute only 2% of the country's total population, they comprise around 27% of the prison population (ABS, 2017a). In the Northern Territory, where over 100 Aboriginal languages and dialects are spoken, Aboriginal people constitute 84% of the adult prison population (ABS, 2017b) and are 13 times more likely to be incarcerated than non-indigenous people. In Western Australia, Aboriginal people are 15 times more likely to be incarcerated than non-indigenous people (ABS, 2017c). Unfortunately no data are publicly available regarding the languages spoken by these populations, or even how frequently interpreters are used, but it is reasonable to assume that many who find themselves in contact with the justice system, particularly in the Northern Territory, speak an indigenous language (Australian Law Reform Commission, 2018; Schwartz & Cunneen, 2009).

As has been well-documented by Blagg (2008), Cunneen (2001), White (2015) and others, the justice system continues to represent a form of colonial control over Aboriginal and Torres Strait Islander peoples. While this is clearly manifested by the hyperincarceration of indigenous peoples (White 2015), Eades (2008) has argued that control also extends to the routine language and communication practices of the justice system, which silence and exclude many indigenous witnesses from any kind of legitimate participation in their own legal matters. For Eades (2008), this is exhibited in the typical practices of a rigid "question-and-answer" format in examinations, which often conflicts with modes of communication used by many indigenous people who often value periods of silence and also use narrative responses to to clarify a situation (Eades, 2008). Common practices of courtroom discourse dictate how and when witnesses are allowed to speak, and what they are allowed to say (Eades, 2008). This has led to perceptions amongst some Aboriginal communities that courts simply do not want to hear what they have to say (Eades, 2000:168). Creating an ongoing need for decolonised approaches that seek to engage indigenous people and their communities in decisions about how to address issues of crime and the administration of justice (Blagg, 2008).

While Eades focused on how courtroom discourse effectively silences witnesses by controlling what they can say and when they can say it, control also extends to the language one is allowed to hear and speak, especially in the justice system. While Australia might no longer openly punish people for primarily speaking a language other than English, it continues to reinforce the hegemonic status of English by ensuring that access to major institutions is limited for speakers of minority languages[1] (Coventry et al., 2015). In the justice system, there are two clear reasons for this: the first, as mentioned, is that there is a shortage of adequately trained legal interpreters in Australia, resulting by default in English monolingualism effectively being imposed on people, irrespective of their proficiency. The second is that English-speaking police and judges often hold discretionary power over when to use the available interpreters. Owing to this, even where interpreters are accessible, they may simply not be used on the belief that English-only communication will suffice. The exercising of this discretion becomes especially important if a person exhibits a superficial level of English-speaking ability, which may be sufficient for everyday conversations but not for the rigours of a police interview or a court proceeding (Cooke, 2002).

The long-standing failure to provide suitable numbers of professional legal interpreters in the justice system, coupled with the discretionary prerogative of officials to decide when (and when not) to use available interpreters, serves to regulate the language choices and preferences of people whose linguistic repertoires do not include English. When an interpreter is not available, a person is forced to act as an English monolingual speaker, irrespective of their relative ability to understand and speak fluently, or of their preference for using their first language to engage according to their own understanding and discretion (Eades, 2012). Conversely, as Cooke (1996) has argued, an interpreter can become a means of linguistic empowerment by allowing minority languages speakers greater access to language choice when giving evidence. It is significant that people's linguistic choices are shaped by the practical logistics of interpreter availability, as well as micro-level decisions which also reflect the broader systemic failure to provide adequate and quality legal interpreting services.

This chapter aims to demonstrate how under-provision of this service in the justice system, together with discretionary use of the available interpreters, emerges from a deep-seated ideological position that privileges and values English monolingualism (and, by extension, English monolingual speakers). Simultaneously, this position devalues and problematises linguistic diversity as a personal deficit, rather than a valuable resource (Ruiz, 1984). This ideological position is in force despite official policy statements claiming to support and celebrate an increasingly diverse Australia. Contemporary government rhetoric around valuing diversity, inclusiveness, tolerance, fairness and equity, often rings hollow in light of such actual practices in the justice system. In this way, the real practice of monolingualism

---

[1] An example of this can be seen in the push by the Strathfield Municipal Council in Sydney for "English only" shop signs; effectively denying the factual existence of community languages other than English. Policies such as this reinforce the primacy of English monolingualism and play a role in the continued subordination of the many languages spoken by local community members (Chik & Benson, 2018).

continues to marginalise linguistic minorities, and to create an environment where miscarriages of justice can and do occur.

The following section of this chapter provides an analysis of the current state of legal interpreting in Australia, and the specific policies and practices of interpreter accreditation, illustrating ongoing shortcomings in the provision of properly trained and accredited legal interpreters in the justice system, despite repeated calls for improvement over the past 30 years. The third part offers an analysis of the discretionary use of interpreters by police during an interview, and by judges during court proceedings, demonstrating how preferring English-only communication simultaneously devalues the appropriate use of a different language. A key case study illustrates the consequences of poorly-exercised discretion in the case of a Pintupi-speaking young Aboriginal man, who suffered a substantial miscarriage of justice after being compelled to undergo multiple police interviews in English. The third part of this chapter discusses how linguistic stratification is embedded in both the law and the institutional discourse of the criminal justice system, a stratification that ensures that English monolingualism remains highly valued, and makes speakers of other languages appear deficient, vulnerable and even disabled in their capacity as communicators. The way the law frames the "right" to an interpreter, and the ways speakers of non-dominant languages are depicted in the legal process, are symptomatic of a system that sees linguistic diversity as a hindrance, a deficit and a "problem" which could be overcome if everyone simply spoke English. Therefore, while Australia claims to celebrate diversity, for at least one of its major institutions, the justice system, linguistic diversity remains an unwelcome and unwanted presence.

Interpreter access and accreditation

Despite repeated calls for improved access to highly qualified legal interpreters since 1988, there are still widespread inadequacies in the system that reveal an ongoing antipathy towards appropriate provision for llanguage diversity in the legal system. It is instructive that, in 1999, the year before the introduction of the Aboriginal Interpreter Service in the Northern Territory (10 April 2000), the then Chief Minister, Dennis Burke, expressed resistance to the idea by claiming that "providing Aborigines with interpreters was like giving a wheelchair to someone who should be walking" (Blundell, 2000). While access to interpreters in general has improved since the 1980s, there remain significant concerns over the both the quantity and quality of the services being provided. Particularly in legal settings, interpreters have to handle unique challenges. The system has not made interpreters readily available, or ensured that legal interpreting is of a suitably high standard, which continues to exclude minority language speakers from legitimate participation in the legal process.

Focusing on the matter of competent interpreting, a national report into multicultural affairs in 1988 found that:

> The provision of competent interpreters with a sound knowledge of the law and the legal system was identified by many of those consulted as a major means towards achieving genuine equality before the law … Accessible, reliable interpreting is often critical to the exercise of justice.
>
> (Australia: Advisory Council on Multicultural Affairs, 1988:2)

Although the final report of the above discussion paper dedicated very little space to interpreting, subsequent recommendations were put forward for a survey to be conducted by the Attorney-General's Department into interpreting requirements in legal contexts. Based on research and discussions that followed, a significant gap between law, policy and practice was revealed which in turn, directed attention to the urgent needs of legal interpreting (Ozolins, 1991:12). Although it has been over 30 years since the publication of the findings, the widespread provision of competent legal interpreting is yet to be achieved.

Reports into the need for specialist training for legal interpreters, in addition to research and reviews into the issues stemming from incompetent interpreting in the legal context, have been widely documented. An important review into appeals on grounds of poor interpreting, conducted by Hayes and Hale (2010), highlighted 119 appellate cases in Australia that led to the questioning of the interpreter's competence and/or qualifications. Moreover, the results of a survey conducted by Hale (2011) showed that, whilst judicial officers in general showed concern for the lack of quality in interpreting, 70% of the survey respondents (judicial officers) expressed their dissatisfaction with the current interpreting services. A number of studies and reviews in the context of court cases and police interviews have also documented examples of incompetent interpreting which have led to wrongful convictions and/or appeals (Nakane, 2009; Roberts-Smith, 2009).

Whilst issues of competence in interpreting in general can be dependent on the individual skills and training of interpreters, the main reason for the prevailing situation can be attributed to the systemic lack of recognition of the importance of specialist legal interpreting training and the lack of an accreditation/certification system that is designed to test the specific skills required for the level and demands of legal interpreting. Based on the findings of a study of interpreting services conducted in the Victorian County Court, Laster and Taylor (1994:14) state the following:

> Many of the deficiencies blamed on individual interpreters, now and in the past, are the result of systemic problems, such as the lack of uniform education and testing to promote high levels of technical competence, and the failure to develop proper mechanisms for service delivery. Underlying these, of course, are inadequacies in the resources for legal interpreting services and levels of pay for interpreters.

Former Western Australian Supreme Court Justice Len Roberts-Smith reviewed several cases of significance in which issues related to poor interpreting resulted in legal complexities (Roberts-Smith, 2009). He discussed these cases on the basis of three main factors, one of which relates to the services of "professional accredited" but untrained interpreters who do not possess the required high-level skills to perform as legal interpreters. The examples he provides support the argument that a generalist NAATI professional level accreditation alone, without specialist training, does not suffice for legal interpreting (Gamal, 2014; Hale, 2004; Hayes & Hale, 2010; Lai & Mulayim, 2013; Laster & Taylor, 1994).

NAATI was initially set up in 1977 to professionalise interpreting and translation services to meet the language needs of new arrivals to Australia during migration in the 1970s, replacing the informal practices followed since the influx of post-war migrants in the late 1940s, in which family or friends of migrants were relied upon to act as ad hoc interpreters (Ozolins, 1991:17). Since then, NAATI has been the body responsible for setting the standards for translating and interpreting (T & I), testing of T & I accreditation, and approval of courses offered at tertiary and vocational training institutions. However, since its inception, NAATI has failed to raise the standards of interpreting and failed to recognise that the current credentialling system does not provide for the specialist skills needed for legal interpreting.

Until recently, NAATI's accreditation system had been awarding interpreter accreditations based on a generalised testing system with no specialist skills required other than candidates sitting a once-off interpreting test. Formal training in the area of interpreting was never compulsory but optional for those who wished to undertake such training through a NAATI-approved tertiary course, subject to the availability of the course in their language pair. The prerequisites for sitting the NAATI Professional-level test included the ability to speak two languages, an undergraduate degree in any field of study (but training in the fields of linguistics, languages, translation or related field was not required), or an interpreting accreditation at Paraprofessional level (for which an undergraduate degree is not needed).

Given that the Paraprofessional level test did not require any formal education at tertiary level, candidates with only secondary education, or perhaps with only primary education, were given the opportunity to attempt the test. A category called "Recognition" has also been awarded to candidates from rare and emerging languages in which there is a demand for interpreting services but a lack of examiner panels for such languages in which testing could be offered. In the Recognition category, candidates are not tested for their bilingual skills or interpreting skills. As mentioned previously, due to the generic structure of the NAATI tests, passing a NAATI test at any given level (Professional or Paraprofessional), or being awarded "Recognition" by NAATI, does not ensure competence in legal interpreting.

Nevertheless, successful completion of the test meant interpreters were qualified to practise in courts and other legal settings (e.g. police interviews, tribunals).

Because compulsory training (as in other professions) was never a prerequisite for becoming an interpreter in Australia, those with formal training or qualifications are not given preference, nor do they receive remuneration commensurate with their formal qualifications. Hale (2007) has pointed out that if the legal system does not recognise appropriate payment for professional interpreting services, fees will not equate to the skills that are required. She also emphasises that until officers in the legal system working in collaboration with interpreters mandate higher standards and show support for an acceptable level of training and pay, nothing will change. The lack of recognition of highly skilled, formally trained interpreters by legal professionals has also resulted in a number of interpreters leaving the workforce and moving into other areas of more lucrative professional work. From the interpreters' standpoint, the central issue is their low status, represented by poor levels of pay; and this has had a serious bearing on the employment and retention of highly skilled, formally trained interpreters, thus in turn affecting the establishment of quality legal interpreting provisions (Laster & Taylor, 1994). The cumulative result of these longstanding approaches has been a pool of interpreters not only underprepared and unsuited to interpreting in the highly specialised legal field, but a dilution of the amount of highly skilled and trained professionals capable of the demands of legal interpreting.

The repeated failure of Australian policy makers, institutions and interpreting organisations to promote greater numbers and higher standards of legally-trained interpreters perpetuates the linguistic exclusion of many from minority language backgrounds. While the provision of interpreters has often been idealised as a means of furthering substantive equality before the law, current policies and practices often render this goal as little more than symbolic rhetoric. As Angermeyer (2015) has suggested, the problems so often associated with access to, and use of, suitably qualified legal interpreters can be tied to broader underlying ideologies which work to demand monolingualism in English. For Angermeyer (2015), these structural and practical constraints mean that it would be better for minoritised language speakers to simply learn English if they wish to be treated fairly in their interactions with the justice system and forego their 'need' for an interpreter. In this way, the justice system further embeds linguistic inequality by privileging English monolingualism even in the face of the linguistically diverse backgrounds of many who find themselves in contact with police, courts and legal services. As the following sections will describe, not only can linguistic discrimination be seen at a policy level through the inadequate provision of services (Beacroft, 2017), but within micro-level discretionary practices of police and courts who act as linguistic gatekeepers (Heydon & Mabasso, 2018) in determining when and under what circumstances a person will be allowed to converse in a language other than English through an interpreter. In the third part, we discuss how the discretionary use of interpreters can give rise to specific problems in practices and institutional discourse.

Discretionary use of interpreters

There is a clear need to provide greater numbers of highly skilled and legally trained interpreters in the justice system. However, it is also important to recognise that in Australia there is no automatic right to an interpreter for someone who does not speak English as a first language. Rather, access is dependent on one's ability (or more accurately, inability) to communicate in English. Legislative frameworks and common law precedent have largely established the use of interpreters as discretionary on the part of both courts and police. For example, Section 30 of Victoria's Evidence Act 2008 states this:

> A witness may give evidence about a fact through an interpreter *unless the witness can understand and speak the English language sufficiently* to enable the witness to understand, and to make an adequate reply to, questions that may be put about the fact (emphasis added).

Similar provisions exist in most other state and territory jurisdictions. This framing of the "right" to an interpreter means that it is the courts that are tasked with deciding whether or not to use them in particular circumstances. While sometimes this decision may be obvious (such as for a monolingual non-English speaker), it becomes more challenging when a person exhibits some capacity to communicate in English, but may be more fluent in their first language (Cooke, 2002). While in theory this decision should be based on a formal assessment of English language proficiency, it can be subject to managerial concerns such as time and cost which are largely unrelated to language (Gibbons, 2003).

Like the courts, police also hold discretionary power regarding the use of interpreters during interviews with suspects and witnesses. While police are legally obliged to provide an interpreter, this only needs to be done in particular circumstances – specifically where a person is demonstrably unable to communicate adequately in English.[2] Again, this assessment is ideally built on some kind of formal assessment of English proficiency (Cooke, 2002), but in reality can be based on superficial observation (Wakefield, Kebbell, Moston & Westera, 2015).

At common law, the case of *R v Willie* (1885) long ago established the importance of interpreters to procedural fairness when Justice Cooper of Queensland's Supreme Court discharged the case against four Aboriginal men facing murder charges because no interpreter could be found to assist (Goldflam, 2012). More recently, the High Court in

---

[2] See Evidence Act 1995 (NSW) s.30 & Division 3 of Law Enforcement (Powers and Responsibilities) Regulation 2005 (NSW); Police Powers and Responsibilities Act 2000 (Qld) s.512; Summary Offences Act 1953 (SA) s.83A; Criminal Law (Detention and Interrogation) Act 1995 (Tas) s.5.

Re East & Ors; Ex Parte Nguyen (1998) reaffirmed this limited right when deciding whether the applicant had been denied procedural fairness because of the absence of an interpreter during the original trial.[3] For the High Court, a trial is effectively conducted in the absence of the accused if they cannot understand the case against them, and are unable to articulate a defence. As such, a person's right to be "present" for their own trial, means not just physical presence, but linguistic presence also.

As Eades (2010) has articulated previously, however, interpreters can be viewed with suspicion, especially if a defendant speaks some English. In this regard, interpreters are not always seen as meeting a basic right, but as an advocate for a defendant or suspect (Eades, 2010). Moreover, the exercising of discretion around interpreters has often been based on flawed assumptions about English proficiency. Courts for example can sometimes rely on basic questions such as, "How long have you lived in Australia?" or "Where did you learn English?" to make this assessment. Not only do these questions not reflect the complexities of spoken language in court, they also assume, for example, that a person who has lived for a certain period in Australia will therefore speak English well enough to navigate the legal process. More significantly, however, is that assessments such as these only see English as worthy of consideration and so neglect any other capacities in one's first language. This means that assessments about the "need" for an interpreter can further reinforce the invisibility of minority languages (Wiley & Lukes, 1996).

Given the discretionary nature of interpreter use, it is important to illustrate the implications for justice when this discretion is questionably exercised. The recent case of Gene Gibson is a stark example of how wrongful convictions can happen when interpreters are deemed unnecessary. In 2012, Gibson, a young Aboriginal man from the remote Pintupi-speaking community of Kiwirrkurra, became a person of interest over the death of Josh Warneke in Broome, Western Australia. Gibson's first language was Pintupi, and his second Kukutja. He also had some English-speaking ability, and used it as a third language. The Pintupi community is known for the strength of its Aboriginal languages, which are often valued over the use of English in the community (*The State of Western Australia v Gene Gibson*, 2014). Gibson underwent two interviews with members of the Major Crime Squad (MCS); and, while the initial interview treated Gibson as a possible witness, he proceeded to make admissions which suggested some involvement in Warneke's death. Gibson was then treated as a suspect for subsequent interviews, during which he made similar admissions that resulted in his being charged with murder.

---

[3] It is worth noting that during the original hearing, the applicant's own lawyer was steadfast in rejecting the need for an interpreter, even where the court repeatedly inquired whether one should be used. The refusal to make use of an interpreter by counsel became central to the High Court's eventual dismissal of the appeal.

During none of the interviews was an interpreter present owing to members of the MCS forming the opinion that, based on informal conversations with Gibson (in English) prior to the interviews, an interpreter was not necessary. It is not clear whether interviewing officers actually knew what Gibson's first language was, or that he spoke a first language other than English. Importantly, a Corruption and Crime Commission review into the investigation process found that the inquiries made into Gibson's English language proficiency were inadequate, and that police had failed to follow specific protocols about testing the suspect's English language proficiency (Corruption and Crime Commission, 2015). Indeed, local Broome police who were assisting the MCS investigation had recommended that an interpreter be used during the second and third interviews, given that English was clearly not Gibson's first language. The absence of an interpreter meant that the interviews were ruled inadmissible, and the admissions unreliable. As a result, the murder charge was downgraded to manslaughter, to which Gibson pleaded guilty.

In 2017, WA's Supreme Court of Appeal exonerated Gibson on the basis that the plea he entered into was not voluntarily made. In large part, this was because he did not have access to an interpreter during key meetings with his own lawyer, meaning that he was limited in his capacity to fully understand the case against him and his lawyer's advice, or to give proper instructions to the lawyer in response. Importantly, Gibson's lawyer had recognised that a Pintupi interpreter was likely to be important, but was not always available. As such, the absence of an interpreter at this stage was not so much based on a decision that one was not needed (such as the decision made by police). After spending five years in prison, Gibson was released and has now received a formal apology from the State, along with $1.3 million compensation.

Of particular note within the Gibson case is the preferential regard for Gibson's third language (English) over his first, or even second, Aboriginal languages. While it would be easy to lay blame solely on the police, it is notable that legislative frameworks themselves can actually contribute to an environment where miscarriages of justice can and do arise. Not only do they require police to act as untrained linguists in making assessments about English proficiency (Cooke, 2002; Cotterill, 2000), but they also frame English monolingualism as the default preference for communication. From this perspective, it is unsurprising that interpreters can be underused, particularly if a person appears to speak English at a conversational level (Powell & Bartholomew, 2003). As Eades (2015) has suggested, by constructing English as a social norm, the barring of access to interpreters can be justified based on untested assumptions that overestimate an individual's English proficiency. More importantly, however, it also reinforces the unwelcomeness of "other" languages in the legal process by rendering them invisible in favour of English monolingualism.

Given that the decisions about interpreters are fundamentally tied to English, minority language speakers must either prove themselves to be sufficiently proficient in English to cope, or be so deficient as to "need" an interpreter (Angermeyer, 2014). It is notable that, in Gibson's case, the appeal court often referred to him as subject to "English language disabilities" (*Gibson v The State of Western Australia,* 2017:2) because he did not speak it as a first or second language. Gibson's Aboriginal languages, Pintupi and Kukutja, as well as his community's preferencing of Pintupi in everyday talk, had now come to be problematised as a contributor to a linguistic "disability", rather than a valuable commodity to be harnessed. The following discussion will further illustrate how linguistic diversity in the justice system frequently becomes viewed as a problem or deficit (sometimes overcome by enforcing English monolingualism), rather than as a valuable resource for promoting the legitimate participation of speakers of minority languages.

Overcoming the "problem" of minority languages

As Bourdieu and Thompson (1991) have argued, the ideology of a dominant language creates a standard by which people's linguistic practices are judged. In Bourdieu's terms, "when one language dominates the market, it becomes the norm against which ... other modes of expression, and with them the values of various competences, are defined" (Bourdieu, 1977:652). This becomes particularly true within social institutions (e.g. the legal system) which not only value particular language practices over others, but also construct these practices as "normal" or unmarked (Heller, 1995). This process of norm-creation is not a neutral one, but often serves the interests of particular groups to the exclusion of others. Language therefore becomes a central means through which symbolic domination is realised (Bourdieu, 1991). In Heller's (1995) words, "language norms are a key aspect of institutional norms, and reveal ideologies which legitimate institutional relations of power" (p. 373). This often serves to reinforce a monoglot standard, which denies and suppresses the actual practices of multilingualism and linguistic diversity (Silverstein, 1996), and also legitimises linguistic discrimination that uniquely affects minority language speakers (Phillipson, 1992). As such, not only do language ideologies in official settings serve the interests of those already wielding institutional authority, but they continue to reflect and legitimise broader social hierarchies that position minoritised language speakers as subordinate.

Moreover, the process of idealising and normalising English monolingualism gives rise to institutional discourses that operate to mark and assess the language practices of minoritised language speakers. This often results in a deficit orientation whereby certain people and groups are framed only in terms of their perceived linguistic failures. Within a legal context, Haviland (2003) suggests that legal ideologies about language depict English as the language of the "standard person" and English monolingualism as the repertoire of the "normal" language user. In comparison, non-English speakers are often marked as inadequate, and that "speaking English in part defines how a person shows him or herself not to be handicapped" (p. 746). In this regard, the use of an interpreter in the legal process is framed as a means of overcoming the perceived language "disabilities" experienced by somebody like Gene Gibson.

Because access to an interpreter is legally tied only to English, attitudes exhibited within the institutional discourse of Australian criminal justice systems are shaped by a "problem" orientation that depicts minority language speakers only as incapable communicators. As Ruiz (1984:16) argues, orientations towards broader language policy which problematise minority languages in this way also condition what is "thinkable" about linguistic diversity at a micro level.

In this sense, not only are minority languages not viewed as valuable, they can be seen only as a hindrance to both their speakers, and the institutions with which they interact (Harrison, 2007; Ruiz, 1984). Indeed, in order for someone to claim that they should be granted an interpreter (e.g. during a criminal appeal like that of Gene Gibson), adopting the status of a "deficient" English speaker is legally necessary, but not always successful. For example, this was exhibited in the following interaction that occurred in the case of *Singh v The Queen* (2014:13):

Singh	What I need, your Honour, I need interpreter because my English is not very well. I need a Punjabi interpreter or maybe Hindi, Indian and national language interpreter please, your Honour.
His Honour	I don't accept that, Mr Singh, your English is sufficient for these purposes.
Singh	But I can't understand the difficult words, you know, some hard words.
His Honour	Well then we will avoid hard words. We'll be dealing with children so we won't be using hard words in any event.

Singh's proficiency in Punjabi is clearly of little importance in a court setting. For this appeal to succeed, he was required to position himself as an incompetent English speaker. It is also notable that, while the court summarily claimed that Singh would understand enough to get by, it then proceeded to infantilise him by saying "we won't be using hard words because children were also involved in the matter".[4] Not only was Singh tasked with attempting to live up to a particular status of deficiency, but, in response, the court rendered his language preferences invisible because he had "sufficient" English language capability to cope, at least to a similar extent as a child. In this way, the means of overcoming the "problem" of another language was to suppress it entirely.

---

[4] It is worth mentioning that Singh had a Masters Degree in Physics from the Lalit Narayan Mithila University.

In the case of *DPP v Natale* (2018), an Italian man who was interviewed by police without an interpreter was described by the court in these terms:

> Many of the answers of the accused are garbled or were expressed in barely understandable terms. Many answers give rise to concerns about his understanding of the situation he was in and the answers he was giving.

This language would be repeated later in the matter:

> There is a real question about what the accused actually meant by various answers that he gave which were highly incriminating in relation to the alleged offending and other uncharged offending. His answers were often garbled and grandiose. (p. 25)

However, while the court was required by law to illustrate Natale's inadequate use of English in order to rule that police should have provided an interpreter, it also reaffirmed that Natale's best language was clearly Italian (p. 39). Simply by establishing this as a relevant practical consideration in favour of interpreter use, discourses that focus solely on English "problems" can be resisted. By articulating and recognising Natale's preferred language, the court also recognised the value of allowing him to use it for the purposes of the interview. Indeed, the court went so far as to suggest that the police's failure to see it in this way constituted discrimination based on national origin. During the interview itself, Natale's efforts to assert a language preference and indicate discomfort in conversing in English were dismissed by interviewing officers.[5] As such, while the court may have recognised Natale's language as a valuable asset for navigating the police interview, officers viewed it as a largely irrelevant concern.

While in Natale's case the court attempted to recognise the value of Natale's first language, the same could not be said about the case of *The State of Western Australia v Cox* (2008), Cox had been denied access to an interpreter during a police interview. His appeal involved a claim that this made the interviews unfair. In its ruling, the court recognised this as follows:

> His preferred language is Kriol which is a dialect made up of a mixture of Aboriginal and English words. He also speaks English and it is not suggested, nor could it be concluded from the evidence, that his capacities in English were so limited as to necessitate an interpreter. However, it is clear from the evidence that his fluency in English is limited, and that he speaks a form of English sometimes described as Aboriginal-English, which may well give rise to issues as to the comprehension of his answers if the video record of interview is admitted into evidence. (p. 4)

They went on to say this:

> The fact that an interpreter is not strictly necessary or essential does not mean that it is not desirable for an interpreter to be provided. There will be many cases – and this is one – in which the interests of justice will be advanced if an interpreter is present and available during police interview of a suspect and during any subsequent trial. (p. 4)

---

[5] Natale had stated during the interview, "I don't know what you say in English. My language is –" before being cut off by officers (p. 8).

While there is a recognition of Cox's preferred language, and even that an interpreter would have been beneficial, it did not result in a ruling that one should have been used by police. In this regard, the court believed that Cox did not present as suitably deficient to warrant access to an interpreter. His preferred language, Kriol, is largely erased as a concern which might justify the use of an interpreter, even if the use of an interpreter might have advanced the "interests of justice". Therefore, an interpreter is not viewed as "strictly necessary or essential" if one does not present as sufficiently inadequate in English. Indeed, the consideration of English alone not only supersedes any consideration of language preference, but even how justice might be better served by allowing a suspect to converse in a language he is most comfortable with an interpreter.

Clearly, having enough English to "get by" (or not being sufficiently deficient) can come to be viewed as inherently more valuable than greater proficiency in a minority language. In this way, the "problem" of linguistic diversity can be overcome simply by erasing it from practical consideration. For Gene Gibson, this meant being denied any opportunity to converse in Pintupi, because an informal conversation led police to believe an interpreter was unnecessary. For David Cox, even where the court acknowledged that justice would have been advanced had an interpreter been used, English-only communication was still preferred because he was not suitably inadequate in English. Upkar Singh was equated to a child when the court promised to "avoid hard words". In these ways, not only does the existence of a hegemonic language frame how language practices are judged (Bourdieu, 1977), but it can also work to render minority languages virtually invisible in official settings (Bourdieu & Thompson, 1991).

Conclusion

The serious shortage of professional interpreters with competence in legal matters, both in indigenous languages and non-indigenous non-English languages, is by now well established, having been the subject of criticism and review for some 30 years. It is also indisputable that use of the available interpreters is subject to the discretion of police during interviews and and judges during court proceedings. These circumstances indicate that linguistic diversity represents an unwelcome and unwanted presence in the justice system, despite Australia's wider claims to celebrate diversity as a valuable part of contemporary Australian society.

The declaration of Chief Minister Dennis Burke in 1999, that providing interpreters was akin to giving a wheelchair to someone who should be walking (Blundell, 2000), is still represented in similar sentiments towards linguistic diversity in the policies and practices of Australian criminal justice systems. The expectation of linguistic unification, which the ideology of a state language demands, has the practical consequence of poorly equipped and understaffed interpreter services, and the problematic exercising of discretion around the use of available interpreters. Further to this, the ideology of an "official" language gives rise to an institutional discourse which marks people from linguistically diverse backgrounds as personally deficient because their value as communicators is tied only to English, and renders any capabilities in another language invisible.

Ultimately, this means that the use of interpreters in legal affairs, and by extension the use of minority languages, can still be viewed as a last resort and only of relevance in circumstances where English-only communication is virtually impossible. This privileging of English monolingualism will invariably mean the continued exclusion of those who do not primarily speak the dominant language; and, in the justice system at least, this will reinforce a social hierarchy that subordinates and stigmatises the language practices of indigenous and ethnic minority peoples.

References

General

Angermeyer, P.S. 2014. Monolingual ideologies and multilingual practices in small claims court: The case of Spanish-speaking arbitrators. *International Journal of Multilingualism*, 11(4):430-448.

Angermeyer, P.S. 2015. *Speak English or what? Codeswitching and interpreter use in New York City Courts*. New York: Oxford University Press.

Beacroft, L. 2017. Indigenous language and language rights in Australia after the *Mabo (No 2)* decision: A poor report card. *James Cook University Law Review*, 19(23):113-134.

Berk-Seligson, S. 1990. *The bilingual courtroom: Court interpreters in the judicial process*. Chicago: University of Chicago Press.

Bianco, J.L. 1987. *National policy on languages*. Canberra: Australian Government Publishing Service.

Blagg, H. 2008. *Crime, aboriginality and the decolonisation of justice*. Annandale NSW: Hawkins Press.

Blundell, H. 2000. A long fight for a basic human right. *Alternative Law Journal*, 25(5):219-223. https://doi.org/10.1177%2F1037969X0002500503

Bourdieu, P. 1977. The economics of linguistic exchanges. *Social Science Information*, 16(6):645-668.

Bourdieu, P. & Thompson, J.B. 1991. *Language and symbolic power*. Cambridge: Polity.

Chik, A. & Benson, P. 2018. *Council wants "English First" policy on shop signs – What does it mean for multicultural Australia?* https://theconversation.com/council-wants-english-first-policy-on-shop-signs-what-does-it-mean-for-multicultural-australia-95777 [Retrieved 5 May 2019].

Cooke, M. 1996. A different story: Narrative versus "question and answer" in Aboriginal evidence. *International Journal of Speech Language and the Law*, 3(2):273-288

Cooke, M. 2002. *Indigenous interpreting issues for courts*. Carlton VIC: Australian Institute of Judicial Administration.

Cotterill, J. 2000. Reading the rights: A cautionary tale of comprehension and comprehensibility. *Forensic Linguistics*, 7(1):4-25.

Coventry, G.; Dawes, G.; Moston, S. & Palmer, D. 2015. *Sudanese refugees' experiences with the Queensland criminal justice system: Report to the Criminology Research Advisory Council*. Canberra ACT: Australian Institute of Criminology.

Cunneen, C. 2001. *Conflict, politics and crime: Aboriginal communities and the police*. Crows Nest NSW: Allen & Unwin.

Eades, D. 2008. *Courtroom talk and neocolonial control*. New York: Mouton de Gruyter.

Eades, D. 2010. *Sociolinguistics and the legal process*. Bristol: Multilingual Matters.

Eades, D. 2012. The social consequences of language ideologies in courtroom cross-examination. *Language in Society*, 41(4):471-497.

Eades, D. 2015. *Language varieties spoken by Aboriginal people in the Northern Territory today*. Paper presented at the Northern Territory Supreme Court Language and the Law Conference, August 2015, Supreme Court, Darwin NT. http://www.supremecourt.nt.gov.au/conferences/documents/presenter-info/Diana%20Eades.pdf [Retrieved 30 May 2018].

Gibbons, J. 2003. *Forensic linguistics. An introduction to language in the justice system*. Oxford: Blackwell Publishing.

Goldflam, R. 2012. *Ngayulu nyurranya putu kulini: The legal right to an interpreter*. Paper presented at the Northern Territory Language and the Law Conference, May 2012, Supreme Court NT.http://www.supremecourt.nt.gov.au/about/documents/r_goldflam_ngayulu_nyurranya_putu_kulini.pdf [Retrieved 25 May 2018].

Hale, S. 2003. *What does "to fully and faithfully interpret the evidence" mean?* Paper presented at the Interpreters and Legal Professionals Working Together in Courts and Tribunals Conference, 21 March, University of New South Wales.

Hale, S. 2004. *The discourse of court interpreting: Discourse practices of the law, the witness and the interpreter*. Amsterdam: John Benjamins.

Hale, S. 2007. The challenges of court interpreting: Intricacies, responsibilities and ramifications. *Alternative Law Journal*, 32(4):198-202.

Hale, S. 2011. *Interpreter policies, practices and protocols in Australian courts and tribunals. A national survey*. Melbourne: Australasian Institute of Judicial Administration.

Harrison, G. 2007. Language as a problem, a right or a resource? A study of how bilingual practitioners see language policy being enacted in social work. *Journal of Social Work*, 7(1):71-92.

Haviland, J.B. 2003. Ideologies of Language: Some reflections on language and US Law. *American Anthropologist*, 105(4):764-774.

Hayes, A. & Hale S. 2010. Appeals on incompetent interpreting. *Journal of Judicial Administration*, 20:119-130.

Heller, M. 1995. Language choice, social institutions, and symbolic domination. *Language in Society*, 24(3):373-405. https://doi.org/10.1017/S0047404500018807

Lai, M. & Mulayim, S. 2013. Interpreter linguistic intervention in the strategies employed by police in investigative interviews. *Police Practice and Research: An International Journal*, 15(4):307-321. https://doi.org/10.1080/15614263.2013.809929

Laster, K. & Taylor, V.L. 1994. *Interpreters and the legal system*. Sydney: Federation Press.

Marmion, D.; Obata, K. & Troy, J. 2014. *Community, identity, wellbeing: The report of the Second National Indigenous Languages Survey*. Canberra ACT: Australian Institute of Aboriginal and Torres Strait Islander Studies.

Nakane, I. 2009. The myth of an "invisible mediator": An Australian case study of English-Japanese police interpreting. *Journal of Multidisciplinary International Studies*, 6(1). https://epress.lib.uts.edu.au/journals/index.php/portal/article/view/825 [Retrieved 2 November 2018].

Ozolins, U. 1991. *Interpreting translating and language policy*. East Melbourne: National Languages Institute of Australia.

Phillipson, R. 1992. *Linguistic imperialism.* New York: Routledge.

Piller, I. 2016. *Linguistic diversity and social justice: An introduction to applied sociolinguistics.* Oxford: Oxford University Press.

Powell, M.B. & Bartholomew, T. 2003. Interviewing and assessing clients from different cultural backgrounds: Guidelines for all forensic professionals. In: D. Carson & R. Bull (eds.), *Handbook of psychology in legal contexts.* Chichester, West Sussex: Wiley. p. 65.

Roberts-Smith, L. 2009. Forensic interpreting: Trial and error. In: S. Hale & U. Ozolins (eds.), *Critical Link 5. Quality in interpreting: A shared responsibility.* Amsterdam: John Benjamins. pp. 13-35.

Ruiz, R. 1984. Orientations in language planning. *NABE Journal,* 8(2):15-34.

Schwartz, M. & Cunneen, C. 2009. Working cheaper, working harder: Inequity in funding for Aboriginal and Torres Strait Islander legal services. *Indigenous Law Bulletin,* 7(10):19-22.

Silverstein, M. 1996. Monoglot "standard" in America: Standardization and metaphors of linguistic hegemony. In: D. Brenneis & R.K.S. Macaulay (eds.), *The matrix of language: Contemporary linguistic anthropology.* New York: Routledge.

Wakefield, S.J.; Kebbell, M.R.; Moston, S. & Westera, N.J. 2014. Perceptions and profiles of interviews with interpreters: A police survey. *Australian and New Zealand Journal of Criminology,* 48(1):72. https://doi.org/10.1177%2F0004865814524583

White, R. 2015. Indigenous young people and hyperincarceration in Australia. *Youth Justice,* 15(3):256-270.

Wiley, T.G. & Lukes, M. 1996. English-only and Standard English ideologies in the U.S. *TESOL Quarterly,* 30(3):511-535.

Official reports and publications

Access & Equity Inquiry Panel. 2012. *Access and equity for a multicultural Australia: Inquiry into the responsiveness of Australian Government Services to Australia's culturally and linguistically diverse population.* Canberra ACT: Commonwealth of Australia.

Advisory Council on Multicultural Affairs. 1988. *Towards a national agenda for a multicultural Australia: A discussion paper.* Canberra: Australian Government Public Service (AGPS).

Attorney-General's Department. 1991. *Access to interpreters in the Australian legal system: Report.* Canberra: Australian Government Public Service (AGPS).

Australian Bureau of Statistics. 2016a. *Media release: Census reveals a fast changing, culturally diverse nation.* http://www.abs.gov.au/ausstats/abs@.nsf/lookup/Media%20Release3 [Retrieved 14 March 2018].

Australian Bureau of Statistics. 2016b. *National Aboriginal and Torres Strait Islander social survey: Language and culture.* http://www.abs.gov.au/ausstats/abs@.nsf/Lookup/by%20Subject/4714.0~2014-15~Main%20Features~Language%20and%20culture~3 [Retrieved 14 March 2018].

Australian Bureau of Statistics. 2017a. *Aboriginal and Torres Strait Islander prisoner characteristics.* http://www.abs.gov.au/ausstats/abs@.nsf/Lookup/by%20Subject/4517.0~2017~Main%20Features~Aboriginal%20and%20Torres%20Strait%20Islander%20prisoner%20characteristics~5 [Retrieved 15 March 2018].

Australian Bureau of Statistics. 2017b. *Aboriginal and Torres Strait Islander prisoner characteristics: Northern Territory.* http://www.abs.gov.au/ausstats/abs@.nsf/Lookup/by%20Subject/4517.0~2017~Main%20Features~Northern%20Territory~24 [Retrieved 15 March 2018].

Australian Bureau of Statistics. 2017c. *Aboriginal and Torres Strait Islander prisoner characteristics: Western Australia.* http://www.abs.gov.au/ausstats/abs@.nsf/Lookup/by%20Subject/4517.0~2017~Main%20Features~Western%20Australia~22 [Retrieved 16 March 2018].

Australian Department of Social Services. 2017. *Multicultural Australia: United, strong, successful. Australia's multicultural statement*. https://www.homeaffairs.gov.au/mca/Statements/english-multicultural-statement.pdf [Retrieved 28 March 2018].

Australian Law Reform Commission. 1992. *Multiculturalism and the law*. Sydney NSW: Commonwealth of Australia.

Australian Law Reform Commission. 2017. *Pathways to justice: An inquiry into the incarceration rate of Aboriginal and Torres Strait Islander peoples*. Canberra, ACT: Commonwealth of Australia. https://www.alrc.gov.au/sites/default/files/pdfs/publications/final_report_133_amended1.pdf [Retrieved 25 February 2018].

Corruption and Crime Commission. 2015. *Report on Operation Aviemore: Major crime squad investigation into the unlawful killing of Mr Joshua Warneke*. Perth WA: Corruption and Crime Commission.

Human Rights and Equal Opportunity Commission. 1997. *Bringing them home: National inquiry into the separation of Aboriginal and Torres Strait Islander children from their families*. Canberra ACT: Commonwealth of Australia.

National Accreditation Authority for Translators and Interpreters. 2016. *Annual Report 2015-2016*. Canberra ACT: NAATI.

Legislation

Criminal Law (Detention and Interrogation) Act 1995 (Tas).

Evidence Act 1929 (SA).

Evidence Act 1995 (NSW).

Evidence Act 1997 (Qld).

Evidence Act 2001 (Tas).

Evidence Act 2008 (Vic).

Evidence (National Uniform Legislation) Act 2016 (NT).

Law Enforcement (Powers and Responsibilities) Regulation 2005 (NSW).

Police Powers and Responsibilities Act 2000 (Qld).

Summary Offences Act 1953 (SA).

Cases

DPP v Natale (2018) VSC 339.

Gene Gibson v The State of Western Australia (2017) WASCA 141.

R v Willie (1885) 7 QLJ (NC) 108.

Re East & Ors; Ex parte Nguyen (1998) HCA 73.

Singh v The Queen (2014) NTCCA 16.

The State of Western Australia v Cox (2008) WASC 287.

The State of Western Australia v Gene Gibson (2014) WASC 240.

MONOLINGUAL LANGUAGE OF RECORD

A critique of South Africa's new policy directive

Zakeera Docrat & Russell H. Kaschula

Introduction

This chapter aims to analyse the 2017 resolution to adopt English as the monolingual language of record that affects high courts in South Africa with reference to the constitutional language framework. We investigate whether the legislative framework enables the Chief Justice to change the language of record; and how a monolingual language of record affects the official status of languages other than English. In this judicial context, the language of record is taken to mean the language, which is used officially to litigate in courts of law, the language in which the judicial process is conducted, the language in which the proceedings are recorded, as well as that of written judgments.

The decision to make English the sole official language of record is also analysed in relation to the constitutional and legislative imperative of transforming the South African legal system, and we aim to show to what extent this decision effectively hinders real transformation. We present statistics to illustrate the importance of language planning in the legal system, which needs to be cognitive and responsive to the language demographics of litigants in their pursuit of access to justice. If a single language (English) is used, as is presently the case, then no utterances made in languages other than English are recorded and only the English interpretations and translations are used and recorded. The injustices that may occur from such a one-sided linguistic approach, and that may emanate from sociolinguistic misunderstandings, a lack of appropriate interpretational skills, and flawed translation, are highlighted in this chapter.

History of language usage in South African courts

The official languages in use determined the use of languages in South African courts at the specific periods when legislation and policies were drafted. Evidence can be traced back to the arrival of Jan van Riebeeck in the Cape (Van Niekerk, 2015:373). During the Dutch occupation, Dutch was imposed on the local population, and the language of the courts was Dutch. English was introduced during the British occupation in the 18th and early 19th centuries, and became the sole official language for use in courts. Arguably, what is happening today is merely a re-enactment of the 19th century colonial, or now neo-colonial, policies. In 1813, Governor Sir John Cradock published his sentiments about the importance of English by making it necessary for all government employees to acquire good English skills (Van Niekerk, 2015:377). Subsequently, on 5 July 1822, he issued a proclamation stating that English had been adopted as the "exclusive official and judicial language" (Van Niekerk, 2015:382). The proclamation applied to all judicial proceedings of the lower and higher courts. The move to have English as the sole official language for legal proceedings was justified on the basis that it would unite "local inhabitants" and those of British origin (Van Niekerk, 2015:383). Van Niekerk questions what he calls the "curious notion that a single language would lead to unity". This point must be borne in mind, specifically in relation to the reasoning behind the recent monolingual language of record decision.

The dominance of English as the language of record was further cemented through the Royal Charters of Justice (Van Niekerk, 2015:386). In 1827, the First Charter of Justice determined that the language medium would be English only, in both the Supreme Court and the circuit courts. The Second Royal Charter, in effect from 1834 and identical to the First Royal Charter, reaffirmed the English-only language of record decision (Van Niekerk, 2015). Section 2 of the Constitution Ordinance Amendment Act 1 of 1882 reintroduced Dutch as an official language and awarded it equal status alongside English. The Dutch Language Judicial Use Act 21 of 1884 permitted the use of Dutch as a language of record, where the parties in court chose Dutch as their language of choice for the case (Van Niekerk, 2015).

The South Africa Act of 1909, which resulted in the establishment of the Union of South Africa in 1910, recognised English as an official language in addition to Dutch. In Section 137 of the Act of 1909, the dual official language status of Dutch and English was recognised. The definition of Dutch was extended to include Afrikaans in the Union Act 8 of 1925. Through Act 8 of 1927, Afrikaans ultimately replaced Dutch as an official language alongside English, and with the onset of apartheid in 1948, the legislative formulations constantly reaffirmed the position of English and Afrikaans as the official languages. The Republic of South Africa Constitution Act 110 of 1983, specifically Section 89(1), entrenched the position of English and Afrikaans as official languages.

It is evident that legislative recognition of African languages in the form of their official, developmental status or use was absent from the beginning, hence the entrenchment of English and Afrikaans and the marginalisation of African languages in terms of formal use in public affairs. It can be argued that the use of African languages for formal purposes was recognised in Act 110 of 1986, in that African languages were to be utilised within the self-governing territories or homelands. In effect, African languages were being developed in the self-governing territories through the schooling system, where linguistic segregation was utilised to achieve racial segregation (Bambust et al., 2012).

Mirroring the above legislative positioning of languages in South Africa, the legal system adopted English and Afrikaans as the language media for court use. According to Bambust et al. (2012:221), the current legislative position regarding the use of language in court was adopted wholly as inherited in the democratic dispensation. Van Niekerk (2015:375) succinctly summarises the historical exclusionary position of African languages and their speakers:

> Indigenous African cultural institutions, including languages, have notoriously been ignored in the history of early South Africa. Thus the needs of the indigenous population played no role in any decisions relating to judicial language both during the Dutch and the English administrations of the Cape, later in the territories beyond the borders of the Cape.

We will discuss the current status of language in the legal system against this historical backdrop of the role, use and status of language in the South African legal system.

The language of record resolution in context

On 16 April 2017, it was reported in the *Sunday Times* that the languages of record, English and Afrikaans, had been changed to English only with immediate effect (Docrat et al., 2017:1). The decision was reported to have been taken by the Heads of Court, comprising all Judge Presidents of all High Courts under the leadership of the Chief Justice of the Constitutional Court, Justice Mogoeng Mogoeng. The Chief Justice was quoted as saying that the removal of Afrikaans as a language of record would contribute to the transformation of the legal system and would reverse the historical discrimination endured during apartheid.

Further communication on the matter was in the form of a directive by the Western Cape Judge President, Justice Hlophe. The directive confirmed the resolution adopted by the Heads of Court. Hlophe JP stated that having English as the sole official language of record would "result in speedier and more efficient adjudication and finalisation of all cases". Hlophe JP stated further that the resolution would apply to all courts, for both civil and criminal cases.

Regarding the submission of court documents, the directive instructed that each document be submitted in English only. The exception was the submission of witness statements in a language other than English, where the witness was not sufficiently conversant in English.

With regard to court proceedings, the directive again prescribed the use of English only, except where a witness not sufficiently conversant in English needed to rely on interpretation. At pre-trial stage, the presiding officer was instructed through the directive to ask the following:

> In terms of a national directive by the Heads of Courts, the official language of record is English. Are you conversant in English? Do you have any objection to the court proceedings continuing in English?

Dealing with the above question, Hlophe JP (2004) states further in the directive that:

> Should the witness not have an objection to the evidence being led in English, the court should continue as such. Should the witness not be conversant in English, the leading of evidence only may be conducted in any other language. In such cases an interpreter should as far as possible be utilised to interpret the evidence into English …. In such cases where there is no interpreter available and there is an indication that the matter is to proceed to appeal or review, the presiding officer should, for the purposes of the court record to be in English, order the Administration of the Office of the Chief Justice and/or the Department of Justice and Constitutional Development to have the portions of the evidence led in any other language simultaneously translated into English whilst it is being transcribed. The translated version of the evidence will form part of the court record.

The facts above raise several issues, which will now be discussed. The primary question is whether the resolution to make English the sole official language of record is constitutionally sound. In turn, subsequent issues and questions arise. These include (but are not limited to):

- Firstly, whether the Chief Justice and the Heads of Courts have the inherent constitutional or legislative authority to take such a decision.
- Secondly, it must be questioned whether the elevation of English to a "super" official language, as a result of being the sole official language of record, fosters transformation for all languages, specifically the nine official African languages being excluded from use in courts (except in instances of interpretation). Furthermore, it must be asked whether this exclusion of African languages does not, in fact, hinder transformation, as it certainly does not redress past linguistic discrimination.
- Thirdly, it must be questioned how cases will be adjudicated in ways that are "more efficient" and "speedier" by using English as the sole official language of record. Does conducting cases in a speedy manner supersede the importance of access to justice?
- Fourthly (and importantly), there is the issue of determining the yardstick of whether someone is "sufficiently" conversant in English, and the question of whether a judicial officer is linguistically qualified to conduct such an enquiry into linguistic competence.
- The fifth issue is linked to the previous point raised: whether, in fact, the resolution or directive has actually diminished the constitutional language rights conferred upon litigants to an interpretational right – specifically the language right conferred upon accused persons through Section 35(3)(k) of the Constitution of the Republic of South Africa (1996).
- The sixth and final issue concerns the statement quoted above, in which Hlophe JP states that the record must be translated into English simultaneously as it is being transcribed. This point is discussed with regard to the practical impossibility of concurrent transcription and translation.

Constitutional language framework

To answer the primary question above and simultaneously to address the issues arising, the constitutional language framework needs to be outlined. The constitutional language provisions commence with Section 6 in the Founding Provisions. Section 6 confers official status on eleven languages, as opposed to the two official languages used during apartheid. Nine African languages are conferred with official status, thereby implying that they should be further intellectualised for such purposes (cf. Sibayan, 1999:72). Subsection (2) provides further that the state is obligated to take "positive and practical measures to elevate the status and advance the use of these languages". Subsection (3)(a) furthermore prescribes a minimum threshold of using two official languages for national purposes. The two languages must be selected based on the criteria prescribed in Subsection (3)(a), namely usage, practicality, expense, regional circumstances, and the balance of the needs and preferences of the population as a whole, or of the province concerned. Important to note is Subsection (4), which states that, as per the provisions in Subsection (2), "all languages must enjoy parity of esteem and must be treated equitably".

What is evident from the linguistic blueprint in Section 6 is the elevation of nine African languages to equal place alongside English and Afrikaans. It is our understanding that Subsection (2) provides an obligation to elevate the African languages through practical and positive measures, meaning that English or Afrikaans alone cannot be used solely, as this would be contrary to the constitutional mandate. This point needs to be borne in mind in the context of the discussion that follows concerning the effect that the monolingual language of record resolution has had on the transformation of the legal system.

According to Du Plessis and Pretorius (2000:507), Subsections (2) and (4) set out the normative guidelines for the drafting and enactment of language policies. Simply put, a policy or directive concerning the language of record must be informed by the constitutional provisions, which call for the elevation of nine African languages – not the elevation of English to a super official language. This interpretation of Section 6, however, is not explicit, given the insertion of discretionary words such as "at least", where "practicable" and "equitable". De Vos (2017) explains that the provisions of Section 6 are ambiguous, given that no definitions are provided for the discretionary words listed, and that this weakens the enforceability of the provisions. Although De Vos (2017) agrees with sentiments published by Constitutional Court Judge Edwin Cameron (2013) that the Constitution is a theoretical framework that requires practical implementation, he points out that Section 6 prescribes minimum thresholds for compliance. This is seen as problematic where the State and persons responsible for implementation are not invested in ensuring the realisation of the status, use, development and elevation of African languages as part of the further intellectualisation of African languages in order for them to be used in high status domains such as law.

The provisions of Section 6 inform the language rights, and the equality provision of Section 9, all housed in the Bill of Rights (BOR). Section 9 of the Constitution, the equality provision, applies squarely to the discussion at hand, given that this chapter discusses the constitutionality of the resolution taken on the language of record. The point of determining constitutionality would, in our minds, entail determining whether or not the resolution unfairly discriminates against all litigants and legal practitioners who are not conversant in English (see Chapter 5 in this volume for a full discussion on the linguistic competencies of legal practitioners). The following provisions of Section 9 are of relevance:

(1) Everyone is equal before the law and has the right to equal protection and benefit of the law.

(3) The state may not unfairly discriminate directly or indirectly against anyone on one or more grounds, including ... language ...

(4) No person may unfairly discriminate directly or indirectly against anyone on one or more grounds in terms of Subsection (3). National legislation must be enacted to prevent or prohibit unfair discrimination.

(5) Discrimination on one or more of the grounds listed in Subsection (3) is unfair unless it is established that the discrimination is fair.

What is evident from the provisions of Section 9 is that language is a listed ground upon which discrimination is automatically unfair, where alleged and successfully proven by the Applicant. Discrimination may be deemed fair as per Subsection (5), and this would occur where the Respondent proves that either no discrimination was present, or that discrimination was present, in which instance evidence is to be led to prove the discrimination was fair. With regard to the latter, the Respondent must provide evidence showing that there is no possible alternative to achieve the purpose and which could have averted the discrimination.

In accordance with Section 9(4) of the Constitution, the Promotion of Equality and Prevention of Unfair Discrimination Act No. 4 of 2000 (hereafter, the Equality Act) was enacted and expands on the constitutional equality provisions. The Equality Act (2000) is not a replacement of Section 9 of the Constitution, but rather provides an expansion and greater clarity. The Equality Act (2000) also includes guidelines for the court to determine if discrimination was present and, if so, whether it was fair or unfair. When bringing an application on grounds of discrimination, such discrimination must be alleged directly in terms of the Equality Act (2000). According to Ngcukaitobi (2013:245), direct reliance on Section 9 of the Constitution will only be permitted in exceptional circumstances where the discrimination is beyond the scope of the Equality Act (2000) or is based on a listed ground in Section 9(3) of the Constitution.

Furthermore, according to Ngcukaitobi (2013:245), the primary question the court should determine is whether the discrimination, if found to have occurred, results in:

> ... systemic disadvantage; or undermines human dignity; or adversely affects the equal enjoyment of a person's rights and freedoms in a serious manner that is comparable to discrimination on a prohibited ground in Section 9(3) of the Constitution.

Moreover, the Equality Act (2000) defines discrimination as:

> ... any act or omission including a policy, law, rule and practice, condition or situation which directly or indirectly –
> (a) Imposes a burden, obligation or disadvantage on; or
> (b) Withholds benefits, opportunities or advantages from any person on one or more of the prohibited grounds ... including language.

The issue of discrimination on grounds of language was considered in the case of *Lourens v Speaker of the National Assembly and Others* (2015) (see Docrat, 2017a for a full discussion). Briefly, the case dealt with Lourens, the Applicant, alleging that Parliament was discriminating against persons on grounds of language by failing to publish legislation in all eleven official languages; and that such discrimination was unfair, given the provisions of Section 6 of the Constitution. Parliament, acting as the first Respondent, argued that there was no onus created through Section 6 of the Constitution to use all eleven languages and that two languages were being used. The court found that discrimination on grounds of language was indeed present; however, that such discrimination was fair, given Parliament's defence.

It is surprising that in the *Lourens* (2015) case the judiciary accepted the restrictive interpretation of Section 6 of the Constitution, adopted by Parliament. Docrat (2017b) argues that restrictive interpretation limits the application of the rights of African language speakers, where the judiciary fails in its mandate to interpret purposively the constitutional provisions. Furthermore, the reasoning in the *Lourens* (2015) judgment resonates with De Vos's (2017) observation that Section 6, by prescribing minimum thresholds for compliance, will see those responsible for implementation finding a loophole within the system, as they are not committed to the development and elevation of the status and use of African languages.

In our opinion, Section 6 specifically provides that African languages be elevated; and this in turn means treating the African languages as equal to English and Afrikaans and encouraging the further intellectualisation of these languages. If not, then what would have been the purpose of conferring official status on the nine African languages and stating that practical and positive measures be taken to elevate the status and use of these African languages? The constitutionality of the monolingual language of record policy directive needs to be considered against Section 35(3)(k) of the Constitution. Section 35(3)(k) is informed by the provisions of Section 6 and essentially constitutes the language right in the legal system. The right is conferred upon accused persons and states that:

> (3) Every accused person has a right to a fair trial, which includes the right
> (k) to be tried in a language that the accused person understands, or if that is not practicable, to have the proceedings interpreted in that language; ...

Section 35(3)(k) confers a language right on accused persons to be tried in a language they understand, where practicable. Our understanding of the qualifier "where practicable" is that it should mean that, where that language is spoken by the majority in the province and it is a provincial official language, then it should be used. Applying the monolingual language of record policy directive to the language right in Section 35(3)(k) would mean that, where English is not your mother tongue and you are not conversant in English, your right is automatically downgraded to an interpretational right. We use the word "downgraded" here, as English is regarded as the "normal" and the other ten official languages as the "abnormal". In effect, as an accused person, you have to conform with a policy that ensures the language rights of only 9.8% of the population, those who are English mother tongue speakers, this is evident from Table 4.1 (Census, 2011).

TABLE 4.1 National language demographics of South Africa

Language	EC	FS	GP	KZN	LP	MP	NC	NW	WC
Afrikaans	10.6	12.7	12.4	1.6	2.6	7.2	53.8	9.0	49.7
English	5.6	2.9	13.3	13.2	1.5	3.1	3.4	3.5	20.2
IsiNdebele	0.2	0.4	3.2	1.1	2.0	10.1	0.5	1.3	0.3
IsiXhosa	78.8	7.5	6.6	3.4	0.4	1.2	5.3	5.5	24.7
IsiZulu	0.5	4.4	19.8	77.8	1.2	24.1	0.8	2.5	0.4
Sepedi	0.2	0.3	10.6	0.2	52.9	9.3	0.2	2.4	0.1
Sesotho	2.5	64.2	11.6	0.8	1.5	3.5	1.3	5.8	1.1
Setswana	0.2	5.2	9.1	0.5	2.0	1.8	33.1	63.4	0.4
Sign Language	0.7	1.2	0.4	0.5	0.2	0.2	0.3	0.4	0.4
SiSwati	0.0	0.1	1.1	0.1	0.5	27.7	0.1	0.3	0.1
Tshivenda	0.1	0.1	2.3	0.0	16.7	0.3	0.1	0.5	0.1
Xitsonga	0.0	0.3	6.6	0.1	17.0	10.4	0.1	3.7	0.2
Other	0.6	0.6	3.1	0.8	1.6	1.0	1.1	1.8	2.2

Census, 2011

TABLE 4.2 Legal Aid South Africa: 2016 survey on the primary spoken language in criminal matters

Province	WC	KZN	GP	EC	FS	NW	MP	NC	LP	Total
Resp.a	9 302	7 031	6 278	5 392	3 113	2 631	2 558	2 065	1 988	40 358
					Proportions (%)					
Zulu	0	85	37	0	5	4	39	2	1	24
Afrikaans	66	0	8	15	5	6	3	58	1	22
Xhosa	26	3	7	82	6	7	1	6	1	20
Sotho	0	1	15	2	74	9	4	2	9	10
Tswana	0	0	9	0	5	69	1	31	3	8
English	7	10	7	1	3	1	1	1	0	5
Pedi	0	0	8	0	0	2	14	0	48	5

TABLE 4.2 Continued

Province	WC	KZN	GP	EC	FS	NW	MP	NC	LP	Total
Resp.a	9 302	7 031	6 278	5 392	3 113	2 631	2 558	2 065	1 988	40 358
				Proportions (%)						
Tsonga	0	0	5	0	0	2	3	0	20	2
Swati	0	0	1	0	0	0	27	0	0	2
Venda	0	0	2	0	0	0	0	0	15	1
Ndebele	0	0	1	0	0	0	6	0	1	1
Other	0	0	0	0	0	1	1	0	1	0

a = Number of respondents

TABLE 4.3 Legal Aid South Africa: 2016 survey on the primary spoken language in civil matters

Province	KZN	GP	EC	WC	FS	NW	LP	MP	NC	Total
Resp.a	1 083	1 045	797	758	480	374	318	313	188	5 356
				Proportions (%)						
Zulu	68	24	0	0	1	2	1	31	1	21
Afrikaans	1	12	23	63	12	20	8	8	59	20
Xhosa	1	6	67	18	8	6	1	1	10	16
English	29	11	9	18	1	3	1	5	5	12
Sotho	0	19	1	0	70	9	3	4	6	11
Tswana	0	9	0	0	8	58	2	0	20	7
Pedi	0	11	0	0	0	2	44	26	0	6
Tsonga	0	4	0	0	1	1	19	2	0	2
Venda	0	2	0	0	0	0	21	0	0	2
Ndebele	0	1	0	0	0	0	0	12	0	1
Swati	0	1	0	0	0	0	0	11	0	1
Other	0	1	0	1	0	0	0	1	0	0

a = Number of respondents

TABLE 4.4 Legal Aid South Africa: 2016 language survey on English proficiency in criminal cases

Prov	Understand %			Speak %			Read/Write %		
	Good	Satisfactory	Poor	Good	Satisfactory	Poor	Good	Satisfactory	Poor
EC	15.9	27.7	56.4	14.2	24.6	61.2	13.8	23.6	62.6
FS	26.8	39.7	33.4	24.0	34.9	41.1	22.7	33.1	44.2
GP	33.8	41.7	24.5	30.7	40.9	28.4	30.3	38.5	31.2
KZN	21.9	37.0	41.0	20.1	33.4	46.5	18.8	31.2	50.0
LP	27.2	36.3	36.6	21.1	35.4	43.5	21.5	31.9	46.6
MP	25.4	38.2	36.4	21.4	36.7	41.9	21.5	35.1	43.4
NW	28.3	40.4	31.3	24.0	39.3	36.7	24.6	37.3	38.0
NC	15.0	42.4	42.6	12.3	37.9	49.8	11.9	33.2	54.9
WC	24.4	43.5	32.2	21.4	40.6	38.1	19.4	37.7	42.9
Total %	24.4	38.7	36.8	21.5	36.1	42.4	20.7	33.8	45.6

TABLE 4.5 Legal Aid South Africa: 2016 language survey on English proficiency in civil cases

Prov	Understand %			Speak %			Read/Write %		
	Good	Satis-factory	Poor	Good	Satis-factory	Poor	Good	Satis-factory	Poor
EC	44.8	30.0	25.2	41.5	30.4	28.1	43.4	27.1	29.5
FS	46.9	30.2	22.9	43.8	32.1	24.2	44.2	30.8	25.0
GP	52.6	31.4	16.0	48.5	34.4	17.1	49.6	30.8	19.6
KZN	47.7	29.8	22.4	44.1	29.7	26.1	46.8	25.5	27.7
LP	35.2	40.9	23.9	33.0	40.6	26.4	35.2	36.8	28.0
MP	37.4	30.7	31.9	36.4	28.8	34.8	35.5	27.8	36.7
NW	48.1	28.3	23.5	43.6	28.6	27.8	47.3	25.4	27.3
NC	32.4	33.0	34.6	31.9	32.4	35.6	31.9	27.7	40.4
WC	39.7	40.4	19.9	37.7	38.0	24.3	37.9	36.0	26.1
Total %	45.2	32.4	22.4	42.1	32.7	25.2	43.5	29.6	26.9

At this stage of the discussion, the statistics shown in these tables are relevant in illustrating that the majority of persons in courts are not English mother-tongue speakers. Moreover, Table 4.1 illustrates that the majority in each of the nine provinces does not speak English. Most persons per province speak either an African language or Afrikaans as their mother tongue. The statistics for the legal system are similar to the provincial language demographics, as evidenced in Tables 4.2 and 4.3, in both criminal and civil courts. Although we acknowledge that the Legal Aid Language Survey (2016) does not account for every single litigant in the legal system during 2016, these were the latest statistics available at the time the monolingual language of record policy directive was made, so we argue that these language demographics should not have been overlooked. They provide proof that English is a minority language of litigants in South African courts. The choice of English-only is therefore apparently one of convenience, rather than one providing for social justice. Tables 4.4 and 4.5 provide further compelling language statistics supporting why English must not be the sole language of record, given that in criminal cases, as per Table 4.4, litigants' English proficiency in the categories of understanding, speaking, reading and writing was shown to be overwhelmingly "poor" or merely "satisfactory". There is an improvement in the figures for these categories for civil courts, but there remain more than 20-25% of litigants whose English proficiency is "poor" or "satisfactory". These statistics speak for themselves and cannot be ignored.

The point is that the monolingual language of record decision will result in most litigants being conferred with an interpretational right, rather than the right to be heard in their mother tongue in instances where they are not proficient in English. This addresses the fifth issue highlighted earlier in this chapter: being conferred with an interpretational right only places a litigant, in our opinion, at a disadvantage. Gibbons (2003:202) explicates this point in the following excerpt:

> A second language speaker who does not speak the language of the court, and who is not provided with interpreting services may receive the same treatment as native speakers, but such a process is clearly unjust, in that s/he can neither understand the proceedings, nor make a case.

Hlophe (2004:46) states that interpreters lack consistency due to their inadequate level of training, resulting in possible miscarriage of justice. The Section 35(3)(k) constitutional right could then be curtailed where a litigant is not proficient in English, the language of record (Ndlovu, 2002).

The aforementioned leads to the third issue, highlighted earlier, namely the justification by Hlophe that the monolingual language of record will result in the "speedier and more efficient adjudication and finalisation of all cases". The irony and contradictions by Hlophe are evident where he acknowledges the issues plaguing the poor quality of interpretation in South African courts, yet his directive entrenches the interpretational system. In the language rights case of *State v Pienaar* (2000), (discussed fully in Chapter 5 in this volume by De Vries and Docrat), the court reasoned that communication in the accused's mother tongue should take place directly, unless in exceptional circumstances through an interpreter. The court furthermore explained that the Department of Justice's language of record would have "phenomenal cost and quality implications" (*State v Pienaar*, 2000:145) where sole reliance would be placed on interpreters. The implications would exceed the financial burden due to interpretation, where the court advanced that the policy position would be in direct conflict with Section 6(4) of the Constitution (2000:145). From a point of practice, interpretation is problematic; and, in our opinion, there should be a move away from such practices with the aim of giving meaning to the constitutional language provisions where the language right in Section 35(3)(k) is not diminished to an interpretational right.

By reducing the Section 35(3)(k) language right to an interpretational right, the Chief Justice and Heads of Court are, in effect, limiting that right. The limitations analysis, as espoused in Section 36 of the Constitution, is thus applicable. Section 36 states:

> (1) The rights in the Bill of Rights may be limited only in terms of law of general application to the extent that the limitation is reasonable and justifiable in an open and democratic society based on human dignity, equality and freedom, taking into account all relevant factors, including –
> (a) the nature of the right;
> (b) the importance of the purpose of the limitation;
> (c) the nature and extent of the limitation;
> (d) the relation between the limitation and its purpose; and
> (e) less restrictive means to achieve the purpose.
> (2) Except as provided in Subsection (1) or in any other provision of the Constitution, no law may limit any right entrenched in the Bill of Rights.

Based on the provisions above, Section 36 comprises a two-stage enquiry. Similar to the enquiry in the Equality Act (2000), Section 36 requires a certain amount of balancing. Balancing becomes relevant where there are competing rights. According to Woolman (1998-2003:53-54) balancing can take place in two ways. Firstly, one right may simply outweigh the other competing right. A clear example was in the case of *S v Makwanyane* (1995) where, on the one hand, the accused had a right to life, while on the other, the state's interest was the death penalty. There was no possible justification for a decision that would enable a balance of some sort to be struck, nor for the death penalty to outweigh the right to life (Woolman, 1998-2003:55). It is, however, a difficult task and, in some instances, it may be impossible to strike a balance. To this effect, Woolman (1998-2003:61) states that it boils down to how we wish the world to look, and in what kind of world we wish to live.

This brings into question the intention of the Chief Justice and Heads of Courts when changing the language of record. Currie and De Waal (2013:154) emphasise that the reasonability and justifiability of a limitation cannot be decided abstractly. This determination requires evidence, in the form of sociological or statistical data, of the impact that the restriction will have on society. This would include taking into consideration the language statistics (advanced in the tables in this chapter) which prove that the English proficiency of accused persons is poor, and that the majority of South Africans are not English mother tongue speakers. Furthermore, evidence could have been sought from forensic linguists on both the legal and linguistic implications of limiting the Section 35(3)(k) right. Evidence can be in the form of both facts and/or policies; and this can be extended to include academic research on the impact a monolingual language of record has on the right to a fair trial, the right to equality on linguistic grounds, and ensuring compliance with the provisions of Section 6(2) of the Constitution. The lack of consultation is evident from the directive, highlighted as a sixth issue above, wherein Hlophe prescribes that the evidence being led in a language other than English be translated simultaneously while being transcribed. Merely from a practical point of view, this, in our opinion, is impossible and illustrates Hlophe's minimal linguistic insight when issuing such a directive.

The element of "reasonable practicability" is missing from the monolingual language of record policy directive. Simply put, to limit the Section 35(3)(k) right requires that cognisance must be taken of the fact that language is not an isolated characteristic. De Vos (2017) acknowledges that language is not an isolated characteristic, but cautions against racialising languages as the apartheid regime did. In our opinion, the current language of record position is, in fact, perpetuating apartheid's racial discrimination and, in this instance, advocating for linguistic marginalisation of other languages in favour of English.

There is a further irony regarding issue four above, where a litigant is to be asked during the pre-trial stages whether they are linguistically competent in English. It is nonsensical to ask a non-mother tongue English speaker, who has little or no proficiency in English, whether the trial can proceed in English. There is also no yardstick by which judicial officers can determine the linguistic proficiency of litigants. Furthermore, the directive states that the litigant or witness should be asked if they object to the proceedings being conducted and recorded in English. There is no indication as to what would happen if there were such an objection. The litigant or witness would be provided with interpretation services and the right would therefore be limited. Thus, in reality, there is no choice: if you are not proficient in English, you have an interpretational right and not a language right.

Legislative framework

The constitutional framework and discussions in this chapter have illustrated that the monolingual language of record is contrary to the constitutional provisions. The question arising is whether the Chief Justice and Heads of Court were, in fact, enabled to change the language of record. Simply put, does the enabling legislation, in the form of the Superior Courts Act 10 of 2013, confer authority on the Chief Justice and or Heads of Court to determine the language of record policy? Chapter 3 of the Superior Courts Act (2013), dealing with governance and administration of all courts, is relevant, specifically Section 8(3) to (6), which reads as follows:

8   Judicial management of judicial functions
   (3) The Chief Justice may, subject to Subsection (5), issue written protocols or directives, or give guidance or advice, to judicial officers –
      (a) In respect of norms and standards for the performance of the judicial functions as contemplated in Subsection (6); and
      (b) regarding any matter affecting the dignity, accessibility, effectiveness, efficiency or functioning of the courts.
   (4) (a) Any function or any power in terms of this section, vesting in the Chief Justice or any other head of court, may be delegated to any other judicial officer of the court in question.
      (b) The management of the judicial functions of each court is the responsibility of the head of that court.
      (c) Subject to Subsection (2) and (3), the Judge President of a Division is also responsible for the co-ordination of the judicial functions of all Magistrates' Courts falling within the jurisdiction of that Division.
   (5) Any protocol or directive in terms of Subsection (3) –
      (a) May only be issued by the Chief Justice if it enjoys the majority support of the heads of those courts on which it would be applicable; and
      (b) must be published in the Gazette. [our emphasis]
   (6) The judicial functions referred to in Subsection (2) and Subsection (4)(b) include the –
      (a) determination of sittings of the specific courts;
      (b) assignment of judicial officers to sittings;
      (c) assignment of cases and other judicial duties to judicial officers;
      (d) determination of the sitting schedules and places of sittings for judicial officers;
      (e) management of procedures to be adhered to in respect of –

(i) case flow management;
(ii) the finalisation of any matter before a judicial officer, including any outstanding judgment, decision or order; and
(iii) recesses of Superior Courts.

In accordance with these provisions, specifically Subsections (3) and (4) read together with Subsection (6), there is no inclusion of the language of record as a function, which can be determined or changed by the Chief Justice, with or without the support of all Heads of Court. Furthermore, such a decision, must be in accordance with the provisions, specifically Section 8(5)(b) which prescribes that the decision be published in the *Government Gazette*. To date, there has been no publication of any sort in the *Government Gazette*. In our opinion, no further engagement is needed regarding the provisions of the Superior Courts Act (2013), given there is neither a direct nor indirect provision conferring power on the Chief Justice or the Heads of Court to determine the language of record policy. It is a decision that must be taken by the executive branch of government. However, the Minister of Justice and Constitutional Development has remained silent on the matter, confirming the sentiment stated by De Vos (2017) that the language provisions of the Constitution will not be interpreted purposively and implemented by the State who are not invested in the development, intellectualisation and use of African languages. The constitutional and legislative frameworks illustrate that the policy decision on the language of record is contrary to the Constitution and cannot be determined by the judiciary, but rather by the executive.

African languages in the transformational agenda

We now turn our focus to the last issue, namely transformation. The term "transformation" continues to arise in all spheres of society and across disciplines. It is a word that has become common and which De Vos (2010:1) states "has become a buzzword that is much bandied about and much abused, but few people explain what they mean when they use the word".

Wesson and Du Plessis (2008:187) define transformation as a "change from a state of affairs that existed previously". Furthermore, it has been stated that transformation cannot and should not be understood to carry one static meaning (Wesson & Du Plessis, 2008:187). According to Kaschula (2016:199), when it comes to using language as part of transformation, there are still policy implementation challenges. Kaschula (2016:199) argues further that language is pivotal in the transformation process, where it enables the African voice to emerge. The use of African languages needs to inform the discussions on how to enhance access to justice in order to transform the legal system (Docrat, 2017b:54). Linguistic transformation can be achieved where language is used in an empowering way (Kaschula, 2016:201). Although no actual reference is made in the Constitution to the word "transformation", the Constitution emits the theme of transformation throughout its provisions (Budlender, 2005:716). Ntlama (2014:15) goes further by quoting from Chief Justice Mogoeng Mogoeng on how to achieve judicial transformation. These include:

- ensuring the demographic representation of the country without sacrificing the quality of justice that has to be delivered;
- taking into account awareness of the injustices that were often meted out by courts to black people during the Apartheid era;
- the inaccessibility of the courts and real justice;
- our commitment to a nation to make a decisive break from the institutionalised evil of the past; and
- to hold our new constitutional values and the related imperative to bring into being a justice system that South Africans can relate to and proudly call theirs.

It is ironic and contradictory that the same Chief Justice, who five years earlier listed inaccessibility of the courts and justice, later announces a decision to make English the sole official language of record, thereby excluding all other ten official languages on the basis of so-called transformation. Language has to feature as a measure of transformation for the judiciary and legal system. The current monolingual language of record directive prohibits any form of linguistic transformation. As De Vos (2010) has stated, we need to go back and ask ourselves what is meant by the word transformation when we use it and what kind of transformation the judiciary and the entire legal system are actually aspiring to.

Moerane (2003:716) acknowledges the complexities of the language of record but, in the same breath, states that this reaffirms the need for sound language policies to grapple with the language question facing the legal system and the need to draft and implement a language policy successfully. Moerane (2003:716) explains that factors such as costs of translation of the record for appeal are not reasons for the absence of language policies that encourage the promotion and creation of conditions for the development and use of African languages in the legal system. Cowling (2007:94) explains that the courts function in terms of national legislation and, as such, their rules and procedures must be provided for by national legislation. This is evident from the Superior Courts Act (2013). This might be stating the obvious, but it is important, as the legislature has the constitutional mandate of transforming the legal system linguistically by drafting legislation to bring about change in the current framework, still perpetuating apartheid-era thinking (Cowling, 2007:94). The monolingual language of record policy directive undermines the status of African languages and hinders real transformation in favour of a select few. De Vos (2010) succinctly conveys this point in the following quotation:

> Sadly, few lawyers and judges have embraced this vision of a transformative constitutional project. While most pay lip service to the need for transformation and claim to endorse the transformative vision of the Constitution, it is as if the old had colonised the new by co-opting them in the oppression of the majority of citizens. The concept of "transformation" is now often used – so it seems to me – as a Band-Aid to hide and legitimise the continued injustice and inequality that is perpetrated by the old business elite and the new political business elite.

Conclusion and recommendations

This chapter has clearly articulated the grave injustices that the directive to make English the sole language of record will bring within the legal system. The resolution on the language of record is a decision made for the sake of the convenience of the legal and social elite. It is a top-down decision that is non-consultative and constitutionally questionable. It does not take into account the linguistic proficiencies of the average South African. It again amounts to a "one-size-fits-all" policy; and such policies, in our opinion, have proven to be unworkable in the South African context. Grandiose "one-size-fits-all" policies and dictates abound in every sector of South African society from the legal to the educational spheres, cannot be implemented in the context of diversity that makes up South African society. What we argue for in this chapter is a context-driven, bottom-up approach, a meaningfully engaged approach to the challenges of linguistic diversity in the legal system, and a workable approach to the language(s) of record. Appropriate decision- and policy-making can only issue from meaningful engagement (Docrat & Kaschula, 2015) in the situation on the ground within certain courts and within the contexts of the language demographics of the various provinces, as outlined in this chapter. If this is not done, then the judicial system will continue to foster court decisions based on grave linguistic and cultural misunderstandings, given the present lack of linguistic, interpreting and translation skills (Ndlovu, 2002). It makes sense that people can only fairly give evidence and defend themselves in a language they fully understand – and ordinarily that would be their mother tongue. This is a logical and unquestionable language right that has underpinned well-developed justice systems worldwide, and which underlies the framework of our Constitution. Nevertheless, it still eludes many previously colonised societies, such as those on the African continent, and it is becoming increasingly problematic even in European in societies experiencing increased waves of immigration.

References

Bambust, I.; Kruger, A. & Kruger, T. 2012. Constitutional and judicial language protection in multilingual states: A brief overview of South Africa and Belgium. *Erasmus Law Review*, 5(3):211-232.

Budlender, G. 2005. Transforming the judiciary: The politics of the judiciary in a democratic South Africa. *South African Law Journal*, 122(4):715-724.

Cameron, E. 2013. Constitution holding steady in the storm, *Sunday Times*, 30 June 2013.

Cowling, M.J. 2007. The tower of Babel – Language usage and the courts. *South African Law Journal*, 87:84-111.

Currie, I. & De Waal, J. 2013. *The Bill of Rights Handbook*. 6th Edition. Cape Town: Juta.

De Vos P. 2010. What do we talk about when we talk about transformation? *Constitutionally Speaking*. http://constitutionallyspeaking.co.za/what-do-we-talk-about-when-we-talk-about-transformation-2 [Retrieved 10 February 2016].

De Vos, P. 2017. Formal interview with Zakeera Docrat on 25 April 2017, Cape Town.

Docrat, Z. 2017a. The fissure between law and language in a multilingual constitutional democracy exposed in the case of Lourens v Speaker of the National Assembly and Others. In: M.K. Ralarala, K. Barris & S. Siyepu (eds.), *Interdisciplinary themes and perspectives in African language research in the 21st Century*. Cape Town: Centre for Advanced Studies of African Societies. pp. 279-298.

Docrat, Z. 2017b. The role of African languages in the South African legal system: Towards a transformative agenda. Unpublished MA thesis, Rhodes University, Grahamstown.

Docrat, Z. & Kaschula, R.H. 2015. Meaningful engagement: Towards a language rights paradigm for effective language policy implementation. *South African Journal of African Languages,* 35(1):1-9.

Docrat, Z.; Kaschula, R.H.; Lourens, C.J.A.; Bailey, A. & Ralarala, M.K. 2017. Courts should promote all languages. *News24,* 17 September 2017. https://www.news24.com/Columnists/GuestColumn/courts-should-promote-all-languages-20170917-2

Du Plessis, T.L. & Pretorius, J.L. 2000. The structure of the Official Language Clause: A framework for its implementation. *SA Public Law (SAPR/PL)*, 16(1):513-515. http://www.scielo.org.za/scielo.php?script=sci_arttext&pid=S1727-37812013000100010&lng=en&nrm=iso

Gibbons, J. 2003. *Forensic linguistics. An introduction to language in the justice system*. Oxford: Blackwell Publishing.

Hlophe, J.M. 2004. Receiving justice in your own language — The need for effective court interpreting in our multilingual society. *Advocate Journal*, 17(1)42-47. https://www.sabar.co.za/law-journals/2004/april/2004-april-vol017-no1-pp42-47.pdf [Retrieved 5 December 2018].

Kaschula, R.H. 2016. In search of the African voice in higher education: The language question. *Stellenbosch Papers in Linguistics Plus,* 49:199-214. http://dx.doi.org/10.5842/49-0-658

Legal Aid South Africa. 2016. *Language Survey 2016*. http://www.legal-aid.co.za/wp-content/uploads/2017/04/Legal-Aid-SA-Language-Policy.pdf [Retrieved 10 December 2018].

Moerane, M.T.K. 2003. The meaning of transformation of the judiciary in the new South African context. *South African Law Journal*, 120:708-71.

Ndlovu, T. 2002. Black languages and the South African courts. *De Rebus,* 20(410).

Ngcukaitobi, T. 2013. Equality. In: I. Currie & J. Waal (eds.), *The Bill of Rights Handbook*. Cape Town: Juta. pp. 229-271.

Ntlama, N. 2014. *Transformation of the judiciary: A measure to weaken its capacity*. Paper presented at a conference, Twenty years of South African constitutionalism: Constitutional rights, judicial independence and the transition to democracy. New York Law School, 13-16 November 2014. https://nylssites.wpengine.com/nylslawreview/wp-content/uploads/sites/16/2014/10/Ntlama.pdf [Retrieved 18 January 2016].

Sibayan, B.P. 1999. *The intellectualization of Filipino and other essays on education and sociolinguistics*. Manila: Linguistic Society of the Philippines.

Statistics South Africa. 2016. *2011 Census*. http://www.statssa.gov.za/?page_id=3836 [Retrieved 21 October 2016].

Van Niekerk, G. 2015. Multilingualism in South African courts: The legislative regulation of language in the Cape during the nineteenth century. *Fundamina,* 21(2):372-391.

Wesson, M. & Du Plessis, M. 2008. Fifteen Years On: Central Issues Relating to the Transformation of the South African Judiciary. *South African Journal on Human Rights*, 24(2):187-213. https://doi.org/10.1080/19962126.2008.11864952

Woolman, S. 1998-2003. Limitations. In: M. Chaskalson, J. Kentridge, J. Klaaren, G. Marcus, D. Spitz & S. Woolman (eds.), 1st Edition, *Constitutional Law of South Africa*, Cape Town: Juta Law. 12-1-12-66 [this is a loose-leaf publication].

Case law

Lourens v Speaker of the National Assembly and Others 2015 (1) SA 618 (EqC).
State v Makwanyane & Another 1995 (3) SA 391 (CC).
State v Pienaar 2000 (2) SACR 143 (NC).

Legislation

Constitution of the Republic of South Africa Act, No. 108 of 1996.
Constitutional Ordinance Amendment Act, No. 1 of 1882.
Dutch Language Judicial Use Act, No. 21 of 1884.
Official Languages of the Union Act, No. 8 of 1925.
Promotion of Equality and Prevention of Unfair Discrimination Act, No. 4 of 2000.
Republic of South Africa Constitution Act, No. 110 of 1983.
South Africa Act of 1909.
Superior Courts Act, No. 10 of 2013.

MULTILINGUALISM IN THE SOUTH AFRICAN LEGAL SYSTEM

Attorneys' experiences

Annelise de Vries & Zakeera Docrat[1]

Introduction

There is currently a judicial, academic and political move to entrench the use of English in the broader populace across all spheres of public life in South Africa. Our focus in this chapter is the entrenchment of English in the South African legal system. The constitutional language imperatives contained in Section 6, as well as the constitutional language rights, prescribe that all languages be treated "equitably" and that the status of the nine African languages be elevated to ensure that they are placed alongside English and Afrikaans. The monolingual language of record policy directive of April 2017, which affects high courts undermines the constitutional provisions by elevating English to a super official language – and this under the guise of transformation and enhancing access to justice.

This chapter builds on the discussions in Chapter 4 in this volume, being concerned with the language attitudes of legal practitioners, in addition to their linguistic competencies. We engage with a 2017 language survey aimed at ascertaining language attitudes and experiences of attorneys across all nine provinces in South Africa, via four specific law societies, which was conducted in light of the Chief Justice's 2017 language of record policy directive to make English the sole official language of record in South African high courts. The survey captured the language attitudes and experiences of approximately 2 500 registered attorneys in South Africa. One of the primary purposes of this survey was to gauge whether attorneys felt obliged to communicate in English with their clients and colleagues, regardless of their mother tongue.

---

[1] The financial assistance of the National Research Foundation's (NRF) South African Research Chairs Initiative (SARChI) Chair for the Intellectualisation of African Languages, Multilingualism and Education at Rhodes University, towards this research is hereby acknowledged. Opinions expressed and conclusions arrived at are those of the authors and are not necessarily to be attributed to the NRF.

In this chapter, we argue that although attorneys revealed that they are not averse to the use of multilingualism, they do not see the value of using the ten official languages, given the heightened status of English in the South African legal system. We aim to explicate how the entire legislative framework governing the legal system fails to recognise language as a tool to enhance access to justice if that language is not English, and to show that the attitude of the legal practitioners is one of the primary issues contributing to the failure to recognise, elevate and use all official languages equally. To achieve transformation of legal practitioners' attitudes towards language as a tool to enhance access to justice, and also to ensure that the language rights in Section 35(3)(k), (f) and (g) are fully realised, we propose, firstly, that language requirements that are responsive to the constitutional mandate be legislated for attorneys, other legal practitioners and judicial officers. Secondly, we propose that the linguistic competency of attorneys should be responsive to the language demographics of the populace, as well as the linguistic competencies of litigants accessing the legal system.

Forensic linguistics and language planning

The language survey that was undertaken is located within the area of forensic linguistics, which itself is a branch of applied linguistics. The International Association of Applied Linguistics describes the field of applied linguistics as follows:

> Applied linguistics is an interdisciplinary field of research and practice dealing with practical problems of language and communication that can be identified, analysed or solved by applying available theories, methods or results of linguistics or by developing new theoretical and methodological frameworks in linguistics to work on these problems.
> (Wei 2013:2)

According to Wei (2013), language planning and forensic linguistics are common branches of applied linguistics. Forensic linguistics can be defined as "the application of linguistic knowledge to a particular social setting, namely the legal forum" (Olsson, 2008:3). Expanding the definition, Olsson states that

> forensic linguistics is the interface between languages, crime, law, where law includes law enforcement, judicial matters, legislation, disputes or proceedings in law, and even disputes which only potentially involve some infraction of the law or some necessity to seek legal remedy.

Grant (2017) summarises the definition by Olsson (2008), explaining that forensic linguistics is an attempt to improve the delivery of justice. It furthermore involves linguistic analysis of legal texts, contexts and processes. The definition by Grant (2017) will be used for the purposes of this chapter.

Monolingual language of record policy directive: an overview

On 16 April 2017, it was reported that Chief Justice Mogoeng Mogoeng, together with the Heads of Court, had changed the language of record to English only (Docrat et al., 2017:1). It was reported that the decision to remove Afrikaans as a language of record was taken on grounds of transformation and the need to redress past discrimination. Western Cape Judge President, Justice Hlophe, released a directive reaffirming this pronouncement, stating further that the resolution would apply to both civil and criminal cases. Hlophe stated that having English as the sole official language of record would "result in speedier and more efficient adjudication and finalisation of all cases". (For further discussion, see Chapter 4.)

Constitutional language imperative

The Constitution of the Republic of South Africa of 1996 informs the legislative framework. Section 6 of the Constitution, the linguistic blueprint, provides the linguistic principles which are to be reflected in the legislation to provide a practical framework for language use. Subsections (1) and (2) are relevant through their conferring official status on all eleven languages, whereas previously there were only two official languages. According to Lourens (2012), this official status means that the State is obliged to use the languages conferred with official status for all official business across all spheres of public life. Lourens explains that this would include their official use in the judiciary and in the legal system more broadly. This understanding correlates with Subsection (2), which obligates the State to "take practical and positive measures to elevate the status and use" of African languages, given their historical marginalisation. This mandate is to be implemented practically through the creation of legislation as per Section 6(4) and through the implementation of language rights contained in the Bill of Rights (BOR), specifically Section 35(3)(k).

Legislative language framework

In terms of Section 6(4), the State is required to ensure the enactment of primary language legislation. The constitutional mandate was not fulfilled until the judgment in the case of *Lourens v President of South Africa* (2013). The court ordered that legislation be drafted in response to the constitutional imperative; and, to this effect, the Use of Official Languages Act 12 of 2012, was drafted and enacted. This Languages Act (2012), being the primary language legislation of the Republic, is of further relevance to this chapter as a result of its application through Section 3(1) to the following departments and entities:

(a) national departments;
(b) national public entities; and
(c) national public enterprises.

Docrat et al. (2017:8) argue that the application of the Languages Act (2012) is limited to government (thus in accordance with the doctrine of separation of powers) and that it, therefore, does not apply to the judiciary. However, it applies to national departments, including the Department of Justice and Constitutional Development, and the South African Police Services.

The Languages Act (2012) necessitates that each national department and entity should draft a language policy to comply with its provisions. Section 4 more specifically provides directives for the drafting of a language policy, with specific constitutional compliance, whilst including practical measures for publicising it in the broader community. Docrat et al. (2017:7) observe that the language policy directives are progressive, extending beyond the ambit of the linguistic framework created in Section 6 of the Constitution in acknowledging the importance of other languages besides the official languages. To this effect, Section 9.1 of the Department of Justice's draft language policy (2015) is relevant. It reads as follows:

> The use of official languages in court proceedings including court interpretation services, court process, documents and recordings of court proceedings shall be regulated by rules of court or any other applicable legislation.

Based on this excerpt, the Draft Policy on Use of Official Languages of the Department of Justice and Constitutional Development (2015) does not comply with the Languages Act (2012), nor with Section 6 of the Constitution. The draft language policy of the Department of Justice (2015) fails to develop the law and to bridge the legislative and policy gaps which were pointed out by Yekiso J (2004) in the case of *State v Damoyi* (2004). In his judgment, Yekiso J (2004:123) explained that he wrote to the Director of Public Prosecutions in the Western Cape to enquire whether a language policy existed for the Department of Justice, and what it said concerning the use of any one of the official languages in criminal proceedings in both the High Court and lower courts. It is evident that Yekiso J (2004:123) specifically asked what the capacity of the office of the Director of Public Prosecutions was concerning the use of any official language other than English and Afrikaans in criminal proceedings, in both the High Court and lower courts. In response to this, the Director of Public Prosecutions stated that there was no language policy in place for the Department of Justice at the time the case was heard. The draft language policy of the Department of Justice (2015) promotes what Heugh (2002:451) refers to as "linguicism," where a high status is placed on English and a low status on other languages. By not addressing the practical role and use of African languages in the draft language policy of the Department of Justice (2015), the status quo is maintained and African languages are continuously accorded a low status, perpetuating the exclusion of these languages.

Legislative language requirements for attorneys

We now examine primary legislation regulating the admission of attorneys to the Side Bar, to assess whether it includes language requirements for attorneys, and the extent of development of these requirements in terms of amendments in compliance with the constitutional language provisions.

At the onset of democracy, the existing legislation governing admission to the Side Bar was the Attorneys Act 53 of 1979, which included language requirements in the form of English, Afrikaans and Latin, all of which needed to be acquired at university level as part of the Bachelor of Laws (LLB) degree. In the Attorneys Amendment Act 115 of 1993, the Latin requirement was removed, but for English and Afrikaans (the official languages at the time), the requirements remained unchanged (Bambust, Kruger & Kruger, 2012).

Given the attention paid to language requirements under apartheid, it might be assumed that the multitude of amendments flowing from democratic changes would result in the insertion of appropriate linguistic requirements, in giving effect to Section 6 of the Constitution, representative of the nine official African languages that were previously excluded.

Chapter 1, Sections 2-24 of the Attorneys Amendment Act (1993), concerns qualifications, admissions and removal from the roll. In perusing these provisions, no language requirements are specified for admission to the roll, as apparent in Sections 4 and 15. Sections 13(b) and 14 concern the completion of training in legal practice management and practical examinations. Of relevance, given the absence of language requirements amongst the requirements for inception into the articles programme, is Section 2 of the Attorneys Amendment Act (1993) which deals with the duration of service under articles. Here too, there were no African language requirements in line with the new constitutionally recognised official languages, under consideration at that period, when promulgation of the (interim) Constitution of the Republic of South Africa, 1993) was in process.

With regard to the legislation governing the professions, there are also no language requirements in the form of language policies for the South African Law Society.

It must be noted, however, that in November 2016, a report was released pertaining to a review of the attorneys' profession (Thebe, 2016). It highlights the state of the attorneys' profession in relation to briefing patterns and demographics in terms of a more racially and gender diverse profession. Although there is reference to transformational issues, the report does not include language and is limited to race and gender (Thebe, 2016).

With reference to the attorneys' profession, the legislative frameworks illustrate a linguistically exclusionary legal system. Four questions and sub-issues arising from the above theoretical framework will be discussed further.

Firstly, does the absence of language requirements for attorneys adversely affect broader citizenry when they access the legal system, in terms of communicating with their legal practitioners? In turn, the question raises further points as to whether a litigant really has the right to communicate with a legal practitioner in a language the litigant fully understands. Specifically, does Section 35(3)(k) of the Constitution extend to communication between clients and their legal representatives?

Secondly, does the legal system really provide an interpretational right in practice and a language of choice right in theory? Simply put: should there be a differentiation between theory and practice? It is our opinion that these questions should not be limited to an accused person in the criminal justice system. A complainant is also required to engage with the prosecutor, discharging the onus.

Thirdly, in the context of a province where a majority speaks one of the other ten official languages, how practical it is for a monolingual English-speaking prosecutor to be expected fully to comprehend a complainant's factual explanation of an event in question?

Fourthly, is the complainant being linguistically prejudiced?

It is our opinion that these issues affect the level of substantive justice that the legal system is delivering.

With reference to the questions and issues noted, Sections 35(3)(f), (g) and (k) of the Constitution state:

> (3) Every accused person has a right to a fair trial, which includes the right –
> (f) to choose, and be represented by, a legal practitioner, and to be informed of this promptly;
> (g) to have a legal practitioner assigned to the accused person by the State and at State expense, if substantial injustice would otherwise result, and to be informed of this promptly;
> (k) to be tried in a language that the accused person understands or if that is not practicable, to have the proceedings interpreted in that language; ...

The dictum, in the case of *State v Pienaar* (2000), dealt succinctly with the questions above. The court held that Subsections (f) and (g) are to be read together with Section 35(3)(k). In this assertion, the case of *S v Pienaar* is relevant where the accused had a right to a fair trial which included the right to assistance of a legal representative with whom the accused could communicate in his/her own language (*S v Pienaar*, 2000:145). A further important point emanating from the Pienaar case (2000:144-145) is that the court held that the right to legal representation includes the right to communicate directly with the legal representative in the accused's own language of choice, and that this may only occur indirectly through interpretation in exceptional cases.

In this instance, the court in *S v Pienaar* (2000) found that the right in Section 35(3)(k) did not confer a default interpretational right, but rather a language right where the accused should be tried directly in his or her own language. Furthermore, the court explained that Section 35(3)(k) obligated government and, in particular, the Department of Justice (as it was then) to ensure, in terms of Section 6 of the Constitution, that the languages used overwhelmingly in the Northern Cape (the province in which the Pienaar [2000] case was heard) be promoted in a manner in which they would eventually achieve equality of status alongside English and be treated equitably (*S v Pienaar*, 2000:145).

It is clear then that what would be required are linguistically competent legal practitioners who are competent in one or more of the languages of the province in which they practise. This means that such language requirements should have been legislated in the Attorneys' Amendment Act (1993). Docrat's research (2017) provides an in-depth discussion which captures the views of Justice Lex Mpati (2017), retired Judge President of the Supreme Court of Appeal, Bloemfontein, who cautions against inserting "new" African language requirements into the Attorneys' Amendment Act (1993). Mpati (2017) emphasises the importance of guarding against the emulation of Apartheid-era thinking, where the legislature would be forcing attorneys to learn an African language. This, according to Mpati (2017), is contrary to the ideals and purpose of the Constitution and does not foster transformation. Mpati (2017) agrees, however, that African languages are important and that practical ways need to be developed to ensure their use in the legal system. Mpati (2017) recommends that the starting point would be to create awareness of the importance of language in the legal system, where the attitudes of legal practitioners should be altered to see language as a tool that enhances access to justice.

Docrat (2017) argues that, in addition to an attitudinal change and awareness campaigns, practical approaches, as required in Section 6 of the Constitution, need to be implemented, as the impasse in terms of language rights or interpretational rights needs to be addressed. Docrat (2017) further maintains that the interests of the majority are to be prioritised, and proposes that the right in Section 35(3)(k) can be implemented fully where legal practitioners are linguistically competent in a language spoken by the majority in the province. This will, furthermore, give effect to Section 35(3)(f) and (g). The right in Section 35(3)(k) will thus not be an interpretational right, but rather a language right, as it ought to be. (See Chapter 4 for statistics emanating from the 2011 National Census, illustrating that, in each province, three primary languages are spoken by the majority of that province's inhabitants.) In the case of *S v Pienaar* (2000:145), the court advanced the importance of language demographics and held that language policies should be developed in response to these demographics.

Based on the theory and case law presented in this chapter, it is our opinion that what is practically happening in the legal system regarding the recent language of record policy directive conflicts with the decision in the case of *S v Pienaar* (2000). Rather, legal practitioners need to *be* the linguistic change in the legal system. The following discussion of the language survey concerning the attitudes of attorneys towards language, particularly multilingualism in the legal system, will illustrate the readiness of the profession to embrace this challenge.

The language survey

Contextual and methodological overview

Approximately 25 900 attorneys in South Africa are currently registered respectively with four statutory law societies (Cape Law Society, KwaZulu-Natal Law Society, Law Society of the Free State, and the Law Society of the Northern Provinces). Of the four associations' 14 500 members who are registered legal practitioners, 2 157 completed a computerised self-administered questionnaire (CSAQ), a response rate of 14.9%. We the authors of this chapter compiled and managed the survey. This quantitative language survey made use of non-probable purposive sampling. To ensure that the questions yielded statistically sound results, the questionnaire was referred to an independent statistical consultant beforehand. Participants were informed of the study through an electronic covering letter that included a link to a questionnaire which they could then choose to complete. The language of the questionnaire was English; and participants had three weeks in which to complete the questionnaire.

The first section of the questionnaire comprised biographical questions focusing on aspects such as gender, age, provincial location in South Africa, undergraduate legal qualification and institution(s) of study. Questions excluded race. In the second section, participants answered questions about their language ability, their use of two official South African languages in which they were fluent, as well as the languages used most often, and secondarily most often, in these contexts: at home; in their social circles; during written and oral communication with clients; and during communication with colleagues. Participants were also asked about these aspects: the language in which they mostly conducted their research; the language of documentation and/or correspondence with clients, courts and opponents; the language of legal training; the practitioner's competence in English; and the clients' competence in English (as evaluated by practitioners). The final section of the questionnaire included 18 Likert-scale questions on practitioners' language attitudes, needs and choices. There were four response options for the Likert-scale questions, where the value of 1 indicated that the participant strongly disagreed with the applicable statement, while a value of 4 indicated that the participant strongly supported the applicable statement.

Biographical details illustrated the following: 57.18% of participants were male, and participants generally fell in the age group of 26 to 35 years; the highest number of participants (70.7%) were practising attorneys in Gauteng, with the second highest number of participants (7.29%) practising in the Free State, and then the North West (5.54%). Of the participants, 69.93% indicated that they had received their legal education in their mother tongue. Given that race was excluded as a criterion for biographical details, it appeared that all attorneys completing the questionnaire – whether Black, Indian, Coloured or White – recorded their mother tongue as English or Afrikaans, as law qualifications are only offered in English and Afrikaans at universities in South Africa. The exception was vocation-specific courses. Those participants who obtained an LLB degree as a legal qualification accounted for 55.7% of the group. Regarding higher education institutions attended, 22.27% of participants obtained their legal qualifications at the University of Pretoria, 18.07% at the University of South Africa and 12.08% at the North-West University.

Apart from calculating descriptive statistics, such as frequencies and averages, multiple analyses of variance (MANOVAS) were done under the guidance of an independent statistician. The relationships between variables in the data set were calculated in several ways, as determined by the measurement level of the variables involved. It included t-tests and ANOVAs. McMillan and Schumacher (2010:299) describe the t-test as a comparison between two or more populations or topics to determine any statistically significant differences. ANOVA analyses are similar to t-tests but are used if a heterogeneous population group uses the same data collection instrument. The effect size was also included for an indication of practical significance, since statistical significance alone is insufficient, especially in the case of large samples.

Language survey results

Quantitative results

In the category of language ability and choices, a clear majority of 97.11% of legal practitioners who participated in this study could read, speak and write English, while 71.99% possessed these skills in Afrikaans; and 4.72% had reading, speaking and writing skills in Sepedi. It is important to note that these results were determined by a standardised language ability test but were the result of the participants' subjective evaluation of their own language ability.

The high percentage attributed to the use of English was also clearly visible in the languages in which the legal practitioners communicated with their clients. According to the participants, 84.11% of written correspondence with clients occurred in English, while 63.09% of oral communication with clients took place in English. This tendency extended to the language in which these participants undertook research: 90.87% of the participants in this study indicated that research was mainly conducted in English. These percentages are inconsistent with the languages used primarily at home by the participants: 52.52% indicated that they used Afrikaans as a home language, while 31.91% used English as a home language, and another 3.82% recorded that they spoke Sepedi at home. In addition, 49.06% of participants indicated that they used Afrikaans as their primary communication medium in social circles, while 40.98% used English in these circles; and 3.25% used Sepedi when communicating with friends. From these findings, it can be deduced that legal practitioners felt compelled to use mainly English in the ordinary course of their daily tasks, whether or not English was their mother tongue language or second language.

Regarding language skills, participants rated their English reading and writing skills at 2.77 out of 3; and their English oral skills at 2.69 out of 3. These ratings can be attributed to the fact that the legal practitioners conducted business primarily in English, thus it reflected their perception of their English proficiency.

TABLE 5.1 Clients' English proficiency from the perspective of the legal practitioner

Proficiency in reading and writing	100	N = 1 915
Measured average	2.16/3	
Reasonable	20.94	401
Good	41.83	801
Excellent	37.23	713
Proficiency in oral communication	100	N = 1 915
Measured average	2.15/3	
Reasonable	19.74	378
Good	45.43	870
Excellent	34.83	667
N = total number of participants answering this question		

TABLE 5.2 Summary of clients' English proficiency from the perspective of the legal practitioner

	Three-point scale		
	Reasonable	Good	Excellent
Reading and writing	20.94	41.83	37.23
Oral communication	19.74	45.43	34.83
Total	20.34	43.63	36.03

Participants were asked to evaluate their clients' English language skills on a scale of 1 to 3. The legal practitioners gave their clients an average of 2.15 out of 3 for their reading, writing and speaking skills in English. It should be noted that the percentages reflected in Table 6.1 are not necessarily a reflection of the actual skills, as data was gathered from the legal practitioners' point of view. When these percentages are compared to a survey conducted by Legal Aid South Africa (2016) amongst their clients, the picture looks very different, as shown in Table 5.3.

TABLE 5.3   Legal Aid South Africa's 2016 survey on English skills in criminal and civil cases

Skill	Criminal cases			Civil cases		
	Good	Satis-factory	Poor	Good	Satis-factory	Poor
Understand	24.4	38.7	36.8	45.2	32.4	22.4
Speak	21.5	36.1	42.4	42.1	32.7	25.2
Read and write	20.7	33.8	45.6	43.5	29.6	26.9
Total	22.2	36.2	41.6	43.6	31.57	24.83

Table 5.3 indicates that, in terms of litigants who were assigned legal practitioners at the State's expense, 41.6% of participants in criminal cases indicated that their English language skills were poor. This is concerning, especially in the light of Section 35(3)(k) of the Constitution (1996) and the recent policy directive to make English the sole official language of record.

When Tables 5.2 and 5.3 are compared, it can be deduced that legal practitioners overestimate the litigants' English language proficiency: on a three-point scale, legal practitioners (participants in the relevant study) indicated that 36.03% of their clients had excellent English language skills, whereas in the survey conducted by Legal Aid South Africa (2016), clients receiving State representation indicated that only 22.2% had good English language skills.

Language attitudes, needs, and choices of legal practitioners

Table 5.4 includes the statements that were measured regarding the language attitudes, needs and choices of participants in this study, and the average of the statistical analyses of these statements. Average scores of 1-2 are considered to reflect a more negative attitude, while average scores of 3-4 are considered to reflect a more positive attitude in response to a statement (as measured on a four-point scale).

TABLE 5.4 Results of questionnaire on attorneys' language attitudes, needs and choices

Legend: 1 = Strongly disagree; 2 = Disagree; 3 = Agree; 4 = Strongly Agree

Statement		1	2	3	4	Total
The general language of use in the legal profession should be English.	No.	443	196	320	821	1 780
	%	24.89	11.01	17.98	46.12	2.85
Transformation in the judicial system is fair.	No.	419	468	481	399	1 767
	%	23.71	26.49	27.22	22.58	2.49
Transformation in the judicial system takes place at a satisfactory rate.	No.	345	498	563	358	1 764
	%	19.56	28.23	31.92	20.29	2.53
The judicial system cannot transform adequately if multilingualism is sought	No.	684	397	324	367	1 772
	%	38.60	22.40	18.28	20.71	2.21
It is in the best interests of the client to consult with him/her in English.	No.	760	441	291	278	1 770
	%	42.94	24.92	16.44	15.71	2.05
It is in the best interests of the client to consult with him/her in his/her home language.	No.	180	257	365	970	1 772
	%	10.16	14.50	20.60	54.74	3.2
I have experienced communication problems with clients before because we did not properly understand each other's language.	No.	469	354	410	538	1 771
	%	26.48	19.99	23.15	30.38	2.57
I had to translate legal documents from another language into English before.	No.	798	221	256	490	1 765
	%	45.21	12.52	14.50	27.76	2.25
The translation of legal documents can influence the speed at which a case is settled.	No.	173	223	415	952	1 763
	%	9.81	12.65	23.54	54.00	3.22
Multilingualism can create confusion in the legal profession.	No.	365	270	344	787	1 766
	%	20.67	15.29	19.48	44.56	2.88
In a multilingual country, multilingualism in the courts should be a given.	No.	496	401	372	486	1 755
	%	28.26	22.85	21.20	27.69	2.48
It can be confusing to the client if an attorney does not litigate in his/her home language.	No.	378	367	463	558	1 766
	%	21.40	20.78	26.22	31.60	2.68

TABLE 5.4 Continued

		1	2	3	4	Total
I regularly use language practitioners to translate legal documents.	No.	1 208	310	110	133	1 761
	%	68.60	17.60	6.25	7.55	1.53
		1	2	3	4	Total
I regularly use translators during court proceedings.	No.	650	344	325	422	1 741
	%	37.33	19.76	18.67	24.24	2.3
		1	2	3	4	Total
In a criminal case it is fair that a victim should pay for translation services himself if he/she cannot make a statement in English.	No.	1 279	188	96	185	1 748
	%	73.17	10.76	5.49	10.58	1.53
		1	2	3	4	Total
I have experienced before that interpreters' translations cause confusion during court proceedings.	No.	288	356	486	605	1 735
	%	16.60	20.52	28.01	34.87	2.81
		1	2	3	4	Total
In my profession I will benefit from learning another indigenous South African language.	No.	325	183	382	876	1 766
	%	18.40	10.36	21.63	49.60	3.02
		1	2	3	4	Total
During the translation process, I found that legal concepts could not be translated meaningfully and in context in other languages.	No.	252	390	494	596	1 732
	%	14.55	22.52	28.52	34.41	2.83

The highlighted percentage under "Total" is a "measured mean".

The data in Table 5.4 reflecting legal practitioners' language attitudes, needs and choices can be divided into four themes: (1) multilingualism in the legal profession; (2) translation and interpretation; (3) client interests; and (4) transformation in the legal profession. These themes will now be discussed.

Multilingualism in the legal profession

Legal practitioners' language attitudes and experiences regarding multilingualism in the legal profession are presented in Figure 5.1. Based on the data in Figure 5.1, two codes can be identified: participants' attitudes toward multilingualism in the legal profession as a whole; and participants' attitudes towards multilingualism in the courts.

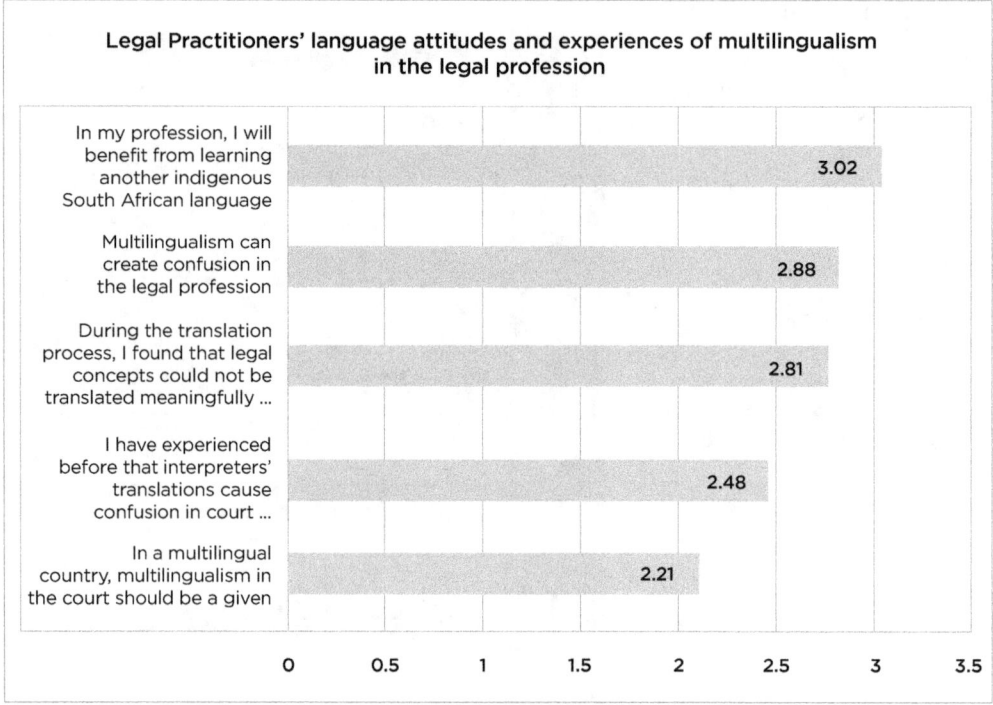

FIGURE 5.1 Legal practitioners' language attitudes and experiences of multilingualism in the legal profession

The data in Table 5.4, as well as in Figure 5.1, indicate that participants in this study regard multilingualism as a key factor in the transformation of the judiciary (61% *do not agree* that the judicial system can transform adequately if multilingualism is not sought). The latter is aligned with the finding that 71% of participants in this study agree that multilingualism in this profession is beneficial (high score of 4 regarding the statement: "In my profession I will benefit from learning another indigenous South African language"). Although participants thought it would be favourable to learn an additional official language, they did not agree that multilingualism in courts should be a result of courts being in a multilingual country: 2.48 out of 4 (51%) disagreed, while 49% of participants agreed. The results show that 64% of participants agreed that multilingualism could create confusion in the legal profession (2.88 out of 4) – owing to a lack of confidence in interpretation and translation.

Translation and interpreters

Legal practitioners' language positions and perceptions of interpretation and translation are presented in the graph in Figure 5.2. From the data in Table 5.4, as well as in Figure 5.2, it is clear that participants do not use language practitioners to translate legal documents. The reason for this may be that 77.5% of participants indicated that they were under the impression that the translation of legal documents obstructed the speed it took to settle a case (3.22 out of 4) and that it might cause confusion (as explained in the previous section). The latter is especially illustrated in the well-known South African case of the *S v Pistorius* (2014) (Pienaar & Cornelius, 2015:186-206), where interpreting and/or translating had extremely negative consequences. Media reports on the state of court interpretation and translation in South Africa further highlighted the negative impressions regarding this issue (Pienaar & Cornelius, 2015:188), for example, the following news headlines:

"Renosterstroper" dalk vry oor tolk (Van Heerden, 2012).

Joburg courts face foreign language problems (Monnakgotla, 2012).

Bad interpreters ruin court cases, says Mogoeng (*City Press*, 2014).

Ralarala (2012, 2014) and Mpahlwa (2015) also address problems regarding the inefficiency of interpreters and translators in South African courts. Their research is consistent with participants' negativity regarding translation and interpretation in the legal profession.

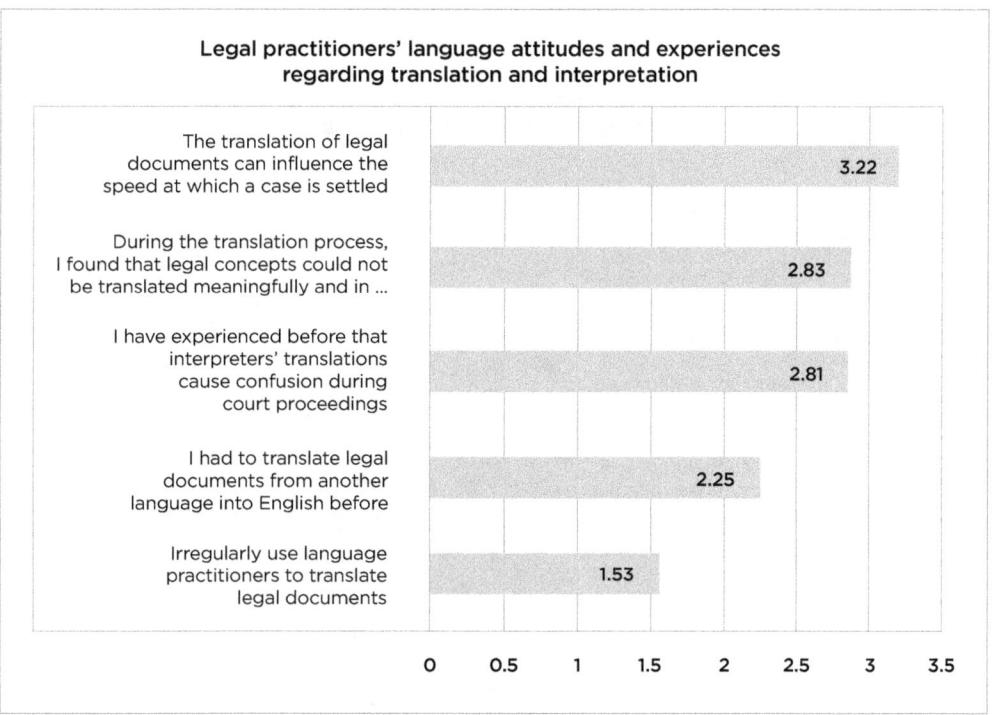

FIGURE 5.2 Legal practitioners' language attitudes and experiences regarding translation and interpretation.

Pienaar and Cornelius (2015:189) further note that public and media galleries in the Gauteng Provincial Legislature are still not equipped with earphones. Another problem with the court interpreting system that requires attention is the quality of training currently available for court interpreters (*Pretoria News*, 2014). This discussion links to preceding paragraphs of this chapter where we highlighted the issue that the language rights in Section

35(3)(k) should not be reduced to a default interpretational right, where the litigant is not fully conversant in English.

Client interests

Legal practitioners' perceptions about the interests of the client are explained in Figure 7.3. The data in Table 5.4, as well as in Figure 5.3, illustrates that 75.3% of the participants who completed the language survey were more positive about the fact that it is better to consult with a client in the client's home language (3.2 out of 4), given that 57.8% of participants indicated that they had experienced that it could be confusing to a client if an attorney did not litigate in the client's home language (2.68 out of 4). This correlates with the participants' more negative attitude towards consultation with a client in English, regardless of the client's home language (2.05 out of 4). It is also noteworthy that 67.9% of the participants indicated that they did not agree that it was in the best interests of the client to consult with him/her in his/her home language.

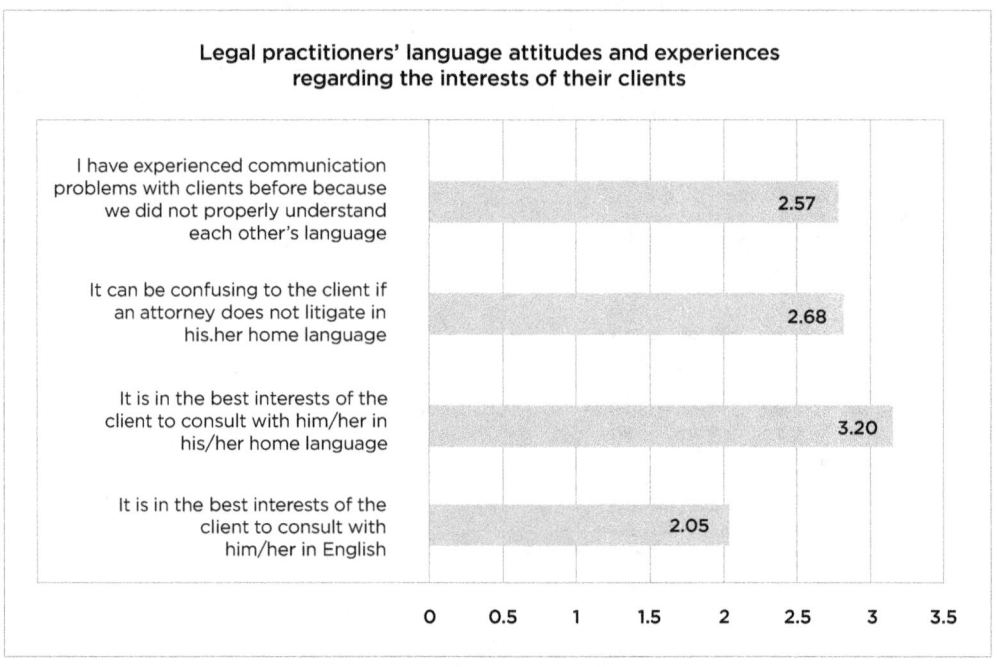

FIGURE 5.3 Legal practitioners' language attitudes and experiences regarding the interests of their clients

Transformation in the legal profession

Legal practitioners' perceptions of the transformation in the legal profession are set out in Figure 5.4. Although most participants agreed that multilingualism should be a key aspect of transformation, 64.1% of participants agreed that English should be the general language of use of the legal profession (2.85 of 4). This can be attributed to the fact that 62.9% of participants indicated that they had had bad experiences with translation and interpreters in the legal profession and in the courts (see Table 5.4). For a full discussion on language as part of the transformational agenda of the legal system, see Docrat and Kaschula's chapter in this volume, or Docrat (2017).

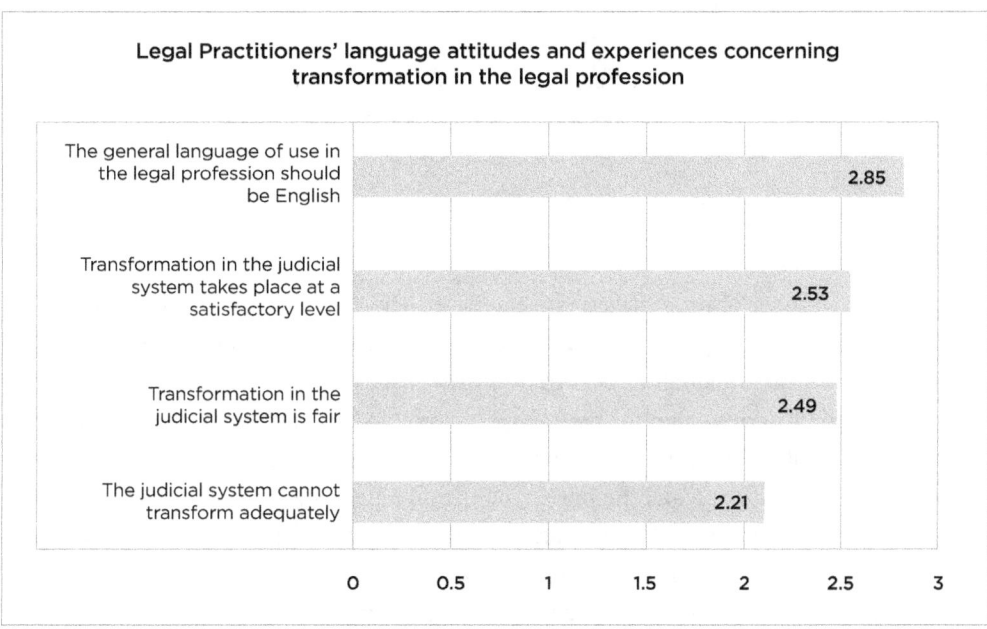

FIGURE 5.4 Legal practitioners' language attitudes and experiences concerning transformation in the legal profession

TABLE 5.5 Summary of the Lickert scale data from the questionnaire

More than 50% of the participants ...
• agree that the translation of legal documents impedes the time it takes to settle a case;
• agree that it is better to consult with a client in his/her home language;
• agree that they will benefit from learning another official South African language;
• agree that it is NOT in the best interests of the client to consult with him/her in English;
• are positive about English being the common language of use in the legal profession;
• agree that multilingualism can create confusion in the legal profession;
• agree that interpreters and translators can create confusion in the legal profession;
• consider multilingualism as a key factor in the transformation of the South African judicial system;

TABLE 5.5   Continued

•	agree that it may be confusing to the client if the attorney does not consult with him/her in his/her home language;
•	do not really agree that multilingualism in the judicial system is a natural outcome of a multilingual country.

From this summary, it can be deduced that participants realise the value of multilingualism in the legal profession, but that certain frustrations (emphasised in bold font in the table) in certain instances illicit a negative response to multilingualism amongst participants.

Quantitative results: Inferential statistics

Relation between variables: Provinces

Owing to the number of provinces represented, an ANOVA would not be meaningful, as an impractical number of post-hoc comparisons would have to be done. Therefore, only the average scores for multilingualism per province are reported here. It appears that the average scores are within a narrow margin (between 2.46 and 2.84) on a scale of 1 to 4. There seems to be a minimal difference between the provinces. Although the Free State Province scored the highest and KwaZulu-Natal the lowest, no actual difference can be deduced from this. The conclusion can therefore be drawn that there is no significant difference between the provinces regarding their attitudes towards multilingualism. It is also important to note that most respondents (64%) were from Gauteng. Too few respondents were from the other provinces for a meaningful comparison between provinces to be possible.

TABLE 5.6   Average scores for multilingualism per province

Province	Median	Standard deviation
Western Cape	2.6595	0.45264
KwaZulu-Natal	2.4637	0.46244
Free State	2.8352	0.42586
North West	2.8139	0.39678
Gauteng	2.5266	0.44861
Mpumalanga	2.7831	0.3892
Limpopo	2.8184	0.37301

Language preferences

Questions were asked concerning the respondents' language preferences in various contexts: amongst others, the language used at home and at work was of interest. Respondents' choices were divided into three categories, namely Afrikaans, nine official African languages, and English. These groups were then compared regarding multilingualism through a one-way ANOVA.

It is important to note that it cannot be deduced that one group has a "high" or a "low" score – the scores are to be evaluated in the context of the underlying four-point scale.

TABLE 5.7 Statistical relation between attorneys' language preference and multilingualism: Most used at home

Choice	No. speakers	Average	Significant difference?	Effect size
Afrikaans	956	2.6502	Yes ($p < 0.01$)	0.093 Medium
English	557	2.4064		
African languages	269	2.8026		
Post-hoc analysis: All groups differ significantly from one another. English has the lowest score, followed by Afrikaans, with African languages being the highest.				

TABLE 5.8 Statistical relation between attorneys' language preference and multilingualism: Most used in social circles

Choice	No. speakers	Average	Significant difference?	Effect size
Afrikaans	899	2.6614	Yes ($p < 0.01$)	0.083 Small
English	713	2.4530		
African languages	170	2.8609		

TABLE 5.9 Statistical relation between attorneys' language preference and multilingualism: Most used in oral communication

Choice	No. speakers	Average	Significant difference?	Effect size
Afrikaans	508	2.7469	Yes ($p < 0.01$)	0.104 Medium
English	1 116	2.4875		
African languages	158	2.8888		

TABLE 5.10 Statistical relation between attorneys' language preference and multilingualism: Most used in communicating with colleagues

Choice	No. speakers	Average	Significant difference?	Effect size
Afrikaans	626	2.7081	Yes ($p < 0.01$)	0.058 Small
English	1 064	2.5104		
African languages	92	2.8429		

TABLE 5.11 Statistical relation between attorneys' language preference and multilingualism: Most used in written communication

Choice	No. speakers	Average	Significant difference?	Effect size
Afrikaans	265	2.8252	Yes ($p <0.01$)	0.62
English	1 498	2.5521		
African languages	sample too small			
Post-hoc analysis: English lowest, followed by Afrikaans.				

Language skills

Respondents were asked to evaluate their own language skills, as well as those of their clients, on a three-point scale, with 1 being "reasonable" and 3 "very good". The three groups which thus emerged were compared in terms of their perceptions of multilingualism by way of one-way ANOVAs.

It seems that, regarding respondents' own language skills, that those with a skill choice of 3 had a significantly lower score on multilingualism (that is, a more negative attitude towards multilingualism) than those who chose 1 and 2, respectively.

With regard to participants' assessment of their clients' language proficiency, there was a significant increase in negative attitude towards multilingualism as skills increased. Higher levels of language English proficiency (as judged by the legal practitioner), both of the practitioner and clients, have been associated with more negative attitudes towards multilingualism.

TABLE 5.12 Statistical relation between language proficiency and multilingualism: Attorneys' English reading and writing skills

Choice	No. participants	Average	Significant difference?	Effect size
(1) Reasonable	43	2.7456	Yes ($p <0.01$)	0.022 Small
(2) Good	318	2.7298		
(3) Very good	1 421	2.5628		
Post-hoc analysis: Group 3 scored significantly lower than Groups 1 and 2.				

TABLE 5.13 Statistical relation between language proficiency and multilingualism: Attorneys' English-speaking skills

Choice	No. participants	Average	Significant difference?	Effect size
(1) Reasonable	58	2.7529	Yes ($p <0.01$)	0.036 Small
(2) Good	433	2.7378		
(3) Very good	1 291	2.5428		
Post-hoc analysis: Group 3 scored significantly lower than Groups 1 and 2.				

TABLE 5.14 Statistical relation between language proficiency and multilingualism: Clients' English reading and writing skills

Choice	No. participants	Average	Significant difference?	Effect size
(1) Reasonable	377	2.8152		
(2) Good	747	2.6091	Yes (p <0.01)	0.083 Small
(3) Very good	658	2.4584		
Post-hoc analysis: All three groups differ from one another – the higher the skill, the lower the score.				

TABLE 5.15 Statistical relation between language proficiency and multilingualism: Clients' English-speaking skills

Choice	No. participants	Average	Significant difference?	Effect size
(1) Reasonable	354	2.834		
(2) Good	809	2.6213	Yes (p <0.01) (t-test)	0.102 Large
(3) Very good	619	2.4297		
Post-hoc analysis: All three groups differ from one another – the higher the skill, the lower the score.				

Language of research versus language used in practice

Respondents were asked if the language in which they conducted research differed from the language in which they drafted documents. A mere 17% of respondents indicated that there was a difference. The relation of this variable to multilingualism was investigated by means of a t-test for independent groups. Results showed a significant difference between the groups (p <0.01). Amongst those for whom there was a difference, the attitude toward multilingualism was more positive (average = 2.85) than amongst those for whom there was no difference (average = 2.55). The effect size is 0.72, which is medium.

Legal training in a mother tongue

Respondents were also asked if they had received their legal training in their mother tongue. Only 30% indicated that this was not the case. The relation of this variable to multilingualism was investigated by means of a t-test for independent groups. Results were that there was a significant difference ($p < 0.1$) between the groups (those who had received their legal education in their mother tongue compared to those who had not received their legal education in their mother tongue). Amongst those who had not received mother tongue education, the attitude towards multilingualism was slightly more negative (average = 2.64) than amongst those who received training in their mother tongue (average = 2.58). The small effect size amounts to 0.15.

Conclusion and recommendations

This chapter has provided an empirical insight, with reference to South Africa's constitutional, legislative and policy frameworks. The constitutional framework, specifically Section 6 (although discretionary in nature), provides a linguistic blueprint which informs the language rights in the BOR, but which is also to be given practical meaning through legislation and policies. We argued in this chapter that there is an absence of practical language regulations, which results in a default monolingual English position for the legal system, as evidenced by the language of record policy directive. What is blatantly evident from this chapter is the prevailing silence of the State, broader citizenry and attorneys. It is as if English is being forced onto attorneys (as is evident from the language survey). Although these attorneys acknowledge the need and desire for legal practitioners to acquire an additional official South African language, they do not view it as practicable, given that the language of record is English only. In our opinion, this undermines the provisions of Section 6 of the Constitution and automatically results in the limitation of Section 35(3) (f), (g) and (k).

In the context of this chapter, premised on the language survey, the conflicting and indecisive opinions and attitudes of attorneys towards the ten official languages other than English, and towards multilingualism, need to be addressed from both a legal and linguistic perspective. It is our recommendation that the issues highlighted in this chapter should be addressed in three ways. Firstly, language awareness campaigns must be undertaken, where the important role of language as a tool to enhance access to justice is highlighted. Such initiatives are not the sole responsibility of the judiciary, State or Department of Justice and Constitutional Development. It is the collective responsibility of all these departments and stakeholders; as well as of the Pan South African Language Board (who are mandated to promote, and ensure the use and development, of all eleven official languages). Collective initiatives will result in broader participation and buy-in, where the South African Law Society can be included. A collective approach can also circumvent the default excuse that language initiatives and language implementation are financially constraining (Muller 2017). Secondly, Section 6 of the Constitution needs to be interpreted purposively and implementation should be achieved through the equal use of all eleven official languages. Thirdly, tangible language requirements need to be legislated in the amended statutes and policies, to reflect the constitutional imperative: to ensure that the African languages are elevated in status and of equivalent force alongside Afrikaans and English. There needs to be a consultative discussion – followed by implementation – of the proposal by Mathole Motshekga, chairperson of the parliamentary Portfolio Committee on Justice and Correctional Services. He contended that proficiency in at least one indigenous African language should be demonstrated before law students are awarded a law degree" (Ndenze, 2017:4).

This chapter has illustrated that the transformational agenda of the legal system has resulted in past linguistic marginalisation and discrimination adopting a new face called *transformation*. True transformation has been distorted with the primary intention of benefiting an elite to the exclusion of the majority, where English is seen as the language of aspiration, while the African languages – and, most recently, Afrikaans – have been downgraded to be used in the home. This point is succinctly captured by De Vos (2010) in the following quotation:

> Sadly, few lawyers and judges have embraced this vision of a transformative constitutional project. While most pay lip service to the need for transformation and claim to endorse the transformative vision of the Constitution, it is as if the old had colonised the new by co-opting them in the oppression of the majority of citizens. The concept of "transformation" is now often used – so it seems to me – as a Band-Aid to hide and legitimise the continued injustice and inequality that is perpetrated by the old business elite and the new political business elite.

References

Bambust, I.; Kruger, A. & Kruger, T. 2012. Constitutional and judicial language protection in multilingual states: A brief overview of South Africa and Belgium. *Erasmus Law Review*, 5(3):211-232.

City Press. 2014. Bad interpreters ruin court cases, says Mogoeng. *City Press*, 25 January. https://www.news24.com/Archives/City-Press/Bad-interpreters-ruin-court-cases-says-Mogoeng-20150429 [Retrieved 31 January 2018].

De Vos, P. 2010. *What do we talk about when we talk about transformation? Constitutionally Speaking.* http://constitutionallyspeaking.co.za/what-do-we-talk-about-when-we-talk-about-transformation-2 [Retrieved 10 February 2016].

Docrat, Z. 2017. The role of African languages in the South African legal system: Towards a transformative agenda. Unpublished MA thesis, Rhodes University, Grahamstown.

Docrat, Z.; Kaschula, R.H.; Lourens, C.J.A.; Bailey, A. & Ralarala, M.K. 2017. Courts should promote all languages. *News24*, 17 September 2017. https://www.news24.com/Columnists/GuestColumn/courts-should-promote-all-languages-20170917-2 [Retrieved 9 February 2018].

Grant, T. 2017. *The usefulness of investigative linguistic analysis in the courts and beyond.* Paper presented at the 13th Biennial Conference of the International Association of Forensic Linguists: New challenges for forensic linguists, Porto, Portugal.

Heugh, K. 2002. Recovering multilingualism: Recent language-policy developments. In: R. Mesthrie (ed.), *Language in South Africa*. Cambridge: Cambridge University Press. pp. 449-475.

Legal Aid South Africa. 2016. Language Survey. http://www.legal-aid.co.za/wp-content/uploads/2017/04/Legal-Aid-SA-Language-Policy.pdf [Retrieved 9 February 2018].

Lourens, C. 2012. Language rights in the constitution: The "unborn" language legislation of subsection 6(4) and the consequences of the delayed birth. In: C. Brohy, T. du Plessis, J.G. Turi & J. Woehrling (eds.), *Law, Language and the Multilingual State. Proceedings of the 12th International Conference of the International Academy of Linguistic Law*, Bloemfontein: SUN MeDIA. pp. 269-290

McMillan, J.H. & Schumacher, S. 2010. *Research in education: Evidence-based inquiry*. 7th Edition. London: Pearson.

Monnakgotla, M. 2012. Joburg courts face foreign language problems. *Sowetan*, 27 March. https://www.sowetanlive.co.za/news/2012-03-27-joburg-courts-face-foreign-languages-problems [Retrieved 31 January 2018].

Mpahlwa, M.X. 2015. Language policy and practice in Eastern Cape courtrooms with reference to interpretation in selected cases. Unpublished MA thesis. Rhodes University, Grahamstown.

Mpati, L. 2017. Formal interview with Zakeera Docrat, Grahamstown, 1 February, as recorded in Z. Docrat, The role of African languages in the South African legal system: Towards a transformative agenda. Unpublished MA thesis, Rhodes University, Grahamstown. http://vital.seals.ac.za:8080/vital/access/manager/Repository/vital:27833 [Retrieved 4 December 2018].

Muller, G. 2017. Telephonic interview with Zakeera Docrat, Pretoria. 28 July, as recorded in Z. Docrat, The role of African languages in the South African legal system: Towards a transformative agenda. Unpublished MA thesis, Rhodes University, Grahamstown. http://vital.seals.ac.za:8080/vital/access/manager/Repository/vital:27833 [Retrieved 4 December 2018].

Ndenze, B. 2017. No law degree without fluency in indigenous language proposed, *The Herald* (Port Elizabeth), 30 March.

Olsson, J. 2008. *Forensic Linguistics: An introduction to language, crime and the law.* 2nd Edition. New York: Continuum.

Pienaar, M. & Cornelius, E. 2016. Contemporary perceptions of interpreting in South Africa. *Nordic Journal of African Studies*, 24(2):186-206.

Ralarala, M.K. 2012. A compromise of rights, rights of language and right to a language in Eugene Terre'Blanche's (ET) trial within a trial: Evidence lost in translation. *Stellenbosch Papers in Linguistics*, 41:55-70. https://doi.org/10.5774/41-0-43

Ralarala, M.K. 2014. Transpreters' translations of complainants' narratives as evidence: Whose version goes to court? *The Translator*, 20(3):377-395.

Thebe, M. 2016. 2016 Review of the attorneys' profession, *De Rebus*, 24 October. http://www.derebus.org.za/2016-review-attorneys-profession [Retrieved 29 November 2018].

Van Heerden, S. 2012. "Renosterstropers" dalk vry oor tolk. *Maroela Media*, 16 March. https://maroelamedia.co.za/nuus/renosterstropers-dalk-vry-oor-tolk [Retrieved 31 January 2018].

Van Zuydam, L. 2014. Moves to improve court interpreting. *Pretoria News*, 26 March.

Wei, L (ed.). 2013. *Applied linguistics*. Hoboken NJ: Wiley Blackwell.

Legislation

Attorneys Act, No. 53 of 1979.

Attorneys Amendment Act, No. 115 of 1993.

Constitution of the Republic of South Africa, 1996.

Use of Official Languages Act, No. 12 of 2012.

Language policy

Draft Policy on Use of Official Languages of the Department of Justice and Constitutional Development. 2015. *Government Gazette*, No. 38778.

Case law

Lourens v President of the Republic of South Africa and Another 2013 (1) SA 499 (GNP).

State v Damoyi 2004 (1) SACR 121 (C).

State v Pienaar 2000 (2) SACR 143 (NC).

State v Pistorius 2014 ZAGPPHC 793 (12 September 2014)

Yekiso J presiding. 2004. *State v Damoyi* 2004 (1) SACR 121 (C).

JUSTICE IN THE MOTHER TONGUE

The task of court interpreters in Ghanaian law courts

Mercy Akrofi Ansah & Prince Ofei Darko

Introduction

Ghana is characterised by societal as well as individual multilingualism. In the administration of justice, more so when there is incongruence in the language of communication amongst the parties, an interpreter serves as a bridge. In this chapter, we investigate the role of the court interpreter as a mouthpiece in the exercise of the linguistic rights of parties or witnesses in a lawsuit in a Ghanaian law court. Although the literature is replete with similar studies in multilingual communities elsewhere, in the case of Ghana there is inadequate documentation.

In our research we made use of qualitative methods, namely interviews, group discussions, and observation, to acquire data. We conducted our research within the framework of the 1992 Constitution (Republic of Ghana, 1992): Articles 19(2), sub-clauses (d) and (h); 26(1); 39(3); and the Interpreter's Oath under the Oaths Act (Ghana Legal, 1972), examining practice at five magistrate courts and two high courts in Accra, by means of interviews and discussions with court interpreters, magistrates, judges and lawyers, and augmenting our data by observation notes of court proceedings. As with studies elsewhere, we found that in the execution of their duties, court interpreters are faced with linguistic and non-linguistic challenges that result in poor quality interpretation; which in turn has led to detrimental legal outcomes. In our study we argue that court interpreters who lack the necessary skills of interpretation impede the smooth running of court proceedings, and could affect the outcome of a trial.

The Constitution of Ghana (Republic of Ghana, 1992), Article 19(2), states that:
>   A person charged with a criminal offence shall
>   (d) be informed immediately in a language that he understands, and in detail; of the nature of the offence charged;
>   (h) be permitted to have, without payment by him, the assistance of an interpreter where he cannot understand the language used at the trial.

Granted that the law is unequivocal on linguistic rights,[1] the language of the courts is English, and so a litigant or witness who does not speak English can only exercise their linguistic rights via an interpreter. The full enjoyment of one's linguistic rights therefore depends on the efficiency of the court interpreter. It therefore goes without saying that the court interpreter's role in the adjudication of cases is crucial.

The literature demonstrates a wealth of studies carried out on issues related to the role of court interpreters in the administration of justice where the litigants or witnesses speak languages other than the language of the court, and there is reliance on the court interpreter to act as a spokesperson to ensure that the litigants or witnesses are able to exercise their linguistic rights. In African multilingual communities where colonial languages have been assigned official status, a court interpreter is expected to be skilled in the colonial language, which is usually also the language of the court, and also in the indigenous language spoken by the litigant or the witness. In Africa, studies like those of Lebese (2011), Hlophe (2004) and Moeketsi (1999), amongst others, have been done in the context of South Africa's linguistic terrain where, in the midst of "favoured" languages, linguistic rights of non-speakers of English and Afrikaans are ultimately denied; which, according to the South African Constitution, they ought to enjoy (Republic of South Africa, Act 108 of 1996, Subsection 6(2)). In the context of this paradox, such studies have interrogated the exercise of language rights vis-à-vis the role of the interpreter in the South African judicial system.

Similarly, outside of Africa, in communities where there is language heterogeneity, studies have been carried out regarding the interpreter's role in the adjudication of cases. Typical instances may be cited from Europe and America, where studies have shown that non-English speakers, especially amongst Spanish-speaking Latinos in America, have had to deal with obstacles when trying to access justice (Berk-Seligson, 1990; Hale, 2004, 2008; Mikkelson, 2014). The studies have highlighted the important role of the interpreters and, consequently, the need for commensurate specialised training for them.

In Ghana, where our study was conducted, no research on the present subject matter has been documented. We therefore seek to examine the work in Ghanaian law courts of court interpreters designated to support non-English speakers in exercising their linguistic rights.

Amongst other findings, our research revealed that the role of court interpreters in the execution of justice is critical in the multilingual milieu of Ghana; and that their being often faced with linguistic and non-linguistic challenges, is indicative that they would be more efficient if they were professionally trained.

---

[1] In this chapter, language rights and linguistic rights are used interchangeably.

The linguistic landscape of Ghana affiliate

The United Nations Statistical Department (2016) states that Ghana's population is approximately 27 670 000. According to Simons and Fennig (2018), Ghana is constituted by 75 ethnic groups which speak about 81 languages: 73 indigenous languages and eight non-indigenous languages. The 73 indigenous languages are affiliated to the Niger-Congo group which is broadly divided into three subgroups: Kwa, Mande and Gur families.[2] English is a colonial language, as well as the official language of Ghana, and is used for government business. Hausa is another widely-spoken, non-indigenous language which serves as a lingua franca in several Muslim communities. It is also commonly used for a number of commercial activities in the urban areas of Ghana.

Of the 81 languages, nine enjoy the status of being state-sponsored languages; they have official orthographies and are used as languages of instruction, according to the language-in-education policy of Ghana. The sponsored languages are Akan (the most widely spoken, and made up of three major dialects: Asante, Akuapem, Fante); Ewe, Ga, Nzema, Dangme, Dagbani, Gonja, Dagaare, and Kasem. Akan is spoken by about 8 100 000 as a first language, and by 1 000 000 as a second language (United Nations Statistical Department, 2013). Of the nine sponsored languages, four, namely Dagbani, Gonja, Dagaare and Kasem, belong to the Gur family, and are spoken in the northern parts of the country. The other five are Kwa languages, spoken in southern Ghana.

In Ghana, language policies which steer various spheres of public life generally favour the English language. The language policy-in-education, for instance, stipulates that the language of instruction from kindergarten to year 3 of primary education, in respective linguistic areas, should be one of the sponsored languages widely spoken in the community. During these five years (i.e. two years of kindergarten and three years of primary education), English is taught alongside the indigenous language as a school subject. From year 4 up to the tertiary level, English is used as the language of instruction. Ghanaian languages are taught as school subjects from year 4 to year 10, which is the final year of Basic Education. From the secondary level to the tertiary level of education, one may study a Ghanaian language as one of a few electives. In some universities in Ghana, students are offered Ghanaian language proficiency courses.[3] At the University of Ghana for instance, four Ghanaian languages (Akan, Ewe, Dagbani and Ga) are amongst a number of electives from which students may select during one of the semesters of the second year of their various programmes (University of Ghana, 2017). Although the language proficiency option is often recommended to students whose professional training and career would demand

---

[2] Ligbi and Bisa are the only Mande languages spoken in Ghana.
[3] It is a one-semester course designed for non-speakers of one of four selected Ghanaian languages. It is anticipated that, by the end of the semester, the student should have attained a low to intermediate proficiency level.

oral skills in Ghanaian languages, it has been reported that many such students have not taken advantage of the courses (Ansah, in press).

English, being the official language used for government business and trade, and serving as the language of instruction from the fourth year of school, is thus also the language of record in the law courts. Although a judge may speak and understand the mother tongue of a litigant or a witness he or she is expected to speak only English, and to communicate via an interpreter if the litigant or witness does not speak any English or decides not to use English. Although the adult literacy rate in Ghana stood at 76.6 % in 2015 (Knoema, 2019), it has been observed that the preferred language of litigation in the lower courts is one's mother tongue. This is not surprising, because a number of studies on the use of mother tongue (Cummins, 1981; Kioko, Ndung'u, Njoroge & Mutiga, 2014; Skutnabb-Kangas, 2008) have confirmed that using one's mother tongue affords the speaker emotional stability; which a litigant or witness usually requires in a courtroom situation.

In the Ghanaian parliament, although the requirements for a parliamentarian do not include English proficiency, parliamentary discussions are held in English.

Although the use of indigenous languages is encouraged by Ghana's Constitution (Republic of Ghana, 1992), English occupies a prestigious position in national affairs, while indigenous languages are mostly used for unofficial transactions. Minority languages do not receive much attention.

Ghana shares borders with three francophone countries: Burkina Faso in the north; Togo in the east; and Côte d'Ivoire in the west. There are therefore pockets of French speakers found within Ghana's borders. Several other foreign languages are also unofficially spoken in Ghana, primarily due to the presence of immigrants who operate in both the private and public sectors of the economy.

The linguistic landscape of Ghana is therefore characterised by a multiplicity of languages of which only the nine government-sponsored languages are privileged with recognition as official languages. However, in the course of our research, we also discovered that there are educated Ghanaians who, apart from English, speak only their mother tongue. English, the colonial language, continues to enjoy a prestigious position in almost all public settings.

A survey of related literature

The work of the court interpreter

Language is central in the communication process in all legal proceedings, so understanding the language used in these court proceedings is vital in ensuring fairness. Recognising the importance of interpretation in providing a fair trial, the 1992 Constitution of Ghana

(Republic of Ghana, 1992), for example, guaranteed the right to interpretation and translation for charged or accused persons who do not speak or understand the language of court proceedings (Nartowska, 2015). Despite the multicultural diversity in several societies, English continues to prevail as the language of record in courts (Hlophe, 2004). This has implications for the exercise of linguistic rights.

Generally, interpreters have been viewed as helpers, conduits, communication facilitators and bilingual and bicultural specialists (Roy, 1993). Lebese (2011) describes the court interpreter as one who is neutral, competent and a professional facilitator of communication in the judicial process, who is expected to interpret from one language into the listener's familiar language in a clear manner. Therefore, the interpreter must only function as a transmitting medium (Gonzalez, Vasquez & Mikkelson, 1991). The interpreter may be likened to a mechanical device which changes non-English speech into English for the benefit of the judge, attorney and court records (Berk-Seligson, 1990).

However, the view of the court interpreter as a non-social participant overlooks the complexity and the deeply social nature of the communication process (Ahmad 2007; Berk-Seligson 1990; Colley & Guéry, 2015; Morris, 2010; Pöchhacker, 2008). Interpreters can control the flow of information produced during legal proceedings and have a radical effect on the "manufacture" of a case (Aliverti & Seoighe, 2017). Beyond merely demonstrating proficiency in interpreting for an individual who speaks a language other than English, the interpreter must be sufficiently familiar with terminology and procedures of a particular judicial system to ensure accurate interpretations (Pawlowsky, 1996). In her work involving Spanish speakers who appear as defendants in criminal proceedings in the United States, Pawlowsky cautions against oversimplification and incorrect assumptions about the Spanish language being monolithic. She argues that regional dialects, as well as differences in pronunciation, may result in different words being used for the same object.

Despite the importance of interpreters in court proceedings, they are faced with a myriad of challenges that can have implications for the delivery of justice. Berk-Seligson (1990) identifies the problem of vocabulary as an important issue in the sphere of court interpreting. During a criminal trial for example, the interpreter must demonstrate the capacity to interpret the expert testimony of a physician (which may include professional jargon), while at another point in the trial, the interpreter may have to interpret slang-laden testimony of a narcotics pusher (Berk-Seligson, 1990). Unfortunately, some interpreters either do not have a wide range of speech varieties in their linguistic repertoire, or they establish a particular style – regardless of the particular way a given witness, defendant, lawyer or judge is speaking (Berk-Seligson, 1990). The use of uncontracted forms and the insertion of implied material also affect the register of witnesses' utterances and produce a significant effect on persons judging the testimony (Berk-Seligson, 1990:41). Berk-Seligson (1990) describes a situation where a citizen is asked of what country he is a citizen. His answer is a two-word, "De Mexico". The interpreter conveyed the message as, "I am a citizen of Mexico" (Berk-Seligson 1990:40). For Berk-Seligson, the nearest corresponding translation in English should have been, "of Mexico" or "Mexico".

In examining the nature of verbal interaction in the courtroom, including court interpreting in South Africa, Moeketsi (1999) observed that poor training and improper definition of the interpreter's role were responsible for their dismal performance. Sociolinguistic studies of variation in the courtroom have shown that individuals whose language variety or speech style differs from that of legal professionals are likely to be evaluated negatively by judges or jurors (Berk-Seligson, 1990; Wodak, 1980). In addressing the challenges faced by Spanish speakers who appeared as defendants in criminal cases, Pawlowsky (1996) cautioned against oversimplification and making inappropriate assumptions that there is only one Spanish language and that the language is monolithic: she provides an instance of a case in the United States involving a worker's compensation benefits for a back injury. Apparently, the Salvadorian interpreter interpreted "cintura" as "waist", rather than "lower back", which was what the Mexican-dialect worker intended (Pawlowsky, 1996). When questioned by the judge about the injury, the worker denied having any other injury than to his back. The worker subsequently lost the hearing because the judge found his account to be unreliable and elusive (Pawlowsky, 1996).

Notwithstanding the usefulness of the court interpreter, lapses in their work have been reported and have had dire consequences in the outcome of trials. Poor quality interpretation has been adduced to a number of factors, mostly emanating from differences in the makeup of the source and target languages. Amongst the challenges that have been reported are: the non-existence of equivalences of legal terms in the target language; lack of precision in the target languages; interpretation of idioms and metaphors from one language to the other; and the numerous speech varieties that confront the interpreter (Hlophe, 2004; Kasonde, 2016; Roy, 1993).

Although the works reviewed in this section are from outside Ghana, they nevertheless have implications for the work of the interpreter in Ghanaian law courts. We will therefore examine the role of the court interpreter as a key actor, or agent, in court proceedings in Ghana, and the implications for justice delivery in our judicial system.

Methods

Data sources

The study reported in this chapter covered the Magistrate Court at Madina; and the Central and La Magistrate Courts in Accra. Tools commensurate with a qualitative study were employed: semi-structured interviews, focus-group discussions and observation. In all,

13 interpreters (Table 8.1) were interviewed on their experience as court interpreters. We held discussions with nine magistrates and one judge of the high court. There were one-to-one interviews with four magistrates and one high court judge. There were two group discussions: the first involved four magistrates; and the second involved two magistrates. We held discussions with the magistrates about their experience of working with court interpreters. The researchers also observed 12 court proceedings. As audio recordings were not permitted in the courtrooms, mental notes of proceedings were made and recorded in writing immediately after every session. The interviews and observations were completed between 20 September and 28 November 2014.

We also visited the Judicial Training Institute (JTI) in Accra to acquaint ourselves with their activities, particularly about training programmes on offer for court interpreters. The Judicial Service of Ghana court interpreter's handbook (Judiciary of Ghana, 2011), was a helpful resource. Literature on studies that have been done on language, law and court interpretation was also consulted.

We transcribed the audio-recorded interview texts verbatim and did a qualitative content analysis of the texts on the model proposed by Mayring (2000).

Framework

The study is situated within the framework of language rights-related provisions found in Ghana's 1992 Constitution (Republic of Ghana, 1992): Article 19 (2), (d), (h); Article 26 (1); Article 39 (3); and the Ghana Interpreter's Act under the Oaths Act (Ghana Legal, 1972). The language rights of all persons in relation to access to justice and the pledge by the government of Ghana to develop indigenous languages are spelt out as follows:

Article 19 (2)
A person charged with a criminal offence shall be:
(d) informed immediately in a language he understands, and in detail; of the nature of the offence charged;
(h) be permitted to have, without payment by him, the assistance of an interpreter where he cannot understand the language used at the trial.

Article 26 (1)
Every person is entitled to enjoy, practise, profess, maintain and promote any culture, language, tradition or religion subject to the provisions of this constitution.

Article 39 (3)
The state shall foster the development of Ghanaian languages and pride in Ghanaian culture.

While the 1992 Constitution of the Republic of Ghana is explicit regarding the language rights of persons who appear at the law courts as litigants or witnesses, the full enjoyment of one's language rights is dependent to a large extent on the efficiency of the court interpreter. Thus, the court interpreter's role in the adjudication process cannot be underestimated.

Under the Oaths Act (Ghana Legal, 1972), court interpreters of Ghanaian courts take the Interpreter's Oath, swearing to interpret the testimony of litigants and witnesses verbatim. The Interpreter's Oath (Oaths Act 1972) is as follows:

> I, [interpreter's name], swear by the Almighty God that I will well and faithfully interpret and explain to the Court [the Jury] and the witnesses the matters and things that are required of me to the best of my skill and understanding.

Our research investigated the extent to which court interpreters are able to abide by the Interpreter's Oath, and what obstacles, if any, prevent them from doing so. Data collected for the study was intended to address the following research queries:

- What is the magistrate or judge's experience of working with a court interpreter?
- What language or linguistic obstacles does the interpreter encounter in transferring meaning from one language to another?

Findings and discussion

Professional background of interpreters

Table 6.1 is an overview of information gathered from interviews with the 13 court interpreters.

TABLE 6.1 Professional background of interpreters in Ghanaian courts

Interpreters	Highest qualification	Language repertoire	Years of experience
Int. 1	Middle School Leaving Certificate (MSLC)	English, Ewe, Ga, Akan	25
Int. 2	Ordinary Level Certificate	English, Akan, Ga, Akan	15
Int. 3	Ordinary Level Certificate	English, Akan, Ga	14
Int. 4	Post Middle Technical School certificate	English, Dangme, Leteh, Akan	20
Int. 5	Diploma in Business Studies, Accounting	English, Ga, Ewe, Akan	10
Int. 6	Post-Secondary Vocational, Auto Mechanics	English, Ewe, Dangme, Akan	5
Int. 7	Higher National Diploma, Human Resource Management	English, Dagbani, Akan, Ga, Ewe	2
Int. 8	BSc Home Economics	English, Ga, Dangme, Akan, Dagbani	3
Int. 9	Ordinary Level Certificate	English, Mamprusi, Hausa, Dangme, Akan	16
Int. 10	Advanced Level Certificate	English, Ewe, Akan, Ga	15

TABLE 6.1   Continued

Interpreters	Highest qualification	Language repertoire	Years of experience
Int. 11	Higher National Diploma, Purchasing and Supply	English, Ga, Dagbani, Akan	2
Int. 12	Higher National Diploma, Marketing	English, Ga, Dangme, Akan	1
Int. 13	Diploma, Management Studies	English, Ga, Akan, Ewe	3

Data gathered indicate that the ratio of men to women court interpreters in the study sample is 5:1, with an age range of 25-60 years. Whereas the lowest level of education was Middle School Leaving Certificate or Technical School, which is post Middle School, the highest level of education was a bachelor-level degree at university. School subjects that the interpreters studied at the highest level of their education included these: Accounting; Auto Mechanical Engineering; Human Resource Management; Law; Business Management; and Home Economics. Data indicate that, although English language is integral to the discharge of their duties, none of the interpreters had any specialised background in English language; neither did any have any qualification or training in any Ghanaian language.

The language repertoire of interpreters included Ga, Ewe, Akan, Dagbani, Mamprusi, Hausa, Dangme and English. Whereas five of these are government-sponsored languages, Mamprusi and Hausa are not. Speakers of Akan dominated, followed by Ga, and then Ewe and Dagbani. From the interviews we held with them, it was found that none of the interpreters had had any formal training in court interpretation; they had acquired the skill while working.

The interpreters were rather evasive when it came to stating their salaries; they preferred to state a range rather than be specific. Their salaries ranged from GHS 250 to GHS 1 050 per month, an equivalent of USD 50 to USD 210 per month (at the exchange rate at the time of calculating).

The Judicial Training Institute is responsible for training court interpreters. The courses are usually run in the regional capital cities for court interpreters who are employees of the Judicial Service of Ghana. Course subjects that have been taught in recent years are Court Ethics, and Management.

If parties to a suit depended on court interpreters to exercise their linguistic rights in order to receive justice, then the requisite qualification for engaging interpreters has to be adhered to. It is also important for interpreters to receive remuneration commensurate with the services they render.

The opinions of judges and magistrates

During our interviews and discussions with the judge and magistrates, it was observed that, to a large extent, the work experience that each of them had had with interpreters hinged on the language background of the former. The language background of the judge and magistrates who were interviewed is provided in Table 6.2.

TABLE 6.2 Language backgrounds of judge and magistrates

Office-bearer	Language repertoire
Judge	English, Akan, Ewe
Magistrate 1	English, Ga, Ewe
Magistrate 2	English, Akan
Magistrate 3	English, Dangme, Guan
Magistrate 4	English, Akan
Magistrate 5	English, Akan, Ewe
Magistrate 6	English, Ga, Ewe, Akan
Magistrate 7	English, Akan, Ga,
Magistrate 8	English, Ga, Ewe, Akan
Magistrate 9	English, Ewe, Akan

In Table 6.2, languages spoken by the judge and magistrates are listed from most proficient to least proficient. The language repertoire of those interviewed comprised Akan, Ga, Ewe and Guan. It is interesting to note that there were two magistrates (2 and 4) who spoke one Ghanaian language only, Akan, in addition to English. As table 2 indicates, the remaining eight were multilingual and they spoke a combination of two or more indigenous languages. It is also noteworthy that none of the Northern languages from the Gur language group were represented, which meant that, if a witness, litigant or interpreter spoke any of the Gur languages in their courts, they would be at a loss as to the content of the communication.

In the one-to-one interviews with the judge and Magistrates 1-5, each of them agreed that interpreters were indispensable to their work. Whilst each expressed some satisfaction with some interpreters, the challenge on which the judge, and Magistrates 1, 3 and 5 commented was non-alertness on the part of some interpreters. When they were asked how they confirmed interpretation given by interpreters, especially when they were not proficient in the language used, Magistrates 2 and 4 said they confirmed with lawyers, or judged by the length of the sentence spoken by the interpreter. They would also request a repetition of the rendition by the interpreter, a practice which often delayed proceedings. The code of conduct of interpreters required that the latter admitted whenever they had challenges interpreting some statements, in order to prevent the recording of misrepresentations which could affect the outcome of a trial. If a judge needed to adjourn the case, they would do so, and get the right interpreter at another sitting. Furthermore, when court interpreters are employed, they are required to abide by the Oaths Act (Ghana Legal 1972); the magistrates and judges therefore trusted that they would discharge their duties accordingly. Without exception, the four magistrates in the group discussion (6, 7, 8, and 9) unanimously recommended that professional training for interpreters could enhance their skills.

Challenges faced by court interpreters

Court interpreters face both linguistic and non-linguistic challenges. Most of the linguistic challenges confronting them are related to the differences in the structure of the source and target languages. Other challenges they mentioned were instances of legal jargon whose equivalence did not exist in the target language, as well as the interpretation of idioms and metaphors between the two languages. They admitted that they sometimes felt that their Ghanaian language renditions lacked precision. An example which one interpreter cited was the distinction between words like "manslaughter" and "murder". Other terms they found difficulties in distinguishing were "rape", "defilement" and "unnatural carnal knowledge". In their attempt to interpret such terminologies, they had to use phrases and sentences which rather described the acts, and sometimes in the process they found that the meanings were either exaggerated or understated. It was concluded that several Ghanaian language expressions lacked the nuances of the legal register in English. Legal terms whose equivalents the interpreters could not find in the target language included "prima facie", "appellant", "plaintiff", "defendant", "litigant", "party", and "docket".

Challenges posed by differences at various linguistic levels between the source and target languages could have adverse effects on the performance of the interpreter. Although none of the magistrates nor the judge admitted to a miscarriage of justice due to inaccurate interpretation, one cannot rule out such happenings; in studies conducted in some other countries, such cases have been reported. Examples cited in the report of the Committee to Study Interpreter Issues in Arizona Courts (2002) gave detailed information to the Arizona Judicial Council on Interpreter Issues in Arizona Courts, 2002 (see *US v Gómez* 1990, FL CA II (902 F2d 809); and *US v Mata* 1999 (4th Cir. Virginia)). The lack of such in-depth studies in Ghana could be the reason that such cases have not been documented.

During court proceedings that formed part of our study, some observations were made by researchers of factors that could influence the outcome of the cases. There were instances of a mixed use of direct/first-person and reported speech/third-person, which is against the accepted rules of court interpretation. Participants in a judicial process are expected to address one another in direct speech. The use of indirect/third-person could create miscommunication, delay proceedings and take away the illocutionary force of a testimony.

The following (Extract 1) is an example illustrating the interpreter's using indirect speech/third-person. The defendant spoke Akan.[4]

EXTRACT 1

Defendant	*Menni fɔ.*	[I am not guilty.]
Interpreter	He says he's not guilty.	

The English rendition and the defendant's statement differ in meaning whereas the defendant used direct speech, the interpreter's rendition is reported speech. The act is in contravention of the Interpreter's Oath which mandates the interpreter to interpret faithfully. If the interpreter fails to render the litigant or witness's testimony faithfully, by using indirect speech/third-person, there could be interference with preservation of the record, and the integrity of the record is consequently compromised. The record will reflect the conclusion of the interpreter and not the words of the litigant or witness.

Secondly, the use of the third person creates ambiguity. In this instance, the judge had to seek clarification by asking: "Who is not guilty?" Such back-and-forth interactions delay legal process. If the judge had not sought clarification, and the statement had been part of the official record, transcripts that would be prepared from the recordings afterwards would be less intelligible. In court interpreting, direct speech/first-person is therefore generally preferred.

Another observation was that, sometimes, the interpreter appeared to have guessed that the witness could understand English, and did a partial interpretation (see Extract 2).

EXTRACT 2

Magistrate	Did you see the accused climbing over the fence wall or you saw him at the site and assumed that he climbed over the fence wall?	
Interpreter	(omits first part) *Wuhuu no wɔ "site" hɔ anaa?*	[Did you see him/her at the site?]
Witness	*Mihuu no sɛ ɔreforo "wall" no, "my lord".*	[I saw him/her climbing over the wall, my lord.]
Interpreter	[I saw him climbing over the wall, my lord.]	

The magistrate observed that a partial interpretation had been given. Consequently, in order to ascertain the answer given by the witness, the interpreter was asked to repeat the rendition. The witness repeated the answer. It is clear that the witness did not depend on the wrong rendition given by the interpreter.

---

[4] Akan is the Ghanaian language in the Extracts. In some instances, there was Akan-English code mixing/code switching.

EXTRACT 3

Magistrate	Did you see the accused climbing over the fence wall or you saw him at the site and assumed that he climbed over the fence wall?	
Interpreter	Wuhuu no sɛ ɔreforo "wall" no anaa wuhuu no wɔ "site" hɔ na wodwen sɛ ɔforoo "wall" no?	[You saw him climbing the wall or you saw him at the site and you assumed that he climbed over the wall?]
Witness	Mihuu no sɛ ɔreforo "wall" no, "my lord".	[I saw him/her climbing over the wall, my lord].
Interpreter	[I saw him climbing over the wall, my lord].	

The magistrate had to repeat her question, and she insisted on complete interpretation. This lapse could hinder both communication and the judicial process. It is important for the interpreter to remember that the legal equivalent he provides constitutes the record which will be relied on as part of evidence, contributing to the outcome of the trial. Training in interpretation skills could correct such an unprofessional act.

Furthermore, the interpretation of colour terms was noted to present problems to interpreters. In many Ghanaian languages, apart from the primary colours, no distinctions are made with secondary colours and other colour shades. The challenge of imprecise translation is evident in the following Extract (4).

EXTRACT 4

Magistrate	What was the colour of the shirt he was wearing when you met him?	
Interpreter	Wohyiaa no no, na ataade a ɔhyɛ no su te sɛn?	[When you met him, what was the nature/colour of the clothing he had on?]
Witness	Na ɔhyɛ ataade a ani dum, "my lord".	[He was wearing a dark-coloured dress/clothing, my lord.]
Interpreter	[He was in a black dress, my lord]	

The witness did not describe the dress/shirt as black, he said "dark colour" which could refer to the dark shade of any colour. The translation here is therefore imprecise.

Yet another difficulty the interpreter had to grapple with was distinguishing between different types of clothing. In many Ghanaian languages, such as in Akan, *ataade* is a general term representing all types of clothing; there is no term for "shirt". The interpreter was therefore faced with the challenge of interpreting "shirt". This interpretation was therefore fraught with imprecision, emanating from the use of a culturally bound term which is non-existent in the target language.

In yet another instance, the interpreter failed to distinguish between personal pronouns based on gender which could result in misrepresentations (Extract 5).

EXTRACT 5

Witness	"My lord", ɔne no na ɛbaa me dan mu hɔ.	[My lord, he/she came with him/her to my room.]
Interpreter	[My lord, she came with her to my room.]	

The gender of the referent in the witness's statement was not certain. The gender of the "intruders" was very necessary for maintaining a clear record. Consequently, the magistrate had to pose further questions to ascertain the gender; it was realised that, contrary to the interpreter's rendering, the intruders were male. This error seemed to have originated from the grammar of the target language which does not make gender distinctions in the pronoun class.

Finally, another grammatical issue the interpreter had to deal with was the correct use of tenses (Extract 6).

EXTRACT 6

Witness	mekae sɛ mɛsesa "key" no.	[I said that I will change the key.]
Interpreter	My lord, I changed the key.	

The correct rendition should have been, "I said that I will change the key". Such an inaccurate rendition is bound to affect the veracity of the transcripts that will be prepared from the recordings.

In all such cases of inaccurate renditions, if care is not taken, poor quality interpretation could lead to injurious legal outcomes. A judge or magistrate relies on evidence (interpreted into English) and the law to arrive at judgment. Challenges faced by interpreters must therefore be addressed to ensure that citizens really do receive justice in their own language. Litigants and witnesses have the right to be linguistically present at their own legal proceedings; interpreters are to make this possible.

In addition to the cited linguistic challenges, the interpreters mentioned other non-linguistic challenges. They recounted challenges such as harassment from lawyers and litigants. In some cases, lawyers and litigants complained that the interpretations lacked clarity. Such behaviour frustrated the efforts of interpreters and slowed down proceedings. In such cases, interpreter 3, for instance, believed that such accusations were only excuses on the part of their accusers.

During the one-to-one interviews held with the interpreters, they unanimously suggested two means to improve their services, and to make them more efficient in representing the voice of litigants and witnesses: these were professional training, and higher salaries.

Recommendations arising from the study

In our study, using interviews and observation, challenges that court interpreters face were unearthed. It is desirable that the impact of poor interpretation on trial outcomes in Ghanaian law courts, as revealed in court documents, will cause the authorities concerned to pay more attention to the litigant, defendant or witness who must be able, with confidence, to exercise their linguistic rights to access justice via their intermediary, a court interpreter.

Out of this study, we offer recommendations for court office-bearers and interpreters that could ameliorate the services of court interpreters. Although the study is situated in Ghana, the recommendations have implications for communities that are multilingual in Africa and beyond.

Recommendations for interpreters

For interpreters, it is recommended that they:
- have a pass in English at intermediate level;
- are equally competent in at least three of the indigenous languages spoken in the region where they are stationed to work; and have proof of courses that they have taken in those indigenous languages;
- have acquired a university degree in Interpretation Skills;
- undergo regular refresher courses for interpreters, while in service, to help sharpen their skills. In that regard, the Judicial Training Institute of Ghana could collaborate with the School of Languages (for training in Interpretation Skills) and the Language Centre (English and Communication Skills) at the University of Ghana;
- have a component in their professional training that includes legal education. This can be handled directly by the Judicial Service.

Recommendations for the Judicial Service

We further recommend that:
- the professional training of judges and magistrates includes courses in Ghanaian languages at the undergraduate level. The target proficiency level should be intermediate. The language skills will enable them at least to confirm the rendition of accounts given by court interpreters who work with them;
- the Judicial Service of Ghana considers the Ghanaian language repertoire of judges and magistrates before they are posted to stations;
- the Judicial Service of Ghana sets strict criteria for the engagement of court interpreters. The educational background of the interpreters (Table 6.1) suggests that this is currently not the case;
- the Service also need to set adequate levels of remuneration in order to attract and retain well-trained and effective interpreters.

Recommendations for academics

African Languages linguists need to take up the challenge of developing equivalents for English legal terms in the indigenous languages. The work of Agyekum (2011), who deals with Akan terms in the fields of punctuation, phonetics, phonology, morphology, syntax, semantics and literature, could serve as the impetus for work to be done on legal terms in Ghanaian languages. When such work has been done, the knowledge must be published for stakeholders.

Conclusion

This chapter has examined practices of court interpreters for non-English speakers in Ghanaian courts operating in terms of the Interpreter's Oath (under the Oaths Act – Ghana Legal, 1972). Because the language of record is English, under the Constitution of Ghana (Republic of Ghana, 1992), litigant and witness have the right to use their mother tongue in the law courts, but can only do that through an interpreter. In this chapter we have argued that, if the litigant and witness must exercise their language rights via an interpreter, then it behoves the Judicial Service of Ghana to ensure that court interpreters are able to abide by the oath they take to act professionally and effectively.

It is possible in Ghana to receive justice in one's mother tongue, provided the Judicial Service of Ghana ensures that court interpreters are competent and are adequately remunerated, and that judges and magistrates are also linguistically suitably equipped.

References

Agyekum, K. 2011. *Akan linguistics: Metalanguage and terminology*. Saarbrücken: Lambert Academic Publishing.

Ahmad, M. 2007. Interpreting communities: Lawyering across language difference. *UCLA Law Review*, 54:999-1086.

Aliverti, A. & Seoighe, R. 2017. Lost in translation? Examining the role of court interpreters in cases involving foreign national defendants in England and Wales. *New Criminal Law Review*, 20(1):130-156.

Ansah, M.A. At press. The indigenous language factor in professional training. *Contemporary Journal of African Studies*, 6.

Berk-Seligson, S. 1990. *The bilingual courtroom: Court interpreters in the judicial process*. Chicago: University of Chicago Press.

Berk-Seligson, S. 2015. The importance of linguistics in court interpreting. *Berkeley La Raza Law Journal*, 14(2):14-48.

Colley, H. & Guéry, F. 2015. Understanding new hybrid professions: Bourdieu, illusion and the case of public service interpreters. *Cambridge Journal of Education*, 45(1):113-131.

Committee to Study Interpreter Issues in Arizona Courts. 2002. *Report to the Arizona Judicial Council on Interpreter issues in Arizona Courts*. https://www.migrationpolicy.org/sites/default/files/language_portal/Report%20to%20the%20Arizona%20Judicial%20Council%20on%20Interpreter%20Issues%20in%20Arizona%20Courts_0.pdf [Retrieved 8 November 2018].

Cummins, J. 1981. The role of primary language development in promoting educational success for linguistic minority students. In: A. Mohanty, M. Panda, R. Philipson & T. Skutnabb-Kangas (eds.), *Multilingual education for social justice: Globalising the local*. New Delhi: Orient Blackswan. pp. 21-35

Ghana Legal. 1972. *Oaths Act 1972*. (NRCD 6). http://laws.ghanalegal.com/acts/id/382/oaths-act [Retrieved 8 November 2018].

Ghana Statistical Service. 2012. *2010 Population and housing census: Summary report of final results*. Accra: Author. http://www.statsghana.gov.gh/gssmain/storage/img/marqueeupdater/Census2010_Summary_report_of_final_results.pdf [Retrieved 8 November 2018].

González, R.D.; Vasquez, V.F. & Mikkelson, H. 1991. *Fundamentals of court interpretation. Theory, policy, and practice*. Durham NC: Carolina Academic Press.

Hale, S. 2004. *The discourse of court interpreting: Discourse practices of the law, the witness and the interpreter*. Amsterdam: John Benjamins.

Hale, S. 2008. Controversies over the role of the court interpreter. In: C. Valero-Garcés & A. Martin (eds.), *Crossing borders in community interpreting: Definitions and dilemmas*. Amsterdam: Benjamins Translation Library. pp. 99-121.

Hlophe, J.M. 2004. Receiving justice in your own language – The need for effective court interpreting in our multilingual society. *Advocate Journal*, 17(1):42-47. https://www.sabar.co.za/law-journals/2004/april/2004-april-vol017-no1-pp42-47.pdf [Retrieved 5 December 2018].

Judiciary of Ghana. 2011. *Interpreters Handbook, 2011*. http://www.jtighana.org/downloads/publications/Interpretershandbook.pdf [Retrieved 8 November 2018].

Kasonde, A. 2016. The changing role of the court interpreter-translator in Africa: The case of Zambia. *Comparative Legilinguistics*, 27(2):21-32. http://dx.doi.org/10.14746/cl.2016.27.2

Kioko, A.N.; Ndung'u, R.W.; Njoroge, M.C. & Mutiga J. 2014. Mother tongue and education in Africa: Publicising the reality. *Multilingual Education*, 4(1):18. https://doi.org/10.1186/s13616-014-0018-x

Knoema. 2011. Adult literacy rate of Ghana. *World Data Atlas* https://knoema.com/atlas/Ghana/topics/Education/Literacy/Adult-literacy-rate [Retrieved 12 January 2019].

Lebese, S. 2011. A pilot study on the undefined role of court interpreters in South Africa. *Southern African Linguistics and Applied Language Studies*, 29(3):343-357.

Mayring, P. 2000. Qualitative content analysis. *Forum: Qualitative social research*. 1(2). http://www.qualitative-research.net/index.php/fqs/article/view/1089/2385 [Retrieved 8 November 2018].

Mikkelson, H. 2000. *Introduction to court interpreting*. Manchester: St. Jerome/Routledge.

Moeketsi, R.H. 1999. *Discourse in a multilingual and multicultural courtroom: A court interpreter's Guide*. Pretoria: Van Schaik.

Morris, R. 1995. Pragmatism, precept and passion: The attitudes of English-language legal systems to non-English speakers. In: M. Morris (ed.), *Translation and the Law*. Amsterdam: John Benjamins. pp. 263-279.

Morris, R. 2010. Images of the court interpreter: Professional identity, role definition and self-image. *Translation and Interpreting Studies*, 5(1):20-40.

Nartowska, K. 2015. The role of the court interpreter: A powerless or powerful participant in criminal proceedings? *Interpreters Newsletter*, 20(20):9-32.

Pawlowsky, M.M. 1996. When justice is lost in the "translation": *Gonzalez v United States*, and "Interpretation" of the Court Interpreters Act of 1978. *DePaul Law Review*, 45(2):435-492.

Pöchhacker, F. 2008. Interpreting as mediation. In: C. Valero-Garcés & A. Martin (eds.), *Crossing borders in community interpreting*. Amsterdam: John Benjamins. pp. 9-26.

Republic of Ghana. 1992. Constitution of the Republic of Ghana. https://www.ghanaweb.com/GhanaHomePage/republic/constitution.php [Retrieved 8 November 2018].

Republic of South Africa. 1996. Constitution of the Republic of South Africa. https://www.gov.za/documents/constitution/constitution-republic-south-africa-1996-1 [Retrieved 10 January 2019].

Roy, C. 1993. The problem with definitions, descriptions and the role of metaphors of interpreters. *Journal of Interpretation*, 6(1):127-154.

Simons, G.F. & Fennig, C.D (eds.). 2018. *Ethnologue: Languages of the world*. 21st Edition. Dallas TX: SIL International. https://www.ethnologue.com [Retrieved 8 November 2018].

Skutnabb-Kangas, T. 2008. Human rights and language policy in education. In: S. May & N. Hornberger (eds.), *Encyclopedia of Language and Education*, Vol. 1: *Language policy and political issues in education*. 2nd edition, New York: Springer. pp. 107-119.

United Nations Statistical Department. 2013 and 2016. https://unstats.un.org/unsd/databases.htm [Retrieved 21 October 2018].

University of Ghana. 2017. *Handbook for the Bachelor's Degree Course Descriptions for Programmes in the Humanities*. University of Ghana: Public Affairs Directorate. http://www.ug.edu.gh/sites/default/files/aad/Humanities%20handbook%202017%20%28website%29-min.pdf [Retrieved 11 January 2019].

Wodak, R. 1980. Discourse analysis and courtroom interaction. *Discourse Processes*, 3(4):369-380. https://doi.org/10.1080/01638538009544498

LANGUAGE AND THE RIGHT OF ACCESS TO PROCEDURAL JUSTICE IN SOUTH AFRICA

Noleen Leach

Introduction

This chapter addresses the concepts of literacy, legal literacy and access to procedural justice in South Africa, and explores how access to procedural justice is measured; it examines language and the right to a fair trial with reference to relevant cases; and identifies the emerging principles and practices. Access to justice is essential for the establishment and the maintenance of the rule of law and has been an imperative in South Africa since before 1994. According to the Commission on Legal Empowerment of the Poor (CLEP), four billion people are excluded from the rule of law globally (Open Society Justice Initiative, 2010). South Africa is no exception, as serious barriers to access to justice still remain in the country. These barriers include poor literacy levels, poverty, delays in concluding legal disputes, inadequately sourced legal aid systems, limited public participation in reform programmes, excessive number of laws, formalistic and expensive legal procedures, and avoidance of the legal system due to economic reasons. Poverty deepens the legal isolation of the poor, and language, in particular, presents a formidable barrier to the country's poverty-stricken multicultural and multilingual society. Insufficient knowledge of the language in which legal information is available (mainly English and Afrikaans) and the complexities of the language of the practice and discipline of law prevent individuals and communities from claiming, enforcing and defending their legal rights. This power imbalance prevails, not only when the individual is a party to proceedings in a criminal, civil or administrative matter, but also when engaging in other activities that have legal consequences.

The right of access to procedural justice in criminal matters and the right to choose a language of communication intersect expressly in Section 35 of the Constitution of the Republic of South Africa (1996) and implicitly in Section 34. These provisions guarantee the right of access to adjudicating fora in criminal and civil matters. An essential element of that right is the fairness of the proceedings, whether in a court of law or another dispute resolution forum. One of the pillars of natural justice is the principle of *audi alteram partem* (literally "let the other side be heard as well"), which requires parties to a dispute to be afforded a fair opportunity to present their cases. However, the right of access to the courts or other tribunals in a society that is not legally literate is practically meaningless, especially without the right to legal assistance. In most instances, parties in court proceedings are obliged to rely on legal representation and the assistance of interpreters when proceedings are conducted in a language that they do not understand.

The decision of the heads of court in 2017, to make English the language of proceedings in the courts (Chabalala, 2017), raises questions about the constitutional protection afforded by the right to be tried in a language one understands and the right of access to procedural justice, amalgamated in Section 35(3)(k) of the Constitution.

What is literacy?

Language is considered to be the key to literacy, which could be described, in its simplest form, as the ability to read and write. However, attempts to formulate a common definition of literacy and to attribute any specific cognitive effects to it have been criticised by anthropologists and researchers of New Literacy Studies, notably Brian Street. This school of thought views literacy more as a "social practice" than an autonomous set of skills (Street, 1984, 1995). Barton and Hamilton (2000:8) not only noted that "Literacy practices are purposeful and embedded in broader social goals and cultural practices" but that "Literacy practices are patterned by social institutions and power relationships, and some literacies are more dominant, visible and influential than others".

The position in this article is that literacy as an ability to functionally read and write remains an essential element of legal literacy, whether it is viewed as a technical skill or, ideologically, as a social practice.

What is legal literacy in South Africa?

Knowledge of the law is a cornerstone of a true democracy. It is therefore essential for a functioning member of contemporary, highly regulated South African society to have a rudimentary understanding of the law to claim its protection or obey it. Various definitions of legal literacy have been advanced over the years (White, 1983; Manley-Casimir et al., 1986; American Bar Association, 1989; Canadian Bar Association, 1992; Hassan, 1994; Bilder, 1999). Yet the central tenet in all those definitions is the focus on the capacity to embark on an appropriate response to legal problems.

Legal literacy, therefore, enables individuals and communities to obtain the information, develop the knowledge and acquire the capability to navigate the various domains of social interaction, legal and otherwise, without having to rely completely on legal assistance in the form of legal aid, legal representation and an interpreter.[1] Literacy in South Africa, as a technical skill, is thus a pre-requisite for legal literacy as most laws are reduced to writing and legal disputes are resolved through oral and written communication.

Literacy as a social practice, on the other hand, has equal importance for legal literacy as the latter has been considered historically to be the domain of the law professionals and individuals within the justice system. Proceedings in most adjudicating fora are formal and legalistic but continue to be conducted in the languages of record prior to 1996: Afrikaans and English. Legal and social cultures influence the way evidence is viewed, conveyed and applied, whilst communication across these cultures affects the credibility of witness testimony and increases errors in translation. These factors shape the cultural context for the social practice of making meaning and interpretation of the law.

However, South African society is not only multicultural and multilingual (with eleven officially recognised languages), but is also characterised by poverty, disadvantage and low literacy levels (Statistics South Africa, 2016). Barriers such as language and social practice within the legal domain deprive citizens of meaningful access to the law. These barriers may continue to deny meaningful access even where an individual receives legal assistance, as illustrated below. Individuals or communities who are not familiar with the historical languages of record have to overcome a double barrier, that of the language of proceedings as well as the language of law. This has particular significance for access to justice as these conditions encourage the perception in the minds of affected individuals and communities that the law is the problem. It sows mistrust in adjudicating fora and renders peace and stability in South Africa tenuous.

What is access to procedural justice in South Africa?

Jacques Derrida held that "justice is relative to social meanings and that these meanings are relatively fluid and contestable" (Litowitz, 2009). In this view, a universal definition is elusive and the construct must be contextualised. It is thus argued that an examination of the meaning of access to procedural justice in contemporary South Africa involves an examination of the capacity of citizens to "pursue, claim and enforce their rights" (Leach, 2018:25). Measuring access to justice involves an evaluation of the extent to which the substantive legislative framework, the institutions, human resources, infrastructure, knowledge, values and attitudes reflect and support that access (OHCHR, 2011). Access to procedural justice thus concerns itself with whether the legal framework creates an environment through which people, in terms of their rights, are empowered to access the mechanisms that facilitate delivery of justice. In South Africa, this legal framework

---

[1] See the discussion on *Kruse v S* further in this chapter.

is informed by the knowledge, values and attitudes enshrined in the Constitution, which represents an intention to shape a culture of respect for human rights that should be inviolable.

Constitutional values and knowledge of the law

The values of human dignity, equality and freedom are not only firmly entrenched in the preamble and founding provisions of the Constitution but are also given explicit expression in the text. This indicates that these values have exceptional foundational significance: they permeate every right in the Bill of Rights to a greater or lesser extent and influence the way in which each right in the Bill of Rights is to be interpreted (Constitution of the Republic of South Africa, Section 39). The pervasiveness of these values is not accidental but is founded in the mandate of social transformation that is explicitly articulated in the Preamble, to:

- Heal the divisions of the past and establish a society based on democratic values, social justice and fundamental human rights;
- Lay the foundations for a democratic and open society in which government is based on the will of the people and every citizen is equally protected by law;
- Improve the quality of life of all citizens and free the potential of each person.

The values of human dignity, equality and freedom thus present the prism through which Section 35(3)(k) is to be interpreted.

Two of the factors that accelerate the decline in the use of a specific language are the "ideology of contempt" and the "prestige of transfer" (Dorian, 1998:7-9). These two remnants from South Africa's colonial and apartheid eras continue to influence the values and attitudes towards indigenous languages in the country. The "ideology of contempt" for indigenous languages in South Africa was characterised by an attitude of disrespect and condescension towards these languages by users of the dominant languages such as English and Afrikaans (Fredericks, 2011) and cemented into the substantive legal framework of the country. This is further exacerbated by the prestige that is afforded to a language by virtue of its use by successful persons. Therefore, in spite of the statutory protection afforded to indigenous languages, the use of an indigenous language might nevertheless decline as preference is given to the prestigious language(s).

It is clear that the value attributed to the nine official indigenous African languages and the attitudes expressed towards these languages in South Africa often do not align with the values entrenched in the Constitution. This presents a formidable barrier to access to justice in South Africa and contributes to the decline in the use of some of its indigenous languages. This decline is exacerbated by the lack of resources available to protect these languages adequately, and consequently the functional limitations of institutions such as the Pan South African Language Board (PanSALB).

The Pan South African Language Board

Section 6(5) of the Constitution makes provision for the establishment of a Pan South African Language Board. PanSALB became a reality with the enactment of The Pan South African Language Board Act of 1995 which was subsequently amended by the Pan South African Language Board Amendment Act of 1999. The extent to which PanSALB is empowered to support access to procedural justice for persons whose language rights have been violated is doubtful, as its own standing to approach the court on matters related to a violation of language rights was called into question in 2007 in *PanSALB v MEC for Roads, Transport and Community Safety*.

PanSALB approached the High Court seeking a declaratory order to the effect that the decision of the North-West provincial government to allow printing of the provincial logo "The Platinum Province" on vehicle number plates in English only was unconstitutional and unlawful, and that the declaratory order allow for number plates to be displayed in Afrikaans and Setswana. The High Court ruled that PanSALB has no standing to approach the court and advised that "the general tenor of the Language Board Act militates against the Board litigating on complaints or on behalf of complainants" (Paragraph 22). It is clear from this decision that the court was of the view that PanSALB should achieve its objectives through non-litigious means.

The problem with denying PanSALB standing to access the courts on behalf of persons whose language rights have been violated is illustrated by the case of *Lourens v President van die Republiek van Suid Afrika en Andere*. Fourteen years after the adoption of the final Constitution, a blind, white, male, Afrikaans-speaking attorney successfully approached the court seeking an order compelling the legislature to enact legislation that would regulate and monitor the use of official languages by the national government in compliance with Section 6(4) of the Constitution. The order of court resulted in the enactment of the Use of Official Languages Act, No. 12 of 2012, two years later. This demonstrates the importance of access to the courts to ensure substantive justice. As much as the above ruling is a step in the right direction and the action by Mr Lourens is nothing short of admirable, it must be noted that the applicant is a practitioner of the law with the means and the legal literacy to approach the courts. It is not hard to imagine that someone without that level of legal literacy and resources would not be able to enforce their language rights in a similar fashion.

Noting how slowly the wheels of justice turn, it is unconscionable that PanSALB is denied the standing to approach the courts on behalf of those whose language rights are violated, especially those who are not in a position to do so for the very reasons of language empowerment and means. The lack of standing of PanSALB and the slow pace of legal reform are outweighed by the lack of available resources when parties to legal proceedings wish to assert the guarantees in respect of their language rights when proceedings are conducted. It results in justice being delayed, which, according to the established legal maxim is "justice denied". This raises questions about the way in which the substantive legal framework of the right to language and access to procedural justice is framed.

Language and the right to a fair trial

The founding provisions of the Constitution of the Republic of South Africa, 1996, expressly recognise and mandate linguistic pluralism, and the right to language and culture are entrenched as substantive rights in the Bill of Rights.

The founding provisions (Section 6)

Section 6(1) confers the status of official language on eleven languages in the country. These are, Sepedi, Sosotho, Setswana, siSwati, Tshivenda, Xitsonga, Afrikaans, English, isiNdebele, isiXhosa and isiZulu. Section 6(5) expressly calls for the enactment of national legislation for the purpose of establishing a Pan South African Language Board (PanSALB). The Constitution delivers the mandate of PanSALB in imperative terms by stating that PanSALB "must" promote and develop not only official languages but also sign language, the Khoi, Nama and San languages (Section 5(a)). Linguistic pluralism is further recognised in Section 6(5)(b) by imposing a duty on PanSALB to promote respect for all languages that are commonly used in South Africa.

The Constitution also places a positive obligation on national, provincial and local government to advance indigenous languages. Section 6(2) is couched in peremptory terms and places an obligation on the State not only to recognise the disadvantage suffered by indigenous languages in the past but also to take practical and positive measures to improve the status of these languages and to promote their use. Section 6(3)(b) places a positive obligation on municipalities to take into consideration the language practices of those citizens who reside within their municipal borders. In addition, Section 6(4) imposes a duty on national and provincial government to regulate and monitor their own use of official languages and to ensure equitable treatment and parity of esteem of official languages. The national and provincial governments are thus constitutionally bound to give effect to the objective envisaged in the Constitution when conducting their affairs.

However, it would seem that this bold imperative to recognise and promote multilingualism in South Africa is subject to cost, attitude and demographics. Although a positive obligation is imposed on national and provincial government to use at least two official languages, Section 6(3)(a) entrenches the use of language for the purpose of government at national and provincial level in permissive terms. These two levels of government "may" make use of any official language for the purpose of government. This use firstly, is subject to usage and regional circumstances, in other words, demographics. Secondly, it is subject to economic factors, in this case "practicality and expense"; and finally it is subject to attitude, embodied as the "preferences of the population as a whole or in the province concerned". It would thus seem that, even in the founding provisions, the right to language is diluted.

The case of *Lourens v Speaker of the National Assembly of Parliament* illustrates how the inherent limitations that the founding provisions contain are interpreted by the courts. Lourens challenged the practice of Parliament of introducing and publishing Bills, and preparing the official text sent to the President for assent, in English only. He argued that this practice amounted to unfair discrimination against all citizens who do not speak English and that the failure to translate Acts of Parliament into the eleven official languages identified in Section 6 of the Constitution amounted to unfair discrimination on the basis of language, and violated the Promotion of Equality and Prevention of Unfair Discrimination Act 4 of 2000.

The Supreme Court of Appeal made short shrift of this argument, pointing out that the practice of Parliament is compliant with Section 6 of the Constitution and can therefore not amount to discrimination, let alone unfair discrimination. Lewis, Justice of Appeal, concluded that "one must accept that the Constitutional Assembly intended that not all official languages have to be employed in the process of government. The text of s 6 says so expressly" (paragraph 12). The court further held that "the Constitution itself requires that acts of government, including the passing of Acts of Parliament, be conducted in only two of the official languages. Thus the Constitution itself would be guilty of unfair discrimination on Mr Lourens' argument, which is plainly absurd" (paragraph 29).

The right to language and culture

On the contrary to the outcome of the above case, the imperative language used in parts of Section 6(3)(a), sections 6(3)(b), 6(4) and 6(5) appears to reflect the seriousness with which the drafters of the Constitution viewed the right to language and culture in South Africa, so much so that this right has been entrenched as a freestanding substantive right in the Bill of Rights. This clothes the right to language and culture with particular foundational importance.

Section 30 of the Constitution of the Republic guarantees the right of the individual to use the language of their choice, and reads as follows:

> Everyone has the *right to use the language* and to participate in the cultural life of their choice, but no one exercising these rights may do so in a manner inconsistent with any provision of the Bill of Rights (my emphasis).

Section 30 thus codifies the protection of the right of the individual to the use of their language of choice subject to the inherent limitation that it may not conflict with any other provision of the Bill of Rights. This right is not restricted to the private domain only, but may be exercised in public, including during interactions with state agencies.

The right to language is further entrenched in Section 31(1), which reads:
> Persons belonging to a cultural, religious, or linguistic community may not be denied the right, with other members of that community –
> (a) to enjoy their culture, practise their religion and *use their language*; and
> (b) to form, join and maintain cultural, religious and *linguistic* associations and other organs of civil society (my emphasis)

This provision in the Bill of Rights codifies the protection of the collective to enjoy their culture, practise their religion and use their language in association with each other.

The right to a fair trial

The right to language and the right of access to procedural justice are represented expressly in Section 35(3) and implicitly in Section 34 of the Constitution. The focus here is on Section 35(3)(k). Effective communication through language and/or interpretation or translation is an essential element of a fair trial. It is through effective communication that an accused can exercise rights pertaining to a fair trial, such as the right to be fully present, to cross-examine witnesses, and to prepare a defence. The rights of an accused in criminal matters is comprehensively and expressly contained in Section 35 of the Constitution, which guarantees the right of an accused to be tried in a language that they understand, and the right to an interpreter in the event that it is not practicable for the criminal proceedings to be conducted in a language that the accused understands. Section 35(3)(k) reads as follows:
> Every accused person has a right to a fair trial, which includes the right–
> (k) to be tried in a language that the accused person understands or, if that is not practicable, to have the proceedings interpreted in that language.

Much could be opined about the content, nature and scope of Section 35(3)(k). However, a series of key court decisions since the adoption of the final Constitution provide valuable insight into the complexities that emerge in practice when the courts are called upon to give effect to this right.

Key court decisions

The parity of esteem of the eleven official languages has been the subject of a number of court decisions since the enactment of the South African Constitution. The court decisions represented here reflect divergent views of the content, nature and scope of Section 35(3)(k) of the Constitution.

S v Matomela

In *S v Matomela* an automatic review was brought before the Ciskei High Court in 1998 following a conviction and sentence in a lower court. It transpired that the entire record was in isiXhosa as there was no interpreter available on the day that the matter was heard in the Magistrates' Court. All the parties to the proceedings as well as the presiding officer could speak isiXhosa. The decision was further influenced by the hardship that a postponement of the trial would bring to bear on the complainant, the fact that no prejudice would ensue if proceedings were conducted in isiXhosa, and the fact that the presiding officer would have had to interpret the proceedings for the record. The senior magistrate relied on Section 6(1) of the founding provisions as well on Section 35(3)(k) of the Constitution as authority for his decision in the absence of any express directive from the Department of Justice.

The High Court endorsed the conviction and sentence and found the reasons given by the senior magistrate to be fair and reasonable. The principle was therefore established in practice that proceedings in a court of law could be conducted in any of the eleven official languages. Judge Tshabalala, with Justice Pickard (as Judge President) concurring, strongly supported the introduction of one official language for the courts. The Court stated that, "All official languages must enjoy parity of esteem and be treated equitably but for *practical reasons* and for *better administration of justice* one official language of record will resolve the problem" (*S v Matomela*, p. 4; my emphasis).

It is clear from the record that Judge Tshabalala's view was influenced by factors such as the potential inconvenience of translating court proceedings and the time-consuming nature thereof, possible delays and the resultant cost to the State and the litigants (*S v Matomela*, p. 4).

Mthethwa v De Bruin NO

In *Mthethwa v De Bruin NO*, the High Court considered the question as to whether Section 35(3)(k) allows for proceedings to be conducted in the accused's language of choice. The accused, Mr Mthethwa, was an isiZulu-speaking teacher who, by his own admission, understood English. He nevertheless requested that his trial be conducted in isiZulu in the Regional Court, a request which the regional magistrate refused. The regional magistrate directed the trial to be conducted in English or Afrikaans. The matter was taken upon review to the Natal High Court. The High Court dismissed the application and made it clear that Section 35(3)(k) does not confer the right upon an accused to have a trial conducted in the language of his choice. Justice Howard, presiding judge, with Judge Mthiyane concurring, relied heavily on the practical considerations to justify a restrictive interpretation of Section 35(3)(k). The Court concluded that the refusal of the lower court to have the proceedings conducted in isiZulu "could not possibly constitute unfair discrimination when the provisions of Section 35(3)(k) expressly provided for constraints imposed by the dictates of *practicality*" (*Mthethwa v De Bruin NO*, p. 337; my emphasis).

S v Pienaar

S v Pienaar stands in contrast with *Mthethwa v De Bruin NO*. Mr Pienaar, the accused, was Afrikaans-speaking and was represented by a public defender who did not speak Afrikaans. Mr Pienaar requested the public defender to withdraw and she complied. The magistrate did not inform him that he could get another legal representative, nor was he informed that he had the right to an interpreter.

Judge Buys, with Judge Majiedt concurring, set aside the conviction and sentence handed down by the lower court in this case. The High Court, in arriving at its decision, did not only rely on the constitutional directive to consult foreign law, but quoted with approval the decision in *S v Matomela* to conduct proceedings in isiXhosa, which was the language that all parties to the proceedings understood.

The Court also criticised *Mthethwa v De Bruin NO* for reading Section 35(3)(k) in isolation from the founding provisions contained in Section 6 of the Constitution. Judge Buys nevertheless concurred that, based on the facts that were presented, the Natal High Court in this instance made the correct decision to conduct the proceedings in English.

The Northern Cape High Court in *S v Pienaar*, in my view, adopted a holistic and comprehensive approach when it considered a complex, multifacetted matter. It considered foreign judicial precedent and quoted with approval the dictum in *Reference re Public Schools Act (Man), s 79(3), (4) and 7*. The Canadian court held that, "Firstly, the courts should take a purposive approach to interpreting the rights. ... Secondly, the right should be construed remedially, in recognition of previous injustices that have gone unredressed and which have required the entrenchment of protection of minority language rights" (paragraph 850).

The Northern Cape High Court was further persuaded by judicial precedent set in the case of *S v Matomela* in which the senior magistrate ordered the trial to proceed in one of the official languages, namely isiXhosa, a language that lacked parity of esteem with the existing languages of the court, namely English and Afrikaans.

The High Court also gave due consideration to an ecosystem of laws guided by the constitutional principles. The Court had regard to the accused's right to a fair trial. It specifically considered Section 35(3)(f) and (g) of the Constitution, which guarantee the right to have legal representation; and Section 35(3)(k), which guarantees the right to have a trial conducted in a language that the accused understands, and alternatively, to have the proceedings interpreted. The Court further relied on Section 6(1) of the Magistrates'

Court Act 32 of 1944, which allows proceedings to be conducted in either English or Afrikaans. This provision was read with Section 6 of the Constitution, which contains the founding provisions.

The High Court further adhered to the principles of statutory interpretation as prescribed by Section 39 of the Constitution. The Court thus interpreted the constitutional and statutory provisions through the prism of the constitutional values of freedom, equality and dignity as directed by Section 39. Hence, it cited again with approval the dictum in a number of Canadian cases. In *Reference re Public Schools Act (Man), s 79(3), (4) and 7*, the Canadian court stated, "The importance of language rights is grounded in the essential role that language plays in human existence, development and *dignity*" (paragraph 850; own emphasis). In *Ford v Quebec (Attorney-General)* the court held that, "Language is so intimately related to the form and content of expression that there cannot be true *freedom* of expression if one is prohibited from using the language of one's choice" (paragraph 748; own emphasis).

Judge Buys therefore concluded that the accused had the right to a fair trial which included the right to be tried in a language that the accused understood, which in this instance, was Afrikaans. The Court also held that the right to a fair trial includes the right to a legal representative who could communicate in the accused's own language either directly or by means of an interpreter and that the magistrate had an obligation to inform the accused of these rights. The failure of the magistrate to explain these rights to the accused amounted to a procedural irregularity which compromised the fairness of the proceedings. Hence, the conviction and sentence were set aside.

S v Damoyi

S v Damoyi share similar circumstances to those of *S v Matomela* as the magistrate proceeded to conduct the trial in isiXhosa and the matter became the subject of an automatic review by the High Court. The High Court endorsed the decision of the lower court to conduct the proceedings in isiXhosa, which is one of the eleven official languages, and held that the proceedings were fair. The court adhered to its own precedent set in *S v Matomela* but agreed with the restrictive interpretation of Section 35(3)(k) in *S v Mthethwa*, citing cost, quality of service and efficiency in the administration of justice: all practical considerations.

The High Court further distanced itself from the decision to invoke Section 6(1) of the Magistrates' Court Act in *S v Pienaar*. Judge Yekiso stated that "the provisions of Section 6 of the Magistrates' Court Act were superseded by the provisions of Section 6 of the Constitution so that reliance on Section 6 of the Magistrates' Court Act in support of the view that the accused had a right to be tried in the Afrikaans language, in my view, is not in conformity with the provisions of Section 6 of the Constitution" (p. 8). It has to be pointed out that the record shows that the court in *S v Pienaar* had due regard to Section 6 of the Constitution, in fact, Section 6(1) of the Magistrates' Court Act *was* read with the founding provisions (Section 6, p. 154).

Unfortunately, Judge Yekiso did not provide an exposition for his view, which reduces an interpretation of his statement to mere speculation. It is nevertheless my view that both judges are correct. Judge Buys was correct in stating that Section 6(1) of the Magistrates' Court Act, as it stands, still refers to "Either of the official languages". This phrase refers to Afrikaans and English as the language of record and reflects the position prior to 1996, which I am assuming is what Judge Yekiso is attempting to point out. Relying on Section 6(1) of the Magistrates' Court Act as authority for Afrikaans as the preferred language of record, falls foul of Section 6 of the Constitution, which confers official status on ten other languages. This is not, in my view, what Judge Buys was propagating. The founding provisions (Section 6) refer to eleven official languages, which includes Afrikaans. Whether read with Section 6 of the Constitution or in isolation, the accused is entitled to have his trial conducted in a language which he understands, and if that is not practicable, to have the proceedings interpreted. If the language that he understands is Afrikaans, the Constitution, as well as Section 6(1) of the Magistrates' Court Act, as it stands, provide for it, whether read within the context of a pre- or post-constitutional dispensation.

S v Van der Merwe

S v Van der Merwe shared similar circumstances to *S v Pienaar*. The High Court, likewise, set aside the conviction and sentence as the proceedings were conducted in English, although the accused and some of his witnesses requested repeatedly for the proceedings to be conducted in Afrikaans. Judge Smit, with Judge Mynhardt concurring, stated the following: "*Dis 'n skending van beskuldigde se getuie en van beskuldigde se reg om in 'n taal van hul keuse die geding te voer*" (at p. 4: translated as "It is a violation of the right of the accused's witness and of the accused to have proceedings conducted in a language of their choice"). Although no mention is made of Section 35(3)(k), the court in *S v Van der Merwe* applied a liberal interpretation to this provision as it expressed the view that the failure to allow the proceedings to be conducted in the language of choice of the accused, constituted a violation of his language rights.

S v Prince

In *S v Prince* the legal representative of the accused could not speak Afrikaans. He requested an interpreter and the magistrate denied his request although an interpreter was provided for one of the State witnesses during the trial. The trial therefore proceeded in Afrikaans. Judge Moshidi held that the accused had not received a fair trial as he did not have effective legal representation. This constituted a violation of Section 35(3) of the Constitution. The convictions against him were therefore set aside. As was the case in *S v Pienaar*, the court made it clear that it would not tolerate a situation where the violation of the accused's language rights guaranteed by Section 35(3)(k) is compounded by a violation of his/her right to legal representation which compromises his/her right to a fair trial.

S v Damani

The use of any of the eleven official languages at any stage during criminal proceedings was again the subject of an automatic review by the KwaZulu-Natal High Court in *S v Damani*. The proceedings were conducted in isiZulu except for the charge sheet and the cover page of the review case. Judge Ndlovu, with Judge Nkosi concurring, adhered to the precedent set in *S v Matomela* and *Mthethwa v De Bruin* and concluded that Section 35(3)(k) does not confer the right upon an accused to be tried in the language of his or her own choosing. The court stated that, "The provision simply means that an accused is entitled to understand the language used during the proceedings either directly or through an interpreter" (paragraph 10). Judge Nkosi read Section 6(1) of the Magistrates' Court Act with Section 6 of the Constitution and stated that reference to "official languages" included all official languages in the Republic, not only English and Afrikaans, which were the language of record prior to 1996. The High Court nevertheless expressed a sobering perspective on the ideal to have any of the eleven official languages used at any stage of the proceedings by stating that, "from an empirical perspective, that the realisation and implementation of this constitutional ideal has, thus far, proved elusive and impracticable" (paragraph 12).

Kruse v S

The Western Cape High Court again had the opportunity to consider the application of Section 35(3)(k) in *Kruse v S* upon appeal from the Regional Court following a conviction and sentence for murder. The fact that the accused in this case had a hearing and speech impediment distinguishes it from the preceding cases.

Acting Judge Davis, with Judge Ndita concurring, stated that many of the guarantees provided in Section 35(3) are dependent upon "effective communication by and with the accused" (paragraph 4). These include the right to be present at the trial and the right to adduce and challenge evidence. Judicial precedent defines being present at your trial as the capacity to hear and comprehend the significance of the evidence and the nature of the proceedings. The right to adduce and challenge evidence is contingent upon the capacity of the accused to hear and understand witness testimony. This right also hinges on the ability of the accused to make him or herself understood when providing instructions to counsel and giving evidence. Section 35(3)(k) and Section 35(4),[2] in particular, contain guarantees that have its origin in the recognition of effective communication as an essential element of a fair trial. Acting Judge Davis stated, "These constitutional elements are founded on the recognition that *effective communication is imperative for a fair trial*" (paragraph 4; Court's emphasis). The High Court relied upon judicial precedent when concluding that "A fair trial requires that the accused be able to understand the proceedings at all times" (paragraph 3).

Acting Judge Davis was highly critical of the attempts at interpretation which she described as sub-standard, as they were not continuous, precise, competent and contemporaneous. This impaired the ability of the accused to participate effectively in his own trial, thus not affording him a fair trial. The appeal was therefore upheld and the conviction and sentence set aside.

The above decisions of the courts show the divergence in the views concerning the use of official languages in court proceedings. These disparate views come from courts with equal status and their rulings only hold persuasive value for each other. In spite of this, certain trends seem to emerge.

Emerging principles and practices

A key principle that emerges is that the courts in South Africa do not consider the right to have a trial conducted in the language that the accused understands or, if that is not practicable, to have the proceedings interpreted, as a substantive primary right. This right is rather regarded as an essential element of the right to a fair trial.[3] As a consequence, a second principle developed. Courts are more inclined to enforce Section 35(3)(k) where the violation compromises other essential elements of the right to a fair trial, such as the right to legal representation.[4]

A third principle that emerges is that the main aims of the administration of justice feature prominently in the considerations when the guarantees contained in Section 35(3)(k) are interpreted. These include accessibility, fairness, swiftness, efficiency and effectiveness. The courts seem to favour practical considerations.[5]

A practice that has taken root is the use of the official African languages in the lower courts, when the language used is one that all parties to the proceedings understand. The practice

---

[2] 35(4) Whenever this section requires information to be given to a person, that information must be given in a language that the person understands.
[3] See *Kruse v S, S v Prince, S v Damoyi, S v Pienaar, S v Matomela.*
[4] See *S v Prince and S v Pienaar.*
[5] See *S v Damani, S v Mthethwa, S v Matomela.*

has been endorsed by the higher courts upon review.[6] This practice emerged in the absence of specific guidelines from the Department of Justice.

Most of the court decisions did not favour an interpretation of Section 35(3)(k) that allows for an accused to have proceedings conducted in a language of their choice. Those against such an interpretation cited practicability, cost and limitations inherent in Section 6 of the Constitution as main considerations. The divergent court decisions reveal a rather curious phenomenon. Presiding officers interpreted 35(3)(k) more widely where Afrikaans was the preferred language of the accused. However, where the preferred language of the accused was one of the historically disadvantaged official languages, the presiding officer interpreted the Section more conservatively.

Conclusion

The right to language and culture is a human right which has to be turned into a reality. The right of access to procedural justice, on the other hand, is an imperative if we are to achieve substantive justice. Presiding officers are confronted with a conundrum when presented with the constitutional guarantees contained in Section 35(3)(k). Giving effect to these constitutional principles may have the unintended effect of cementing the dominance of languages that do not only have a historical advantage but continue to enjoy an elevated status in the country. Moreover, considerations of cost and practicability may very well legally sanction discrimination against the historically disadvantaged at a time when their fundamental right to freedom is at stake. This militates against the constitutional values of freedom, equality and dignity. The statutory framework that codifies multilingualism in South Africa, therefore, has to be accompanied by the necessary human and physical resources, to support practices that achieve substantive justice through advancing legal and linguistic literacy.

References

American Bar Association. 1989. *Commission on Public Understanding About the Law. Legal literacy survey summary*. Chicago: American Bar Association.

Barton, D. & Hamilton, M. 2000. Literacy practices. In: D. Barton, M. Hamilton & R. Ivanič (eds.), *Situated Literacies: Reading and writing in context*. London: Routledge. pp. 10-11.

Bilder, M.S. 1999. The lost lawyers: Early American legal literates and transatlantic legal culture. *Yale Journal of Law and the Humanities*, 11:47-112.

Canadian Bar Association. 1992. *Reading the Legal World: Literacy and Justice in Canada*. Report of the Canadian Bar Association Task Force on Legal Literacy. Ottawa: Canadian Bar Association.

---

[6] See *S v Damoyi* and *S v Matomela*.

Chabalala, J. 2017. English will be only language of record in courts – Mogoeng, *News24*, 29 September. https://www.news24.com/SouthAfrica/News/english-will-be-only-language-of-record-in-courts-mogoeng-20170929

Dorian, N.C. 1998. Western language ideologies and small-language prospects. In: L.A. Grenoble & L.J. Whaley (eds.), *Endangered languages: Language loss and community response*. Cambridge: Cambridge University Press. pp. 7-9.

Fredericks, I.N.A. 2012. *The protection of languages and of language rights in the South African Constitution*. LLD thesis, University of the Western Cape, Bellville.

Hasan F.R. 1994. Limits and possibilities of law and legal literacy: Experience of Bangladesh women. *Economic and Political Weekly*, 29(44):69-76.

Leach N. 2018. *The paralegal and the right of access to justice*. LLD thesis, University of the Western Cape, Bellville.

Litowitz, D. 2009. Review of Goodrich, Hoffmann, Rosenfeld & Vismann (eds.), "Derrida and Legal Philosophy." *Notre Dame Philosophical Reviews*, 2(1). http://ndpr.nd.edu/news/23897-derrida-and-legal-philosophy [Retrieved 19 September 2018].

OHCHR. 2011. Access to Justice – Concept Note for Half Day General Discussion https://www.ohchr.org/documents/HRBodies/CEDAW/AccesstoJustice/ConceptNoteAccessToJustice.pdf

Open Society Justice Initiative. 2010. *Community-based paralegals: A practitioner's guide*. New York: Open Society Institute.

Statistics South Africa. 2016. *General Household Survey*. Pretoria: Statistics South Africa.

Street, B. 1984. *Literacy in theory and practice*. Cambridge: Cambridge University Press.

Street, B. 1995. *Social Literacies: Critical approaches to literacy in development, ethnography and education*. London: Longman.

White, J.B. 1983. The invisible discourse of the law: Reflections on the legal literacy and general education. *University of Colorado Law Review*, 54:143-159.

Legislation

Constitution of the Republic of South Africa, 1996.

Pan South African Language Board Act, No. 59 of 1995.

Pan South African Language Board Amendment Act, No. 10 of 1999.

Cases

Ford v Quebec (Attorney-General) [1988] 2 SCR.

Kruse v S (A100/2018) [2018] ZAWCHC 105.

Lourens v President van die Republiek van Suid Afrika en Andere (49807/09) [2010] ZAGPPHC 19.

Lourens v Speaker of the National Assembly of Parliament (20827/2014) [2016] ZASCA 11.

Mthethwa v De Bruin NO 1998 (3) BCLR 336 (N).

PanSALB v MEC for Roads, Transport & Community Safety 2007 (11) BCLR 1258 (B).

Reference re Public Schools Act (Man), s 79(3), (4) and 7, [1993] 1 SCT 839.

S v Damani (DR224/14) [2014] ZAKZPHC 60; 2016 (1) SACR 80 (KZP).

S v Damoyi [2003] JOL 12306 (C).

S v Matomela [1998] 2 All SA 1 (Ck).

S v Pienaar 2000 (2) SACR 143 (NC).

S v Prince [2006] JOL 16730 (W).

S v Van der Merwe [2006] JOL 16498 (T).

PART 3
Language as evidence

JUDGES AS LANGUAGE REFEREES FOR CARIBBEAN ENGLISH VERNACULAR SPEAKERS

How do they score?

Celia Brown-Blake

Introduction

From time to time, judges are required to make decisions that hinge on questions of the degree of linguistic proficiency and knowledge possessed by people involved in the judicial process. A typical scenario in which they may be called upon to make such a decision concerns the appointment of an interpreter for a criminal defendant. Another, which US judges often face, involves the determination of whether a suspect "knowingly and intelligently" waived certain legal protective rights which police officers are required to communicate to a suspect[1] in their custody before interrogating him or her. In many instances, such a determination pivots on the suspect's ability to understand the language used by the police officer. Other circumstances touch on the issue of the credibility of speakers using particular language varieties and how a tribunal may perceive these varieties.

This chapter examines three court cases which exemplify the circumstances described above. These cases involve speakers of Caribbean English vernaculars, specifically Jamaican and Guyanese. The chapter argues that judicial ideology about the nature of these vernaculars can affect the quality of judicial decision-making and, in turn, impinge on the legal notions of due process and fair trial. It begins by contextualising these vernaculars in their home speech communities, outlining the nature of the language situation and its legal context, as well as situating these vernaculars in the global space. It also considers the degree of intelligibility between the vernaculars and English in both the home speech

---

[1] The shorthand label for these rights is the "*Miranda*" warning" named for the US Supreme Court case, *Miranda v State of Arizona* 384 US 436 (1966). They include the right against self-incrimination and the right to have an attorney present during the interrogation. The warning also includes a statement that, if the suspect chooses to speak during questioning, what he says will be recorded and may be used against him or her in any trial of the matter.

communities and in the wider global sociolinguistics. This sets the background for the case studies – the first arising from Jamaica, the second from the US and the third from Canada.

Caribbean English-based vernaculars

Ideology and legal context

Caribbean English-lexicon creoles are vernacular languages spoken natively in many Commonwealth Caribbean territories where their superstrate, English, is the *de facto* official language. Despite being structurally distinct from their superstrate as demonstrated in the nature of their grammars (Devonish and Thompson, 2010, regarding Guyanese or Creolese; Bailey, 1966, regarding Jamaican or Patois), these vernaculars tend to be obscured in the linguistic topography. They have been regarded as "dialects" of English (Görlach, 1991) – a perception induced perhaps by their lexical resemblance to English, but also rooted in an ideology that these creole varieties are not real or proper languages.[2] Indeed, Devonish (2003:163) states that the public generally views Caribbean English creoles as "hidden amongst 'dialects' of English", and Nero (2006:5-6) writes that they are "publicly labeled English due to stigmatization" and that "the perception in the mind of the Caribbean native … is that English is their only language, however different it may be in terms of structure, lexicon, pronunciation, and usage from a standard variety of English".

The fluidity amongst language varieties in creole continuum situations (Rickford, 1987; Bickerton, 1973; Decamp, 1971) characteristic of Jamaica and Guyana, for example, may also be a factor that contributes to the notion that the vernacular varieties under discussion are merely shadow varieties of English. Creole continua display a range of intermediate or mesolectal varieties with varying degrees of similarity to the idealised polar varieties, the most creolised or basilectal variety at one end, and the most socially acceptable variety of English, the acrolect, at the other end. The absence of a patent point of separation between the basilect and the acrolect, by virtue of a string of highly interwoven mesolectal varieties, arguably presents a case for an English dialectal model. Inherent in this model is an assimilation of these vernaculars into the linguistic clan of English and a simultaneous rejection of them as languages in their own right.

The invisibility of Caribbean English vernaculars looms large in the law, which gives no recognition to these language varieties. In none of the territories in the Commonwealth

---

[2] In support of this is the observation by a member of a parliamentary committee in Jamaica considering, inter alia, the question whether language should be included as a basis upon which discrimination is constitutionally prohibited. The committee member commented that this inclusion could lead people to "interpret it to mean that you are actually giving creole the status of a language", which he said was a highly controversial matter in Jamaica. See Verbatim Notes of Joint Select Committee Meeting on the Charter of Rights (Jamaica), 15 March 2001.

Caribbean where these vernaculars are spoken is there legislation that explicitly acknowledges their existence. This is in sharp contrast to the French-based creole of the Republic of Haiti in the Caribbean, which has been constitutionally recognised as the "common language" uniting all Haitians (La Constitution de la République d'Haïti, 1987, Art. 5). In addition, it is notable that the English-based Pacific creole, Bislama, also has national and official language status under the Constitution of the Republic of Vanuatu, 1980, Section 3(1).

It is arguable that the law and the practice of it in Commonwealth Caribbean territories reflect and reinforce the view that Caribbean English vernaculars are a form of English, thereby obscuring their existence as languages. A brief survey of several pieces of legislation in Jamaica indicates several requirements that must be carried out in the English language.[3] Such provisions, particularly those contemplating consumer protection, arguably imply that English is the language generally used and spoken by Jamaicans – a position that subsumes the linguistic identity of the Jamaican vernacular under English. This linguistic blurring is arguably also reflected in the fact that, in relation to Jamaican-dominant or monolingual speakers who are defendants in criminal trials, courts in Jamaica, which operate officially in English, largely ignore the fair trial right to an interpreter for accused persons who do not proficiently speak or adequately understand the language of the court.[4] This is against the backdrop of diminished levels of intelligibility between Jamaican and English which is discussed below.

The vernaculars in the global space

Traditional migration patterns as well as inexpensive and easy mobility in the era of globalisation have led to the establishment of large Caribbean diaspora communities in the US, UK and Canada (International Organisation for Migration, 2017), particularly in the metropolitan centres of London, New York and Toronto. With this, Caribbean English vernaculars have been transported to these destinations where English is the, or an, official language. The speech of members of these diaspora communities has received some attention in the literature. This is exemplified in the works of Sebba (1993) who has addressed the influence of Jamaican on the development of British Creole, of Winer and

---

[3] See, for example, Consumer Protection Act, 2005, Section 8(1) which requires that sellers of goods "provide to the consumer verbally or in writing in the English language, all information concerning the goods being sold"; and regulations under the Standards Act, 1968, which require that labelling information for the relevant goods be in the English language (The Standards (Labelling of Processed Food) Regulations, 1974, r. 3(2)).

[4] Jamaica's Constitution, 1962, Section 16(6)(e), provides that anyone charged with a criminal offence is entitled to have the assistance of an interpreter at the State's expense if he or she cannot understand or use the language used in court. This is in keeping with universally recognised due process right. See, for example, the International Covenant on Civil and Political Rights, 1966, art. 14(3)(f) and the European Convention on Human Rights, 1950, art. 6(3)(e).

Jack (1997) who have examined the nature of Caribbean vernacular use in New York, of Hinrichs (2011) who, amongst other things, has commented on the function that Jamaican performs in the speech of Toronto Jamaicans, and of Moll (2015) who examines Jamaican in the virtual diaspora.

As Mair (2003) and Hinrichs (2011) explain, new Caribbean vernacular-influenced speech forms may be emerging in diaspora communities. However, continual flows of new migrants and itinerants from the Commonwealth Caribbean contribute to a currency of Caribbean English vernaculars in these global spaces. Although these speakers may be linguistically comfortable while embedded in their respective diaspora communities, language communication difficulties surface when they interact with host country institutions or authorities. Devonish (2003), for instance, alludes to the dilemma faced by children in the education system in New York who speak primarily Caribbean English vernaculars. He explains that New York educational regulations provide for bilingual educational programmes or English as Second Language programmes for students who speak a language other than English and who are assessed as limited in their English proficiency. While the results of the assessment indicated that Caribbean English vernacular-dominant students were below the threshold for English proficiency,[5] they were unable to qualify for the bilingual programmes because they were not considered to be speakers of a language other than English. As a consequence of this, Caribbean English vernacular-dominant students were consistently assigned to special education classes where they were disproportionately represented.

It is against this background that Devonish (2003) explains his testimony to the New York State Board of Education in a bid to encourage acceptance by the relevant educational authorities of the language-hood of Jamaican. Although the authorities accepted that Jamaican was a language other than English, Jamaican-dominant speakers remained unable to benefit from the relevant instructional programmes. As Devonish (2007:218) reports, the applicable regulations obliged the students and their families to confirm that they were speakers of a language other than English. They were apparently unwilling to acknowledge this, preferring, according to Devonish, to retain "the perceived advantage of being considered 'English-speaking'". It seems then, that although the social context of vernacular stigmatisation and inferiority may be absent in the interactions between Caribbean vernacular speakers and English-speaking officials in the host countries, vernacular-dominant speakers remain locked into the ideology that they speak English, or are reluctant to admit that they are not, dominantly, speakers of English.

---

[5] This is arguably linked to the question of the degree of mutual intelligibility between Jamaican and English which is discussed in the following section.

Mutual intelligibility with English

The perception that the vernaculars are species of English, coupled with the fact that their vocabulary is largely derived from English, may also mask the issue of their intelligibility with English. There is very little research which has tested and measured the degree of mutual intelligibility between Caribbean English vernaculars and English. A study carried out in Jamaica by Smalling (1983), reported in Devonish (2007), investigated how well a group of Jamaican-dominant or monolingual speakers understood radio news broadcasts delivered in English. Using the content questions method, the study found that the average mark scored by this group was 50.2%. This contrasted with an average score of 70% for the control group and the highest mark in the control group of 93.15%. This – albeit limited – investigation indicates that, despite the lexical relatedness between Jamaican and English, speakers for whom Jamaican is the only or dominant language have only partial understanding of the standard or official English used in broadcasting services in Jamaica.

In support of this conclusion are observations noted in Blake & Devonish (1994:151-152), indicating instances of misunderstanding by Jamaicans[6] of weather reports given in English via the mass media on the threat of a serious hurricane, which eventually ravaged the country in September 1988. In a more recent study involving legal settings in Jamaica, Brown-Blake (2017) hints at some communication wrinkles for speakers of Jamaican not highly proficient in English. This, too, lends support to the notion that intelligibility of English is restricted for speakers of Jamaican with limited or no proficiency in English. A national survey on language competence carried out by the Jamaican Language Unit (2007:12) at the University of the West Indies, Mona Campus in Jamaica, indicates that over one-third of the survey sample were Jamaican monolingual speakers. The suggestion is that a significant fraction of the population may face communication challenges when confronted with speech in English.

Situations in which the degree to which a speaker of English understands a speaker of Jamaican arise, perhaps, much less frequently in Jamaica than situations in which communication gaps occur for vernacular-dominant speakers listening to English speech. This is attributable to the nature of the language situation in Jamaica where one's first language is usually Jamaican. English is acquired as a second language substantially via the education system (Kennedy, 2017:198) with varying levels of proficiency. It is rare to encounter monolingual speakers of English amongst the native population in Jamaica and indeed Guyana. Indeed, Devonish and Walters (2015:225, 231), writing about Jamaica, indicate the improbability of monolingual English speakers amongst the Jamaican

---

[6] The authors report, for example, that most of the 33 informants engaged in the study associated the "eye of the hurricane" – a frequently used term in the weather reports – with the most severe part of the storm. They note that only one informant correctly associated the term, with reduced storm activity.

population, given limited opportunities for learning English as a first language. Speakers bilingually competent in both the vernacular and English are communicatively flexible and diglossically adept, generally capable of adjusting to speech events in either language variety. Insights then about the degree to which speakers of English understand speakers of Jamaican and other Caribbean English vernaculars, like Guyanese, are better gleaned from the experiences of Caribbean English vernacular speakers in the diaspora.

As indicated previously, where Caribbean English vernacular speakers come into contact with host country institutions operating in English, the intelligibility issue is likely to come into focus. This has been demonstrated in Brown-Blake and Chambers (2007), who provide examples of misunderstandings or communication breakdowns that attest to reduced intelligibility between Jamaican-dominant speakers and English-speaking personnel in the UK legal system. The following excerpt highlights the fact that phonological and morphosyntactic distinctions between Jamaican and English contribute to misunderstandings of speakers of Jamaican by speakers of English. As explained in Brown-Blake and Chambers (2007:276-277), the excerpt is from an official written transcript, produced by a UK transcription service, which purported to reflect the audio version of an interview between a UK police officer and a Jamaican-speaking witness to an incident.

| Witness | When I heard the shot (bap, bap) I *drop the gun* and then I run. (emphasis added) |

The authors report that the audio equivalent of this utterance was:

| Witness | Wen mi ier di bap bap, mi *drap a groun* and den mi staat ron. |
| Gloss | When I heard the bap bap [the shots], I fell to the ground and then I started to run.) |

In addition to explaining the differences in linguistic structures which contributed to the mistranscription, Brown-Blake and Chambers point to the potential legal ramifications of such a communication error. Issues of language intelligibility may thus transmute into critical legal problems which may distort the factual foundation and adversely affect fair trial considerations and the proper administration of justice. Rickford and King's work (2016:971-976) on the testimony of a speaker of African-American Vernacular English (AAVE) in a US criminal case helps to validate the proposition that lack of intelligibility between English-based vernaculars and their superstrate can undermine the judicial process. They present differences between the speech of the witness and English and indicate that these features are unlikely to be understood by persons unfamiliar with AAVE, in this case, the majority of the jurors. This, they argue, contributed to negative evaluations of the witness and considerably weakened her credibility.

Intelligibility issues appear to play a role in linguistic disadvantage experienced by Caribbean vernacular-dominant speakers in the US who have had some contact with the legal system there. This has been highlighted in letters to the editor of a local newspaper. In one such letter[7] over the signature of James Martin, whose address is stated as New Jersey State Prison, the author highlights the language barrier that exists for Jamaican, and indeed other Caribbean nationals in US courts and other legal contexts. The letter, which alleges instances of misinterpretations by US law authorities, also alludes to the communication challenges faced by Jamaicans in the US judicial system and the potential implications of such challenges for accused persons:

> there are many Jamaican citizens that do not speak fluent English; nor do they understand the American judicial English ... [We] as Jamaicans have a situation where mere words erroneously interpreted can cause death or life imprisonment ... The importance of the language barrier ... should not be treated lightly, especially when lives are at stake.

In addition, the letter claims that the failure to "legitimise" Jamaican "as an official language in Jamaica" has contributed to the lack of recognition it has in the US as a language; which has led to Jamaicans not being provided with interpreters in American courts. The suggestion is that the prevailing language ideology in the respective home territories of Caribbean English vernaculars has a bearing on whether speakers of these vernaculars are afforded the language related fair trial right to an interpreter in foreign courts. The widely held belief that Caribbean English vernaculars are forms of English, and that they are mutually intelligible with their lexifier, may also infuse trials within the respective home jurisdictions and negatively affect the administration of justice. I attempt to demonstrate this in the first case study, a Jamaican case, *R v Kirk Williams*.[8]

R v Kirk Williams (Jamaica)

This case from Jamaica, in which the accused was charged with stealing[9] an iPad, was tried in the Resident Magistrate's Court in 2012 and subsequently appealed to the Court of Appeal. The data relied on in the discussion of this case is drawn from the following sources: the official notes of evidence in the trial as generated by the Resident Magistrate; her summation and verdict; a copy of the document charging the accused (the indictment); a copy of the pre-trial question and answer; skeleton arguments filed by counsel on appeal; and the judgment delivered by the Court of Appeal.

---

[7] See Martin (2002).

[8] RM Court for the parish of St Catherine, Information No. 454/12; appealed as *Kirk Williams v R* [2013] JMCA 51.

[9] The technical legal charge is "simple larceny" which is reflected on the indictment, the document charging the accused.

The linguistic crux of the case

A critical component of the defence case relied on an appreciation of a feature of the vowel system of Jamaican and the way in which many Jamaican vernacular speakers are likely to modify this feature when attempting to approximate their speech to the socially acceptable variety of English in Jamaica (JamE). In Jamaican, the low central vowel, /a/ occurs in sound environments in which there are at least two possible sound variants in JamE (Devonish & Harry, 2004:463-464). The vowel /a/ in Jamaican is sometimes converted to /ɔ/ in the cognate JamE term, so that Jamaican /afis/ becomes /ɔfis/ (office) in JamE. However, in some cases, no sound change to the Jamaican vowel is required to render the cognate term in JamE, so that, for example, Jamaican /man/ is phonetically the same in the socially acceptable variety of English in Jamaica. In Jamaican then, /aipad/ is homonymous for both iPad and iPod.

Some speakers of Jamaican, however, over-apply the Jamaican /a/ to JamE /ɔ/ conversion rule, or as Devonish & Harry (2004:465) explain, they presume "a one-to-one correspondence" between Jamaican /a/ and JamE /ɔ/. The result of this is that they tend to modify all instances of Jamaican /a/ to /ɔ/ in attempting to approximate their speech to JamE. The tendency has been described as hypercorrection (Pollard, 2001). I suggest that it was a factor in the court case under discussion in relation to the lexeme descriptive of the subject matter of the larceny, an electronic tablet, an iPad. The accused appeared to have confused this with iPod, the smaller device used to store and play audio files. The judicial officers, at the level of both the trial and appellate court, appeared not to have appreciated this confusion. The confusion seemed to have been partly attributable to the nature of Jamaican speech and was compounded by the fact that the accused appeared not to have been at all familiar, at the time of the incident, with iPad devices. I argue that the apparent failure on the part of the judicial officers to appreciate the language-based confusion affected the credibility of the evidence for the accused, and ultimately, the measure of fairness which was brought to the judicial consideration of the case.

Overview of the facts of the case

An understanding of the facts is important to the discussion. A team of policemen, in response to a call for help in connection with a pregnant lady in labour, went to a home just after midnight. Some of the officers, including the accused who was carrying an M16 rifle, entered the house. The accused was asked by his team leader to assist in escorting the lady to one of the police vehicles so that she could be taken to the hospital. By this time, she had given birth. The accused, on his way back outside to relieve himself of his rifle and personal effects to enable him to render assistance, stumbled upon an object. His evidence was that his foot accidentally hit something and it slid across the verandah into the yard.

As he picked up the object, his team leader urgently called for him again. In the rush of the moment, the accused put his rifle, his personal effects and the object (which turned out to be an iPad belonging to one of the occupants of the house, Y) into the vehicle. He quickly doubled back into the house to assist the new mother.

Later that morning back at the police station, there were two conversations in which the accused was confronted about the issue. In the first, the officers who were on assignment at the house, including the accused, were asked by another officer, CC, whether they had seen anything fall from Y as she left the house. They all said they had not. In the second conversation, the accused was again in the presence of some of the officers who had been on the assignment. One of them, S, confronted him revealing that another officer, A, had said that he, A, had seen the accused with something looking like an Apple iPad tablet while they were on the assignment. The accused denied this too. Shortly after, he went to the vehicle, saw the object, and at this time he appeared to have made the connection between the enquiries made of him and the object. He immediately took steps to hand it over to his superior officers.

A formal question and answer of the suspect ensued, during which the suspect exercised his right to silence. He was subsequently charged on indictment with simple larceny, tried, found guilty and sentenced. He appealed, citing as one ground the effect on the fairness of the trial of the Resident Magistrate's under-appreciation of the linguistic ambiguity arising from the homonymous lexeme in Jamaican, *aipad*. His appeal against conviction was dismissed.

Testimony from the accused: The language element

Various aspects of the testimony given by the accused (KW) raise the issue of the ambiguity surrounding the Jamaican lexeme, "aipad". The following testimony from the accused has been extracted from the Resident Magistrate's notes of evidence of the case, the official record of the trial. In his examination-in-chief, the accused was asked about the first conversation to which reference was made in the previous section in which he was confronted about the iPad. His response was:

EXTRACT 1

	She [CC] asked if we saw anything fall from the female as she exited the house ... [CC] did not give full description of what ... she said it was an IPAD. My response was "no".

Part 3 | Language as evidence

The following interaction occurred during cross-examination of the accused by the prosecutor (P):

EXTRACT 2

P	She [CC] said it was an IPAD, CC?
KW	No, an IPOD; not an IPAD.

Prima facie, there appears to be an inconsistency between KW's evidence-in-chief and his evidence in cross-examination in terms of what he reports CC as having said to him. In the following extract, however, some clarification regarding the apparent inconsistency is offered by the accused in his response to a question asked by the Resident Magistrate:

EXTRACT 3

KW	The difference between IPOD and IPAD, I only know of an IPOD. I understood [CC] to be enquiring about an IPOD and not an IPAD.

His explanation is consistent with the fact that there is no phonetic distinction in the Jamaican vernacular between the lexemes used for the smaller electronic device (iPod) and the larger device (iPad). Whether CC had said /aipad/ or /aipɔd/, it would have been reasonable for a Jamaican-dominant speaker to interpret the lexeme as referring to the smaller electronic device. This is so given (a) the homonymous nature of /aipad/ in Jamaican, and (b) the speech phenomenon described as hypercorrection as explained in a previous section, in terms of how it is sometimes exhibited in Jamaican speech. Additionally, KW's explanation reveals a gap in his knowledge – that, at the time, he was not aware of iPad devices ("I only know of an IPOD"). This appears to compound the confusion arising from the ambiguity relating to the Jamaican lexeme, "aipad". It is clear that by the time the case comes for trial, the accused is well aware of iPads. At this time, it appears that he also appreciates the phonological distinction in English. This is reflected in his response to the prosecutor in Extract 2.

It is against this background that evidence of KW's denials about noticing or possessing an iPad might be assessed. In addition to the denial reproduced in Extract 1, in his examination-in-chief he also accounts for his denial in the second conversation in which he is confronted by his colleagues:

EXTRACT 4

KW	[S] told me what [A] had told him, to [sic] which I denied. He told me [A] had seen me with an Apple IPAD Tablet. I denied it because I had no knowledge of what they were speaking about.

Unsurprisingly, the linguistic dimension of his evidence is adversely construed by the prosecutor who suggests that the "distinction between IPOD and IPAD" was designed "to mask intention only", i.e. merely a ploy to conceal the intention to steal, a critical ingredient of the offence.

Judicial treatment of the accused's testimony

This perspective also appears to have been adopted by the magistrate who views the denials by the accused as further evidence of his intent to steal. In her summation, the magistrate states that "the Accused's denial of knowledge about the Ipad [is] inconsistent with and erode[s] any prospect of a finding that he intended to return it". It is noted that in her summation, apart from a repetition of the accused's testimony that he understood CC to have been enquiring about an iPod, not an iPad, the magistrate does not confront the issue of the linguistic ambiguity raised by the defence. She fails to isolate the language point, an important pillar of the defence case. She essentially rejects the totality of the accused's evidence, stating that it was "lacking in truth". This failure on the part of the magistrate to deliberate expressly on the defence case goes to legal fairness which demands that a trial judge provide a balanced consideration of all the evidence presented in a case. A feature of this legal requirement is that a trial judge should identify and even-handedly assess the defence advanced by an accused.

It is arguable that the Resident Magistrate's failure to address the language issue is symptomatic of a discounting of the linguistic realities in Jamaica, and reflective of the general traditional ideology that Jamaican is merely a form of English and that, consequently, all Jamaicans speak and understand English. It is reasonable to assume that a judicial officer in Jamaica belongs to the group of speakers who are bilingual in both Jamaican and English. Given the linguistic adaptability of such bilingual speakers, it may be that, in many cases, they do not readily appreciate the intelligibility gap between Jamaican and English and the misunderstandings that may arise for vernacular speakers whose proficiency in English is not advanced. In this context, confusion rooted in the homonymous nature of the Jamaican lexeme, /aipad/, is likely to appear implausible. This strikes at the credibility of the accused and the evidence he has offered.

I argue that the judicial insensitivity to the language point raised by the defence is particularly glaring in view of the fact that a similar language-based confusion was spawned by the legal system's own personnel. In two documents – the original indictment drafted by the Clerk of Court, and the record of the interrogation of KW – the device in question is represented as "iPod". The official record of the trial generated by the magistrate reveals that, at the end of the case for both the prosecution and the defence, permission was sought and granted to amend the indictment to reflect correctly the subject matter of the larceny. Up to that point in the trial, the particulars of offence in the indictment had read that KW "Did Steal an I-Pod". In the document containing the questions and answers written by the police officer who interviewed KW, there are, in the questions put to him, eight noun references to the subject matter of the larceny. Each reference is recorded as "I pod". These errors on the part of the agents of the state may perhaps be attributable to the phenomenon described as hypercorrection which tends to characterise Jamaican speech and which has been explained in the first section. It is indeed ironic that, in the indictment, the magistrate was clearly confronted with linguistic confusion resembling that relied upon by the defence. This did not, however, seem to prompt her to attach any significance to the linguistic dimension of the defence case. Her blindness to the linguistic confusion arising on the Crown's case and advanced by the defence is compatible with an ideology which denies the linguistic reality and perpetuates the invisibility of the vernacular within the legal structures.

The approach taken by the appellate court mimics that of the trial judge. This court also diminishes the possible effect of the linguistic ambiguity and rationalises the trial judge's failure to address adequately the linguistic point of the defence case. Although the judgment of the Court of Appeal concedes that the magistrate "did not specifically refer to an ambiguity in the use of 'iPad' and 'iPod'", it opines that "whether the stolen item was referred to as 'the iPad', rather than 'the thing', was immaterial".[10] The court emphasises the appropriateness of the trial judge's approach where it states, approvingly, that "[s]he ascribed no great importance to the name of the item alleged to be stolen".[11] This perspective disregards the very complaint made by the appellant, i.e. that the trial judge gave no consideration to the language question, which had a bearing on the credibility of the accused. The appellate court concluded that it was satisfied that the magistrate "fairly assessed the defence and dealt adequately with it".[12]

The discussion suggests that such a conclusion has some basis in judicial insensitivity to the language situation. This arguably arises from a reluctance to recognise the distinctiveness of Jamaican from English. In addition, there is, perhaps, some incapacity on the part of the class of speakers commanding bilingual proficiency, including judicial officers, to appreciate readily the language communication difficulties that may arise for Jamaican-dominant and monolingual speakers in Jamaica's bilingual speech community.

A role for linguistic evidence?

There seems to be an implicit assumption in the case of *R v Kirk Williams*, at the level of both the trial and appeal court, that vernacular-dominant speakers effectually understand English. The upshot of this is that arguments founded on miscommunication stemming

---

[10] [2013] JMCA Crim 51 at paragraph 20.
[11] [2013] JMCA Crim 51 at paragraph 26.
[12] [2013] JMCA Crim 51 at paragraph 28.

from the phonology and grammar of the Jamaican vernacular and the speech behaviour of vernacular speakers come across as being highly incredible and are thus likely to be given short shrift. This brings into focus the issue of the competence of judicial officers in Jamaica as language referees for speakers whose dominant language is Jamaican. It should perhaps be pointed out that no actual expert linguistic evidence was introduced by the defence. Reliance was placed on the magistrate taking judicial notice of the linguistic features of Jamaican. Judicial notice is a concept under which a judicial officer may accept that a fact exists, although it has not been established by evidence brought before the court. Such a fact will normally be one which is so generally well-known that it is not reasonably disputable (Tapper, 2010:75-77).

Although the linguistic crux of the case related to phonological features which are generally well-known to Jamaican/English bilingual speakers, it might have been useful to put expert linguistic evidence before the court, thereby squarely demanding that the magistrate confront the linguistic information central to the defence. Such expert evidence might have addressed not just the nature of the phonology of Jamaican, but the extent of its distinctiveness from English. It might also have provided evidence and professional opinions regarding language competence in Jamaica, the degree of mutual intelligibility between Jamaican and English, including the nature of the linguistic bases of miscommunications encountered by speakers of Jamaican not highly proficient in English. This might have set a stronger evidential foundation on which to challenge notions that Jamaican is a form of English and that English is readily and pervasively understood by Jamaican-dominant speakers. These traditional notions are likely to have inhered in judicial notice of the linguistic facts the court was being asked to accept without the usual course of proof.

United States v Kwame Richardson

The second case study also raises the issue of judicial misconceptions about the nature of Caribbean English vernaculars and about the nature of the speech of speakers of these vernaculars. *US v Kwame Richardson*[13] concerns the question whether a Guyanese-dominant defendant had sufficient understanding of the caution administered by the police before interrogating suspects, referred to in the US as the *Miranda* warning.[14] As indicated, Guyanese is the vernacular language spoken natively in Guyana and is sometimes referred to as Creolese.

---

[13] No. 09-CR-874 (JFB), US District Court EDNY, Memorandum and Order, 23 December 2010. The defendant was charged on indictment with conspiracy to import cocaine, importation of cocaine, conspiracy to distribute cocaine and attempted possession with intent to distribute.

[14] See note 1.

The case study draws largely on information contained in the Memorandum and Order issued by the court on the question whether the suspect-turned-defendant understood the *Miranda* warning. It also relies on information carried in several documents, filed in court in connection with the case, which are available via PACER, an electronic service providing access to a range of documents filed in certain US court cases.

The court's determination of the issue

Prior to trial, the defence moved to exclude from the trial (motion to suppress) post-arrest statements made by the defendant including admissions which implicated him. The motion to suppress was brought on the basis that the defendant had not knowingly and intelligently, and thus not voluntarily, waived his *Miranda* rights. The defence argued that, because the defendant was not an English speaker, he did not understand the *Miranda* warning, which had been told to him in English by the police without the assistance of an interpreter. The court rejected this argument, citing a series of factors:[15]

- That the defendant had never indicated at any time that he did not understand the warnings;
- That he did not ask the special agent to repeat the warnings – in English or otherwise;
- That the defendant had "substantial English language skills that would certainly be strong enough to enable him to understand". This evaluation was based on the interviewing agent's evidence concerning the nature of the interview the special agent had with the defendant;
- That the defendant did not indicate that he did not understand the questions asked of him by the special agent;
- That the defendant was appropriately responsive to questions put to him in English in other situations and reportedly seemed to understand another officer who spoke to him in English in their conversations.

The court, on the basis of these considerations, concluded that the defendant had comprehended the warnings, and had thus knowingly waived his *Miranda* rights in providing statements to the special agent. As a result, the statements were admissible as evidence. In arriving at its conclusion, the court did not have the benefit of expert linguistic testimony. The Memorandum and Order of the case indicates that although the defendant had advised that he would be calling an expert witness at the hearing of the motion to provide opinion evidence on the defendant's ability to understand the *Miranda* warning, this was not ultimately done. The reason for this is unclear from the Memorandum and Order.

---

15   See *US v Richardson*, No. 09-CR-874 (JFB), US District Court EDNY, Memorandum and Order, 23 December 2010, p. 6.

Comprehensibility and comprehension of the Miranda warnings

The defence, had engaged the services of a language expert, Hubert Devonish, then Professor of Linguistics, University of the West Indies, Mona, Jamaica. He had provided an opinion that the defendant, as a Guyanese creole-dominant speaker of limited English proficiency, lacked the linguistic competency to understand and waive his *Miranda* rights communicated to him in English without the assistance of a Creolese-speaking interpreter. His expert opinion was based on a language comprehension test he administered to the defendant and on sociolinguistic data involving the defendant's social contacts in the US as well as his social and educational background in his country of origin, Guyana.

The expert's opinion accords with a growing literature on the comprehensibility and comprehension of the *Miranda* warning, for example, Grisso (1998), Rogers et al. (2007) and Frumkin, Lally and Sexton (2012).[16] This literature shows that some of the difficulty surrounding comprehensibility of the *Miranda* warning is language related, grounded in the structural complexity of the warning and the use of lexical items in unusual ways. Ainsworth (2010:115), having examined some of the literature, stated:

> the researchers concluded that, as used in many jurisdictions, much of the *Miranda* warning would not be properly understood by a considerable percentage of the general public and would be inadequately understood by an even larger percentage of the arrestees, given their statistically lower educational attainment.

This seems to be particularly true for certain vulnerable categories of people, such as juveniles, individuals with mental incapacities (Cloud, Shepherd, Barkoff & Shur, 2002) and those with linguistic impairment (Rost & McGregor, 2012).

The law recognises that comprehension of the warning by the suspect is necessary. Indeed, the principle is that it must be given in "clear and unequivocal language" and that a suspect must "knowingly and intelligently" waive his *Miranda* rights. However, the legal indicators as to whether the rights were "knowingly and intelligently" waived seem very elementary. Thomas (2001:1082) has found that "once the prosecutor proves that the warnings were given in a language that the suspect understands, courts find [knowing and intelligent] waiver in almost every case". It appears then that the law does not put too much weight on whether suspects *appreciably* understand the rights.

Comprehension and comprehensibility studies dealing with the *Miranda* warning have not, for the most part, dealt with scenarios, such as the one in *US v Richardson*, where the suspect speaks a different, though lexically related language to English. The studies

---

[16] There is other evidence of difficulty regarding language related comprehension and comprehensibility of other speech events within the legal system such as jury instructions. See, for example, Charrow and Charrow (1979) and McKimmie, Antrobus and Baguley (2014).

have largely contemplated circumstances where there is a common language between the police officer and the suspect, or where the suspect is a native speaker of a foreign language unrelated to English. There is arguably then a need to reproduce and develop on the kind of test administered by the expert in the course of arriving at his opinion conceived for use in *US v Richardson*. This potentially would provide useful data specific to Caribbean English vernacular languages and speakers that could supplement the existing research on the comprehension and comprehensibility of the *Miranda* warning. This is necessary particularly in view of US law on the admission of expert testimony of which *Daubert v Merrell Dow Pharmaceuticals, Inc*[17] is a leading authority.

A role for language experts?

The law, concerned about the reliability of expert opinions, requires courts to evaluate the scientific validity of the reasoning or methodology informing the expert opinion. According to *Daubert*, such an evaluation may involve a number of lines of enquiry such as whether the technique involved has been tested and subjected to peer review, the scope for error, and its general acceptability within the relevant scientific community. Meintjes-Van Der Walt (2003:100-103; and in Chapter 12 in this volume) elaborates on the nature of these *Daubert* factors, which are largely concerned with the adequacy and reliability of the test method. The methods used to test and determine issues of comprehension and comprehensibility of the *Miranda* warning must therefore satisfy the standards of integrity demanded by the law in order to clear the hurdle for admission into evidence of the test results and the expert opinion emanating from the test.

In the US, the law also provides that "[f]or an expert's testimony to be admissible ... it must be directed to matters within the witness' scientific, technical, or specialized knowledge and not to lay matters which a jury is capable of understanding and deciding without the expert's help."[18] In the *Richardson* case, the Government's Memorandum of Law in Opposition to the Defendant's Motion to Suppress, dated and filed on September 30, 2010, stated that "whether the defendant understands English is an issue that the Court is capable of resolving without an expert's help" and that the Government was "not aware of any case in this Circuit in which a Court permitted an expert to testify at trial or in a hearing about whether a defendant understood English". A difficulty then may be whether this question may even be regarded as a matter for specialist testimony. The fact, too, that the vernaculars under discussion resemble English at the level of vocabulary may beguile judicial officers in US courts into the belief that they, as competent speakers of English, are quite capable of evaluating the English proficiency of Caribbean English vernacular speakers. This presents

---

[17] 509 US 579 (1993).

[18] See, for example, *Andrews v Metro-North Commuter RR Co* 882 F 2d 705 (2d Cir. 1989), paragraph 9.

an additional challenge to overcome the hurdle of the "lay matter" exclusionary rule regarding admission of expert evidence. It also raises the issue of the fitness of the average judicial officer to make such an evaluation. Using sociolinguistic information, the next part explores this issue of the suitability of judges to evaluate a suspect's comprehension of the *Miranda* warning in the context of the *Richardson* case.

Language proficiency factors considered by the court

In the previous section "The court's determination of the issue", the factors upon which the court relied to arrive at its conclusion are outlined. Three of the five factors outlined entail the defendant's neglect to state any lack of understanding on his part or to show any sign of failure to understand, such as requesting repetition. I question the reliability of these factors as indices of comprehension in view of the traditional overt ideology attending Caribbean vernaculars in their home territories. Significantly, and as explained earlier, these vernaculars, in the societies in which they are natively spoken, have been perceived as merely a version of their lexifiers and have not been regarded as genuine languages. In addition, because habitual vernacular speakers have tended to be of low socioeconomic status, the vernaculars themselves have been associated with impecuniosity, lack of education and low intelligence.[19]

This ideology associated with Caribbean English vernaculars is likely to make vernacular-dominant speakers reluctant, particularly in the presence of unfamiliar authority figures, to admit failure to understand, or to provide overt signals of their lack of understanding of the superstrate language. This view is supported by the observations by Nero (2006) cited in a previous section of this chapter ("The vernaculars in the global space") and by Devonish (2003) cited in another section ("Mutual intelligibility with English"). An admission of inability to understand would be tantamount to the speaker stating that he or she is poor and stupid. Given this language ideology, the value of the factors concerning the defendant's failure to signal lack of understanding of the warnings as a gauge of comprehension is problematic.

The other two factors upon which the court relied involved a kind of rough and ready assessment by the court of the defendant's responses and responsiveness in certain

---

[19] This is in tandem with Rickford's (1985) work on language attitudes in Guyana which indicated that participants in a matched guise experiment associated basilectal speech with the least prestigious jobs and acrolectal speech with the more prestigious jobs. Despite attitudinal shifts which indicate more positive popular attitudes to Caribbean vernaculars by their speakers, some negative orthodox attitudes remain. A 2005 national Language Attitude Survey carried out in Jamaica by the Jamaican Language Unit showed that 44% of the sample believed that a speaker of English would have more money than a speaker of Jamaican and that significant sample majorities (61% and 57%) believed that a speaker of English would be more educated and intelligent respectively. The associations may, however, also be reflective of the traditional sociolinguistic reality.

conversations. These conversations were with (a) the special agent who was instrumental in the defendant's arrest and who had administered the warning, and (b) a pre-trial services officer who supervised the defendant over some nine months while he was on bail. The questions in the conversations with the special agent solicited information largely concerning other persons involved in the incident, the type of drugs involved, the origin of the drugs in Guyana, and the location to which the defendant was to deliver the drugs in the US. The pre-trial services officer appeared to have testified that the defendant observed all the terms of his bail which had been communicated to him in English, and that the defendant gave appropriate responses whenever the officer met with the defendant. The court also attached weight to the fact that the defendant, whenever he reported on bail, successfully used an automated kiosk which generated questions in English. These automated reporting kiosks appear to generate basic questions regarding, for example, contact information, name changes, court dates, employment and education information, and arrests (Bauer et al., 2015:46). Some of the questions appear to require merely yes/no responses.

Creole continuum typologies, like those existing in Guyana and Jamaica, raise issues of the range of varieties along the respective continuum in which a speaker is competent. Generally, the varieties in which a speaker will be competent are determined by the speaker's social and educational exposure (Alleyne, 1980:181-185; DeCamp, 1971). Proficiency in the acrolect is typically acquired via formal education for many speakers. Limited formal schooling then, suggests low levels of competence in the socially acceptable variety of English in the speech community. The language expert who had been engaged by the defence assessed the defendant as a lower mesolectal speaker with limited understanding of English. That assessment was supported by information gathered by the expert that the defendant had not finished primary school and that his social contacts, both in Guyana and in the US, would not have provided him with frequent regular exposure to English to enable him to acquire advanced proficiency in English.

The literature (for example Pavlenko, 2008), shows that many non-native speakers of English, though they possess social or interactional language competence, may lack proficiency in registers that incorporate complex sentence structures, a specialised lexicon and that tend to be used in connection with abstract concepts.[20] The nature of the exchanges upon which the court relied to determine the defendant's language skills seems to have required, in the main, interactional competence. Complete comprehension of the *Miranda* warning calls for significantly higher English language proficiency levels, given its assessed levels of reading and listening comprehension difficulty (Brière, 1978). There is thus a mismatch between the linguistic nature of the texts or discourse used by the court to assess the defendant's language skills and the linguistic nature of the warning,

---

[20] See too *US v Hector Rosa et al* 946 F. 2d 505 (7th Cir. 1991) and discussed in Brown-Blake (2006:411-412).

the text constituting the subject of the defendant's alleged lack of understanding. The court's assessment method did not take into account (i) settled notions concerning the possibility of a gap between a speaker's interactional competence and the more advanced proficiency levels needed for comprehension of denser and more complex texts, and (ii) the possibility that such proficiency gaps loom large in speakers from Caribbean English creole continuum situations, despite the lexical similarity between English on the one hand, and varieties of Guyanese on the other. I argue that the method used by the court in assessing the defendant's language proficiency was flawed. The faulty method of proficiency assessment has implications for the correctness of the court's finding and also demonstrates how ill-equipped judicial officers may be to make independent decisions regarding degrees of language proficiency.

Disparate legal standards

Documents[21] filed with the court from the time of the initial appearance indicate that an interpreter was invariably present whenever the defendant made appearances in court. The documents indicate that the language for which the interpreter was engaged was Creole or Guyanese Creole.[22] The practice of providing a Guyanese language interpreter continued even after the ruling on the motion to suppress. This is clear from the court filings and records regarding hearings subsequent to the Memorandum and Order in respect of the motion to suppress. These include the hearing for sentencing of the defendant where an interpreter was present and sworn.

The provision of an interpreter *ex post* the Memorandum and Order on the motion to suppress seems to be inconsistent with the determination in that Order that the defendant had "substantial English language skills" to allow him to understand the *Miranda* warnings. Both the appointment of an interpreter and the determination of whether a suspect knowingly waived his *Miranda* rights are intricately linked to the question of linguistic competence. A court, in arriving at either determination, must engage in an assessment of the degree of proficiency in the particular language, in this case, English, that the defendant is presumed to possess. It would appear, though, that the legal threshold for language proficiency for the appointment of an interpreter is different to the threshold applied for determination of waiver of *Miranda* rights.

---

[21] See, for example, US District Court, Eastern District of New York, Initial Appearance Calendar, Magistrate Case Number M-09-1198 dated 5 December 2009; Calendar: Magistrate's Proceedings, docket number 09-1198M, dated 9 December 2009; Calendar: Magistrate's Proceeding, docket number 09CR874 (JFB), dated 12 January 2010; Criminal Cause for Status Conference, docket number CR-09-00874, dated 4 February 2010, all concerning defendant, Kwame Richardson.

[22] It is noted, though, that in some instances the language specified is Jamaican Patois. See, for example, Criminal Cause for Status Conference, docket number CR 09-00874-JFB, dated 21 March 2011.

Appointment of an interpreter for a defendant or witness in criminal proceedings is permitted where that person "speaks only or primarily a language other than the English language ... so as to inhibit such party's comprehension of the proceedings or communication with counsel or the presiding judicial officer, or so as to inhibit such witness' comprehension of the questions and presentation of such testimony".[23] If this is the legal context in which an interpreter is appointed, then the presence of an interpreter in proceedings is an acknowledgement that the judicial officer is satisfied that the relevant person is insufficiently competent in English to adequately follow the proceedings. It is thus difficult to reconcile a finding that the accused had substantial English language skills to understand the *Miranda* warning with the fact that an interpreter continued to be provided in proceedings subsequent to the ruling on the motion to suppress.

R v Douglas and Bryan (Canada)

This case[24] involved speakers of Jamaican who were the defendants in a Canadian court trial in which the quality of interpretation was questionable. An application for a mistrial was made on the basis that the interpretation was seriously flawed and thereby constituted a violation of the defendants' right to an interpreter under the Canadian Charter of Rights and Freedoms.[25] Evidence in the application for a mistrial was given by an unaccredited interpreter, a native speaker of Jamaican, who was present at the trial. Alluding to this evidence, the judgment reports a number of deficiencies in the interpretation. It indicates that during the testimony of one of the accused, there had been omissions by the interpreter. In addition, the judgment indicates that the interpreter sometimes added to the defendant's testimony, and, at other times, incorrectly interpreted words spoken by the defendant. The court also accepted that, in some instances, "the poor interpretation altered the meaning of the expression used" by the defendant and that critical aspects of the defendant's testimony were "lost in the poor translation". The judgment also reveals that both the trial judge and the jury were aware of the poor quality of the interpretation: the judgment indicates that the trial judge had received a note from the jury during the testimony of one of the accused. The note asked the judge to instruct the interpreter to cease paraphrasing and to interpret verbatim. As the judgment observes, it is clear that at least one juror was familiar with Jamaican.

The application for a mistrial was granted. While the court noted that interpretation need not be perfect, it stated that "the minimum constitutional threshold to meet the obligation

---

[23] US Court Interpreters Act, 1978, 28 US Code, §1827.

[24] 2014 ONSC 2573.

[25] Section 14 of the Charter states that a party or witness in any proceedings who does not understand or speak the language in which the proceedings are conducted or who is deaf has the right to the assistance of an interpreter.

under Section 14 of the Charter must be high". Citing the authority of *R v Tran*,[26] the judge in *R v Douglas and Bryan* stated:

> once poor interpretation is found beyond the relatively narrow limits of imperfection tolerable, it is not appropriate for the Court to second-guess and speculate as to whether there was a breach of s.14 of the Charter. Irrespective of whether the poor interpretation actually affected the accused's right to make full answer and defence, something which could rarely if ever be known with certainty, the accused is entitled to the minimum constitutionally-protected threshold afforded by s.14".

Canadian law, and courts in their application of that law appear to be uncompromising in the treatment of rights grounded in language, particularly where these rights have a bearing on fair trial. In the context of the *Douglas and Bryan* case, it seems reasonable to say that the apparent expediency inherent in the US approach, whereby *Miranda* rights are almost routinely adjudged to have been validly waived by suspects with limited English proficiency, is absent in the Canadian approach. There is an unquestioned presumption in the Canadian approach that Jamaican, despite its lexical similarity to English, is a language, and is sufficiently distinct from English, the language of the court, to raise issues of mutual intelligibility. The judgment notes, for example, that one of the accused, at a point in his testimony, had used the expression "dash wey" which was initially rendered by the interpreter as "throw away". While this is a literal translation, the context of the expression in the testimony made it clear that the correct translation of the expression was "kill". This semantic nuance assumes legal significance in light of the defence of duress advanced by one of the accused.

A Canadian court is thus likely to assume that a Jamaican-dominant speaker's ability to substantially comprehend court proceedings, and indeed the ability of a court and a jury to understand such an accused, are compromised in the absence of satisfactory interpretation. The potential upshot of this is that the legal position of such a speaker may be prejudiced. The *Douglas and Bryan* court expressed particular concern that some of the faulty interpretation occurred at a time when one of the accused was providing testimony that was relevant to his defence of duress. There appeared then to be a likelihood of prejudice in the face of the poor interpretation. But, as the aforementioned quotation from the judgment shows, there is no legal requirement to establish that the faulty interpretation *actually* impaired the accused's legal position in order to determine that the right to an interpreter was abrogated. These liberal legal approaches are arguably justifiable, given (a) the complex nature of a speaker's language proficiency, particularly where a speaker hails from a creole continuum situation, and (b) the unreliability of lay assessments by judicial officers of a

---

[26] (1994) 117 DLR (4th) 7. In this case, the Supreme Court of Canada agreed with the proposition that interpreters should be permitted "unless a court were convinced that the applicant was able to understand the proceedings *to the same degree as if those proceedings were conducted in a language in which the applicant has the greatest facility*" (my emphasis).

speaker's linguistic proficiency. In this context, the Canadian approach is preservative of the law's overarching goal of fairness in criminal proceedings.

The court's keen awareness of, and sensitivity to, the position of Jamaican vernacular speakers is arguably reflected in its lament that in the particular county in which the trial was conducted "the availability of accredited Jamaican Patois interpreters is so slim". Indeed, the judicial sensitivity to the language issues facing Caribbean English vernacular speakers displayed by this Canadian court stands in sharp contrast to the judicial approaches seen in the cases under study from the US and Jamaica. A daily newspaper in Jamaica which reported the *Douglas and Bryan* case declared that "[t]he age-old debate about the legitimacy of Jamaican Patois is bound to be refuelled by revelation from a Canadian judge … that there is a shortage of professional interpreters" (Thompson, 2014) for the Jamaican language in that country. The suggestion is that the recognition of Jamaican and the treatment of its speakers in a foreign justice system may motivate, if not oblige, adjustment to the status of the language in the home country.

Conclusion

The case studies have shown that judicial ideas and beliefs about Caribbean English vernaculars are likely to permeate judicial decision-making, and thus have a bearing on outcomes in cases before the courts involving speakers of these languages. Judges arguably make unsuitable arbiters in matters grounded essentially in language proficiency. This is perhaps what informs even the more generous approach by the Canadian judiciary which compensates for the risks of unsound judicial assessments regarding speakers of Caribbean English vernaculars and their languages.

This chapter has argued that expert linguistic testimony has the potential to introduce more objectivity and empiricism into the determination of language issues in cases. However, it also reveals that judges, by virtue of the application of legal rules governing admission of expert evidence, also perform the role of gatekeepers in respect of such testimony. Linguists specialising in Caribbean English vernaculars, as they develop measures to evaluate proficiency and comprehensibility in the context of legal settings, have the task of ensuring that the techniques they employ have the highest chance of withstanding the judicial scrutiny for admission where, as in the US, the law establishes such conditions for admission of expert evidence. Even in jurisdictions where the conditions may not be so rigorous, *Daubert*-type factors are likely to be important in determining the probative weight of an expert's opinion where it has been admitted into evidence.

References

Ainsworth, J. 2010. *Miranda* rights: Curtailing coercion in police interrogation – the failed promise of *Miranda v Arizona*. In: M. Coulthard & A. Johnson (eds.), *The Routledge handbook of forensic linguistics*. New York: Routledge. pp. 111-125.

Alleyne, M. 1980. *Comparative Afro-American*. Ann Arbor: Karoma.

Bailey, B. 1966. *Jamaican Creole syntax: A transformational approach*. Cambridge: Cambridge University Press.

Bauer, E.; Hagen, C.; Greene, A.; Crosse, S.; Harmon, M. & Claus, R. 2015. *Kiosk Supervision: A guidebook for community corrections professionals*. Rockville MD: Westat.

Bickerton, D. 1973. The nature of a Creole continuum. *Language*, 49(3):640-669.

Blake, C. & Devonish, H. 1994. Developing technical vocabulary for Jamaican Creole. In: I. Fodor & C. Hagège (eds.), *Language reform: History and future*, Vol. 6. Hamburg: Helmut Buske Verlag. pp. 149-161.

Brière, E. 1978. Limited English speakers and the *Miranda* rights. *TESOL Quarterly*, 12(3):235-245.

Brown-Blake, C. 2006. Fair trial, language and the right to interpretation. *International Journal on Minority and Group Rights*, 13(4):391-412.

Brown-Blake, C. 2017. Supporting justice reform in Jamaica through language policy change. *Caribbean Studies*, 45(1&2):183-215.

Brown-Blake, C. & Chambers, P. 2007. The Jamaican Creole speaker in the UK criminal justice system. *International Journal of Speech, Language and the Law*, 14(2):269-294.

Charrow, R. & Charrow, V. 1979. Making legal language understandable: A psycholinguistic study of jury instructions. *Columbia Law Review*, 79(7):1306-1374.

Cloud, M.; Shepherd, G.; Barkoff, A. & Shur, J. 2002. Words without meaning: The constitution, confessions and mentally retarded suspects. *University of Chicago Law Review*, 69(2):495-624.

DeCamp, D. 1971. Toward a generative analysis of a post-creole speech continuum. In: D. Hymes (ed.), *Pidginization and Creolization of Languages*. Cambridge: Cambridge University Press. pp. 349-370.

Devonish, H. 2003. Language advocacy and conquest diglossia in the "anglophone" Caribbean. In: C. Mair (ed.), *The politics of English as a world language*. Amsterdam: Rodopi. pp. 157-177.

Devonish, H. 2007. *Language and liberation: Creole language politics in the Caribbean*. Kingston Jamaica: Arawak Publications.

Devonish, H. & Harry, O. 2004. Jamaican Creole and Jamaican English: Phonology. In: B. Kortmann & E. Schneider (eds.), *A handbook of varieties of English*, Vol. 1. Berlin: Mouton de Gruyter. pp. 450-480.

Devonish, H. & Thompson, D. 2010. *A concise grammar of Guyanese Creole (Creolese)*. Munich: Lincom Europa.

Devonish, H. & Walters, K. 2015. The Jamaican language situation: A process, not a type. In: D. Smakman & P. Heinrich (eds.), *Globalising sociolinguistics: Challenging and expanding theory*. London: Routledge. pp. 223-232.

Frumkin B.; Lally, S. & Sexton, J. 2012. The Grisso tests for assessing understanding and appreciation of *Miranda* warnings with a forensic sample. *Behavioral Sciences and the Law*, 30:673-692.

Görlach, M. 1991. Jamaica and Scotland: Bilingual or bidialectal? In: M. Görlach (ed.), *Englishes: Studies in varieties of English 1984-1988*. Amsterdam: John Benjamins. pp. 69-89.

Grisso, T. 1998. *Instruments for assessing understanding and appreciation of Miranda rights*. Sarasota FL: Professional Resource Press.

Hinrichs, L. 2011. *The sociolinguistics of diaspora: Language in the Jamaican Canadian community*. Proceedings of the 19th Annual Symposium About Language and Society, Austin, April 15-17. http://salsa.ling.utexas.edu/proceedings/2011/01TLF54-Hinrichs.pdf [Retrieved July 2018].

International Organisation for Migration. 2017. *Migration in the Caribbean: Current trends, opportunities and challenges*. Working Papers on Migration/WP1.

Jamaica. Parliament. 2001. Verbatim notes of the Joint Select Committee Meeting on the Charter of Rights, March 15.

Jamaican Language Unit. 2005. *The language attitude survey of Jamaica*. http://mona.uwi.edu/dllp/jlu/projects/Report%20for%20Language%20Attitude%20Survey%20of%20Jamaica.pdf [Retrieved July 2018].

Jamaican Language Unit. 2007. *The language competence survey of Jamaica*. https://www.mona.uwi.edu/dllp/jlu/projects/The%20Language%20Competence%20Survey%20of%20Jamaica%20-%20Data%20Analysis.pdf [Retrieved July 2018].

Kennedy, M. 2017. *What do Jamaican children speak?* Kingston Jamaica: University of the West Indies Press.

Mair, C. 2003. Language, code, and symbol: The changing roles of Jamaican Creole in diaspora communities. *Arbeiten aus Anglistik und Amerikanistik,* 28(2):231-248. http://www.jstor.org/stable/43025702 [Retrieved July 2018].

Martin, J. 2002. Patois as judicial problem. Letter to the editor, *The Gleaner,* 28 December.

McKimmie, B.; Antrobus, E. & Baguley, C. 2014. Objective and subjective comprehension of jury instructions in criminal trials. *New Criminal Law Review,* 17(2):163-183.

Meintjes-Van Der Walt, L. 2003. The proof of the pudding: The presentation and proof of expert evidence in South Africa. *Journal of African Law,* 47(1):88-106.

Moll, A. 2015. *Jamaican Creole goes web: Sociolinguistic styling and authenticity in a digital "Yaad"*. Amsterdam: John Benjamins.

Nero, S. 2006. Introduction. In: S. Nero (ed.), *Dialects, Englishes, Creoles, and education*. Mahwah NJ: Lawrence Erlbaum.

Pavlenko, A. 2008. "I'm very not about the law part": Nonnative speakers of English and the *Miranda* warnings. *TESOL Quarterly,* 42(1):1-30.

Pollard, V. 2001. "A singular subject takes a singular verb" and hypercorrection in Jamaican speech and writing. In: P. Christie (ed.), *Due respect: Papers on English and English-related Creoles in the Caribbean in honour of Professor Robert Le Page*. Kingston: University of the West Indies Press. pp. 97-107.

Rickford, J. 1985. Standard and non-standard language attitudes in a Creole continuum. In: N. Wolfson & J. Manes (eds.), *Language of Equality*. Berlin: Mouton. pp. 145-160.

Rickford, J. 1987. *Dimensions of a Creole continuum*. Redwood City CA: Stanford University Press.

Rickford, J. & King, S. 2016. Language and linguistics on trial: Hearing Rachel Jeantel (and other vernacular speakers) in the courtroom and beyond. *Language,* 92(4):948-988.

Rogers, R.; Harrison, K.; Schuman, D.; Sewell, K. & Hazelwood, L. 2007. An analysis of *Miranda* warnings and waivers: Comprehension and coverage. *Law and Human Behavior,* 31(2):177-192.

Rost, G. & McGregor, K. 2012. *Miranda* rights comprehension in young adults with specific language impairment. *American Journal of Speech-Language Pathology,* 21(2):101-108.

Sebba, M. 1993. *London Jamaican*. London: Longman.

Smalling, D. 1983. An investigation into the intelligibility of radio news broadcasts in Jamaica. Caribbean Studies paper. Mona, Jamaica: University of the West Indies.

Tapper, C. 2010. *Cross & Tapper on evidence,* 12th Edition. Oxford: Oxford University Press.

Thomas, G. 2001. Separated at birth but siblings nonetheless: *Miranda* and the due process notice cases. *Michigan Law Review*, 99(5):1081-1120.

Thompson, K. 2014. Patois interpreter shortage in Canada. *Jamaica Observer*, 19 May.

Winer, L. & Jack, L. 1997. English Caribbean Creole in New York. In: O. Garcia & J. Fishman (eds.), *The multilingual Apple: Languages in New York city*. Berlin: Mouton de Gruyter. pp. 301-337.

Legal sources

(i) International Conventions
European Convention on Human Rights, 1950.
International Covenant on Civil and Political Rights, 1966.

(ii) Constitutions
Constitution de la République d'Haïti, 1987.
Jamaica Constitution, 1962.
Republic of Vanuatu Constitution, 1980.

(iii) Statutes
Canada

Charter of Rights and Freedoms, Part 1 of the Constitution Act, 1982.

Jamaica

Consumer Protection Act, 2005.
Standards Act (Jamaica), No. 57 of 1968.
Standards (Labelling of Processed Food) Regulations, 1974.

USA

Court Interpreters Act, 1978, 28 U.S.C. § 1827.

(iv) Cases
Andrews v Metro-North Commuter RR Co 882 F 2d 705 (2d Cir. 1989).
Daubert v Merrell Dow Pharmaceuticals Inc, 509 US 579 (1993).
Kirk Williams v R (2013) JMCA 51.
Miranda v State of Arizona, 384 US 436 (1966).
R v Douglas and Bryan 2014 ONSC 2573.
R v Tran (1994) 117 DLR (4th) 7.
US v Hector Rosa et al 946 F. 2d 505 (7th Cir. 1991).
US v Kwame Richardson, No. 09-CR-874 (JFB), US District Court EDNY, Memorandum and Order, December 23, 2010.

A ZIMBABWEAN PERSPECTIVE ON THE EFFECT OF INTERPRETER-INITIATED TURNS

Interactional dynamics in the adversarial courtroom

Paul Svongoro & Kim Wallmach

Introduction

This chapter examines the conversational dynamics involved in consecutively interpreted interactions in Zimbabwean courtrooms. Drawing on authentic courtroom data from Zimbabwean courtrooms, and using the approaches of discourse analysis and interpreting studies, we investigate the nature of interpreter-mediated trials in Zimbabwean courtrooms, which essentially involve two primary interlocutors and an interpreter. By law, court officials have power to regulate turns of speaking, ask questions and manipulate question forms by means of various rhetorical devices. Our principal objective is to investigate how this power of the court officials may be diminished if the meanings of questions are not reproduced in the interpreted version. We achieve this objective by analysing the occurrence and use of specific conversational phenomena (turn-taking and questioning, for example) by the different court players, as well as how these were rendered by interpreters during court proceedings.

A trial in the adversarial courtroom is notably marked by what critical discourse analysts refer to as "power asymmetry", with magistrates and public prosecutors as questioners enjoying institutionalised power and control over lay participants as answerers (Cotterill, 2003; Gibbons, 2008; Walker, 1987). Walker (1987), for instance, identifies three sources of power enjoyed by the legal professionals:

- a "sociocultural base of power" stemming from their roles as authorised participants who resolve disputes in a recognised societal institution;
- a "legal base of power", which stipulates counsel's right to ask questions and impose sanctions against those refusing to answer;
- and a "linguistic base of power", which originates from the right to ask questions and thus to manipulate the form of a question in order to control the answer to the question posed.

However, in interpreter-mediated trials like those that take place in Zimbabwean courtrooms, counsel may lose some of this power (and thus control) over the proceedings. Ng (2009:162) suggests that the use of the consecutive mode during court interpreting gives counsel an extra layer of control over witnesses who cannot tell their stories and interact with counsel as freely as their counterparts in a monolingual court, as they have to pause frequently for interpretation, and their interaction with counsel occurs through the interpreter. Consecutive interpreting is a mode of interpreting commonly used in the courts and other community settings. During consecutive interpreting, the person with limited English proficiency speaks, and this is followed by the interpreter's conversion of what was said to the English speaker. During these sessions, there are pauses or breaks between sentences when each party is speaking. In other words, the interpreter listens then interprets.

Due to the language mediation role that interpreters play in the legal process, coupled by the fact that bilingualism is a rare skill, the interpreter is inevitably cast "in a highly important role vis-à-vis his clients"; and the interpreter's position in the middle "has the advantage of power inherent in all positions which control scarce resources" (Anderson & Bruce, 2002:212). However, Anderson and Bruce (2002:214) point out at the same time that the interpreter's monopolistic power disappears "if a client happens to be bilingual". In the context of the Zimbabwean courtroom, most court players generally have varying levels of bilingualism. This applies both to officers of the court and, at times, to the accused persons and witnesses. It could thus be argued that the linguistic power of the interpreter depends, to a large extent, on the co-present court actors' degree of bilingualism.

Anderson and Bruce (2002:215) suggest that the potentially monopolistic power and "relative ambiguity" of their role allows interpreters considerable latitude in defining their own behaviour vis-à-vis their clients; and, as a result, introduces the possibility of translating selectively without their monolingual clients knowing the difference – unless an interpreter oversteps rather wide bounds. It could thus be argued that, being the only "proficient bilingual" in the encounter, the interpreter has the power to depart from the ethical code that requires interpreters to be faithful and impartial, amongst other things. Owing to the presence of other bilinguals, however, a staff interpreter working between English and Shona in the present-day Zimbabwean courtrooms, however rarely enjoys the monopolistic power of an interpreter in a typical bilingual setting, except in trials involving a witness speaking another language of which the other court actors have little knowledge. In that case, the court would function as a typical bilingual setting for as the duration of the testimony of that particular witness.

The norm in interpreter turns

Accuracy is accorded the highest significance in court interpreting, as it matters considerably in the administration of justice. Misinterpretation of witness testimonies may lead to miscarriages of justice (see Koo, 2009; Morris, 2010). The interpreter, as González, Vasquez and Mikkelson (1991:475-476) point out, acts as the voice of the non-English speaker and is very often the only bilingual person in court. As such, the interpreter has "an overriding obligation to ensure that the target language (TL) rendition meets the highest standards of accuracy" so that the witnesses' testimonies can be conveyed precisely and completely. González et al. (1991) contend that, to attain this highest level of accuracy, interpreters must opt for verbatim interpretation (what Mikkelson, 2000:17, also terms "literal interpretation"), and must "conserve every single element of information" in the source language message, including both linguistic and paralinguistic elements, such as the source language register, word choice, obscenities, repetitions, self-corrections, slips of the tongue, pauses, false starts and tone of voice. On the other hand, interpreters must not try to enhance the clarity of the source language message through addition and elaboration; and they must not lengthen the testimony or improve on any nonsensical or non-responsive testimony. Mikkelson (2000) points out that the emphasis in verbatim interpretation, therefore, is on adhering strictly to the form of the source-language message rather than meaning. What González et al. (1991) are proposing is, in essence, that accuracy in interpreting necessitates close adherence to both the propositional content and the style of the source language message. This is the generally established definition for "accuracy" in various codes of ethics governing the practice of court interpreting; and it emphasises the importance of a faithful rendition of the source language speaker's message without addition, omission or distortion, as well as the requirement for the interpreter to conserve not only linguistic, but also paralinguistic, elements. Similarly, the National Association of Judicial Interpreters and Translators (NAJIT) defines accuracy in the following way:

> Source-language speech should be faithfully rendered into the target language by conserving all the elements of the original message ... and there should be no distortion of the original message through addition or omission, explanation or paraphrasing. All hedges, false starts and repetitions should be conveyed; [...] the register, style and tone of the source language should be conserved. (NAJIT, 2016:12)

In Zimbabwe, Hoffman's (1994:21) rules for interpreters (Rules 1 and 3, for instance) emphasise that "court interpreters must interpret faithfully – without addition or omission – everything said in court"; and the rules state that, if a witness is speaking incoherently and unintelligibly, interpreters should refrain from clarifying for the witness and are "expected to try his/her utmost to interpret accurately and faithfully what was said in full". Unfortunately, these rules emphasise word-for-word interpretation which reveals a preoccupation with form of the source-language message rather than meaning transfer.

Verbatim interpreting is a highly controversial issue, and has been challenged by standards of functional equivalency and meaning-based translation that are now almost universally accepted by translation and interpretation scholars. However, it is generally agreed amongst researchers (Berk-Seligson, 1990; De Jongh, 1992; González et al., 1991; Hale, 2002) that interpreters should convey not only the content of the utterance, but also the style in which the utterance is made, if participants in the court proceedings who do not speak the language of the court are to be placed on an equal footing with those who do. Accurate interpretation means that all words, including slang, vulgarisms, and epithets, should be interpreted to convey the speaker's intended meaning (Mikkelson, 2000). Unfortunately, though, most members of the legal profession are not aware of the distinction between a literal translation and an accurate one. Thus, Hale (2002) clarifies that the style in which a message is delivered affects how it is received by listeners because not only the content of an utterance but also the style is essential to the ultimate meaning communicated.

Participant roles in interpreter-mediated trials

To explore the interactional dynamics in an interpreter-mediated courtroom, it is essential to examine the institutional and participant roles taken up by court interactants. This helps demonstrate not only the participation status of individual court actors but also the power relations amongst them. It will also show how power is maintained and realised in the roles ascribed to, or taken on by, these actors. In this regard, Goffman's (1981) participation framework provides a useful analytical tool.

One can participate in a communicative act as a speaker or a hearer. In his production format, Goffman (1981) deconstructs the speaker role into that of "animator" (sounding box or talking machine), "author" (the agent who composes or scripts the lines uttered), and "principal" (someone whose position or belief is established by the words spoken).

Regarding hearer roles, Goffman (1981) identifies two basic categories: the ratified and the unratified. According to Goffman, ratified hearers are official listeners comprising both the addressed recipients, who are being directly spoken to, and the unaddressed recipients, who may or may not be listening. Goffman regards the unratified hearers or participants as "bystanders" whose presence is, however, considered the rule, not the exception. Those "bystanders" who follow the talk and "catch bits and pieces of it, all without much effort or intent" are categorised as "overhearers", whereas those who "surreptitiously exploit the accessibility they find they have" will qualify as "eavesdroppers" (Goffman, 1981:132).

In monolingual courtroom examinations, the examining lawyer has a speaker role as both animator and author but may or may not be principal, because the lawyer's words may not attest to his/her own position but to that of the client or the prosecution. The witness's speaker role, on the other hand, usually combines animator, author and principal, except perhaps in a case where the witness is made to say something which does not attest to his own stance or belief. Both the examining lawyer and the witness are, by default, each other's addressed recipient. The defendant, the magistrate, the judge, the jury (in the case of a jury trial) and the non-examining lawyers, can be categorised as the unaddressed recipients. Those in the public gallery as bystanders can be regarded as unratified participants (either as overhearers or eavesdroppers) because they are, as a rule, not allowed to take part directly in the talking event, but only to act as silent observers. However, when one considers interactions in bilingual courtrooms where court proceedings are interpreter-mediated, these participant roles by Goffman (1981) are slightly modified, according to Wadensjö's (1998) model (to be explained shortly).

The interpreter's participant role

According to the conduit model of interpreting, the interpreter is not considered a participant proper in an interpreted interaction but a transparent presence. Goffman's citation of the provision of "simultaneous translation of a speech" (Goffman, 1981:146), as an example of the speaker animating someone else's speech, is contentious, because it is tantamount to confirming the mythical conduit model for the interpreter and the suggestion that interpreting is a mechanical process in which a message can be transferred intact from one language to another, without the interpreter having to insert personal knowledge, effort and judgement in creating a new version of the talk. In producing the target language version of the message, the interpreter, as suggested by Wadensjö (1998), necessarily also becomes the author, although not the principal author. At times, the interpreter may even go beyond the strictest sense of relaying or translating, assuming the role of a coordinator and creating his/her own talk in the course of coordinating the talk between the interlocutors, thus qualifying also as principal (Wadensjö, 1998). Wadensjö suggests that Goffman's analytical distinction of recipientship fails to consider the different listener roles taken by, or ascribed to, a participant in an interaction. To complement Goffman's production format in his participation framework, Wadensjö (1998) proposes a reception format, which identifies three listener roles: reporter, recapitulator and responder. Wadensjö suggests that, as reporter, one may listen and memorise (for repetition) words just uttered by another speaker, as in a "say-after-me" language lesson. Alternatively, someone can listen as recapitulator and recapitulates what was said by the preceding speaker when he takes over the floor; finally, the person who listens as responder introduces content of his own or "back-channels" and gazes like a direct addressee. Back channelling is a part of conversation and speech. It is the part a listener plays in a conversation. There are both verbal and non-verbal back channelling signals. A non-verbal example of back channelling is a head nod. Throughout a conversation, the listener may nod their head periodically to show that they are listening. Another way to indicate attentiveness is through verbal signals such as *yeah*, *ok*, *uh* and *huh*.

Applying Goffman's "production" format, and her own "reception" format to interpreter-mediated encounters, Wadensjö (1998) suggests that an interpreter taking, or being given, a reporter's role in the reception format would be expected to speak only in the restricted sense of animator of someone else's speech; by taking or being given a recapitulator's role, an interpreter would be expected to speak as both animator and author of the production format; whereas interpreters taking the role of responder would relate to their talk as animator, author, principal and as the ultimate addressee, as in the case of clarifications with the preceding speaker. Wadensjö suggests that, in the course of interpreting, interpreters with the "mandate and responsibility to compose new versions of utterances", always take the reception role of recapitulator and thus the production role of animator and author.

Interpreter-initiated turns and the role of the interpreter

Corpus-based studies on interpreting in court and other community settings have proven that the notion of the court interpreter as a "conduit" is more of a myth than a reality. In a study of the American courts at various levels, Berk-Seligson (1990), for instance, found that interpreters played an active role: they interrupted and clarified with attorneys and witnesses the meaning of their utterances; they accounted for the side comments of witnesses and defendants; and they prompted the witness or defendant to speak (or otherwise silenced them). Thus, they drew attention to themselves and made themselves highly visible through the turns they assumed during the trial process.

Similarly, in her study of interpreter interruptions in South Wales (Australia) courtrooms, Hale (2001) argues that interpreter interruptions introduce the interpreter's own voice, rendering the interpreter more of an active participant than a mouthpiece of the interlocutors. Hale suggests that interpreter interruptions are unexpected by counsel; and they may interfere with questioning strategies or a line of questioning, taking away some of counsel's power and control over a witness.

In a study of asylum hearings in the Federal Asylum Office in Graz, Austria, Pöllabauer (2004) found that interpreters assumed an active role in the hearings by taking the initiative to elicit information they deemed necessary for the outcome of the hearings and omitting or condensing information they considered irrelevant. Other activities included seeking clarifications from the asylum seekers without asking for the investigating officers' approval, thus taking over the functions of the officers. All these studies and others (e.g. Angelelli 2003; Jacobsen, 2003; Roy, 2000; Wadensjö, 1998) demonstrate that interpreters, whether in legal or other community settings, take on a co-participant role in facilitating talk during an interpreted encounter.

Data and methodology

During court proceedings in Zimbabwe, all interpreter-assisted trials are audio-recorded. The audio files are later transcribed and filed in the language of the court, i.e. English. The testimonies of the accused or defence and witnesses are thus in the interpreted language and not in their first language(s). The data for our study are thus extracts from a corpus of court transcripts heard at two regional courts in Zimbabwe: Harare and Mutare. In Zimbabwean courtrooms, all serious cases, e.g. rape, are audio-recorded for record purposes and for review at the high court. With permission from the Chief Magistrate in the Judicial Service Commission, we as researchers were allowed to access audio-recorded interpreter-mediated interactions which, with the assistance of transcribers from the courts mentioned, were then transcribed into writing for purposes of analysis. The extracts presented in this chapter were carefully selected from 19 transcripts of cases involving alleged rape. The cases were heard in English (the official language of the court) which therefore necessitated the use of interpreters so as to allow speakers of other languages – witnesses and accused persons – to take part in the trial process. These extracts total 49 313 words. The study uses speakers' turns at talk as the unit of analysis; and the transcripts of the courtroom interactions are presented in this chapter using modified versions of Du Bois's (1991) transcription method for oral discourse, with annotation conventions from the Jeffersonian method (Jefferson, 2002). To enable a closer analysis of talk in interaction, Jefferson (2002) and Du Bois (1991) developed systems where specific symbols were used to transcribe:

- time, place and date of the original recording;
- participant identifications;
- words as spoken;
- sounds as uttered;
- inaudible or incomprehensible words or syllable;
- silences;
- overlapping speech and sounds; and
- prosodic features (how something is said) such as pace, stretching, stress and volume.

Borrowing from the two aforementioned systems, the researchers were able to transcribe interactions, using some of the symbols by Du Bois and Jefferson, which feature the following dimensions: turns at talk, prosody, vocalisms and other non-verbal features and events. In the interaction examples that follow in the rest of the chapter, a few of these symbols are demonstrated, as follows:

Table 9.1   Elements of transcription notation used in the Extracts

Symbol	Meaning
↑	Up arrow indicates rising pitch or intonation.
ALL CAPS	Capitalised text indicates shouted utterance, or increased volume of speech.
°	Degree symbol indicates whisper, reduced volume, or quiet speech.
((Italic text))	Italic text in double parentheses indicates annotation of non-verbal activity.

The language scenario that obtains in the Zimbabwean courtroom, where English is the official language of the court and where participants who are not conversant with the language of the court participate in the proceedings through an interpreter, reflects the assumption that "the English interpretation of the court interpreter is a faithful rendition of what has been said in the source language" (Berk-Seligson, 1999:31). However, Berk-Seligson finds this assumption unwarranted. It could be argued, quite to the contrary, that this approach in itself manifests an assumption that there may well exist a discrepancy between the interpreter's rendition and the source language version, and that different court players paying attention to different versions of the same testimony would necessarily come to different conclusions about the trial. In other words, this approach reflects the judicial view that the two versions are not necessarily "identical"; and it has been proven true, as is evidenced in studies, conducted over the past two decades, that have been devoted to the investigation of how court interpreters deal with the style of speakers in the courtroom (Berk-Seligson, 1990; Hale, 2004; Hale & Gibbons, 1999; Rigney, 1999).

Analytical framework

The data collected were analysed using the principles of discourse analysis and interpreting studies, in line with Mason's (2001) observation that the recent advances of research in interpreting studies (e.g. in the courtroom) has helped foster an understanding of the convoluted nature of interpreter-mediated interactions, the focus of our investigation. In the context of interpreter-mediated trials in Zimbabwean courtrooms, the interactions involve two primary interlocutors and an interpreter.

From methods of discourse analysis, the researchers were able to analyse the dynamics of interpreter-mediated interactive discourse (Roy, 1996). In particular, Critical Discourse Analysis (CDA) as an approach (Fairclough, 1992; Van Dijk, 1999; Wodak, 1984) provided the researchers with an analytical framework for analysing court interpreting as a social practice, and enabled a critical social standpoint. Another discourse analytic method from which the study drew insights is Goffman's (1981) participation framework. Goffman's discourse analytic method was used to examine how and why court interpreters may change their participant role during the course of interpreting, and how this may influence other co-present court interactants in the court proceedings. In the context of Goffman's participation framework, we make suggestions regarding the implementation of some of our findings in interpreter training. For instance, we address such questions as whether, when, and how interpreters should intervene during court proceedings. Our data analysis was informed by Goffman's (1981) analytical framework, together with methods of conversation analysis (with a special emphasis on turn-taking processes), the role of context, footing (which is how the speaker and the hearer align during the interpretation process), and other aspects of non-verbal communication, as well as the role of interactivity in face-to-face (interpreter-mediated) communication (Wadensjö, 1998).

The aforementioned discourse analytic methods, together with approaches rooted in pragmatics (see Tkacůkova, 2010), enabled us to analyse how hearers infer meaning during interpreter-mediated question-answer dialogues in the courtroom. Discourse analytic and pragmatic approaches were also used to analyse the strategies that a court interpreter may be assumed to resort to when confronted with an ambiguous situation in a source language utterance. This enabled us to discuss the implications of the inference process that court players undergo during court proceedings.

We also applied Brown and Levinson's (1987) aspects of politeness, which Halliday and Hassan (1976) refer to as "tenor" (and Mason and Stewart, 2001, term "face"), to the investigated interpreter-mediated interactions. According to Hale and Gibbons (1999), in the context of the courtroom, politeness is used for negotiating social relationships amongst participants. Politeness manifests in relations of status and these may be modified when interpreters change politeness strategies used by interactants, or when interpreters introduce changes in tenor absent in the source utterance. Thus, Hale and Gibbons (1999) argue that changes in politeness or tenor may cause changes in the pragmatic force of the interpreted text.

Finally, the above discourse analytic approaches were further complemented by approaches from interpreting studies. The researchers were able to extend Wadensjö's (1998) and Roy's (1996, 2000) "interpreting as interaction" approach by analysing the interpreters' role in Zimbabwean courtrooms beyond the "ideal interpreting norm" of "just translating" and included the function of "coordinating" the primary parties' utterances (Wadensjö, 1998:105). Such an approach acknowledges that the translating and coordinating aspects are simultaneously present in dialogue-interpreting encounters. The eclectic analytical approach adopted for this chapter helped the researchers weave more informed analyses about what interpreters do, and why they do what they do, in the context of their social, ethical and professional environment.

Results and discussion of interpreter-initiated turns

In the sections below, we use Berk-Seligson's (1990) and Hale's (2001) typologies as points of reference to identify and quantify the types of interpreter-initiated turns that were found to be recurring in the data. First, Table 9.2 presents a summary of the interpreter-initiated turns identified in the corpus. Figure 9.1 then graphically demonstrates the relative occurrence of the identified interpreter-initiated turns which were found to be recurring in the data. The examples presented and explained in Table 9.2 were part of a total of 21 interpreter-initiated turns that we identified in the corpus, with a distribution as shown in Table 9.2 and Figure 9.1.

TABLE 9.2 Types of interpreter-initiated turns and frequency of occurrence

Type of interpreter-initiated turns	Frequency of occurrence	Percentage of occurrence
Seek further information (TSFI)	7	33
Seek confirmation (TSCn)	4	19
Seek clarification (TSCl)	6	28
To prompt witness (TPW)	1	5
To identify speaker mistake (TIM)	1	5
To instruct witness/accused (TIWA)	1	5
To intervene in a conflict (TIC)	1	5

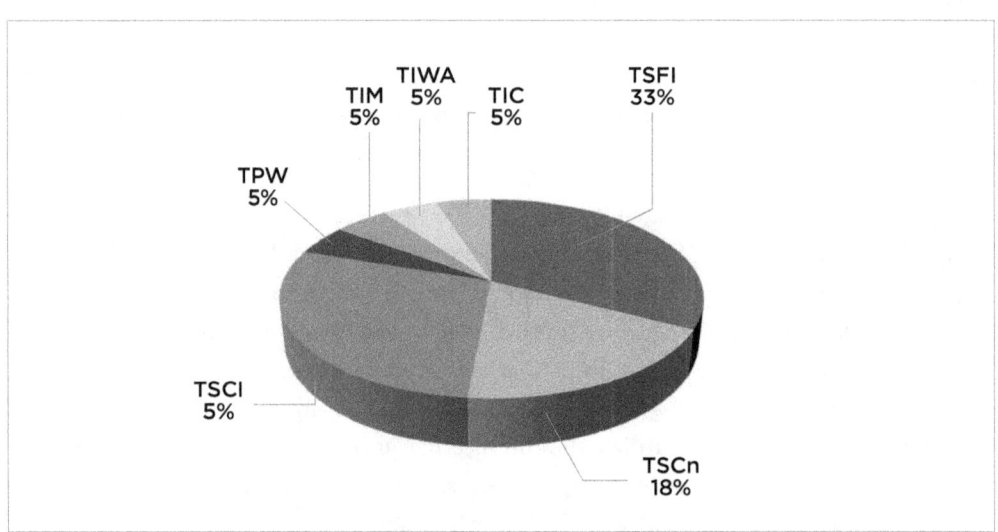

FIGURE 9.1 Relative occurrence of interpreter-initiated turns

In the following section, we illustrate and explain each sub-type of the identified interpreter-initiated turns.

Turns to seek clarification

Turns to seek clarification are used when the interpreter interrupts the proceedings frequently to clarify the meaning of the previous speaker's utterances.

EXTRACT 1 Turns to seek clarification

Legend: PP = Public Prosecutor; I = Interpreter; W = Witness

	Utterance	English gloss
PP	And did he completely remove your pants?	
I	*Saka pant wakaribvisa zvachose here kana kuti wakaridzikisa kana kudii* ↑	So did he completely remove your pants or he simply lowered them or what exactly did he do?
W	*Wakaribvisa.*	He took them off.
I	*Rese?* ↑	Completely?
W	*Ehe*	Yes
I	He completely removed my pants.	
PP	And then what happened next?	
I	*Ndokubva zvazoita sei?*	What then transpired?
W	*Wakavhara muromo wangu* and inserted his penis into my vagina ...	He blocked off my mouth and ...
I	*Akabva adii?* ↑	What did he do?
W	He inserted his penis into my vagina without an agreement with me.	
I	After covering my mouth, he inserted his penis into my vagina without my consent.	

EXTRACT 2 Turns to seek clarification

Legend: M = Magistrate; I = Interpreter; W = Witness

	Utterance	English gloss
M	What time of the day was it?	
I	*Dzakange dziri nguwai*	What time was it?
W	*Kuma two pm*	Around two pm
I	Around two pm	
W	*Ehe*	Yes
I	*Masikati?* ↑	In the afternoon?
W	*Ahh* two am	
I	Around two am instead, Your Worship	

The three **bolded** questions asked by the interpreters in Extracts 1 and 2 are clarification questions. The interpreters sought to clarify a certain position before proceeding and thus claimed another turn before it could be claimed by either the magistrate or the public prosecutor. In this example, the turns the interpreter assumed were aimed at clarifying issues with the witness and these demonstrate that, apart from just translating, interpreters also assume the responsibility of coordinating participants for whom they interpret. While these interpreter-initiated turns aimed at clarifying information seem to confirm Wadensjö's (1998) view that translating and coordinating aspects are simultaneously present in dialogue interpreting encounters, in a court of law, repeatedly requesting clarification from the witness may convey the impression that the witness is being evasive and uncooperative, which in turn, may affect the credibility of that witness. The interpreter therefore has to minimise the frequency with which he or she assumes such turns, to avoid jeopardising the witness's testimony.

Turns to seek further information

While the extracts provided illustrate interpreter-initiated turns to seek clarification, the next two examples illustrate interpreter-initiated turns to seek further information.

EXTRACT 3   Turns to seek further information
Legend: PP = Public Prosecutor; I = Interpreter; W = Witness

	Utterance	English gloss
PP	May you proceed and chronicle the events of the second time that accused had sexual intercourse with you.	
I	*Ko kechipiri kacho chiyi chakaitika?*	How about on the second encounter? What happened?
W	*Wakapindazve mu*bedroom *medu sepakutanga.*	He entered our bedroom like he did the first time.
I	*Wapinda ndokubva waita sei?* ↑	After entering what did he do?

EXTRACT 4   Turns to seek further information
Legend: M = Magistrate; I = Interpreter; A = Accused

	Utterance	English gloss
M	What are you alleging ↑ Are you alleging that this is what happened? Why are you not saying so? ↑	
I	*Uri kutii?* ↑ *Nemhaka yei uchizvitaura? Uri kuti ndizvo zvakaitika here kuti wakakurova?* ↑	What are you saying and why are you saying it? Are you saying this is what happened, that they assaulted you?
A	*Ndiri kutaura kuti wakandirova, kuti waindirova kuti ndibvume nyaya.*	I am saying they assaulted me so that I admit to committing the offence.

EXTRACT 4 Continued

	Utterance	English gloss
I	*Wana ani* ↑	Who exactly?
A	*Iwo ma*complainants.	The complainants.
I	Yes, Your Worship, the complainants were assaulting me forcing me to admit I had committed the offence.	
M	Who assaulted you? ↑	
I	*Akakurova ndiani? Reva kuti nhingi nanhingi.*	Who exactly assaulted you? Name the person.
A	*Babamunini wavo, anenge anonzi musoja.*	Their uncle who is said to be a soldier.
I	*Minin'ina wababa wemumhan'ari?* ↑	Is he young brother to the accused?
A	*Ehe.*	Yes.
I	The complainant's uncle, her father's younger brother who is a soldier.	

In any interpreter-mediated interaction, problems of communication, such as incomplete, ambiguous or unclear responses, do arise from time to time, and thus the need for clarification is sometimes unavoidable. It is, therefore, unrealistic to prescribe, as the conduit model of interpreting does, that interpreters should under no circumstances clarify an issue with the speaker. The interpreter in the aforementioned triadic exchange exercises control over the ongoing interaction and asks the witness a follow-up question, shown in the **bolded** phrases of Extracts 3 and 4 above, for further information before interpreting her utterance, possibly in an attempt to make a more complete and grammatically adequate rendition, although such utterances could still have been interpreted without the requested information. The discourse function of questions is to seek information on a specific point (Quirk et al., 1985), from a CDA point of view; however, this seeking is not always unbiased or neutral, because questions can be formed in a way that shows bias of expectation to a given response. For this reason, questions may be conducive, i.e. they may indicate that the speaker is predisposed to the kind of answer he wants or expects. When the interpreter does so, he or she effectively takes on the examining role by controlling not only the form, but also the content, of the interaction.

However, an interpreter who initiates too many turns to seek further information may be evaluated adversely as lacking competence. With this in mind, too many interpreter-initiated turns aimed at gaining further information should be avoided where possible. It is therefore essential that student interpreters are taught when and how to intervene. For instance, trainee interpreters may be advised to use interpreter-initiated turns aimed at seeking further information when:

- there is a clear case of ambiguity;
- when a question or request from the accused or witness arises and requires the interpreter's immediate action;

- in cases where the witness or accused person is inaudible; and
- when the witness or accused person does not respond to a magistrate or judge's question.

Turns to seek confirmation

Most of the interpreter-initiated turns occurring during the witness's examination-in-chief are confirmation turns used by the interpreter to check her understanding of the witness's utterance by repeating or rephrasing what is said by the witness – they are also the second most frequently used type of interpreter-initiated turns in the witness's cross-examination. In Extract 5, the interpreter takes over from the magistrate and asks two questions to seek confirmation. These questions are indicated by superscripted numbers 1, 2 and 3 respectively.

On the surface, it would appear that the interpreter is making use of these turns to check the accused's understanding of the magistrate's meaning; but it may well be the case that the interpreter uses these turns as a delaying strategy to "buy time" to reformulate her interpretation. As shown in the extract, the interpreter's first turn is immediately followed by her second rendition, without waiting for the witness's confirmation.

EXTRACT 5 Turns to seek confirmation

Legend: PP = Public Prosecutor; M = Magistrate; I = Interpreter; A = Accused

	Utterance	English gloss
PP	Thank you, Your Worship. What is contained there actually is his previous record and can be read, with due respect.	
M	Thank you. Give it to the interpreter please.	
M	(to interpreter) If the record may be read in respect of accused person two.	
I	[1]*Ndinoda kuti uteerere musungwa wechipiri nezvemhosva yawakabatwa nayo ukatoipika mumashure inowa CRB nhamba ...*	I want you to listen carefully accused two about your previous conviction which is CRB number ...
I	[2]*Wanzwa zvandakuverengeraka iwe K.?*	Did you understand what I read in connection with you, K.?
A	*Hongu.*	Yes.
I	[3]*Ndizvoka kuti wakabatwa ukatopikira mhosva iyoyi?* ↑	It is true that you were convicted and served a jail term for this previous crime?
A	*Hongu.*	Yes.

When the interpreter takes over the role of questioning as shown here, he/she assumes greater control and assumes the power of the court officials to ask questions. Questioning is one aspect that differentiates courtroom exchanges from everyday conversation because, when one speaker is given the right to question and another can only respond, an imbalance in power is created. When the interpreter assumes the questioning role, he or she assumes the power to persuade and influence other participants' behaviour (Gibbons, 2003). This potential influence can be achieved through the inclusion of desired information in the question and then structuring the question in a way that makes it difficult to deny. In this way, the interpreter would have control over both the information and the answer.

Turns to prompt the witness

Prompting mostly occurs after the interpreter has rendered an obviously unfinished utterance by the witness. This can be seen as a repair strategy on the part of the interpreter, as in Extract 6, where the interpreter starts interpreting before the witness is able to finish her turn.

EXTRACT 6 Turns to prompt witness or accused
Legend: M = Magistrate; I = Interpreter; A = Accused

	Utterance	English gloss
M	To start with, accused, were you ever served with a copy of this medical report? ↑	
I	*Chekutanga wakamboratidzwa kana kupiwa gwaro iri*, medical report *iyi*? ↑	First of all, were you served or at least shown this document, the medical report?
A	*Kwete Ndatopuhwa izvozvi ndakagara pano.*	No, I have just received it now while sitting here.
I	No Your Worship, I only received it today when I was seated here in court	
A	*Zvakare tichiri ipapo* medical report *iyoyo* ...	Still regarding that medical report ...
I	Besides regarding this medical report ...	
I	Medical report *iyoyo ehe* ...	Yes, that medical report ...
A	... *ndinopokana nayo semaziwire andinoitawo mutemo.*	I disapprove of it based on my own understanding of the law.
I	... I object to the medical report based on how I understand the law.	

After rendering her answer in English, the interpreter recapitulates it in Shona: "Medical report *iyoyo ehe* ..." (Yes, that medical report ...) for the witness, as a reminder of what the witness has said, and before prompting her to carry on with her testimony. The interpreter may have deemed it necessary to prompt the witness to go on with her testimony, knowing very well that the turn might be taken over by the examining officer.

Part 3 | Language as evidence

Turns to instruct the witness or accused

In Extract 7, we illustrate interpreter-initiated turns intended to instruct the witness and the accused person.

EXTRACT 7   Turns to instruct the witness or accused
Legend: M = Magistrate; I = Interpreter; W = Witness

	Utterance	English gloss
M	((*Gesturing to the witness to keep quiet*)) That is not for her to answer. It is for the police to answer to that.	
I	*Mubvunzo iwowo hawangaupinduri ungatopindurwa nemapurisa.*	That question is not for her to respond to but rather the police
W	*Aiwa ndinopindura mibvunzo Ndinofanira kutomupindura.*	No, I will respond to the questions. I have an obligation to answer him.
I	*Imbomirai imi mhamha.*	Just wait, mother.
M	Madam, be patient. We are the court. We know what evidence has to be led here. You understand?	
I	*Munofanirwa kuziwa kuti isu ndisu tinenge tichiziwa zvamunenge muchifanirwa kuti mupindure nezvamusingakwanisi Handiti manzwisisa?* ↑	You should know that it is up to us to determine which questions you should respond to or not. Do you understand that?

EXTRACT 8   Turns to instruct the witness or accused
Legend: A = Accused; I = Interpreter; W = Witness

	Utterance	English gloss
A	*Kusvika kumasix baba wangu pawakadzoka nemotokari.*	Up to around 6 pm when my father came back home in his car.
I	Up to about 6pm when my father returned driving his vehicle.	
W	*Ndodaira here?*	Should I respond to that?
I	*Pindurai henyu.*	Respond to that.
W	*Ndine mubvunzo wekuti paati baba wangu ...*	I have a question relating to her earlier allegation that his father ...
I	*Musabvunze Ino inguwa yekuti mungopindure zvabvunzwa.*	Do not ask question. At this point just respond to what has been asked.

In Extracts 7 and 8, the interpreter assumes the court's power by intervening during the interactions to direct the witnesses about the appropriate course of action to take during a cross-examination. In Extract 7, for instance, the magistrate realised that the question asked by the accused was only relevant if it were directed at the police and not at the witness. However, the witness insisted she was supposed to answer every question, including the irrelevant ones, to which the interpreter intervened by saying "*Imbomirai imi mhamha*"

(Just wait, mother). In Extract 8, the witness directs a question to the court when she says "*Ndodaira here?*" (Should I respond to that?); instead of interpreting the question to the court, the interpreter provides a response: "*Pindurai henyu*" (Respond to that). However, instead of providing a response to the question asked, the witness asks another question and the interpreter again intervenes and directs the witness not to ask questions, but to provide answers to questions, as expected during cross-examination. In the course of these exchanges, the magistrate's voice disappears and the interpreter once again assumes the court's role of issuing directives and making decisions.

When the interpreter assumes the magistrate's role of giving instructions and making decisions, contrary to the conduit model of interpreting, the interpreter can achieve control of the witness and the accused persons by structuring the instructions in ways that may restrict the extant range of possible behaviours. The interpreter could also manipulate the modality of instructions, with this varying from very polite to very brusque. The choice of instruction modality (i.e. the strength with which an instruction is given) depends on the power relations between two people, with more powerful individuals expecting compliance with their instructions (Gibbons, 2003).

Finally, from the extract, apart from his or her role as a primary participant, the interpreter assumes much latitude in negotiating meaning with the speaker. This is what Wadensjö (1998) refers to as translating and coordinating aspects of dialogue-interpreting encounters. In the preceding cases, the interpreter ceases to be the voice of the key interlocutors, but speaks in his or her own voice, combining the roles of animator, author and principal, in Goffman's (1981) production format; and as reporter, recapitulator and responder, in Wadensjö's (1998) reception format. By initiating talk with the witness, he or she has also made herself a direct addressee of the witness's response.

Turns to intervene in a conflict

Apart from the interpreter-initiated turns, interpreters were also found to initiate turns aimed at helping to resolve a conflict, as shown in the next extract.

EXTRACT 9 Turns to intervene in a conflict

Legend: M = Magistrate; I = Interpreter; W = Witness; A = Accused

	Utterance	English gloss
A	Do you recall that you said you were sleeping next to M?	
I	*Uchiri kuyeuka kuti wamboti wanga wakarara pedyo naM?*	Do you still remember that you have already said you were sleeping next to M?
M	(to witness) Who retired to bed first? ↑	
I	*Ndiani* ↑ *akatanga kurara?*	Who went to bed first?

EXTRACT 9 Continued

	Utterance	English gloss
W	*Takatanga kurara.*	We went first.
I	We slept first before accused.	
A	*Hausi kutaura chokwadi.*	You are not telling the truth.
I	You are not telling the truth.	
W	*NDIMI MURI KUTONYEPA.* We went first.	IT IS YOU WHO IS LYING INSTEAD. We went first.
I	*NDIMI MURI KUTONYEPA tisu. Takatanga kurara. Zvisinei, hamufaniri kuitisana nharo Chenyu kubvunzana nekupindurana chete Zviri kudare kuona chokwadi kana manyepo.*	IT'S YOU WHO IS LYING. We were the first to go to bed. Nevertheless, you two should not argue about issues here. Your responsibility is limited to asking and responding to questions only. It is the court's duty to decide on what is true and what is false.
A	Would someone come and fit where you were sleeping?	

In this extract featuring cross-examination of a state witness by the accused, a conflict situation emerged between the accused person and the witness regarding which of the two had retired to bed first. Although the interpreter continued to interpret as expected, she went beyond her role of relaying messages by intervening in the conflict, reminding the two parties of their responsibilities and that of the court – to judge which of them was telling the truth or lying: "*Zvisinei, hamufaniri kuitisana nharo Chenyu kubvunzana nekupindurana chete Zviri kudare kuona chokwadi kana manyepo*" (Nevertheless, you two should not argue about issues here. Your responsibility is limited to asking and responding to questions only. It is the court's duty to decide on what is true and what is false). This reminder is contained in the interpreter's last rendition above.

While the power to intervene in a conflict situation is normally the preserve of the magistrate or judge and not the interpreter, it is interesting to note that the interpreter in the last exchange assumes that power. According to Gibbons (2003:75), "the justice system is arguably the most directly powerful institution in societies subject to the rule of law". Because interaction in the courtroom is mainly linguistic, the researchers note that an important manifestation of power relations is language behaviour. In the extract, the interpreter wields this power by taking over the role of reminding the witness and the accused persons of what to do or not do in the court. In sociology, power is defined as the ability of an individual or a group of individuals to carry out their will, even in the face of resistance from others; and it includes the ability to control the behaviour of others, at times against their will (Giddens, 2009). With regard to discourse, Wang (2006:531) notes that, "Power can be characterised as the ability to control and constrain others; as the capacity to achieve one's aim; as the freedom to achieve one's goals and as the competence to impose one's will on others." According to Fairclough (1989), power exists in various modalities, with physical force (or violence) being just one of these modalities. More subtle and perhaps more difficult to detect, is power exercised "through the manufacture of consent to or at least acquiescence towards it" (Fairclough, 1989:4). Fairclough further argues that language is one of the means through which inequality in the distribution of power is created and perpetuated, and through which this inequality can be remedied. This is because it is through the use of language, especially in institutional settings, that conventions are created; and, through their recurrence, that conventions are developed into ways of behaving that are deemed correct.

In the context of the definitions of power provided by Giddens (2009), Wang (2006), and Fairclough (1989), in the aforementioned interaction the interpreter (who is averagely powerful) assumes the role of the most powerful interactant in the courtroom (i.e. the magistrate) as, through the use of language, she intervenes in a conflict situation and demands that the less powerful interactants (i.e. the accused and witness) conduct themselves in ways deemed proper by the court.

Turns to identify a speaker mistake

Data from the transcripts also revealed that 5% of the interpreter-initiated turns were directed at identifying a speaker's mistake. This could be argued to be in line with court interpreters' primary objective, namely, to achieve successful communication. Extract 10 is the first example to illustrate this.

EXTRACT 10 Turns to identify speaker mistake
Legend: PP = Public Prosecutor; I = Interpreter; W = Witness

	Utterances	English gloss
PP	But you have already testified in this court that you reported the matter to the police in September who then asked you to take the child to the doctor for medical examination.	
I	° Your Worship, with due respect I wish to correct you on the correct month the matter was reported. The witness said August and not September.	
PP	(to witness and interpreter) My apologies for the error madam. Can you go ahead and interpret to her with the correct month in context.	

EXTRACT 10 Contined

	Utterances	English gloss
I	IMI maziwisa dare muno nechekare kuti mhosva iyi makaimhan'ara kumapurisa muna August iwo mapurisa achibva ati muende kuchipatara nemwana kuti aongororwe	YOU have already told the court that you reported this crime to the police in August and the police advised you to take the child to the hospital for examination.
W	Ndizvozvo, asi wakange uri musi wa31 Saka patazoenda rechimangwana racho tanga tatobata September	Yes, it is true but it was on the last day of August. When we took the child to the hospital on the following day it was already the first day of September.
I	Yes, Your Worship but the report was made on the last day of August. When we took the child to the hospital the following day it was already on the first of September.	

In the example, the court has made an obvious mistake about the date on which the accused person made her statement to the police. As the month in question was August, not September, the interpreter is sure that the public prosecutor has made a mistake and alerts him to it in a whisper. The interpreter's intervention in this case is presumably to avoid the confusion which might be attributed to the witness if the mistake is preserved in the rendition. This might also be regarded as the interpreter's face-saving strategy, because any confusion caused by the court might be seen later as an interpreting problem. In any case, this is evidence that the interpreter does not regard herself as a copying machine (the conduit myth), but one who plays an active role in coordinating talk and facilitating communication, taking into consideration the participant roles of court actors, as well as the consequences of their power and control over the triadic communication.

However, interpreter interruptions of this kind, if allowed to take place frequently, may interfere with the magistrate's questioning strategies or line of questioning, taking away some of the magistrate's inherent power and thus control over the testimony of the witness. While the example of the interpreter's intrusive behaviour did not have an immediate effect on the ongoing interaction, court officials, witnesses and accused persons who are interrupted by the interpreter more frequently may be deemed to be less competent, credible and trustworthy. In addition, an interpreter who interrupts too often might suffer negative appraisal, judged by others in the courtroom as incompetent and unprofessional.

Conclusion

This chapter has analysed different court players' frequency and use of different conversational features, as well as how these were interpreted by court interpreters during court proceedings. We analysed the occurrence of interpreter-initiated turns to explain how different court players strategically use various aspects of language in the courtroom and how these aspects are interpreted during trials. The researchers have illustrated that, through the use of various types of interpreter-initiated turns, the power of a participant, and thus his or her control over a triadic exchange, is realised not only in the role(s) he or she is capable of playing, but also through the roles of the co-present court actors.

We have illustrated how and why the participant role assumed by the interpreter inevitably influences the court proceedings in one way or another. On the one hand, by assuming a primary participant role in the proceedings through interrupting a speaker to seek clarification or further information, or even to intervene in a conflict, the interpreter takes away some of the inherent power of the magistrate or prosecutor and hence may exercise greater control over the discourse in the courtroom. On the other hand, by adhering strictly to the prescribed role as mouthpiece for the key court players and refraining from clarifying anything the speaker says, even in the face of ambiguous and contradictory utterances, the interpreter risks misinterpreting the speaker's meaning and may, as a result, be accused by the court of being incompetent and unprofessional.

In light of the above dilemma, the researchers therefore argue that, by assuming roles other than "relaying" utterances, the interpreter can become an active and more influential player in the triadic speech event, as well as a critical actor in successful communication. However, although interpreters, like other interlocutors, should be given the right to clarify ambiguous situations in the course of their interpreting, through assuming interpreter-initiated turns, they should also be well informed about how to exercise this right and be warned of the potential impact of their interventions.

Further, the extracts presented here peripherally suggest that an interpreter, working with bilingual court officials and interpreting for bilingual lay people, sees his or her power considerably reduced by these other bilinguals (the magistrate and the public prosecutor, on one hand, and the witness(es) and accused on the other). These bilingual court players for whom the interpreter interprets take on not only the roles of speakers (questioners) and addressees of witnesses' interpreted evidence, but also of overhearers of the witnesses' answers and then judges of the accuracy of the interpretation. However, we see this interesting situation as an essential, naturally occurring, check-and-balance mechanism that is critical in the continuous evaluation of the interpreter's quality of work. Trainee interpreters in Zimbabwe can therefore be forewarned that the presence of other bilinguals in the courtroom essentially means that the quality of their work is always under scrutiny.

The findings discussed illustrate changes in the pragmatic force in the interpreter's renditions of court officials' strategically formulated questions. These findings show that court officials' power to manipulate questions in order to exercise control over witnesses' answers can be reduced, or even lost, when the questioning is performed through an interpreter. The findings presented in this chapter seem to corroborate earlier findings by Hale (2001) who points out that a way counsel may lose control of the evidence is when interpreters move away from their strict role as mouthpiece to become active participants, by interrupting the proceedings and thus assuming "power by virtue of the control they take away from the examining lawyer or the witness" (Hale, 2001:1). In other words, when the interpreter does not adhere to his or her prescribed role as a mere "conduit" of words; when he or she assumes a more active role in interrupting and negotiating meanings with the speaker, or responding to questions from witnesses; when he or she casts him- or herself in a lawyer-like position, counsel may lose to the interpreter some of their "legal base of power".

References

Anderson, R. & Bruce, W. 2002. Perspective on the role of the interpreter. In: F. Pöchhacker & M. Shlesinger (eds.), *The interpreting studies reader*. London: Routledge. pp. 234-251.

Angelelli, C. 2003. The interpersonal role of the interpreter in cross-cultural communication: A survey of conference, court and medical interpreters in the US, Canada and Mexico. In: L. Brunette, G. Bastin, I. Hemlin & H. Clarke (eds.), *The critical link 3: Interpreters in the community*. Selected papers from the third international conference on interpreting in legal, health and social service settings, Montréal, Quebec, Canada 22-26 May 2001. Amsterdam: John Benjamins. pp. 15-26.

Berk-Seligson, S. 1990. *The bilingual courtroom: Court interpreters in the judicial process*. Chicago: University of Chicago Press.

Berk-Seligson, S. 1999. The impact of court interpreting on the coerciveness of leading questions. *Forensic Linguistics*, 6(1):30-56.

Brown, P. & Levinson, S. 1987. *Politeness*. Cambridge: Cambridge University Press.

Cotterill, J. 2003. *Language and power in court*. New York: Palgrave Macmillan.

De Jongh, E. 1992. *An introduction to court interpreting: Theory and practice*. Lanham MD: University Press of America.

Du Bois, J.W. 1991. Transcription design principles for spoken discourse research. *Pragmatics*, 1(1):71-106.

Fairclough, N. 1989. *Language and power*. London: Longman.

Fairclough, N. 1992. *Discourse and social change*. Cambridge: Polity Press.

Gibbons, J. 2008. Questioning in common law criminal courts. In: J. Gibbons & M.T. Turell, *Dimensions of forensic linguistics*. Amsterdam: John Benjamin. pp. 115-130.

Giddens, A. 2009. *Sociology*. 6th Edition. Cambridge: Polity Press.

Goffman E. 1981. *Forms of talk*. Oxford: Blackwell.

González, R.D.; Vasquez, V.F. & Mikkelson, H. 1991. *Fundamentals of court interpretation. Theory, policy, and practice*. Durham NC: Carolina Academic Press.

Hale, S. 2001. The complexities of the bilingual courtroom. *Law Society Journal*, 39:68-72.

Hale, S. 2002. How faithfully do court interpreters render the style of non-English speaking witnesses' testimonies? A data-based study of Spanish-English bilingual proceedings, *Discourse Studies*, 4(1):25-47. https://doi.org/10.1177/14614456020040010201

Hale, S. 2004. *The discourse of court interpreting: Discourse practices of the law, the witness and the interpreter*. Amsterdam: John Benjamins.

Hale, S. & Gibbons, J. 1999. Varying realities: Patterned changes in the interpreter's representation of courtroom and external realities. *Applied Linguistics*, 20(2):203-220. https://doi.org/10.1093/applin/20.2.203

Halliday, M.A.K. & Hasan, R. 1976. *Cohesion in English*. London: Longman.

Hoffman, J. 1994. *A guide to interpreting in judicial proceedings*. Harare: Government Printers.

Jacobsen, B. 2003. Pragmatics in court interpreting: Additions. In: L. Brunette, G. Bastin, I. Hemlin & H. Clarke (eds.), *The Critical Link 3. Interpreters in the community*. Selected papers from the third international conference on interpreting in legal, health and social service settings, Montréal, Quebec, 22-26 May 2001. Amsterdam: John Benjamins. pp. 223-238.

Jefferson, G. 2002. Is 'no' an acknowledgement token? Comparing American and British uses of (+)/(-) tokens. *Journal of Pragmatics*, 34(10/11):1345-1383.

Koo, A. 2009. Truth through court interpreters. *International Journal of Evidence & Proof*, 13:212-224.

Mason, I (ed.). 2001. *Triadic exchanges: Studies in dialogue interpreting*. Manchester: St Jerome.

Mason, I. & Stewart, M. 2001. Interactional pragmatics, face and the dialogue interpreter. In: I. Mason (ed.), *Triadic exchanges: Studies in dialogue interpreting*. Manchester: St Jerome. pp. 51-70.

Mikkelson, H. 2000. *Introduction to court interpreting*. Manchester: St. Jerome/Routledge.

Morris, R. 2010. Images of the court interpreter: Professional identity, role definition and self-image. *Translation and Interpreting Studies*, 5(1):20-40.

National Association of Judiciary Interpreters and Translators. 2016. *The notion of accuracy in interpreting*. http://www.najit.org [Retrieved 20 December 2018].

Ng, E. 2009. The tension between adequacy and acceptability in legal interpreting and translation. In: S. Hale, U. Ozolins & L. Stern (eds.), *The critical link 5: Quality interpreting – a shared responsibility*. Amsterdam: John Benjamins. pp. 37-54.

Pöllabauer, S. 2004. Interpreting in asylum hearings. *Interpreting: International journal of research and practice in interpreting*, 6(2):143-180.

Quirk, R.; Greenbaum, S.; Leech, G. & Stravik, J. 1985. *A comprehensive grammar of the English language*. London: Longman.

Rigney, A.C. 1999. Questioning in interpreted testimony. *Forensic Linguistics*, 6(1):83-108.

Roy, C.B. 1996. An interactional sociolinguistic analysis of turn-taking in an interpreted event. *Interpreting: International journal of research and practice in interpreting*, 1(1):39-67. https://doi.org/10.1075/intp.1.1.04roy

Roy, C.B. 2000. *Interpreting as a discourse process*. New York: Oxford.

Tkacůkova, T. 2010. Representing oneself: Cross-examination questioning – Lay people as cross-examiners. In: M. Coulthard & A. Johnson (eds.), *The Routledge handbook of forensic linguistics*. New York: Routledge. pp. 333-346.

Van Dijk, T.A. 1999. Critical discourse analysis and conversation analysis. *Discourse & Society*, 10(4):459-460.

Wadensjö, C. 1998. *Interpreting as interaction*. London: Longman.

Walker, A.G. 1987. Linguistic manipulation, power and the legal setting. In: L. Kedar (ed.), *Power through discourse*. Norwood NJ: Ablex Publishing. pp. 57-80.

Wang, J. 2006. Questions and the exercise of power. *Discourse & Society*, 17(4):529-548.

Wodak, R. 1984. Determination of guilt: Discourse in the courtroom. In: C.S. Kramarae, M. Schulz & W.M. O'Barr (eds.), *Language and power*. Beverly Hills CA: Sage. pp. 89-100.

Woodbury, H. 1984. The strategic use of questions in court. *Semiotica*, 48(3-4):197-228.

CONFLICTS EMANATING FROM THE TRANSLATION AND INTERPRETATION OF THE TERM "DOMICILE"

For consumers in the South African context

Stanley Madonsela

Introduction

The main intention of this chapter is to amplify the legal implications stemming from the inappropriate translation and interpretation of the legal concept of "domicile", and the potential impact of this on consumers, whose rights to be granted credit are in this way compromised. When consumers find their right to apply for credit in terms of Section 60 of South Africa's National Credit Act (NCA) being repudiated, it is often because they have been listed with credit bureaus, as a result of not receiving any notice of the intention to list them.

This chapter further argues that the translation of the word "domicile" in various available resources typically does not provide for a full understanding of the concept. The translation and interpretation of texts in the field of law sometimes poses problems since law is a culture-dependent subject field. When translating a legal text, the legal system in which the source text (ST) is grounded should be considered, as it is structured in a manner that suits the culture concerned, and this is reflected in the legal language used. Similarly, it is assumed that the target text (TT) will be read by a person who is familiar with the legal system corresponding to the jurisdiction for which the TT is prepared. Since the term and concept of "domicile" constitutes an important connecting factor in issues pertaining to private-law status in South Africa, I seek here to disinter the factors that bring about conflict emanating from the translation and interpretation of this concept relative to the South African legal system.

In recent decades, researchers in the field of translation studies have seen a shift in their understanding of translation, in the traditional sense, in step with developments that have taken place in other disciplines. Translation is no longer viewed simply as a cross-linguistic activity, but rather as an essential tool for inter-disciplinary communication. There is also no longer an automatic assumption that a person who speaks two or more languages well, will be able to translate between them with ease. In the legal field in particular, in fact, the appropriate understanding and rendering of a text is more likely to hinge on interpretation than on purely semantic differences. Meanwhile, the mistranslation of a concept or clause in a contract could lead to litigation and loss of money. The term "domicile" is a case in point. Since an incorrect translation and interpretation of this term could potentially lead to lawsuits being instituted or to other legal action being taken, it is important that, where the term is employed, it is clearly defined, along with the rights and duties of the parties involved, to ensure the precise correspondence of these rights and duties as they appear in both the source text (ST) and in the translation.

This chapter argues that, whilst the work of legal translation is not necessarily linguistically transparent, the translator has to be guided by certain standards of linguistic, social and cultural equivalents between the languages used in the ST and TT in order for the TT to be accurate. This is discussed with particular relevance to the inappropriate translation and interpretation of the concept of "domicile", which has led to prejudice to the consumer, and also results in a decrease in consumer spending; which in South Africa is one of the key drivers of the economy. Since simple translation of the concept "domicile" does not provide for a full understanding of its legal implications, we need to re-examine the definition, in a bid to mitigate the implications of not rendering its actual meaning correctly.

The field of translation

Literature on translation

The shift in translation studies from linguistics to other forms of communication is closely connected to the development of the discipline of Translation Studies as a critical tool – as much in the legal field as in others. That Translation Studies has become a complex field with wide-ranging relevance, can be seen in reviews of the literature dedicated to translation competence (see, for instance, Orozco, 2000; Rothe-Neves, 2007; Schäffner & Adab, 2000). In the area of translator education and training, what makes a translator "competent" is a factor of primary concern. Toury (2001) focused on differentiating between different types of translation, such as semantic translation, adaptive translation and communicative translation, to mention but a few. The translation of text requires more than accurate rendering from one language to another: amongst other characteristics, it requires an understanding of the metonymic of a translation and its function in a culture (Even-Zohar, 1990; Kelly, 2005); the construction of similarity (Arduini & Hodgson, 2004; Tymoczko, 2007); and it must be linked to the appropriate strategies of form and content (Hatim & Munday, 2004).

Theoretical framework

A number of theories of translation derive from scholars who also work in comparative literature and, for that reason, comparative literature and translation studies are housed within a single programme in many institutions. Though there have been a number of attempts to arrive at an integrated theory of translating, linguists and translation theorists are still in doubt about such a possibility. The idea behind the creation of an integrated theory of translation is of great importance, as it would suggest systematised methods and procedures used in translation: what translators have had to say about their art/craft/science; how translations have been evaluated during different periods; what kinds of recommendations translators have made; or how translation has been taught; and how this discourse is related to other discourses of the same period (Baker, 2006). There seems to be no unanimity on the role played by theory in translation practice. In this regard, some academics who work on translation have adopted the view that "theory" has no place in most university translation programmes, going so far as to declare that it should be discarded in favour of more practical work. However, such a view is easily countered, both as scientifically and empirically unfounded, as well as on the basis that any translation programme requires some sort of principled theoretical background to guide practice. In this regard, Bahumaid (1996), writing in the context of his own environment, considers the lack of a theoretical component as a serious drawback in most Arab university translation programmes.

Translation theory concerns itself with determining suitable translation methods for the widest possible range of texts or text-categories (Newmark, 1981). A translation theory should be concerned with translation strategies adopted to address difficulties and problems in complicated texts. The observation by Nida (1976) indicates that, because translation is an activity involving language, there is a sense in which any and all theories of translation are linguistic. He suggests a three-stage model of the translation process. In this model, ST surface elements (grammar, meaning, connotations) are *analysed* as linguistic kernel structures that can be *transferred* to the target language (TL) and *restructured* to form TL surface elements. This linguistic approach bears some similarities to Chomsky's (1980) theory of syntax and transformational generative grammar. Apposite to linguistic theories is Newmark's (1981) binary classification of translation into semantic and communicative aspects, which somehow resembles Nida's formal and dynamic equivalence. Newmark (1981) avers that communicative translation attempts to produce in its readers an effect as close as possible to that obtained by the original. Semantic translation, on the other hand, attempts to render an effect as close to the exact contextual meaning of the original as the semantic and syntactic structures of the second language allow.

Comprehending translation in context

> Translation can be regarded as a legitimate offspring of the phenomenon of language since, originally, when humans migrated over the earth, their languages differed, so they needed a means by which people speaking a certain language could interact with others who spoke a different language. (Abdellah, 2002)

Despite this affirmation of "legitimacy", our discussion thus far indicates that translation has been defined differently in different contexts and that each definition reflects the theoretical approach underpinning it. The translation phenomenon has been variously delimited by formal descriptions, echoing the frameworks of the scholars proposing them (El-dadi, 2011). In addition, scholars view translation as a representation or reproduction of thoughts from an original to a target source (see Brooks-Lewis, 2009; House, 2008; Malmkjær, 2005; Manfredi, 2008; Zakhir, 2008). What seems to be a common view amongst scholars of translation is that the purpose of translation is the rendering of the original text (ST) in the language of the TT. In other words, as Bell (1991) avers, it is the *transformation* of a text originally in one language into an equivalent text in a different language while retaining, as far as is possible, the content of the message and the formal features and functional roles of the original text.

Contextualising "domicile" as a term

Dictionary definition of "domicile"

This brings us to consideration of the term "domicile", which is a translation into English from the Latin term *domicilium*, meaning "residence, home, dwelling, abode" (*Latdict*). Yet we find it has different meanings in different contexts. For the purposes of jurisdiction, "domicile" refers to the legal dwelling or place of residence at which a person has his or her fixed or permanent home. While the term is often used interchangeably with "residence", and while the two terms are related, they may not mean the same thing in the context of legal dealings. Although "residence" does refer to the place where a person is living, it does not necessarily refer to this being a permanent arrangement. "Domicile", however, refers definitively to a place where a person intends to settle permanently. In an attempt to provide a clearer understanding of the two concepts, it can be said that a person can have only one "domicile", but multiple residences. The term "domicile" is a general term which applies mostly to matters such as the serving of legal process and the validity of wills and intestacy law. However, in the translation of this term from the Latin, *domicilium*, there is confusion, which often leads to the incorrect interpretation of it.

What help might the consumer hope to get from consulting an ordinary dictionary? It would seem that dictionaries for a general readership do not cater for the legal meaning of the term. Even between two classic isiZulu dictionaries, one bilingual and the other monolingual, the term "domicile" is defined differently. By Doke, Malcolm and Sikakana (1972), in their isiZulu-English dictionary, it is defined as *ikhaya* (home) and as *indawo lapho kuhlalwa khona* (a place to stay). Mbatha (2006), in his monolingual dictionary, defines the same word, *ikhaya*, as:

1. *indawo lapho umuntu ezalwa khona* (a person's birth place);
2. *umuzi lapho umuntu ehlala khona* (a place to stay); and
3. *indawo enabantu abakhe kuyo* (a place with people living in it).

These definitions have lent meaning to the term, but without providing the full legal understanding of it. They have somehow created the impression that the term refers to "any place" where a person lives. A consumer relying on such a definition, when a contract is signed between consumer and credit provider, or between the consumer and a merchant, may easily provide an incorrect address, not understanding the significance of the requirement.

Indeed, definitions used in any particular discipline tend to reflect an understanding which is suited to the focus and scope of that discipline.

Comprehending "domicile" in the legal framework

As noted, whereas the simple dictionary definition of "domicile" pegs it as a place of residence, the term also has a specific legal meaning. The legal definition is not contained in statute law, but rather has developed through a long line of cases. "Domicile", which is normally referred to as *domicilium* in legal usage, is not a concept unique to South African law: it is widely used throughout the world in the area of common law and serves as a connecting factor between the fields of jurisdiction and choice of law. However, the apparent uniformity regarding the use of the concept in the common law "family" is deceptive, since *domicilium* has acquired an own identity in the several jurisdictions constituting this family of laws, both as regards how the concept is interpreted and how it has developed. *Domicilium* as a legal application had its early origins in Roman law and was developed and adapted to meet the needs of a growing Roman Empire. Once it had been well and truly established as a connecting factor for conflict-of-laws purposes, it was Dutch law that provided clear definitions of "domicile". Dutch jurist Johannes Voet (1698-1704) provides a clearer understanding of the concept of "domicile" by explaining it in terms of one's intention to settle permanently:

> Everyone can also be sued by virtue of domicile, in the place, that is to say, in which he has set up his home and the main body of his property and fortunes, from which he is not likely to depart if nothing calls him away, and which when he has left he appears to be travelling abroad. (Gane, 1955)

This legally constituted definition of "domicile" provides a clearer understanding of the concept than do the ordinary English or African language dictionaries. It thus becomes clear that "domicile" should be understood to be the place where a person is legally deemed to be constantly present for the purpose of exercising their rights and fulfilling their obligations, even in the midst of their factual absence. Eventually, the domicile of an individual should indicate the community to which the person truly belongs – only then will "domicile" constitute a connecting factor which satisfies the conflicting demands of justice.

"Domicile" thus locates itself within the discipline of private law, which is primarily concerned with the rights and duties of individuals towards each other. The state's involvement in this area of law is confined to providing a courteous method of resolving any dispute that has arisen. Thus, the legal process is begun by the aggrieved citizen and not by the state. Figure 10.1 illustrates the areas covered by private law, in comparison to the scope of public law which deals mainly with constitutional, administrative and criminal issues.

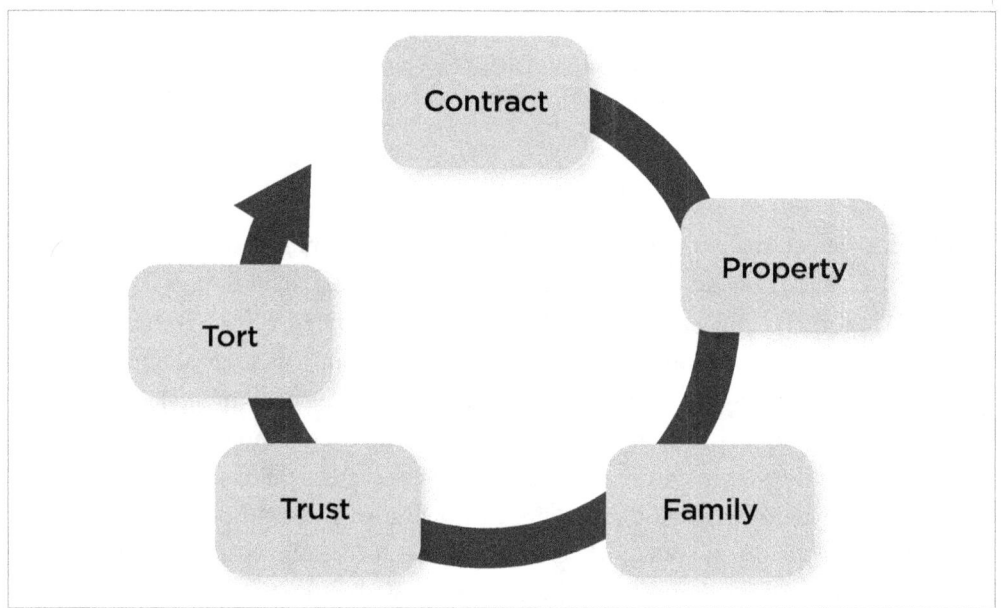

FIGURE 10.1 The partitions of private law

It is in the context of these areas of private law that the term "domicile" is often used and where its inappropriate or incorrect representation usually has implications that reach further than would appear on the face of it.

"Domicile" thus combines two factors, namely "residence" and "intent to remain". Since the term "domicile" includes residence, the scope and significance of the term is overarching and takes precedence over the term "residence". For example, a person may have several residences but would have only one "domicile". Therefore, "domicile" is mostly used in reference to personal rights, duties and obligations.

Credit, consumer rights and commitment

When consumers enter into a credit agreement with a credit provider, they generally come across a clause that requires them to record their *domicilium citandi et executandi*. This clause is normally found towards the end of the agreement form. When translated into isiZulu in a translated contract, the clause reads, *Indawo ohlala kuyo* (A place where you stay). If the consumer were to be asked for his or her understanding of the clause, or of the term "domicile", the answer would very likely be "my address". Is it just a person's address that is required here, though? Is this a correct understanding of the intricacies of the clause? It is in failing to adequately answer this question that consumers end up misunderstanding the requirements of this clause. Basing their understanding of the clause on the inadequate translation they see before them might mean that consumers simply provide a current address, with no insight into the meaning and intent of the original clause.

The protection of consumer rights is vital in ensuring a credit market that is accessible to and sustainable for all South Africans, particularly those who have, for historical reasons, been unable to access credit. The National Credit Act (NCA) (Republic of South Africa, 2005) was introduced to promote and advance the social and economic welfare of South African consumers and to offer them a level of protection. The Act was also aimed at promoting a fair, transparent, sustainable and accessible credit market and industry. To meet its objective of protecting the consumer, the NCA gives consumers various rights. For every right that this Act gives to the consumer, it also places a corresponding duty on the credit provider who is party to a credit agreement with that consumer, to ensure that the application of the law is just, fair and even-handed in as far as consumer rights are concerned. Credit is a key driver of modern capitalism, as it lubricates the economy and promotes commercial activities. The benefits implied by these initiatives are easily derailed, however. Growing economies – such as South Africa's – rely on spending as a major source of their income. The future of consumer spending in such economies will be bleak if there is no effective means to deal with the issue of judgments based on previous dealings, and that occur due to non-receipt of letters of demand. This means that there is a critical need to revisit the understanding of the term "domicile". Where a consumer is unable to honour his or her obligations in terms of a credit agreement, the NCA gives him or her the right to be informed by the credit provider concerned that it intends to report such adverse information to a credit bureau. Such notice must also be provided to the consumer at least 20 business days before the reporting takes place. This right includes, but is not limited to, the consumer being furnished with a copy of the information concerned upon request. The issue of the provision of the correct domicile at the time of concluding a credit agreement becomes crucial in this regard.

The rights and duties of consumers

In discussing the rights and duties of consumers under the National Credit Act (NCA) (Republic of South Africa, 2005), special attention is given to Section 60 of the Act, which speaks to the rights of adult individuals who apply to a credit provider for credit. Consumers who have been listed by credit bureaus find it difficult to exercise their rights in this regard due to their previous dealings with creditors having led to their names being submitted without their knowledge. This problem often arises from their having provided incorrect addresses when entering into credit agreements. The provision of incorrect addresses usually emanates from their misunderstanding, or an incorrect translation, of the term "domicile" and then, ultimately, the clause which deals with domicile when signing a consumer contract. The rights and duties of consumers are aimed at promoting equity in the credit market by providing a balance between the rights and responsibilities of credit providers and those of consumers. In view of the large number of illiterate and less educated consumers exposed to the South African credit industry, extensive protection in the form of a wide variety of consumer rights is essential to ensure a credit market that is accessible to and sustainable for all South Africans, particularly those who, historically, have been unable to access credit (Vessio, 2015). Consumers have an important role to play in uplifting South Africa's economy and, especially in view of the current economic conditions and the prevalence of debt, they should be vigilant and arm themselves with appropriate information rather than "going in blind" when signing up for credit.

Consumers whose credit records suggest that they are a threat to credit providers face challenges when trying to exercise their right to apply for credit. As explained, their negative credit records are often due to their misunderstanding of the concept of "domicile" at the time when the relevant agreements were concluded. Although it may be considered common knowledge that one has to inform one's creditors when changing one's address, this assumption often does not apply to less aware consumers. However, if the concept were clearly understood from the outset, the consumer could use the appropriate address and thus receive their correspondence, irrespective of their having spent time at other, temporary, residences.

Prescripts of the National Credit Act

The NCA (Republic of South Africa, 2005) forms part of the broad legislation overhaul aimed at protecting the consumer in the credit market and in making credit services accessible. The NCA was introduced as part of a drive to promote and advance the social and economic welfare of South African consumers and to promote a fair, efficient and accessible credit market. The NCA is important in this discussion as it makes provision for how credit-related issues with regard to consumers are to be considered. Prior to its promulgation, consumers were not always aware of the implications of signing credit agreements, or of what such agreements contain. The Act created several rights for consumers. Specific reference is made here to Section 60 of the NCA which provides that every adult natural person and every juristic person or association of persons has a right to apply to a credit provider for credit. However, it should be stressed here that Section 60 provides for the right to *apply* – not for any rights in respect of credit having to be *granted*. Subject to Sections 61, 62 and 66 of the Act, a credit provider has a right to refuse to enter into a credit agreement with any prospective consumer on reasonable commercial grounds consistent with its customary risk-management and underwriting practices.

Thus there is nothing in the Act that obliges the credit provider to grant credit or to enter into a credit agreement with a person. In a case where a credit application has been denied by the credit provider, Section 134 provides for the creditor to lodge a complaint with a view to resolving the dispute through the National Consumer Tribunal. It has been observed that it is often only at this stage of the proceedings that consumers discover that they have been blacklisted with credit bureaus based on their previous credit record. Section 72 of the Act provides the right of every affected person to be advised by the credit provider, within a prescribed time, before any adverse information concerning that person is reported to a credit bureau. However, as noted, the listing of consumers without their knowledge is often because the notice of the creditor's intention to blacklist them has not reached them. In examining such claims, the question remains: Did they provide the appropriate *domicilium citandi et executandi* when entering into a credit agreement with their previous credit providers?

Considerations when entering into a contractual agreement

It is important that consumers who have chosen a *domicilium* address at the time of concluding a contractual agreement are in a position to receive any legal notice that is delivered to that chosen address. It must be noted further that, should any change of address occur after the signing of an agreement, the party concerned should notify the other contracting party of that change of address, preferably in writing. That this happens cannot be taken for granted, as some consumers, wittingly or unwittingly, do not adhere to this requirement. The consequences of the latter are not clearly expressed when the contract is concluded; and consumers then usually find themselves on the wrong side of the law when action has already been taken against them. In terms of the law, the delivery of a legal notice to the chosen *domicilium* by any party to an agreement or contract will be considered sufficient for the purposes of legal action and such party will be deemed to have received the legal notice or document.

This last-mentioned condition becomes crucial in that it determines the extent to which a party can challenge a decision based on non-receipt of a legal notice given by a credit provider. This basically means that a contracting party may deliver a summons to the *domicilium* address chosen by the other party; and, even in a case where such a summons was not received, the issuer may proceed to obtain a judgment, as the notice shall be deemed to have been delivered at the correct address.

The understanding of "domicile" is further explained by dispute resolution attorney, Corné Lewis (2017), when he states in simple terms that *domicilium citandi et executandi* means the address one elects for the purpose of receiving all legal notices and processes. He further explains that this declaration of *domicilium* address is applicable to entering into all contractual arrangements including, amongst others, lease agreements, loan agreements and financial agreements. Here, special reference is made to the appeal made to the Gauteng Local Division of the High Court of South Africa in Johannesburg which considered the validity of the service of a summons at a contractually chosen *domicilium citandi et executandi* in the matter of *Shepard v Emmerich* (A5066/2013 [2014] ZAGPJHC 120). In this case, the purchaser issued summons against the seller for the payment of money based on information contained in the signed agreement. In the event, the summons never reached the seller, but as service of the summons was assumed to have been effected, judgement by default was subsequently sought and granted. However, showing the importance of the specific terms of the *domicilium* clause, the seller then launched an application for rescission of the default judgement, which was successful because of the enforcement of technicalities of the *domicilium* clause.

Lewis (2017) further stresses that, in a contractual agreement, upon conclusion of the agreement, it is imperative that the parties should, as a standard practice, insert a *domicilium* clause in the agreement to make provision for the contracting parties to elect their address for the receipt of legal notices and processes in relation to the agreement. This includes, but is not limited to, inserting a street and/or postal address upon which notices of breach, letters of demand, or court processes can be served. Lewis (2017: 2) further asks the question, "But is it as simple as that? Should more attention be given to the *domicilium* clause during the drafting stage?"

Conclusion

The focus in this chapter has been on the viability of the concept of *domicilium* as a connecting factor in South African law and in the areas of choice of law and jurisdiction, with particular emphasis on problems arising around the translation and the interpretation of the concept in this context. Since domicile constitutes such an important connecting factor in matters pertaining to private law, it is important that the translation and interpretation of *domicilium* be clearly communicated to consumers, to avoid the problems that arise with the choice of an incorrect address and also to reduce the high number of consumers who are listed with credit bureaus on the basis of non-compliance. Legal writing, and contracts in particular, seek to establish clearly defined rights and duties for certain individuals. Therefore, it is essential to ensure a precise correspondence between these rights and duties in source texts and in their translations. Inappropriate translation of a concept in the field of law can lead to an inappropriate interpretation of that concept. Misinterpretation of a concept can, in turn, lead to inappropriate reaction towards it; and inappropriate reaction can lead to litigation and other forms of legal discourse which cause unnecessary expense and complication. While there is a drive to promote and advance the social and economic welfare of South African consumers, there also has to be a sense of understanding of the legalities that come with the issue of domicile as it is understood by consumers when they enter into contractual agreements with credit providers. By the same token, translators are responsible for providing appropriate translation of the concept – one which will allow for the correct understanding of it. In this way, the promotion of justice, fairness and transparency can be guaranteed, thus allowing a sustainable and accessible credit market to thrive in South Africa.

References

Abdellah, A.S. 2002. What every novice translator should know, *Translation journal* (July). https://translationjournal.net/journal/21novice.htm [Blog retrieved on 30 April 2019].

Arduini, S. & Hodgson, R. Jr (eds.). 2004. *Similarity and difference in translation*. Rimini: Guaraldi.

Bahumaid, S.A. 1996. Yemeni Arabic dialect studies: A critical evaluation. *Journal of Humanities & Social Sciences* (University of Aden), 1:5-26.

Baker, M. 2006. *Translation and conflict*. London: Routledge.

Bell, R.T. 1991. *Translation and translating: Theory and practice*. London: Longman.

Berman, A. 2000. Translation and the trials of the foreign. In: L. Venuti (ed.), *The translation studies reader*. London: Routledge. pp. 284-297.

Brooks-Lewis, K.A. 2009. Adult learners' perceptions of the incorporation of their L1 in foreign language teaching and learning. *Applied Linguistics*, 30(2):216-235.

Chomsky, N. 1980. *Rules and representations*. New York: Columbia University Press.

Doke, C.M.; Malcolm, M.K. & Sikakana, J.M.A. 1972. *English-isiZulu/isiZulu-English Dictionary*. 2nd Edition. Johannesburg: Witwatersrand University Press.

El-dadi, H.M. 2011. Towards an understanding of the distinctive nature of translation studies. *Journal of King Saud University: Languages and Translation*, 23:29-45. https://core.ac.uk/download/pdf/82218600.pdf [Retrieved 30 April 2019].

Even-Zohar, I. 1990. Translation and transfer. In: Special issue on the papers of Itamar Evan-Zohar, Polysystem Studies. *Poetics Today*, 11(1):73-78.

Gane, P. 1955. *The Selective Voet being the Commentary on the Pandects [Paris edition of 1829] by Johannes Voet [1647-1713] and the Supplement to that work by Johannes van der Linden [1756-1835]*. Translated with explanatory notes and notes of all South African reported cases. 8 volumes. Durban: Butterworths.

Hatim, B. & Munday, J. 2004. *Translation: An advanced resource book*. New York: Routledge.

House, J. 2008. Beyond intervention: Universals in translation. *Trans-kom*, 1(1):6-19.

Kelly, D. 2005. *A handbook for translator trainers*. Series: Translation practices explained. Manchester: St. Jerome/Routledge.

Latdict Latin Dictionary and Grammar Resources https://latin-dictionary.net/

Lewis, C. 2017. "Domicilium citandi et executandi" – do you really understand this term? *Dispute Resolution Alert*. pp. 2-3. https://docplayer.net/76549763-Alert-dispute-resolution-issue-in-this-25-january-2017-international-arbitration-*domicilium*-citandi-et-executandi-do-you-really-understand-this-term.html [Retrieved 20 March 2018].

Malmkjær, K. 2005. *Linguistics and the language of translation*. Edinburgh: Edinburgh University Press.

Manfredi, M. 2008. *Translating text and context: Translational studies and Systematic Functional Linguistics*, Vol. 1. Cagliari: CUEC (Cagliari University Cooperative Publishing). http://amsacta.unibo.it/2393/1/Manfredi_2008_Monografia.pdf

Mbatha, M.O. 2006. *Isichazamazwi sesiZulu*. Pietermaritzburg: New Dawn Publishers.

Newmark, P. 1981. *Approaches to translation*. Oxford: Pergamon Press.

Nida, E.A. 1976. A framework for the analysis and evaluation of theories of translation. In: R.W. Brislin (ed.), *Translation: Applications and research*. New York: Gardner Press. pp. 47-79.

Orozco, M. 2000. Building a measuring instrument for the acquisition of translation competence in trainee translators. In: C. Schäffner & B. Adab (eds.), *Developing translation competence*, Vol. 38, Benjamins Translation Library. Amsterdam: John Benjamins. pp. 199-214.

Republic of South Africa. 2005. National Credit Act No 34, 2005. *Government Gazette*, 489(28619). https://www.gov.za/sites/default/files/a34-05_0.pdf [Retrieved 22 October 2018].

Rothe-Neves, R. 2007. Notes on the concept of "translator's competence". *Quaderns*, 14:125-138.

Schäffner, C. & Adab, B. (eds.). 2000. *Developing translation competence*. Vol. 38, Benjamins Translation Library. Amsterdam: John Benjamins.

Shuttleworth, M. & Cowie, M. 1997. *Dictionary of translation studies*. Manchester: St. Jerome/Routledge.

Toury, G. 2001. Translation as a means of planning and the planning of translation: A theoretical framework and an exemplary case. In: S. Paker (ed.), *Translations: (Re)shaping of literature and culture* Istanbul: Bogazici University Press. pp. 148-165.

Tymoczko, M. 2007. *Enlarging translation, empowering translators*. Manchester: St. Jerome/Routledge.

Vessio, M.L. 2015. The National Credit Act 34 of 2005: Background and rationale for its enactment, with a specific study of the remedies of the credit grantor in the event of breach of contract. Unpublished DLegum thesis, University of Pretoria, Pretoria.

Zakhir, M. 2008. *Translation procedures*. http://www.translationdirectory.com/articles/article1704.php [Retrieved 20 June 2018].

INTERPRETERS' RENDITIONS IN ZIMBABWEAN COURTROOMS

A corpus-based analysis from frequency profiles to key semantic domains

Paul Svongoro & Patson Kufakunesu

Introduction

One area in which the law interfaces with linguistics is the study of the interaction of participants in court proceedings, an activity generally called "courtroom discourse". A variety of interactions take place in the courtroom, including interactions between the people who are directly involved in a lawsuit: the plaintiffs, the accused and the magistrates or judges, depending on the context. Such interactions typically involve question-and-answer interactions in the form of examination, re-examination and cross-examination. Other interactions, however, may involve court officials and the interpreter whose role it is to interpret testimonies of parties to a conflict when those parties do not speak or understand the language of the court. The court interpreter's role is to interpret in full what the witness or defendant says, without commenting on it. Although such interactions are characteristic of dialogues, courtroom discourse may also involve the study of monologues (e.g. by lawyers, magistrates and judges), some of which can be very dramatic. One major feature that characterises dialogue is the aspect of turn taking, which is manifest in dialogue participants' contributions. Another is "grounding" as participants strive to establish common ground (Brown & Levinson, 1987). Participants have strategies to signal that they hear speakers, what they hear, what they understand, and what they accept (or do not), although repair (i.e. instances when speakers self-correct themselves during conversations) and misunderstanding may still occur. The last feature concerns identifying and dealing with conversational implicatures, i.e. participants rely on interpreting utterances beyond their literal meaning. Grice (1975) was the first to study cases in which what the *speaker* means differs from what the *sentence* used by the speaker means. With these diverse and interesting areas of research in mind, this study employs a corpus-based approach to examine how different court players in Zimbabwean courtrooms use different grammatical, syntactic, and questioning techniques and how these are interpreted by court interpreters.

Specifically, the chapter aims to analyse lexico-grammatical and syntactic features used by the different court players and how these were rendered by court interpreters during court proceedings. The features we observed include, for instance, lexical items, pronouns and other forms of address, question forms, such as "but"/"so" prefaced and "then" prefaced questions. Borrowing from current trends and advances in corpus-based interpreting studies in other parts of the world, the chapter uses Wmatrix (see Rayson, 2000) to make statistical descriptive analyses of a collection of (1) *machine-readable* (2) *authentic texts* which were (3) *sampled* to be (4) *representative* of language mediation in the Zimbabwean courtrooms. The corpus for the study totalled nearly 89 000 words from transcripts of consecutively interpreted rape trials heard in two regional magistrates' courts in Zimbabwe.

The starting point of the study is the assumption that how these aspects of language are used by the various court actors, and how they are interpreted, may have an impact on the trial process and hence on the administration of justice. This study thus hopes to contribute to the field of forensic linguistics, through an exploration of the interactional dynamics involving different court players in the Zimbabwean courtrooms, by demonstrating how linguistic factors may impact on the participation status of individual court actors and, potentially, on the administration of justice. The study is therefore relevant, not only for court interpreters, but also for those working with them, in that they may become more conscious of the impact of their actions.

Justification for the study

Court procedures in Zimbabwe tend to rely more on oral than written presentations of argument, so hearings tend to be lengthy. Such a unique bilingual courtroom affects the interactional dynamics of the courtroom communicative process and, potentially, the administration of justice. To ensure that the rights of such persons are protected, court interpreters are provided for speakers of Shona, Ndebele and other languages. The nature of the Zimbabwean courtroom and the government's commitment to provide interpreting services are, therefore, interesting areas of forensic linguistics research which this study explores.

While corpus-based studies are increasingly attracting scholarly interest amongst researchers in other parts of the world (Baker, 1995; Dose, 2010; Moropa, 2009), they are still relatively new in Zimbabwe. However, Zimbabwean courts of law have vast amounts of authentic recorded data, comprising audio tapes and transcribed material which researchers can take advantage of and retrieve, select and analyse, using corpus linguistic techniques. Although retrieving this material is largely conducted manually, it is possible for researchers to use software to convert such material into machine-readable format and then analyse data using information technology-related research methods. Most scholars (for instance, Bendazzoli & Sandrelli, 2009; Hale, 2004) concur that the creation of parallel and comparable corpora, comprising discourse relevant to interpreting, is important for empirically verifying general hypotheses about translation and interpreting products and processes. In line with this, we analysed court interpreting data available in Zimbabwe's courts of law by investigating the interpreting process with a view to contributing towards a better understanding of interpreter-mediated exchanges. Once the data for the current study had been compiled, it could be kept in an anonymised machine-readable format. The availability of such a resource could be a positive step in corpus building for future studies and interpreter pedagogy, thus improving the quality of interpreting (Hale, 2004).

The choice of rape cases for interrogation in this study was justified by its scope, as gender and sexual violence is a widespread phenomenon in Southern Africa. Figures from Zimbabwe National Statistics (ZimStat, 2017), for instance, indicate that at least 15 women are raped every day in Zimbabwe. Secondly, rape trials were elected because they seem to present severe challenges related to language use during court proceedings, as attested to by researchers. Mikkelson (2000:88) states, "these cases are particularly stressful to interpret, because explicit testimony must be presented regarding the acts that were performed. Reliving the experience can be traumatic for the victim, and the interpreter must take special care not to be emotionally involved". Besides, rape cases are considered very serious criminal cases in Zimbabwe and often drag on before they are finalised. Because of the frequency of occurrence of rape trials and the fact that the trials drag on eventuating in many court appearances, we were able to collect a sufficient amount of primary data for analysis.

Apart from the seriousness of rape cases in terms of criminal law, dealing with rape cases, as Valero-Garcés (2005) points out, also raises cultural, psychological and emotional issues for all involved. Valero-Garcés (2005) reached this conclusion when she investigated the emotional and psychological impact of rape and other violence-related trials on the Interpreters in Public Service (IPS) in Spain. In addition to the trauma of being exposed to this violence, discussing issues of sexuality in public remains taboo in most African societies. This constraint regarding discussing issues of sexuality in public is exacerbated by the social management of the courtroom, which relies on special rules of language use that, in some cases, restrict what may (or may not) be said (Stubbs, 1996). In view of this, we realised the imperative to carry out a close study of court interpreting involving cases of alleged rape to help find solutions to language and interpreting challenges encountered in Zimbabwean courts of law.

In the context of the current reality of court interpreting in Zimbabwe, this study fills part of the gap that exists in the knowledge about the practice and profession of interpreting in general, and court interpreting in particular. It is therefore anticipated that the corpus and the results of the study will be of service to those interested in compiling interpreting corpora to help support practical interpreter training, and the developing and maintaining of their interpreting skills, as well as ensuring ongoing world-class training.

Theoretical framework

Drawing on methods of discourse analysis (Fairclough, 1992), we were able to analyse the dynamics of interpreter-mediated interactive discourse (Roy, 1996) as a "socially situated practice" (Angelelli, 2004:24). First, we applied approaches from pragmatics, such as Grice's (1975) theory, which emphasises the cooperative principle for effective communication. This approach was used as a framework for analysing how hearers infer meaning during interpreter-mediated question–answer dialogues in the courtroom.

In our research we also applied Brown and Levinson's (1987) aspects of politeness (which Halliday & Hassan, 1976, refer to as "tenor"; while Mason and Stewart, 2001, name it "face") to investigate interpreter-mediated interactions. According to Hale and Gibbons (1999), in the context of the courtroom, politeness is used for negotiating social relationships amongst participants. Politeness manifests in relations of status; and these may be modified when interpreters change politeness strategies used by interactants, or when interpreters introduce changes in tenor that are absent in the source utterance. Thus, changes in politeness or tenor are argued to cause changes in the pragmatic force of the interpreted text (Hale & Gibbons, 1999). Finally, we also used critical discourse analysis (Fairclough, 1992; Van Dijk, 2000) to analyse court interpreting as a social practice and from a critical social standpoint.

The above discourse analytic approaches were then complemented by approaches from interpreting studies. For instance, we were able to extend Wadensjö's (1998) "interpreting as interaction" approach by analysing the interpreters' role in Zimbabwean courtrooms beyond the "ideal interpreting norm" of "just translating" (Wadensjö, 1998:105) and included the function of coordinating the primary parties' utterances. Such an approach acknowledges that the translating and coordinating aspects are simultaneously present in dialogue interpreting encounters. In addition, Gile's (1995) "effort models" of consecutive interpreting helped foster a better understanding of the practice of interpreting in terms of the listening, memory and production efforts involved in the interpreting process. This, together with appreciating the various emotional, linguistic and institutional demands on the interpreter (Dean & Pollard, 2011), helped us develop more informed analyses about what interpreters do (and why) in the context of their social, ethical and professional environment.

Corpus analysis methodology

In the sections below, we explain the methodology of the study. The study is largely qualitative, although it also employs basic descriptive statistics and frequency counts characteristic of the quantitative paradigm. This approach can be explained in two ways. First, descriptive statistics and frequency counts are relevant, considering that the corpus-based approach adopted involves a great deal of quantitative analyses, for example, frequency analyses. Data distribution, because of its numerical format, is reflected in this study in the form of tabular and graphical representation. In other words, data are presented and analysed to reflect the degree and frequency of occurrence of particular forms. Secondly, the qualitative approach, on which the study is primarily based, helped us to describe language use, as we interpreted the language data collected and analysed. It should be pointed out at this stage that early attempts to develop corpus-based interpreting studies (CIS) were based on manual corpora that could not be analysed using corpus linguistics methods (Bendazzoli & Sandrelli, 2009). Observational and experimental studies based on corpus data were therefore analysed manually. This was the methodological approach we initially intended to use, as corpus-based studies are still new in Zimbabwe. However, other researchers in the field, such as Wallmach (2000), Rodriguez-Ines (2010) and Kruger, Wallmach and Munday (2011), directly and indirectly provided the impetus for the researchers to take advantage of the current trends and advances in corpus-based interpreting studies in other parts of the world and to use corpus linguistic methods applicable to electronic analysis of corpora. A number of corpus linguistics computer programmes, such as Wordsmith Tools, ParaConc, Wmatrix and EXMARalDA, make automatic analyses of corpora possible. Of these tools, we adopted Paul Rayson's (2000) Wmatrix for this study, enabling analysis of the distribution and frequencies of lexical items, key word and key domain clouds, as well as the distribution of content words versus grammatical words, and the distribution of question forms.

The sections below further explain the methodological aspects of the study, such as the data, the corpus tool employed, and corpus design.

The data and corpus tool

The main source of data chosen for this study was question/answer transcripts of consecutively-interpreted rape trials heard at two magistrates' courts in Zimbabwe. This choice makes the study principally linguistic, although it employs some aspects of ethnography, such as observation. The transcripts in question totalled 89 124 words and were compiled during a period of PhD study at the University of the Witwatersrand in South Africa from 2012 to 2017. Data from transcripts were supplemented by 92 hours of observation of open court proceedings. The study was conducted at two regional magistrates' courts: one located at the Rotten Row Magistrates' Courts in Harare, and the second at Mutare Magistrates' Courts. The Rotten Row Magistrates' Courts are the biggest and busiest in Zimbabwe, with 20 courtrooms and 20 magistrates, one for each courtroom. There is one other magistrate, the Provincial Magistrate, whose duties are mainly administrative. At the Mutare Magistrates' Courts, there are eight courtrooms, six of which are for criminal matters and two others that hear civil matters. This number of courtrooms translates to eight magistrates, each assigned to a courtroom, plus one Provincial Magistrate who performs administrative duties. The number of public prosecutors and interpreters was found to be slightly higher than that of magistrates at both courts.

Although these courts hear cases that require the services of interpreters for the 16 languages spoken in Zimbabwe, there are also frequently cases that require foreign language interpretation. Due to logistical and language issues, we chose to investigate English and Shona in consecutively interpreted cases heard in the regional courts of the two court centres identified. It is fortunate, in the case of this study, that we as researchers speak Shona as our first language. Researching cases which involved English and other languages spoken in Zimbabwe would have required the services of additional special research assistants.

In this study, we adopted Wmatrix as the corpus querying tool. Wmatrix was built by REVERE (Rayson, 2000, 2009), a United Kingdom-funded project investigating the extraction of information from software engineering documents. It is a web-based corpus-processing environment which allows researchers local and remote access to some corpus annotation and retrieval tools. However, unlike other corpus querying tools which are freely available online for download, Wmatrix can only be used for free in a short-time trial version and a user has to obtain a licence by directly contacting Paul Rayson. Tools available in Rayson's (2000) Wmatrix include: CLAWS (part-of-speech tagger); SEMTAG (word-sense tagger); and LEMMINGS (a lemmatiser). In corpus linguistics, lemmatisation refers to the process of grouping together the inflected forms of a word so they can be analysed as a single item, identified by the word's dictionary form (the lemma). Using Wmatrix, we were able to produce frequency lists, carry out statistical comparisons of those lists, and do "key word in context" (KWIC) concordances. This is because Wmatrix extends the key words method to key grammatical categories and key semantic domains. Wmatrix proved particularly useful in conducting lexical analysis and the study of collocations, clusters and statistics related to the texts within our corpus. Some of the tools found in Wmatrix are WordList (Rayson, 2000), which we used to generate lists of words from the corpus under study; KeyWords, which is responsible for generating lists of key words from the list generated by the WordList; and Concord, which generates lists of concordances, or the occurrences of a specific item. Wmatrix has the advantage that it deals with large amounts of information and can provide information speedily for specific analyses.

Based on this, the study can be said to be data-based linguistic research inspired by the works of Berk-Seligson (1990), Hale (2004) and Mikkelson (2000). The study drew on interpreter-mediated, authentic, tape-recorded and transcribed question-and-answer dialogues, featuring the questioning of defendants and witnesses by magistrates and prosecutors during rape trials. As noted, the languages involved in this study are Shona and English. We conducted a source-text/target-text comparison of the collected data to identify whether changes in linguistic and pragmatic meaning existed. This type of corpus is what Baker (1995) refers to as a "parallel corpus". It consists of original, source-language texts in language A and the translated version in language B. Performance shifts in the form of additions and omissions that were identified were noted and categorised according to their effect on the semantic and/or pragmatic content of the source text and the immediate interaction of participants during the trials. Below, we explain some of the tools of interest found in Wmatrix.

Word-frequency lists

The most basic feature provided by a corpus-analysis tool is a word frequency list which allows users to discover "how many different words are in a corpus and how often each appears" (Bowker, 2002:47). These two features are called "types" (different words identified) and "tokens" (frequency of use of a word) respectively. This list can usually be ordered by frequency or alphabetically and can be used to identify common lexis in a particular corpus. For illustrative purposes, we use a sentence from their corpus of extracts involving cases of alleged rape:

> After raping the complainant, you threatened the complainant with death should she report you to the police.

This sentence contains 17 words, which means the corpus contains 17 tokens. However, some of the words appear more than once (e.g. "the", "you", "complainant"); therefore, the corpus contains only 13 *different* words, and these are known as "types". In a word-frequency list, the types are presented in a list and the number of tokens (the number of times that word occurs) is shown beside the type as shown here:

TABLE 11.1   A word-frequency list showing types on the left and tokens on the right

Types	Tokens
after	1
raping	1
the	3
complainant	2
you	2
threatened	1
with	1
death	1
should	1
She	1
report	1
to	1
police	1

Word-frequency lists can be manipulated in a number of ways. They can be arranged in different orders, including order of occurrence in the corpus, alphabetical order, and order of frequency; and they can be arranged in ascending or descending order. In addition to counting the frequency of words, corpus-analysis tools calculate the ratio of types to tokens. Some corpus-analysis tools can also count the number of sentences and paragraphs, and calculate the average length of words, sentences, and paragraphs in the corpus. This type of information can help interpreters assess some of the stylistic features of the text in the corpus.

Concordance tools

Olohan (2004:63) explains that, once a corpus applicable to a specific research question has been compiled or selected, the researcher has to decide what kinds of data are required from the corpus, and in what form. The most common tool for data retrieval is the concordancer. In addition to the display of corpus excerpts in "keyword in context" format (to be explained shortly), it also incorporates functions to study collocations and words occurring in clusters. A concordancer, in Bowker's (2002:53) terms, is a tool that extracts all the occurrences of a particular search pattern in its immediate contexts and presents these in an easy-to-read format. Zanettin (1998) shares this view and defines a concordance as an index of all the instances of specific words or phrases in a corpus, along with their contexts, as shown in Table 11.2 for the search pattern "pants" from a courtroom corpus of a trial involving alleged rape.

TABLE 11.2 Sample concordances for "pants" from the study's corpus of rape trials

1	fed a cloth in her mouth and forcibly removed her pants which got torn and had sexual intercourse with he	CASE 2.txt
2	room he took with him complainant's torn pair of pants to destroy evidence. On 3 September 2004 accused	CASE 2.txt
3	cloth. Accused proceeded to remove complainant's pants and raped her for the second time. He again threa	CASE 2.txt
4	he report. Accused also took with him complainant pants which again had been torn. Well before the rape	CASE 2.txt

Once a search has been conducted, the results are displayed for the user. The most common display format is known as a KWIC ("keyword in context") display. In a KWIC display, all occurrences of the search pattern are lined up in the centre of the screen, as shown in Table 11.3. The extent of the context on either side of the search pattern is variable and can often be specified by the user. The key word in context displayed in Figure 11.3 shows the concordance produced for the search pattern "complainant" in the same rape trial corpus.

TABLE 11.3 A KWIC display of the concordances retrieved for the search pattern "complainant"

```
1    in which he was sleeping and entered the room the complainant was sleeping with her young sister aged about 6 y CASE 2.txt
2    t 6 years. He got into the same blankets with the complainant who because of fright tried to scream. Accused st CASE 2.txt
3    was fast asleep when this happened. After raping complainant, accused threatened to kill complainant through u CASE 2.txt
4    er raping complainant, accused threatened to kill complainant through undisclosed means should she report the m CASE 2.txt
5    yone. When accused left the room he took with him complainant's torn pair of pants to destroy evidence. On 3 S CASE 2.txt
6    me home some time after midnight. He wakes up the complainant by knocking the main door to be let in. As the co CASE 2.txt
7    nt by knocking the main door to be let in. As the complainant was returning to bed after opening the door, accu CASE 2.txt
8    r mouth with a cloth. Accused proceeded to remove complainant's pants and raped her for the second time. He aga CASE 2.txt
9    ath should she report. Accused also took with him complainant pants which again had been torn. Well before the CASE 2.txt
10   ad been torn. Well before the rape episodes, the complainant used to secure the bedroom door by locking it wi CASE 2.txt
11   , but the accused had withdrawn the keys from the complainant so the door was open during the day and night, th CASE 2.txt
12   d. During these days accused had become strict of complainant's movements. When schools closed complainant ran CASE 2.txt
13   t of complainant's movements. When schools closed complainant ran away from their Dangamvura home using money b CASE 2.txt
14   d that penetration had been effected and that the complainant was three months pregnant. The pregnancy was lega CASE 2.txt
15   legally terminated since it was a result of rape. Complainant later on went to show the Police how and where sh CASE 2.txt
```

As with word-frequency lists, these can be arranged in a variety of ways, such as order of appearance in the corpus (as in the example above), or alphabetically according to the words preceding or following the search pattern. Regardless of the search type pattern entered, the benefit of using concordance lines as a source of linguistic evidence is that they reveal the context in which individual occurrences of words are found. The options for sorting and displaying the data, as Bowker (2002:55) rightly observes, can facilitate the process of observing and distinguishing patterns of linguistic behaviour.

Collocations

Wmatrix also has the ability to compute collocations, which are a characteristic co-occurring pattern of words. Simply put, collocations are words that "go together" or are typically "found in each other's company" (Bowker, 2002:64). More technically, collocations are words that appear together with a greater than random probability. Because language is not random, certain words tend to cluster together, and some of these clusters form collocations.

Corpus design

Another important issue in this study was that of corpus design (Olohan, 2004; Zanettin 1998). The researchers had to consider a number of issues suggested by Olohan (2004) as being critical in corpus-based studies. These factors were corpus representativeness, size and sampling. Issues in corpus design and compilation are fundamentally concerned with the validity and reliability of research based on a particular corpus, including whether the corpus can serve the purpose for which it is intended. Meyer (2002) emphasises that the decisive factor in corpus design is the purpose of a corpus. This purpose largely determines whether a corpus will contain written or spoken language, or both, and what registers and varieties will be represented in it. In relation to this view, three issues need to be considered. The first is whether a corpus is static or dynamic. If a corpus is static, it constitutes a collection of texts that were selected according to some specific principles and for a specific research project, thus providing a snapshot of aspects of the language at a particular point in time. Most corpus-based research is done on static corpora. The British National Corpus (BNC) is static, for example, although very large. According to Hunston (2002:21):

> a dynamic corpus, on the other hand, is also referred to as a monitor corpus since it constitutes an enormous collection of texts that is constantly being added to and that is studied primarily for its ability to reflect language change and to provide data on words that do not occur often.

These huge, dynamic corpora, aimed at tracking language as it changes and develops over time, are more resource-intensive and therefore often less accessible to individual researchers. This aspect of corpus design is called "permanence" by Hunston (2002:25).

Representativeness, though a tricky notion, is the second issue we had to consider in designing the corpus of the study. According to Olohan (2004), researchers would like to be able to make generalisations based on their data analysis, but it is often difficult to confirm with any degree of confidence that their data are depictive of a particular language or genre. When compiling a corpus, a researcher would want to ask him- or herself whether it is representative of written or spoken texts in that language. Compilers of such corpora as the BNC made decisions in an attempt to represent both written and spoken language and different text genres. However, representativeness raises questions about how texts and utterances are produced and used. So, when deciding what texts are to be included in a written corpus, issues to be considered might go beyond judgements about text type and genre, as well as text function or purpose. Regional and temporal factors will often play a part in corpus design. Thus, criteria such as the nationality, ethnicity, age, gender, etc. of a writer or speaker may also be considered in selection of texts, depending on their relevance for the research questions that are to be investigated using the corpus data.

The third aspect we considered in corpus design was corpus size. On the one hand, there is the view that the larger the corpus, the better it is; and, on the other hand, there is the opposing view that a bigger corpus will not necessarily be more useful than a smaller one, particularly when studying high frequency words, since there is a limit to the amount of data a researcher can analyse (Olohan, 2004). A choice is also usually made between using whole texts or samples of text (selected according to some principle, or randomly). There is some acknowledgement that a smaller corpus can be adequate for studying grammar; and that the size of a corpus may ultimately depend on the availability of suitable texts or other factors, such as the need for manual annotation (Hunston, 2002).

From the above it is clear that, in compiling a corpus, researchers need to consider a range of issues and identify criteria that will help them make choices about which material to include or exclude. While multipurpose corpora typically contain texts representative of various genres, specialised corpora can be limited to highlight one genre, or a family of genres. In each case, these criteria are established and choices are made based on the aim of the research, the research questions to be addressed and the hypotheses to be tested. In the final analysis, a corpus is more or less adequate according to the extent to which the corpus matches the purposes to which it is put.

Corpus annotation and mark-up

Bowker (2002:68) states that corpus processing can be done in two ways. The first is when the researcher uses raw corpora. However, it is possible to encode additional information into a corpus, and this information can be either linguistic or non-linguistic in nature. The addition of linguistic information is referred to as "annotation", while the addition of non-linguistic information is known as "marking-up" a corpus.

For the purposes of this study, we attempted linguistic annotation in the form of syntactic annotation, in which each word in the corpus has its associated part of speech specified with tags. Some taggers use very general part-of-speech notations (e.g. verb, noun), while others use more specific notations, such as "imperative verb" and "plural common noun". Punctuation marks were also tagged. While manually adding all parts of speech to a corpus would take a very long time, programmes called "taggers" can do this automatically with over 95% accuracy, which is reasonable for many purposes.

Another type of linguistic annotation we conducted is called "semantic annotation". This was used to distinguish between the various meanings of a word. Semantic annotation can, therefore, be used to distinguish different meanings of homonyms. Homonyms are words that look or sound the same, but have different meanings when used in different contexts. The example cited by Bowker (2002:69) is that of the word "bank", which can refer to (1) a financial institution or (2) the side of a river. Semantic annotation (e.g. bank1 vs bank2) could be used to distinguish between the different senses of a word. The advantage of having a linguistically annotated corpus is that it allows users to focus their searches more narrowly. For example, an interpreter may wish to retrieve all instances of the word "test" where it appears as a verb, but not as a noun; or all instances of the word "bank" when it appears in sense 1, but not as in sense 2. Such retrieval patterns would not be possible in an unannotated corpus.

Adding non-linguistic information could be used to mark-up different structural sections of the texts (e.g. title, subtitle, sentence, paragraph, section and chapter). A researcher working with a corpus involving doctor–patient interaction may mark up different structural sections, uch as history taking, diagnosis and prescription. Similarly, a researcher examining court transcripts may mark up the transcripts into initial arraignment, case outline, examination-in-chief, cross-examination, summation and sentencing. If the transcripts involve the use of an interpreter, they may be marked up further in terms of interpreter's age, gender, training and years of experience. In this way, it would be possible to ask the computer to retrieve only occurrences of a specific search pattern that appears, for instance, in the title of a text.

However, any non-linguistic information would need to be added manually. The advantage of a "raw" corpus is that it is easier and faster to build. Annotating or marking up of a corpus requires a great amount of initial investment time, but subsequently allows for more specific searching options. Consequently, there is a trade-off between the time required to annotate/mark up and the benefits gained by doing so.

Data presentation and analysis

In the sections that follow, we present and analyse various lexical and grammatical aspects of language used by different court interactants and how these were dealt with by court interpreters. Most of these analyses were aided by the corpus tool (i.e. Wmatrix) adopted for the study.

Distribution of words and their frequencies

One way of distinguishing between different speakers is by considering their speaking styles. In this way, distinguishing features of a speaker have to be considered with respect to the other speakers. The analysis of style, also called "stylometry" (Kajzer-Wietrzny, 2013), is an interdisciplinary research area combining literary stylistics, statistics and computer science. For the purposes of this study, style is considered in the context of court interpreting as an individual interpreter's way of interpreting which is characterised by a consistent prominence of one or many linguistic features in his or her interpretations, and which is distinguishable from those of others. According to Kajzer-Wietrzny (2013), style reveals a person's attributes; and these attributes include repetitiveness, questioning strategies, use of fillers, aspects of modality and informativeness. Informativeness is shown by lexical density, i.e. the proportion of lexical/content words to function/grammatical words. A lower lexical density suggests that the text is less informative, as information load is diluted with more function words. In other words, when given two texts that are equal in length, the one which contains more lexical words would be considered more informative than the one with more function/grammatical words. In the following paragraphs, we describe how we analysed the distribution and frequency of content and function words in the source language discourse and in the interpreted target language discourse, and how we then explained the probable underlying reasons for the distribution and frequencies revealed.

Using a tool in Wmatrix (Rayson, 2009) called "frequency profiles", we were able to click on a frequency list to see the most frequent items in the corpus. Then, from the frequency list view, we were able to click on "concordance" and see standard concordances. These can show the usual word-based concordance, as well as all occurrences of words in one part of speech (POS) or semantic category. Frequency lists are available for words in the simple interface, and in the advanced interface for parts of speech, tags and semantic tags, as illustrated in Tables 11.4 and 11.5. The lists can be sorted alphabetically or by frequency. However, we observed that, in both the English-only and the Shona-only corpora, there was generally a higher frequency occurrence of grammatical words than content words. The summaries we present in Tables 11.4 and 11.5 are quite revealing about the distribution and frequency of content and grammatical words.

TABLE 11.4 Shona-only corpus showing the distribution and frequency of the top 10 words

Word	Frequency	Relative frequency
kuti	415	3.16
here	159	1.21
mwana	151	1.15
kana	115	0.87
sei	85	0.65
saka	73	0.56
kubva	71	0.54
pane	65	0.49
asi	64	0.49
uyu	60	0.46

The top 10 words shown in Table 11.4 are a mixture of content and grammatical words in Shona. The content words are *mwana* (child) and *kubva* (a verb in the infinitive) and the rest are grammatical words. In Figure 11.1, we show the proportion of content words versus grammatical words in the Shona-only corpus.

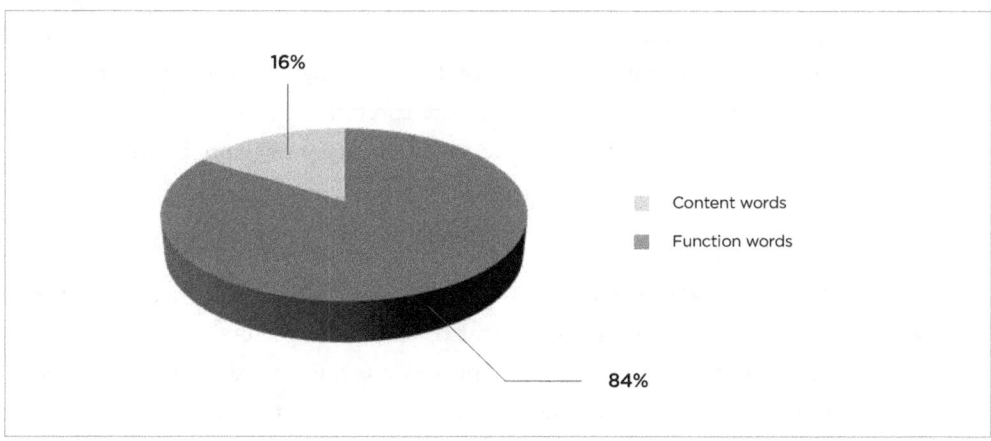

FIGURE 11.1 Proportion of content vs grammatical words in the Shona-only corpus

Distribution and frequency of content words

At a cursory glance, both the English-only and Shona-only corpora would suggest that there is an equal occurrence of "rape" and *chibharo* (rape). However, these forms are only the stems for many possible occurrences.

In the English-only corpus, the word "rape" also occurs as "raping", "raped", and "to rape". Similarly, in the Shona-only corpus, the same semantic item *chibharo* occurs with other words like *kubata chibharo* (to rape) and may have a host of euphemistic synonyms used in its place. Such synonyms include *kubhinywa, kubatwa, kuitwa mukadzi, kurarwa* and *kupindwa*, as well as others which are sexually explicit and taboo words, but which court interpreters sometimes use. Tables 11.5 and 11.6 are used to illustrate this.

TABLE 11.5 Six of the 26 occurrences of the search term "rape" in the English corpus

in relation to	rape 85. <M.Interpreter
possible for me to	rape the child? 255
standing can	rape a woman It has n
I did not	rape complainant? 27
two counts of	rape the first is that
Well before the	rape episodes

TABLE 11.6 Six of the 20 occurrences of the search term *chibharo* (rape) in the Shona corpus

A ndeye kubata	chibharo (.)zvichinzi
Munhu abatwa	chibharo zvanga zvisipo
Achiti abatwa	chibharo 188. <M.Interpreter
)? Dzekubata	chibharo. Yekutanga ndeye
Bva mamubata	chibharo kechipiri Maka
Mubata kwenyu	chibharo vakazopfuurira

Apart from these examples, another content word which was observed as conspicuously recurring in the data is "again" which court interpreters correctly captured, but at times overemphasised as *zvekare* or *zvakare* in their Shona interpretations. Due to space constraints, the frequency of occurrence of these lexical items in the corpora will not be shown.

Distribution and frequency of pronominal forms of address

According to Angelelli (2004), the use of personal pronouns and specific address forms is a useful key for understanding the alignment of court interpreters and the parties for whom they interpret. If, for instance, the third person singular is used, it indicates possible detachment and the intention to deny all responsibility for the utterance. The use of the first person, on the other hand, may suggest a cooperative attitude and an endeavour to share the responsibility about what is being said (Angelelli, 2004). Interpreters investigated in this study had a tendency to shift from one pronominal form to the other, therefore signalling a different level of involvement, which might have been influenced by the witness's or accused's personal story, the attitude of the public prosecutor or the magistrate, as well as the sensitivity of rape cases involved in the trials. The interpreter would decide – often unconsciously – whether to speak *on behalf of* (first person) or *about* (third person) the interlocutors. Resorting to the first person may, moreover, indicate the autonomous intervention of the interpreter, who then becomes a full participant.

In the examples that follow, we show the occurrence of pronominal forms "you" (English) and its Shona counterpart *iwe* (you) which can, however, co-vary, depending on the context of usage.

Occurrences in the corpora of pronominal forms of "you" appear as *iwe, imi* or *imimi*, which, in English, would be "you" (singular), or "you" (plural/honorific), or "you" (emphatic demonstrative pronoun) respectively. Tables 11.7 and 11.8 illustrate this.

TABLE 11.7 Five of the 556 occurrences of the pronoun "you" in the English corpus

from me She said	you have raped my daughter
<F. Magistrate:>	You did not go to work
to go to work but	you were supposed to
NG ELSE, unless	you seriously need the
Or:> When? Were	you born 12. <F.Witness

The pronoun *iwe* ("you" singular form) in the Shona corpus

According to Mashiri (1999:93), terms of address in Shona derive from a multiplicity of sources, both modern and traditional. The choice of terms of address, including pronouns, reflects very broad categories of social meaning. Address forms can therefore be considered screens upon which the Shona project their attitudes towards different aspects of their life. The use of address forms and cultural values are closely interrelated. The pronoun *iwe* can be used as *imi*, which is the honorific/plural form, or as *imimi*, which is the emphatic form, as shown in the following table. (Although the pronoun had 31 occurrences in the corpus, we show just 5 of these.)

TABLE 11.8 Top 5 of the 31 occurrences in the Shona corpus of the pronoun *iwe* ("you" singular)

muno maMutare	iwe E. M. Wakak**** I
Oita idzo ten pm	iwe wakadzoka kumba
Bva aridza mhere	iwe wakazobuda mumba
Interpreter:>Nokudaro	iwe mutongwi hausi kubvum
<M.Interpreter:>	Iwe wanga wakarara

TABLE 11.9 Top 2 of the 33 occurrences in the Shona corpus of the pronoun *imimi* ("you" in the emphatic form)

kunze kwemutemo	imimi mukawanikwa muchi
wake kundorara	imimi makabva mamubata

The pronouns used in Tables 11.8 and 11.9, namely *iwe* and *imimi*, co-varied with the speech situations during trials: i.e. whether it was the accused or witness addressed by the pronouns, the attitude of the addresser to the addressee, and other contextual factors. According to Mashiri (1999:96), Shona speakers' linguistic performance (in this case, the interpreter) is governed by their communicative competence in that it takes cognisance of extralinguistic factors. Knowledge of the latter enables language users to deploy appropriate pronouns of address as determined by the situation. The use of *iwe* to refer to the male accused is probably prompted by the fact that the accused is facing a serious crime and one for which he is seriously condemned by society (and for which the interpreter is not obliged to show respect nor sympathise). However, when another interpreter uses the honorific pronoun *imi* for a different accused of an advanced age, cultural factors, such as considering the accused's advanced age, could explain such a preference. *Imi* is the plural form of *iwe*, which is used for a plural subject or for one when showing respect is required. In the last example, *imimi* is used emphatically to refer to two accused men. In this case, the need to place emphasis takes precedence over other socio-cultural factors, like age, or the need to show respect and sympathy.

Occurrences of the pronominal forms "she" vs *iye*

In Tables 11.10 and 11.11, we explain and illustrate the use of the pronominal forms, "she" in the English-only corpus, versus *iye* (he/she) in the Shona-only corpus.

TABLE 11.10 Top 7 of the 187 occurrences of the pronoun "she" in the English corpus

ers away from me	She said you have raped
raped my daughter?	She was the only woman
aint, I thought	she was joking J is T
J is T's mother;	she is the one who was
d then I thought	she was joking Ts mother
police officer but	she is a female They
the station J said	she did not observe a

TABLE 11.11 Top 5 of the 44 occurrences of the pronoun *iye* ("he/she" or sometimes "now" in English)

I pedyo nerodhi iye	yake yakanga iri
Interpreter:> ((Iye	wenyu uyu)) ang
<F.Witness:> Iye	akati ndaimuonera
Kamwe chete iye	asina kutenderana
<M.Interpreter:>Iye	zvino VaMuchichis

Table 11.11 indicates that the Shona pronoun *iye* has 44 occurrences in the corpus. The pronoun can be the equivalent of "he/she" in English, although it can also be used as an equivalent of "now", which is an adverb of time in English. In the next section, we show the distribution of key word clouds in the corpora.

Distribution of key word clouds

Using Wmatrix (Rayson 2009) as a corpus analysis tool includes key advantages, such as being able to explore part-of-speech tagging (also called "grammatical tagging") and semantic tagging. Thus, using Wmatrix means that one can now not only investigate frequencies and distributions of word forms and lemmas, but also of grammatical word classes and semantic domains. Semantic tagging is especially useful as it can ensure that recurrent themes appear in frequency lists, even if they do not frequently show on the formal level. This means that if we are faced, for example, with a text that any reader would feel is about "a trial" (as in the context of the current investigation), but in which the actual word "trial" is avoided, while words like "charge", "witness", "accused", "complainant", "plead" and "guilty" are used, the word "trial" will probably still emerge in one of the "key word clouds". The tables that follow show key word clouds extracted from the English-only and the Shona-only trial corpora in Zimbabwean courtrooms.

In Figures 11.2 and 11.3, we present key word clouds extracted from the English-only corpus and the Shona-only corpus respectively. These are then compared with the BNC sampler (spoken) which is a larger normative corpus. By clicking on "compare frequency list", a comparison of the frequency list for the English/Shona-only corpus against the BNC sampler (spoken) can be performed. This comparison can be carried out at the word level to see key words, or at the part of speech level (in the advanced interface), or at the semantic level (to see key concepts or domains).

The log-likelihood statistic employed by Wmatrix can be performed using the log-likelihood calculator. In the simple interface, word and tag clouds are shown which visualise the more significant differences in the larger font sizes. In the advanced interface, more detailed frequency information is also displayed in table form. Using Wmatrix, it is also possible to search for collocations (pairs of words that occur together more often than would be expected due only to chance, Zanettin, 1998). Although we did not directly use the log-likelihood and collocation functions of Wmatrix in this study, the log-likelihood function is nevertheless used in Wmatrix to produce key word clouds. In Figure 11.2, we present key words which made analysis at the *word* level possible, and key concepts or domains which made analysis at the *semantic* level possible.

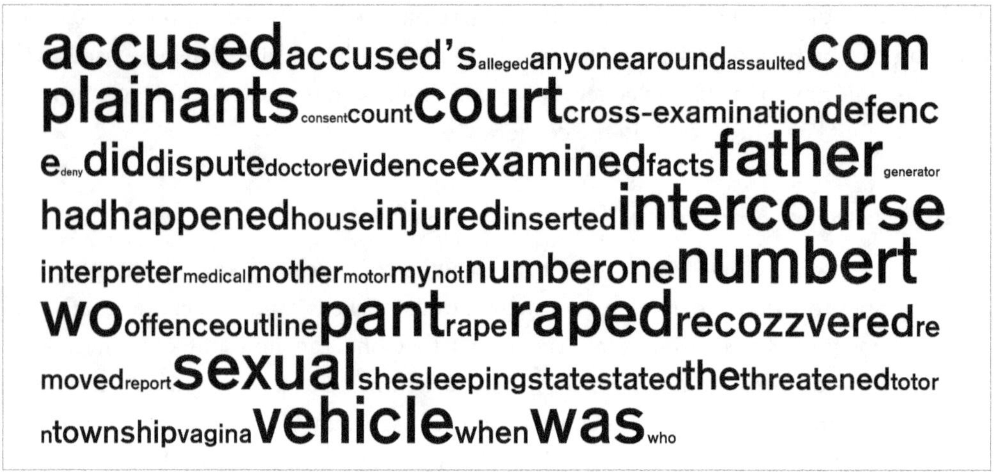

Part 3 | Language as evidence

> accused accused's alleged anyone around assaulted complainants consent count court cross-examination defence deny did dispute doctor evidence examined facts father generator had happened house injured inserted intercourse interpreter medical mother motor my not numberone number t wo offence outline pant rape raped recozzvered re moved report sexual she sleeping state stated the threatened to to n township vagina vehicle when was who

FIGURE 11.2 Key word cloud for the English-only corpus compared to the BNC sampler (spoken) (larger items are more significant)

The first observation was that although pronominal forms featured prominently as grammatical words in the Shona-only corpus shown in Figure 11.3, it is quite clear that most of the content words that appear as key word clouds in the figure are all related to "a trial". Such content words in their order of significance are: *musungwa* (accused); *mhosva* (offence/crime/charge); *mumhan'ari* (complainant); and *chibharo* (rape). Secondly, words expressing denial and admission (and hence consistent with "a trial") were also found to be significant amongst the identified content words. Examples of these words shown in Figure 11.3, to mention a few, are listed in their order of significance: *hongu* (for admission); *handina* (for denial); *kwete* (for denial); and *aiwa* (also for denial). One should, therefore, expect the analysis of semantic tags to throw up semantic domains, as shown in Figure 11.3 (these may not necessarily be congruent with the top key words).

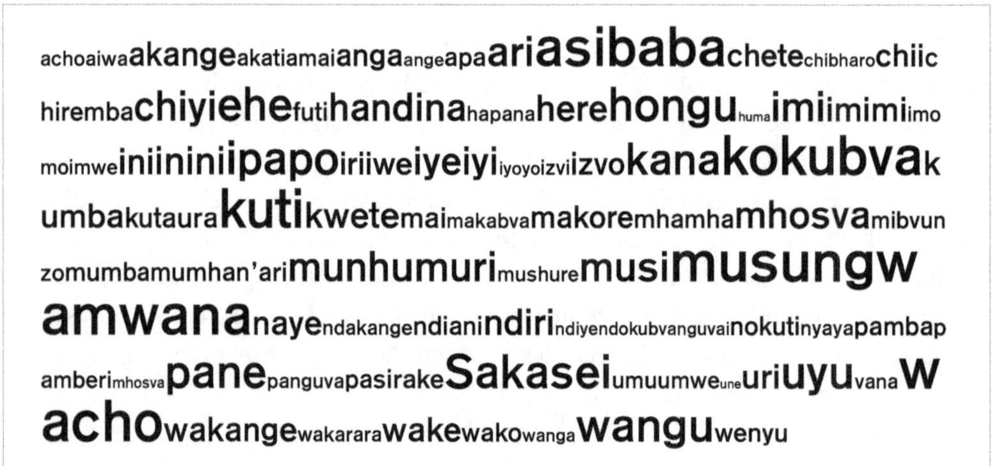

> acho aiwa akange akati amai anga ange apa ari asi baba chete chibharo chiic hiremba chiyiehe futi handina hapana here hongu huma imi imimi imo moi mwe inii nini ipapo irii wei yeiyi iyoyoi zvi izvo kana kokubva k umba kutaura kuti kwete mai makabva makore mhamha mhosva mibvun zo mumba mumhan'ari munhu muri mushure musi musungw amwana naye ndakange ndiani ndiri ndiyendo kubvanguvai nokuti nyaya pambap amberi mhosva pane panguva pasirake Sakasei umuumwe une uri uyu vana w acho wakange wakarara wake wako wanga wangu wenyu

FIGURE 11.3 Key word cloud for the Shona-only corpus compared to the BNC sampler (spoken) (larger items are more significant)

In Figures 11.2 and 12.3, we simply compared frequency and not semantics, as comparing phenomena across two languages would be very strange. Besides, because Shona is an agglutinative language, results might be skewed, as the same word may be recorded as different words, e.g. the word *uraya* which is the verb "to kill" could appear as *akauraya* (he/she killed), *aurayiwa* (he/she has been killed), *tichauraya* (we will kill), *wachauraya* (they will kill), and so on.

Distribution of key domain clouds

In Figure 11.4, Wmatrix was used to analyse key semantic domains for the English corpus.

FIGURE 11.4 Key domain cloud of the English-only corpus compared to the BNC sampler (spoken) (large items are more significant)

In Figure 11.4, the Wmatrix tool enabled us to analyse what was presented in Figure 11.2 as key words, but in this case as "themes" and "topics" (Rayson, 2000), which would otherwise have been difficult to conduct manually.

While most corpus-based tools succeed in describing the linguistic "surface level", Wmatrix can even reach the "below-surface level" through the assignment of semantic tags, which can be regarded as a kind of automatic text interpretation. Hence, Wmatrix as a digital tool can reach the deepest level of interpretation, namely the themes and topics that are often written "between the lines" and which usually only human beings are so successful in finding.

These key domain clouds are part of Wmatrix's complex text interpretation. This allowed us to contrast the results at the word level (key word clouds in Figure 11.2) with the results at the key domains level (semantic tags in Figure 11.4). We were therefore not surprised to observe some of the results at the key domain level reinforcing results at the key words level. For example, in the English-only corpus, "accused", "complainant" and "court" appeared as key words, but "law and order" and "crime" appeared at the semantic level. The same could be said for "inserted", "rape", "intercourse" and "sexual" which also appeared as key words, while "anatomy and physiology" and "relationship and intimacy" appeared at the semantic level. Finally, at the semantic level, "speech acts" appeared for key words like "assaulted", "examined", "injured" and "recovered". This illustrates the advantage of Rayson's (2009) key semantic domains approach over the key words approach, since it allows one to spot further items of interest that otherwise do not appear with other techniques.

While the discussions in the previous sections focused on lexical issues, i.e. the frequency of occurrence of certain lexical items and their distribution, in the sections that follow, we focus on courtroom questions and how they were interpreted during proceedings.

Distribution of question forms

Apart from lexical choices used by the various court players and how they were dealt with by interpreters, as discussed previously, one area of court interpreting research revolves around how some court interpreters may change the pragmatics of courtroom questions, as well as how certain court officials, particularly lawyers, use tools of manipulation to control witnesses. Various scholars (Hale & Gibbons, 1999; Rigney, 1999) have classified courtroom questions in various ways, but we found Rigney's (1999) taxonomy insightful and thus adopted this to analyse two question forms of interest used in this study.

Rigney (1999) examines how courtroom questioning is done through an interpreter using data from the Rosa López testimony during the 1995 O. J. Simpson murder trial in Los Angeles. Rigney's (1999) study shows that, as stipulated by the law, an attorney's power to ask questions and manipulate the questions in order to exercise control over witnesses' answers, is reduced or lost when the questioning is performed through an interpreter, not only because the presence of a third person in the process inevitably changes the flow of communication, but also because the interpreter is found to alter the pragmatics of questions, which are an important tool of manipulation for attorneys.

Rigney (1999) categorises courtroom questions into 13 types according to their degree of control over the witness's testimony, with, at the one end, open "wh–" questions assigned the lowest degree of control, and, on the other end, factual declarative questions assigned the highest degree of control. Rigney's (1999) results show that the interpreter tends to alter the pragmatics of certain types of English questions in the Spanish rendition by, for example, removing the modal question in a request (such as "can you", "would you"), thus turning a polite request into an "unmitigated command" (Rigney, 1999:96). In other cases, a tag question, which is coercive in nature and allows the questioner to exercise more control over the testimony, may be changed into a yes/no question, with a relatively lower degree of control, thus reducing the coerciveness of the original question. Rigney (1999) observed that some of the alterations can be attributed to linguistic differences between English and Spanish. For example, it would be difficult to translate into Spanish an English reverse polarity tag question with a positive tag because of the lack of equivalents. However, other alterations are made, despite the linguistic similarities between the two languages.

The coerciveness of the main types of questions can be ranked in the following order, from least coercive to most coercive (Rigney, 1999):

Least coercive questions
"Wh-" Qs
Routinised "Wh-" Qs
Grammatical Yes/No Qs
Negative grammatical Yes/No Qs
Declarative Qs
Tag Qs
Most coercive questions

Using insights from this classification, we analysed how court interpreters dealt with the pragmatics of courtroom questions in their interpretations. The question forms we found striking are explained and illustrated next.

"But"/"so" prefaced questions

The results of this study showed that coerciveness in cross-examination questions was achieved through the use of "but" prefaced questions which explicitly signal the counter-arguments presented by the parties in a dispute. In a way, out of all the question types, declarative questions were found to be the most convenient for expressing counter-arguments as they have the same syntactic structure as declarative sentences. We thus concur with Rigney's (1999) observation that opinions are expressed through declarative sentences in ordinary conversation.

In Figure 5, "but"/"so" prefaced questions were observed to be typical of the court, i.e. they were mainly used by magistrates and public prosecutors, while lay persons used them sparingly. It was observed that 71% of "but" prefaced questions were used by the court, while 29% were used by lay persons. Similarly, of the total 56 "so" prefaced questions identified, 79% were attributed to the court, while lay persons used 21%, as shown.

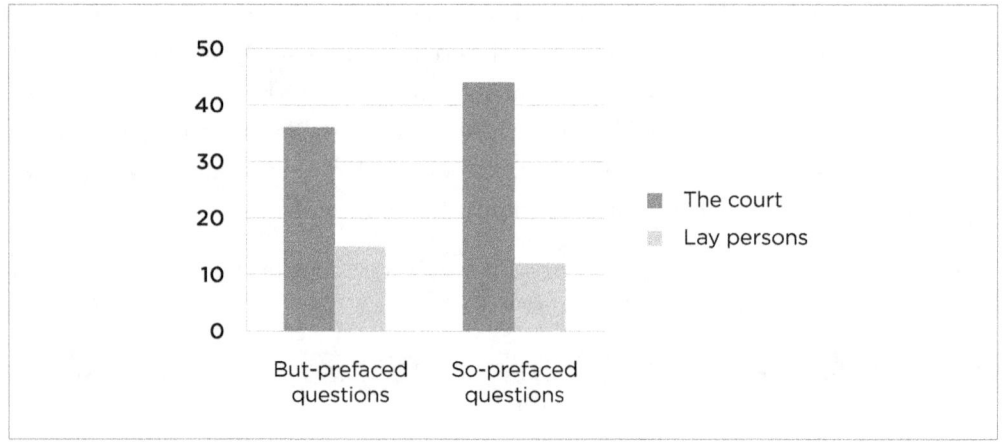

FIGURE 11.5 Comparative occurrence of "but"/"so" prefaced questions

The reason for this scenario is that the court tries to subject "the stories presented by parties in a conflict to various forms of checking" (Hale & Gibbons, 1999:204). First, they are examined for their relevance to the case at hand, as the rules of evidence limit the presentation of evidence to material connected to the case. The stories are then examined for accuracy (Hale & Gibbons, 1999). According to Madhuku (2010), in the Common Law system, particularly in a criminal trial, the customary roles of the prosecution and defence are to construct different representations of the same story. One such representation would lead to a conviction, while the other would lead to a not-guilty verdict. Thus, one way used by the court to examine "these stories" is the use of "but" prefaced questions which explicitly signal the counter-arguments presented by the parties in a dispute. In some cases this occurs because the use of closed questions during cross-examination may be aimed at coercing witnesses, and controlling and constraining their answers to a limited range pre-empted by the leading questions; as well as how the intended effect of the questioner is altered by an interpreter's renditions. These findings are corroborated by the findings of Rigney (1999) and Hale's (2004) investigation into the way in which questions are sometimes used strategically in the courtroom to elicit free narratives from witnesses during the examination-in-chief. The findings are very similar in that they show that there is probably a conscious tendency on the part of the court to use the above question forms strategically to elicit certain responses from the witnesses and the accused persons.

"Then" prefaced questions

Apart from "but"/"so" prefaced questions presented and explained, another interesting occurrence observed in the data were "then" prefaced questions, as shown in the three examples in Table 11.12.

TABLE 11.12 The use of "then"– prefaced questions

No.	Speaker	Utterance	English gloss
C3M	M	Uhu ...	Yes ...
	PP	Then what happened?	
	I	*Chii chakazoitika* ↑	What then happened?
C1H	I	I heard the sound but sounded like it was from afar. I was suddenly shocked when I realised someone was squeezing into my blankets...	
	M	Uhu ...	Yes ...
	PP	And then what happened?	
C2H	W	*Chakaitika ndechokuti ndakashaya mwana masikati acho iwayo asi ndakangoti ari kutamba nevamwe vake semazuva ose.*	During that afternoon in question my child was conspicuously away from home but just thought she was out playing with friends as usual.
	PP	Then what happened?	
	I	*Chiyi chakazoitika?*	What then happened?
	M	Uhu ...	Yes ...

The three examples of "then" prefaced questions were attributed to the court and were used by the court during the examination-in-chief, as well as in the re-examination, to further probe witnesses and accused persons by asking them to recount events under examination in the case. This is referred to as "the eternal reality", in Hale and Gibbons' (1999:207) words. In the three examples presented, it is noted that, after giving an answer to one question, the accused person or witness is further prompted by, "*Then* what happened?"/"And *then* what happened?" to ensure that the court is furnished with further events of the alleged rape encounter in the context of this study.

Discussion

The results presented in this chapter characterise the bilingual Zimbabwean courtroom as being unusual and a unique context, in the sense that the court officials in an English-medium trial also speak the language(s) of the accused or witness, although the officials conduct the trial in the language of the court, i.e. English. This is different from other bilingual settings where court officials do not speak the language of the accused or witness. In the Zimbabwean courtroom, the different court interactants strategically use various aspects of language which, on a daily basis, court interpreters have to deal with in their interpretations. As one of the findings, the study has shown that interpreters tend to shift from one pronominal form to another, thus signalling different levels of involvement during the trial process, perhaps influenced by the witness or accused's personal story, the attitude of the public prosecutor, or that of the magistrate, as well as the sensitivity of the rape cases involved in the trials. The interpreter decides – often unconsciously – whether to speak *on behalf of* (first person) or *about* (third person) the interlocutors. Resorting to the first person, for instance, was seen as indicative of an autonomous intervention by the interpreter, who then became a full participant, contrary to the unchallenged belief system by court officials that interpreters are merely channels for conveying the message uttered by one speaker into another language for another speaker (Wadensjö, 1998).

The study also demonstrated that most of the content words which appeared as key word and key domain clouds in Figures 11.2, 11.3 and 11.4 all collocated with the word "trial". Such content words, in order of significance, included *musungwa* (accused), *mhosva* (offence/crime/charge), *mumhan'ari* (complainant) and *chibharo* (rape). Words expressing denial and admission (and which are, therefore, consistent with "a trial") were also found to be significant amongst the identified content words. Examples of these words included *hongu* (for admission), *handina* (for denial), *kwete* (for denial), and *aiwa* (also for denial). These words, which appeared as key words, were later analysed as semantic domains in terms of themes and topics which were also semantically consistent with the domain of a trial. The study therefore illustrates that, while most corpus-based tools succeed in describing the linguistic "surface level", Wmatrix can even reach the "below-surface level" through the assignment of semantic tags, which can be regarded as a kind of automatic text interpretation. The concept of *keyness* (describing a word that occurs in a text more often than we would expect it to by chance alone) is therefore useful in automatic text analysis and text understanding.

Apart from the above, the study also showed that the force of courtroom questions may be altered during interpreting. This study illustrated that court interpreters sometimes significantly change the pragmatics of courtroom questions that court officials, particularly lawyers, may use as tools of manipulation to control witnesses. Apart from lexical choices used by the various court players and how these are dealt with by interpreters, the findings presented in Section 4.6 demonstrate that, in the Common Law system, particularly in a criminal trial, the normal role of the prosecution and the defence is to construct different representations of the same story. One such representation aims at a conviction, while the other is aimed at a "not guilty" verdict. This objective is achieved through, amongst other things, a conscious tendency on the part of the court to use various question forms strategically to elicit certain responses from the witnesses and the accused. Although the court interpreters investigated tried to preserve the pragmatic force of the questions used by the various court actors, the study illustrates that it was frustrating at times for some court officials who spoke both Shona and English to discover that the interpreters had tampered with the force of this strategic resource.

Conclusion

Using the tools of Wmatrix and observation of open court proceedings, we analysed the frequency and use of different lexical, grammatical, syntactic and conversational features by the different court players, as well as how these were interpreted by court interpreters during court proceedings. In the chapter, we used the tools of Wmatrix, such as frequency profiles, and the keywords and key concepts approaches, to: (1) analyse how different court interactants strategically use various aspects of language in the courtroom; and (2) how these aspects were then interpreted during trials. We have illustrated that, through the use of various lexical items and question forms, the power of a participant, and thus his or her control over a triadic exchange, may be realised not only through the role(s) that he or she is capable of playing, but also through the participant roles of the co-present court actors.

We have shown that the interpreter, working with bilingual court officials and interpreting for bilingual lay people, perceives his or her power considerably reduced by these other bilinguals (the magistrate and the public prosecutor, on one hand, and the witness(es) and accused on the other). All these court actors with their varying degrees of bilingual skill take not only the roles of speakers (questioners) and addressees of witnesses' interpreted evidence, as well as listeners to the witnesses' answers in the vernacular, but they also stand as judges of the interpreters for the accuracy of their interpretation. We have thus illustrated that, through the application of such linguistic factors as lexical items and question forms, the power of each participant, and thus his or her control over a triadic exchange, is realised not only in the role(s) he or she is capable of playing, but also through the participant roles of other co-present court actors.

References

Angelelli, C. 2004. *Revisiting the interpreter's role: A study of conference, court and medical interpreters in Canada, Mexico and the United States*. Amsterdam: John Benjamins.

Baker, M. 1995. Corpora in translation studies: An overview and suggestions for future research. *Target*, 7(2):54-67.

Bendazzoli, C. & Sandrelli, A. 2009. Corpus-based interpreting studies: Early work and future prospects. *Tradumatica* 7. http://www.fti.uab.cat/tradumatica/revista/num7/articles/08/08.pdf [Retrieved 28 December 2018].

Berk-Seligson, S. 1990. *The bilingual courtroom: Court interpreters in the judicial process*. Chicago: University of Chicago Press.

Bowker, L. 2002. *Computer aided translation technology: A practical introduction*. Ottawa: University of Ottawa Press.

Brown, P. & Levinson, S. 1987. *Politeness*. Cambridge: Cambridge University Press.

Dean, R. & Pollard, R. 2011. Context-based ethical reasoning in interpreting: A demand control schema perspective. *The Interpreter and Translator Trainer*, 5(1):155-182. https://doi.org/10.1080/13556509.2011.10798816

Dose, S. 2010. Patterns of growing standardisation and interference in interpreted German discourse. Unpublished MA thesis, University of South Africa, Pretoria. http://hdl.handle.net/10500/4710

Fairclough, N. 1992. *Discourse and social change*. Cambridge: Polity Press.

Gile, D. 1995. *Basic concepts and models for interpreter and translator training*. Amsterdam: John Benjamins.

Grice, H.P. 1975. Logic and conversation. In: P. Cole & J.L. Morgan (eds.), *Syntax and semantics, Vol. 3, Speech acts*. New York: Academic Press. pp. 41-58. https://sites.ualberta.ca/~francisp/NewPhil448/GriceLogicConversation.pdf [Retrieved 12 February 2018].

Hale, S. 2004. *The discourse of court interpreting: Discourse practices of the law, the witness and the interpreter*. Amsterdam: John Benjamins.

Hale, S. & Gibbons, J. 1999. Varying realities: Patterned changes in the interpreter's representation of courtroom and external realities. *Applied Linguistics*, 20(2):203-220. https://doi.org/10.1093/applin/20.2.203

Halliday, M.A.K. & Hasan, R. 1976. *Cohesion in English*. London: Longman.

Hunston, S. 2002. *Corpora in Applied Linguistics*. Cambridge: Cambridge University Press.

Kajzer-Wietrzny, M. 2013. Idiosyncratic features of interpreting style. *New Voices in Translation Studies*, 9:38-52.

Kruger, A.; Wallmach, K. & Munday, J (eds.). 2011. *Corpus-based translation studies: Research and applications*. (Series: Continuum advances in translation.) Manchester: St Jerome/Routledge.

Madhuku, L. 2010. *An introduction to Zimbabwean law*. Harare: Weaver Press and Friedrich-Ebert-Stiftung.

Mashiri, P. 1999. Terms of address in Shona: A sociolinguistic approach. *Zambezia*, 26(1):93-110.

Mason, I (ed.). 2001. *Triadic exchanges: Studies in dialogue interpreting*. Manchester: St Jerome.

Mason, I. & Stewart, M. 2001. Interactional pragmatics, face and the dialogue interpreter. In: I. Mason (ed.), *Triadic exchanges: Studies in dialogue interpreting*. Manchester: St Jerome. pp. 51-70.

Meyer, C.F. 2002. *English corpus linguistics: An introduction*. Cambridge: Cambridge University Press.

Mikkelson, H. 2014. *Introduction to court interpreting*. New York: Routledge.

Moropa, K. 2009. Utilizing "hot words" in ParaConc to verify lexical simplification in English-Xhosa parallel texts. *South African Journal of African Languages*, 29(2):227-241.

Olohan, M. 2004. *Introducing corpora in translation studies*. London: Routledge.

Rayson, P. 2000. *Wmatrix: A web-based processing environment*. Lancaster: University of Lancaster Computing Department.

Rayson, P. 2009. *Key domains and MWE extraction using Wmatrix*. Paper presented at a workshop at Aston Corpus Summer School, Tuesday 28th July 2009. http://ucrel.lancs.ac.uk/people/paul/publications/AstonWorkshop09PRslides.pdf

Rigney, A.C. 1999. Questioning in interpreted testimony. *Forensic Linguistics*, 6(1):83-108.

Rodriguez-Ines, P. 2010. Electronic corpora and other information communication technology tools. *The Interpreter and Translator Trainer*, 4(2):251-282. https://doi.org/10.1080/13556509.2010.10798806

Roy, C.B. 1996. An interactional sociolinguistic analysis of turn-taking in an interpreted event. *Interpreting: International journal of research and practice in interpreting*, 1(1):39-67. https://doi.org/10.1075/intp.1.1.04roy

Stubbs, M. 1996. *Text and corpus analysis:Computer-assisted studies of language and culture*. Oxford: Blackwell Publishers.

Tkacŭkova, T. 2010. Representing oneself: Cross-examination questioning – Lay people as cross-examiners. In: M. Coulthard & A. Johnson (eds.), *The Routledge handbook of forensic linguistics*. New York: Routledge. pp. 333-346.

Valero-Garcés, C. 2005. Emotional and psychological effects on interpreters in public services: A critical factor to keep in mind. *Translation Journal,* 9(3):106-119. http://translationjournal.net/journal//33ips.html

Van Dijk, T.A. 2000. *Ideology: A multidisciplinary study*. London: Sage. http://dx.doi.org/10.4135/9781446217856

Wadensjö, C. 1998. *Interpreting as interaction*. London: Longman.

Wallmach, K. 2000. Examining simultaneous interpreting norms and strategies in a South African legislative context: A pilot corpus analysis. *Language Matters*, 31(1):198-221. https://doi.org/10.1080/10228190008566165

Zanettin, F. 1998. Bilingual comparable corpora and the training of translators. *Meta:Translators' Journal*, 43(4):616-630.

Zimbabwe National Statistics Agency (ZimStat). 2017. *Facts and Figures 2017*. Causeway: Harare.

PART 4

Forensic linguistic evidence

ROAD MARKERS FOR RELIABILITY IN AUTHORSHIP IDENTIFICATION EVIDENCE

Lirieka Meintjes-van der Walt

Introduction

At a time when language rights in South Africa are often grossly neglected; where court proceedings are sometimes at risk of being compromised by less than excellent court interpretation; in a country where the intellectual development of large numbers of children is stifled by the colonial perpetuation of non-mother tongue education; and at a time in the history of our country where, quite rightly, I believe, loud cries are demanding decolonisation and a postcolonial overhaul, the interrogation of the link between the law and linguistics is more than pertinent and urgent. This chapter discusses authorship attribution from a legal perspective and attempts to provide linguists working in this field, particularly those who proffer expert evidence in a court of law, with guidelines that will ensure the reliability and validity of such evidence.

The term "forensic" is broadly a synonym for "legal" or "related to courts". However, the term "forensics" has become so closely associated with the scientific field that many dictionaries include the meaning that equates the word with forensic science. Olsson and Luchjenbroers (2013: xvi) describe forensic linguistics as follows:

> Forensic linguistics is not a single science or study but an umbrella discipline comprised of many facets. Thus, any forensic linguistic inquiry or investigation can draw upon any branch of theoretical or applied linguistics in order to analyse the language of some area of human life which has relevance to the law, whether criminal or civil.

This chapter does not purport to attempt to address the entire field of forensic linguistic science. It focuses specifically on the linking of an author to the production of a particular text, through applying forensic linguistic science as a tool for the purpose of judicial fact finding and dispute resolution.

The discussion below focuses on some pertinent legal aspects regarding authorship attribution. It attempts to provide forensic linguists with road markers that could guide their research design and, hopefully, manifest in useful, and above all reliable, evidence in court that would result in the innocent being exonerated and the guilty being punished. In this chapter I attempt to emphasise that it is essential that the linguistic evidence proffered in a trial is both reliable and valid. This is what Kotzé (2010:1) refers to as the "principle of scientific rigour".

The activity whereby linguists attempt to identify the author of documents by interrogating the language performance style of the authors concerned is called "authorship attribution" (Stamatatos, 2008). Texts that could be subjected to this kind of analysis, and which experts in the field of linguistics may well be called upon to interrogate in an attempt to further the case of a party to litigation, could, inter alia, include documents such as a last will and testament, e-mail messages, online forum messages, blogs, tweets and SMS messages.

Opinion evidence

Opinion evidence is normally not admissible in courts in Anglo-American jurisdictions, as a person giving testimony may only testify to what he or she has personally experienced. However, all Anglo-American jurisdictions make exceptions for instances where the court could benefit from the specialised knowledge of an expert who might testify to some aspect of knowledge which might be outside the common knowledge of the ordinary person (Schwikkard & Van der Merwe, 2016:8.3), including members of a jury in American, English and Australian jurisdictions, or the presiding officers, such as magistrates and judges, in South Africa. For such evidence to be admissible in Anglo-American jurisdictions, it must, first and foremost, be deemed to be relevant and consequently useful to the court in reaching a decision. South Africa inherited the Roman Dutch law tradition, but the Law of Evidence in South Africa is based on English law (Schwikkard & Van der Merwe, 2016:8.3). In *Stock v Stock* (1981:1296E), Diemont, Judge of the Appeal Court, held that an expert "must be made to understand that he is there to assist the Court".

South Africa (like England and Wales, but unlike the USA) does not have clear standards to monitor the admissibility of scientific evidence. South Africa (like England and Wales) has a very lenient approach to the admissibility of evidence; and authorship identification evidence will be allowed if it is potentially relevant. However, the so-called weight attributed to evidence "is a question of fact" (Schwikkard & Van der Merwe, 2016:53); and, as they explain (2016:20), the weight of the evidence refers to "its persuasiveness, alone or in conjunction with other evidence, in satisfying the court as to the *facta probanda* that has to be considered".

In the US courts, the admissibility of expert evidence, including authorship attribution evidence, is a "matter of law" (Berger, 2011:21) and evidence will only be admitted if it is deemed to be not only relevant but at the same time, scientifically reliable (*Daubert v Merrell Dow Pharmaceuticals Inc*, 1993).

Reliability

To provide prospective forensic linguists with road markers to avoid courtroom pitfalls, the discussion that follows briefly interrogates the *Daubert v Merrell Dow Pharmaceuticals* (1993) admissibility criteria and considers how these factors could be applied to determine the weight that should be given to this kind of evidence in South Africa.

In the case of *Frye v United States* (1923), the court ruled that the notion from which the deduction by an expert is made must be sufficiently established to have gained "general acceptance" in the particular field to which it belongs (paragraph 1014), thus establishing the so-called "general acceptance test" (which became known as the "*Frye* rule"). Until 1993, this principle was used by US courts in deciding the admissibility of scientific evidence. A further case, *Kelly v State* (1992), paved the way for the landmark *Daubert v Merrell Dow* decision (1993), which superseded the *Fry* rule. In *Kelly v State*, it was held that a trial court must determine that the evidence is "sufficiently reliable and relevant to help the jury in reaching accurate results" (1993:572). The reliability must be determined by the following:

- The underlying scientific method must be valid;
- The technique applied to the method must be valid; and
- The method must have been properly applied on the occasion in question (1993:572-57).

In *Daubert v Merrell Dow Pharmaceuticals Inc* (1993), which was concerned with product liability, the issue was whether Bendectin, an anti-nausea drug taken during pregnancy, had caused birth defects in children. The epidemiological literature suggested that it did not. The plaintiffs in the *Daubert* case wanted to call experts who would attack the inferences drawn from the data in the published literature on the basis of the results of animal studies. The trial court rejected the expert evidence on the grounds that the work of the experts had not been published and therefore failed to meet the standards of scientific acceptance that the courts had developed under *Frye v United States* (1923). According to the precedent established in the *Frye* case, an important consideration regarding the admissibility of expert evidence was whether the expert evidence proffered in court was generally accepted by other experts in the field. The trial court thus granted summary judgment in favour of the defendant, Merrell Dow (727 F. Supp. 570, 572 (S.D. Cal. 1989)). The court of appeals, in turn, affirmed the trial court's decision (951 F.2d 1128 (9th Cir. 1991)).

However, subsequent to that, the Supreme Court reversed the decision of the court of appeals, holding that the Federal Rules of Evidence (United States Courts, 2017) had replaced the *Frye* standard. It interpreted Rule 702 as requiring courts to engage in a "preliminary assessment of whether the reasoning or methodology underlying the testimony is scientifically valid and/or whether that reasoning or methodology properly can be applied to the facts in issue" (509 U.S. at 592-93). To be scientifically valid, the proffered evidence need not be incontrovertibly accepted in the scientific community. Rather, "the adjective 'scientific' implies a grounding in the methods and procedures of science" (509 U.S. at 590). Thus the *Frye* rule was superseded by the Supreme Court's formulation of new requirements for the admission of expert evidence. The court did not attempt to state the conditions that are both necessary and sufficient for evidence to be scientifically valid. It did, however, herald what I would like to call the "scientific turn" in evaluating expert evidence by formulating the following four non-exclusive indicia:

1. whether the theory offered has been tested;
2. whether it has been subjected to peer-review and publication;
3. whether the rate of error was known; and
4. whether the theory is generally accepted in the scientific community (*Daubert v Merrell Dow Pharmaceuticals Inc*, 509 U.S. 579 (1993) 593-594)).

Subsequent to the *Daubert* case, the *Kumho Tire Co. v. Carmichael* (1999) was heard. This was also a product liability case about automobile tyres. In allowing the inclusion of a tyre expert whose testimony in court was based on his experience in the industry, the court held that "the general principles of *Daubert* apply not only to experts offering scientific evidence, but also to experts basing their testimony on experience" (526 U.S. 137 (1999) 138). Subsequent to the *Kumho Tire* case, Rule 702 of the Federal Rules of Evidence (United States Courts, 2017) was amended to state that:

> A witness who is qualified as an expert by knowledge, skill, experience, training, or education may testify in the form of an opinion or otherwise if:
> (a) the expert's scientific, technical, or other specialised knowledge will help the trier of fact to understand the evidence or to determine a fact in issue;
> (b) the testimony is based on sufficient facts or data;
> (c) the testimony is the product of reliable principles and methods; and
> (d) the expert has reliably applied the principles and methods to the facts of the case.

Based on this, in the case of authorship attribution, for forensic feature comparison to be considered scientifically valid and reliable, its methods must be shown to be repeatable, reproducible, and accurate,[1] and based on empirical studies[2] "at levels that have been measured and are appropriate to the intended application" (National Physical Laboratory, 2010; Pavese, 2009:106; PCAST, 2016:48).

If an examiner states that two samples are similar, without appropriate estimates of accuracy, this is regarded as scientifically meaningless (Edmond & Martire, 2016). This type of statement lacks probative value and it has substantial potential for causing prejudice

---

[1] "By "accurate", we mean that, with known probabilities, an examiner obtains correct results both (1) for samples from the same source (true positives) and (2) for samples from different sources (true negatives)" (PCAST 2016:47).

[2] "By an "empirical study", we mean a test in which a method has been used to analyse a large number of independent sets of samples, similar in relevant aspects to those encountered in casework, in order to estimate the method's repeatability, reproducibility, and accuracy" (PCAST 2016:48).

(Edmond & Martire, 2016). This is so because there is no training or experience that can replace "adequate empirical demonstration of accuracy" (President's Council of Advisors on Science and Technology (PCAST), 2016:143). The scientific method does not need to be perfect, but it is essential that its accuracy must be measured and appropriately based on empirical testing.

A report by the National Research Council (2009) of the US National Academy of Sciences, on strengthening forensic sciences in the United States (also referred to as the "NAS Report"), emphasised the importance of knowing the accuracy of a method. According to the PCAST Report (2016:48), "without an appropriate estimate of accuracy, a metrological method is useless – because one has no idea how to interpret its results"). Additionally, black-box studies,[3] where examiners make decisions about independent tests and determine error rates, are also needed for measuring the accuracy of forensic feature-comparison methods. These studies typically involve decisions based on questioned samples and on one or more known samples to determine the accuracy rate of a method (Edmond & Martire, 2016:373).

In South Africa, presiding officers have to determine what weight should be given to proffered expert evidence with regard to authorship identification. To do so, it is highly likely that an expert witness will have to answer a question as to whether he or she has read the NAS and the PCAST reports; and, more particularly, he or she might be required to indicate to the court what lessons an expert who gives evidence in court should have learnt from the criticism directed at all forensic sciences, with the exception of DNA evidence, in those reports.

From the discussion thus far, it is clear that "scientific validity" and "reliability" require that a method should undergo some empirical testing under conditions which, as set out in the PCAST Report (2016:143), are "appropriate to its intended use and that provide valid estimates of how often the method reaches an incorrect conclusion".

The PCAST Report states that the mere fact that a method is foundationally valid does not necessarily mean that examiners will always get the correct results (PCAST, 2016:57). Referring to an article by Koehler (2016), the report enumerates a number of possible problems which could, in principle, occur:

> features may be mis-measured; samples may be interchanged, mislabelled, miscoded, altered, or contaminated; equipment may be mis-calibrated; technical glitches and failures may occur without warning and without being noticed; and results may be misread, misinterpreted, mis-recorded, mislabelled, mixed up, misplaced, or discarded.
> (PCAST, 2016:57)

---

[3] "By "black-box studies", we refer to empirical studies that assess a subjective method by having examiners analyse samples and render opinions about the origin or similarity of samples" (PCAST 2016:48).

The only scientific way to ascertain that an examiner can apply a foundationally valid method through appropriate empirical testing, basically involves measuring the frequency of getting an accurate answer from an examiner (PCAST, 2016:56). "Proficiency testing" firstly, tests to ascertain whether a practitioner meticulously followed the steps demanded by the prescribed protocol; and, secondly, practice test exercises are carried out to assist practitioners in honing their skills and eliminating error. In PCAST's (2016:57) report, proficiency testing means an ongoing empirical tests to "evaluate the capability and performance of analysts", as expressed in the PCAST Report:

> We note that proficiency testing is not intended to estimate the inherent error rates of a method; these rates should be assessed from foundational validity studies. Proficiency testing should also be distinguished from competency testing, which is the evaluation of a person's knowledge and ability prior to performing independent work in forensic casework. (PCAST, 2016:57)

It is crucially important to understand the validity and reliability of the forensic feature-comparison method because this particular class of method is a "common scientific activity" and in science there must be clear standards for determining reliability (JCGM_200, 2012:200). Furthermore it is important to understand the validity and reliability of a particular field because it has been proven over the past few years that "faulty forensic feature comparisons" can result in miscarriages of justice (Garrett & Neufeld, 2009:3). These kinds of problems could be a result of forensic feature-comparison methods which are not meaningfully evaluated (PCAST, 2016:45). However, the fact that opinion evidence is relevant to a particular set of facts does not necessarily mean that it was derived from a reliable source or that the technique used to produce the results is reliable. Ireland and Beaumont (2015:6) contend that, whenever expert opinion evidence is in question, more is required than just a simple determination of helpfulness. There is a danger in accepting expert opinion evidence without testing or challenging its reliability and validity. Haber and Haber (2008:88) state that reliability "means that a method should produce the same results for the same experiment every time it is used both by many experts and by the same experts knowingly or unknowingly repeating the test".

The reliability of expert opinion is of crucial importance, as unreliable expert opinion evidence may lead to miscarriages of justice and wrongful convictions,[4] as is substantiated by the findings of Saks and Koehler (2005:893) when they reviewed wrongful convictions and DNA exonerations. They discovered that 63% of the cases they scrutinised involved

---

[4] In Roman et al. (2012:9), it is stated that faulty forensic science has contributed to convicting innocent people and will continue to do so if careful steps are not taken to ascertain the reliability of the methods, technique or sources of the evidence presentment in court. Also, the lack of laboratory oversight and forensic standards leaves forensic science distrusted and vulnerable to manipulation.

forensic science testing errors; and 27% involved false or misleading testimony by forensic experts.[5]

Testability

For scientific evidence to be reliable, it must be based on a theory that is testable and falsifiable. Although it is not consistently done, South African courts also require testing of an expert's opinion when the weight of the evidence is decided. This is reflected, many years before the *Daubert* findings, in the South African case of *R v Jacobs* 1940 (TPD 142 at 147) where Judge Ramsbottom held that:

> It is of the greatest importance that the value of the opinion should be capable of being tested and unless the expert states the grounds upon which he bases his opinion, it is not possible to test its correctness so as to form a proper judgment upon it.

A significant factor should be whether the experts "are proposing to testify about matters growing naturally and directly out of research they have conducted independent of the litigation, or whether they have developed their opinions expressly for purposes of testifying" (*In Re Paoli Railroad Yard PCB Litigation*, 1994:741). The court in this case contended that testimony based on "legitimate, preexisting research unrelated to the litigation" constitutes the "most persuasive" grounds for deciding an expert's opinions based on scientific methodology (*In Re Paoli Railroad Yard PCB Litigation*, 1994:742). In the light of this, methods used for authorship attribution need to be tested for reliability.

If a forensic linguist takes cognisance of the kind of questioning that he or she is likely to face in a court hearing, it might significantly enhance the research design utilised in a forensic linguistics field such as authorship attribution. The cross-examination questions that follow, which have been extracted from Edmond et al. (2014:178) and, where necessary, adapted for authorship attribution, may assist in this regard. The following typical cross-examination questions are examples of questions which a forensic linguist is likely to face in court:

- Please direct us to specific studies that have validated authorship identification techniques and indicate to the court what these studies set out to assess.
- Please direct us to the written standard or protocol applicable to your analysis and indicate whether it was followed.
- Considering that the qualitative authorship comparison methodology is highly subjective, do you agree that it is possible that different examiners who use this approach, could come to different conclusions?

---

[5] Upon reviewing 86 DNA exoneration cases, Saks and Koehler (2005:893) noted: "Percentages exceed 100% because more than one factor was found in many cases. In the first study to explore forensic science testimony by prosecution experts in the trials of innocent people, University of Virginia Law Professor, Brandon Garrett and Innocence Project Co-Director, Peter Neufeld, found that, in 139 trials where forensic evidence supported the exoneree's conviction, 61% involved improper testimony by the prosecution's forensic expert." (See also Garrett & Neufeld, 2009.)

- Did you develop your opinions expressly for the purpose of testifying in this court, or did you conduct your research independent of litigation?

Peer-review and publication

According to the *Daubert* case, one of the methods by which a court can determine the scientific validity and reliability of expert testimony, is peer-review. This means that the scientific method of the particular identification process has to be peer-reviewed by other experts in the field. A methodology such as authorship identification, in order to comply with the requirements of the scientific methods, should be published in a professional, peer-reviewed journal. During the peer-review process, experts will evaluate:

> (1) the validity of the hypothesis; (2) how it was formulated and tested; (3) whether the scientific method was followed; and (4) whether proper conclusions were reached.
> (Grzybowski et al., 2003:11)

Error rate and personal proficiency

The third element to determine reliability, as stipulated in the *Daubert* case, is the determination of the error rate of the method that is being used. In cases involving authorship identification, experts are called to give testimony on whether or not the text in question can be identified as having emanated from a particular author. In these instances, presiding officers also want to know "how often such identifications are in error" (Puzniak, 2000:40). In other words, they want to know "how often the profession, using accepted techniques and controls, produces a mistaken identity" (Grzybowski et al., 2003:12).

The fact that science and law define "error" in different ways, could lead to misunderstandings. In the legal sphere, the term "error" is often used to indicate a mistake which would have been avoided if correct procedures were followed, or to indicate a wrong result as a consequence of inadequate calibration. On the other hand, in scientific terms, the term "error" has a wider meaning and could also refer to an inadequacy in the procedure itself, which could result in the production of an incorrect result as a consequence of chance occurrence, despite the proper application of the procedure. When a forensic feature-comparison method is used to ascertain whether two samples were produced by the same source, coincidental matches and human or technical failures are both statistically regarded as "errors" because both can result in an incorrect conclusion (PCAST, 2016:51).

In the field of authorship identification, the experts must be in a position to reveal whether error rates have been reported. The revealing of this information could indicate credibility on the part of the expert. After having given this information, the expert must inform the court on the steps taken by him or her to reduce the occurrence of error in the work he or she presents to the court (Grzybowski et al., 2003: 12). The court in *United States v Diaz*

(2007), with regard to the factor of "known or potential error", held that "it is not possible to calculate an absolute error rate for firearms identification (*US v Diaz*, 2007:8). This is partly because the standards and criteria for traditional pattern matching are subjective" (*US v Diaz*, 2007:8). Furthermore, the court ended by stating that "No true error rate will ever be calculated so long as the firearm-examiner community continues to rely on the subjective traditional pattern matching method of identification" (*US v Diaz*, 2007:8). This means that, currently, even for the long trusted and accepted firearm identification, no true error rate is known. Linguists working in the highly complex field of authorship identification may well heed the warning sounded in the *US v Diaz*, case.

It is difficult to evaluate the validity of the practitioner's evidence when there is no indication of the error rate. The lack of research might prevent appropriate qualifications being made (Edmond et al., 2016:36). The following questions, also borrowed from Edmond et al. (2014:174-197) and, where necessary, adapted for forensic linguistics, are possible questions which a forensic linguist might have to face in court in this regard and they could be borne in mind when an authorship identification investigation is designed and executed:

- Please tell us about the error rate or potential sources of error associated with authorship identification.
- Please indicate specific studies that provide an error rate or an estimation of an error rate for your technique.
- Might someone using the same technique come to a different conclusion?

Non-DNA forensic techniques often rely on subjective judgements; and the proficiency of the expert to make such judgements may become the focus of cross-examination. Forensic linguists could bear in mind the following kind of questions regarding personal proficiency, also informed by Edmond et al. (2014:174-197):

- Have you ever had your own ability for authorship identification tested in conditions where the correct answer was known?
- If not, how can we be confident that you are proficient in this particular field?
- If so, can you provide independent empirical evidence of your performance?

General acceptance by the relevant scientific community

General acceptance refers to "the acceptance by the professional community practicing in a particular field" (Grzybowski et al., 2003: 9). The following would be typical cross-examination questions:

- Please indicate the names and the scientific standing of prominent linguists who use the specific techniques and methods you have used in support of your expert evidence.
- Please refer the court to some prominent publications in the field of authorship attribution which indicate the general peer acceptance of the techniques and methods you have used in reaching the conclusions proffered as expert evidence.

Bias

Forensic techniques that rest on subjective judgments are susceptible to cognitive biases. Cognitive bias refers to ways in which human perceptions and judgments can be shaped by factors other than those relevant to the decision at hand. The phenomenon of "bias" could refer to "contextual bias", where irrelevant background information impacts on attitudes of and decisions by investigators or researchers. It could also include "confirmation bias", where pre-existing beliefs or assumptions prompt researchers to search for new evidence which would confirm their original assumptions. A third manifestation of bias is the so-called "avoidance of cognitive dissonance". In the latter instance, researchers resist, or display a reluctance to accept, new information which does not support their original tentative conclusion (PCAST, 2016:31). Edmond et al. (2014:185) argue that the existence of contextual and confirmation biases "undermine the independence of the analyst's opinion and threaten the validity of their conclusions". Bias may not be intentional, but it is undeniable that it occurs (Edmond et al., 2014:185). A forensic linguist could expect cross-examination questions such as the following, borrowed from Edmond et al. (2014:185):

- Could you explain to the court your understanding of the terms cognitive bias and contextual effects?
- Do you accept that contextual effects can operate unconsciously to such an extent that even an examiner who is carrying out the examination sincerely may be influenced but may not be aware of such influences?
- Did you have any prior knowledge of the details of the case with regard to which you gave expert evidence?
- Could you inform the court what information you had about the accused and about the relevant details of this case before you were asked to analyse the evidence, and before you produced your conclusion?
- Were you provided with any specific information regarding the suspect when asked to undertake your analysis?
- Did your letter of instruction [implicitly or explicitly] indicate the expected outcome of your investigation (e.g. confirm that the suspect is the perpetrator)? Could you indicate whether, and if so, where, in your report, you documented your prior knowledge of the suspect and the circumstances of the case?
- Were you asked to assess whether or not any of the samples provided to you originated from the accused or the defendant?

Conclusion

In her article, "Best Practices and Admissibility for Forensic Linguistics", Chaski (2013:333-378), a prominent forensic linguist, states that "scientifically respectable and judicially acceptable methods" should be used for authorship attribution and that the method should be:

1. Developed independently of any litigation;
2. Tested for accuracy outside of any litigation;
3. Tested for known limits correlated to specific accuracy levels;

4. Tested for any errors of individual testing techniques that could cause accumulated error when combined with other techniques;
5. Replicable;
6. Related to a specific expertise and academic training;
7. Related to standard (generally accepted) techniques within the specific expertise and academic training;
8. Related to uses outside of any litigation in industries or fieldwork in specific expertise.

As far as the required conduct of an expert witness is concerned, the following guidelines could be borne in mind:

1. The witness proffering expert evidence has to establish and prove his or her credentials in order to have the evidence admitted (*Twine and Another v Naidoo and Others*).
2. Expert evidence should only be admitted where it is relevant and reliable (*Twine and another v Naidoo and Others*).
3. The overriding duty of an expert witness is to the court and the administration of justice, and not to the party on whose behalf he is testifying. *(Schneider NO and Others v Aspeling and Another; National Justice Compania Naviera SA v Prudential Assurance Co Limited)*.
4. An expert witness should, at all times, act with honesty, integrity, objectivity and impartiality. (*Schneider NO and Others v Aspeling and Another; National Justice Compania Naviera SA v Prudential Assurance Co Limited*).
5. An expert witness should never assume the role of an advocate (*Schneider NO and Others v Aspeling and Another; Twine and another v Naidoo and Others*).
6. An expert witness should make it clear when a particular question or issue falls outside of his or her expertise (*Twine and another v Naidoo and Others; Nonyane v Road Accident Fund*).
7. An expert witness should declare any personal, financial and/or other interests that could be perceived as a conflict of interest (*Toth v Jarman*).
8. An expert witness should provide expert advice or evidence only within the limits of his or her personal competence. An expert witness should state the facts or assumptions upon which the proffered opinion is based (*Schneider NO and Others v Aspeling and Another*).
9. An expert should take all reasonable steps to maintain and develop his or her professional competence, taking into account material research and developments in the relevant field. (White, 2004:16).
10. An expert witness should state the facts or assumptions upon which his or her opinion is based. The expert should not omit to consider material facts which could detract from his or her concluded opinion (*Schneider NO and Others v Aspeling and Another; National Justice Compania Naviera SA v Prudential Assurance Co Limited*).
11. If an expert's opinion is not properly researched because he or she considers insufficient time to have been allowed, then this must be stated with an indication that the opinion is no more than a provisional one. In the case where the expert witness who has prepared a report could not assert that the report contained the truth, the whole truth and nothing but the truth without some qualification, that qualification should be stated in the report (*Nonyane v Road Accident Fund*).

It would also be wise to remember that a court is neither bound nor obliged to accept the evidence of an expert witness (***R v Nksatlala; R v Theunissen***). This rule of evidence emphasises the grave responsibility which rests on the shoulders of a person proffering evidence in the complex field of authorship attribution. However experienced in the field of linguistics, an expert who proffers evidence that is not proven to be reliable and valid might well negatively affect the course of justice. This by no means implies that the challenges faced by linguistic experts who proffer authorship evidence are graver than those faced by experts from other disciplines. The NAS Report (2009) and the PCAST Report (2016) questioned the scientific reliability and validity of all traditional forensic disciplines, with the exception of DNA evidence.

The selected few forensic road markers discussed in this chapter will hopefully be of some assistance to linguists who negotiate, or who are intending to embark on, the dangerous but exhilarating road of authorship identification evidence. Beware of the unexpected potholes!

References

ASCLD/LAB (American Society of Criminal Laboratory Directors/Laboratory Accreditation Board). 2011. *Supplemental requirements for the accreditation of forensic science testing laboratories*. ASCLD/LAB-International program. http://des.wa.gov/SiteCollectionDocuments/About/1063/RFP/Add7_Item4ASCLD.pdf [Retrieved 25 April 2017].

Ballantyne, K.N.; Edmond, G. & Found, B. 2017. Peer-review in forensic science. *Forensic Science International*, 277:66-76.

Berger, M.A. 2011. The admissibility of expert testimony. In: National Academy of Sciences, *Reference manual on scientific evidence*, 3rd Edition. Washington DC: The National Academies Press. pp. 11-36. https://www.nap.edu/read/13163/chapter/3 [Retrieved 2 January 2019].

Bernstein, D.E. & Jackson, J.D. 2004. The *Daubert* trilogy in the States. *Jurimetrics*, 44. https://ssrn.com/abstract=498786 [Retrieved 11 April 2018].

Chaski, C.E. 2013. Best practices and admissibility of forensic author identification. *Journal of Law and Policy*, 21(2):333-376. http://brooklynworks.brooklaw.edu/jlp/vol21/iss2/5

Dror, I.E.; Charlton, D. & Peron, A.E. 2006. Contextual information renders experts vulnerable to making erroneous identifications. *Forensic Science International*, 156(1):74-78. https://doi.org/10.1016/j.forsciint.2005.10.017

Edmond, G.; Cole. S.; Cunliffe, E. & Roberts, A. 2013. Admissibility compared: The reception of incriminating expert evidence in four adversarial jurisdictions. *University of Denver Criminal Law Review*, 3:31-109. https://commons.allard.ubc.ca/cgi/viewcontent.cgi?article=1078&context=fac_pubs

Edmond, G.; Martire, K.; Kemp, R.; Hamer, D.; Hibbert, B.; Ligertwood, A.; Porter, G.; Roque, M.S.; Searston, R.; Tangen, J.; Thompson, M. & White D. 2014. How to cross-examine forensic scientists: A guide for lawyers. *Australian Bar Review*, 39:174-197. http://netk.net.au/Forensic/UNSW1.pdf.

Edmond, G. & Martire, K. 2016. Forensic science in criminal courts: The latest scientific insights. *Australian Bar Review*, 42(3):367-384. http://www.austlii.edu.au/au/journals/UNSWLJ/2017/22.html

Edmond, G.; Tangen, J.M.; Searston, R.A. & Dror, I.E. 2015. Contextual bias and cross-contamination in the forensic sciences: The corrosive implications for investigations, plea bargains, trials and appeals. *Law, Probability and Risk*, 14(1):1-25. https://academic.oup.com/lpr/article/14/1/1/1820089

Edmond, G.; Towler, A.; Growns, B.; Ribeiro, G.; Found, B.; White, D.; Ballantyne, K.; Searston, R.A.; Thompson, M.B.; Tangen, J.M.; Kemp, R.I. & Martire, K. 2017. Thinking forensics: Cognitive science for forensic practitioners. *Science and Justice*, 57(2):144-154. https://www.ncbi.nlm.nih.gov/pubmed/28284440

Garrett, B.L. & Neufeld, P.J. 2009. Invalid forensic science testimony and wrongful convictions. *Virginia Law Review*, 95(1):1-97. http://www.virginialawreview.org/sites/virginialawreview.org/files/1-2.pdf

Grzybowski, R.; Miller, J.; Moran, B.; Murdock, J.; Nichols, R. & Thompson, R. 2003. Firearm/Toolmark Identification: Passing the Reliability Test under Federal and State Evidentiary Standards. *AFTE Journal*, 35(2):209-241 https://afte.org/uploads/documents/position-nas-2009.pdf [Retrieved 5 January 2019]. https://www.researchgate.net/publication/267774341_FirearmToolmark_Identification_Passing_the_Reliability_Test_Under_Federal_and_State_Evidentiary_Standards_a

Haber, L. & Haber, R.N. 2008. Scientific validation of fingerprint evidence under *Daubert*. *Law, Probability and Risk*, 7:87-109. https://doi.org/10.1093/lpr/mgm020

Ireland, J. & Beaumont, J. 2015. Admitting scientific expert evidence in the United Kingdom: Reliability challenges and the need for revised criteria – proposing an abridged *Daubert*. *Journal of Forensic Practice*, 17(1):3-12. https://doi.org/10.1108/JFP-03-2014-0008

Joint Committee for Guides on Metrology: 200 (JCGM: 200). 2012. *International vocabulary of metrology: Basic and general concepts and associated terms (VIM)*. 3rd Edition. Sèvres: JCGM. https://www.bipm.org/utils/common/documents/jcgm/JCGM_200_2012.pdf [Retrieved 2 January 2019].

Koehler, J.J. 2016/2017. Forensics or Fauxrensics? Ascertaining accuracy in the forensic sciences. *Arizona State Law Journal*, 49:1369-1416. http://dx.doi.org/10.2139/ssrn.2773255

Kotzé, E.F. 2010. Author identification from opposing perspectives in forensic linguistics. *Southern African Linguistics and Applied Language Studies*, 28(2):185-197. https://doi.org/10.2989/16073614.2010.519111

National Physical Laboratory (NPL). 2010. *Good practice guide No. 118: A beginner's guide to measurement*. Queen's Printer and Controller of HMSO. Teddington: National Physical Laboratory. https://www.npl.co.uk/special-pages/guides/gpg118_begguide2measure [Retrieved 7 May 2017].

National Research Council. 2009. *Strengthening forensic science in the United States: A path forward*. Washington DC: The National Academies Press. https://doi.org/10.17226/12589

Olsson, J. & Luchjenbroers, J. 2013. *Forensic linguistics*, 3rd Edition. London/New York: Bloomsbury.

Pavese, F. 2009. An introduction to data modeling principles in metrology and testing. In: F. Pavese & A.B. Forbes (eds.), *Data modeling for metrology and testing in measurement science*. Boston MA: Birkhäuser Boston. https://doi.org/10.1007/978-0-8176-4804-6_1

President's Council of Advisors on Science and Technology (PCAST). 2016. *Report to the President. Forensic science in criminal courts: Ensuring scientific validity of feature-comparison methods* (Forensic Science report in the Executive Office of the President). https://obamawhitehouse.archives.gov/sites/default/files/microsites/ostp/PCAST/pcast_forensic_science_report_final.pdf [Retrieved 10 April 2018].

Puzniak, J. 2000. Expert evidence: The road from *Daubert* to *Joiner* and *Kumho Tire*. *Court Review*, 32-41.

Roman, J.; Walsh, K.; Lachman, P. & Yahner, J. 2012. *Post-conviction DNA testing and wrongful conviction*. Justice Police Center, Research Report. Washington DC: Urban Institute. https://www.urban.org/sites/default/files/publication/25506/412589-Post-Conviction-DNA-Testing-and-Wrongful-Conviction.PDF [Retrieved 3 January 2019].

Saks, M.J. & Koehler, J.J. 2005. The coming paradigm shift in forensic identification science. *Science*, 309:892-895. http://ssrn.com/abstract=962968 [Retrieved 23 July 2016].

Schwikkard, P.J. & Van der Merwe, S. 2016. *Principles of evidence*. 4th Edition. Cape Town: Juta.

Stamatatos, E. 2008. A survey of modern authorship attribution methods. *Journal of the American Society for Information Science and Technology*, 60(3):538-556. https://doi.org/10.1002/asi.21001

United States Courts. 2014. *Federal rules of evidence*. 113th Congress, second session, No. 10. Committee of the Judiciary, House of Representatives. Washington DC: US Government Printing Office. https://www.uscourts.gov/sites/default/files/evidence-rules-procedure-dec2017_0.pdf [Retrieved 22 May 2018].

White, P.C. 2004. *Crime scene to court: The essentials of forensic science*. 2nd Edition. Cambridge: Royal Society of Chemistry.

Case law

Daubert v Merrell Dow Pharmaceuticals Inc, 509 US 579 (1993).

Frye v United States 293 F. 1013 (D.C.Cir.1923).

In Re Paoli Railroad Yard PCB Litigation, 35 F.3d 717 (3rd Cir. 1994). https://law.resource.org/pub/us/case/reporter/F3/035/35.F3d.717.92-2014.92-2016.92-2011.92-1999.92-1997.html [Retrieved 2 January 2019].

Kelly v State 824 S.W.2d 568 (Tex. Crim. App. 1992).

Kumho Tire Co. v. Carmichael 526 U.S. 137 (1999).

National Justice Compania Naviera SA v Prudential Assurance Co Ltd 1993 (2) Lloyds Reports. 1993(2) 68.

Nonyane v Road Accident Fund (3126/2016) [2017] ZAGPPHC 706 (10 November 2017).

R v Jacobs 1940 TPD 142.

R v Nksatlala 1960 (3) SA 543 (A).

R v Theunissen 1948 (4) SA 43 (C).

Schneider NO & Others v AA & Another 2010 (5) 203 WCC. 8675/09) [2010] ZAWCHC 3; 2010 (5) SA 203 (WCC); [2010] 3 All SA 332 (WCC) (8 January 2010).

Stock v Stock 1981 (3) SA 1280 (A).

Toth v Jarman [2006] EWCA Civ 1028, Times 17-Aug-2006, [2006] 4 All ER 1276.

Twine and another v Naidoo and Others case no 38940/14 High Court Gauteng Division.

United States v Diaz No. CR 05-00167 WHA, 2007 WL 485967 (N.D. Cal. Feb. 12, 2007).

THE ACT OF THREATENING

Applying Speech Act Theory to threat texts

Karien van den Berg & Michelle Surmon

Introduction

Threats are a part of our daily lives, ranging from mild warnings to death threats. Threats on the more violent extreme of the continuum sometimes become the object of legal inquiry. In such cases, linguists may be able to support the investigation based on forensic linguistic analysis. Similar to authorship attribution and the language of police interviewing, in such cases, the language of textual threats, as potential linguistic evidence, becomes an important area of interest for linguists. Like police investigations and court proceedings (Gibbons, 2003), threats are complex linguistic entities to be characterised and evaluated accordingly. However, apart from work by Gales (e.g. 2010, 2011, 2015a, 2015b) on interpersonal stance in threatening discourse, and by Muschalik (2018), who presents a mixed methods approach to analysing textual threats as speech acts, the latter has received considerably less attention than the former. Currently, the literature (cf. Gibbons, 2003; Grant, 2008; Olsson, 2008 and 2012; Shuy, 2014) provides some general discussion but lacks depth and a more specific framework for linguistic analysis. This lack – likely to be attributed to the fact that forensic linguistics is still a new and developing field of research – leaves linguists with little if anything of a systematic and comparable working method for analysing threatening texts, rendering linguists and linguistic evidence subject to criticism to the extent that evidence is deemed inadmissible in court (cf. Chaski, 2013). Therefore, more research is necessary to achieve a comprehensive understanding of the language used in threat texts, as threats contain more than aggressive direct demands (Gales, 2011). This leads to the general question: How may written textual threats be characterised for forensic linguistic enquiry in order to:

a) confirm the authenticity of a threat text;
b) evaluate the urgency of a response in terms of the author's commitment to the threat; and
c) assist in attributing authorship of threatening texts?

This chapter addresses the greater issue, with the focus of this discussion linking to the work by Gales (2011) in relation to evaluating the urgency of threat and the author's commitment to the text. This is achieved by specifically addressing the question: How may the pragmatic theory of speech acts (SAT) (Austin, 1962; and Searle, 1975) contribute to a more comprehensive understanding of the language used in written textual threats? Apart from Tiersma (1986), SAT has not been readily applied in forensic linguistic context. Salgueiro (2010), Jacobsen (2010) and Kravchenko (2017) consider threats from a SAT perspective, but in different contexts.

The chapter is structured by first considering the notion of "threat", before reviewing literature on the general features of the language of written textual threats. Then we consider the application of SAT to an authentic example of a threat text, the letter sent to the *New York Times* in 1995 by Theodore Kaczynski (TK), the Unabomber. We conclude this chapter with an argument that SAT may indeed enhance the description of the language of written textual threats to aid an evaluation of urgency and author commitment as part of a greater framework for forensic linguistic analysis of written textual threats. The characterisation that follows in this paper may serve as additional scaffolding for linguistic analysis, rather than as hard and fast rules of conduct. Referring to the text of the Unabomber as a case study, the aim is to establish a means of discussing what the author does with language to execute a threat of a certain nature. Such a description may serve as starting point for similar forensic linguistic investigations.

Threats

Linguists work with any text that is of interest in legal enquiry (Shuy, 2014:10-11) to provide insight into likely scenarios as supporting evidence, based on linguistic cues from the text. Forensic linguistic text types include various forms and genres of text, written or spoken, with some being less context-independent, like wills and business letters, and others being more so, like SMS text messages and written textual threats (Grant, 2008:216; Olsson, 2012:13; Shuy, 2014:11).

The Oxford English dictionary online (OED, 2019) defines a threat as "a statement of an intention to inflict pain, injury, damage, *or other hostile action* on someone in retribution for something done or not done"" [our emphasis]. The threat may also be the thing or person itself. The word originates from an Old English term that carries a sense of "oppression". Often, threats are socially conditioned in that they manifest personal feelings and emotions, or intentions, as shaped by social structures (Gales, 2010:23). Threats are statements that something of a negative nature will happen to a recipient, or group of recipients (Fitzgerald, 2006:2). As such, threats embody linguistic acts of power between the threatener and the threatened, signalling the endowment of one party with power over another (Gales, 2010:23; 2015a:3). Failing to recognise and adhere to this power by not complying with stipulated requirements in written textual threats, in most cases, will result in the perpetrator carrying out a promise that was made in the text (Olsson & Luchjenbroers, 2013:162). Thus, threat is a type of promise, though distinguishable from a promise based on prepositional use:

a promise suggests that something will be done "for" you, while a threat is that something will be done "to" you. A sense of promise to carry out an act, if a demand is not fulfilled, is inherent in threat; therefore, the intention of a threat is classified as something done to the reader of the message (Searle, 1971:11).

We can thus define a threat as a statement uttered in a given social context in which one party – the threatener – attempts to exert their power over another by means of language that promises harm to the subjected or threatened party, with the intent of producing a specific effect, e.g. payment of ransom. This power may be exerted via various forms of communication, such as ransom notes, blackmail and bribery, which may be more or less context-dependent.

The language of written textual threats

As mentioned, various genres of written textual threats can be distinguished, including ransom notes, bribes and blackmail, hate mail, and hate speech (Gibbons, 2003; Olsson, 2008, 2012; Olsson & Luchjenbroers, 2013). The construction of such texts is based on an interplay of linguistic features and contextual elements. Both must be taken into account when analysing a certain threat text. Often the linguistic features of a threat are the only clues left by the threatening party. Warning signs of violence may be embedded within the language as the first indication of threat. The person extending the threat would select linguistic features in response to the social circumstances, in which one party (i.e. the sender) wishes to imply power over another (i.e. the receiver) (cf. Gales, 2010:3); there is also a choice of genre, and interpersonal stance conveying "a speaker or writer's feelings, opinions, and attitudes about a person or proposition" (Biber, 2006). Olssen & Luchjenbroers suggest starting an analysis of written textual threats with an evaluation of the threat text itself, focusing on "the language of the hostage communication" (2013:161) in the form of tenses, lexical and structural choices that reveal hidden semantic meanings. An overview of the literature, presented briefly here, reveals general similarities between written textual threat types, such as the development of these texts in terms of four stages (Olsson & Luchjenbroers, 2013): the notion of cause-and-effect; the presence of violence (Davies, 2006); a lack of room for negotiation, to a lesser or greater extent (Olsson, 2008); and purporting to put the author in a position of power over the receiver (Gales, 2010:3; Gibbons, 2003:268). We argue that these general features are useful, but do not ensure a comprehensive analysis of threats on a pragmatic level.

Threats typically develop in four stages or rhetorical moves: (1) leverage; (2) demand; (3) threat; and (4) promise (Olsson & Luchjenbroers, 2013:163). These stages may be explicitly identifiable or implied; they are not necessarily distinct. Leverage refers to the power of one party to influence another party – as mentioned before, putting the receiver of a threatening note at a disadvantage. This places the threatener in a position of power to stipulate demands. For example, ransom notes typically threaten injury to the hostage (a high-level threat) if the specified requirements are not met. The element of violence in the threat toward the receiver puts the threatened at a disadvantage, yielding the author or kidnapper the dominant party in the equation. This leverage typically initiates the "cause and effect" structure, likely specifying the demand, threat and promise. Demands may often be directly stated orders (Olsson & Luchjenbroers, 2013). The third and fourth stages, threat and promise, are usually executed as the effect resulting from the cause – that is, promising harm to the hostage if conditions are not met (threat); or a promise that the hostage will be returned safely, be it a trustworthy promise or not. Development in terms of these four stages is illustrated as in Figure 13.1, with reference to the Unabomber letter (see Appendix; and this will be discussed in more detail later).

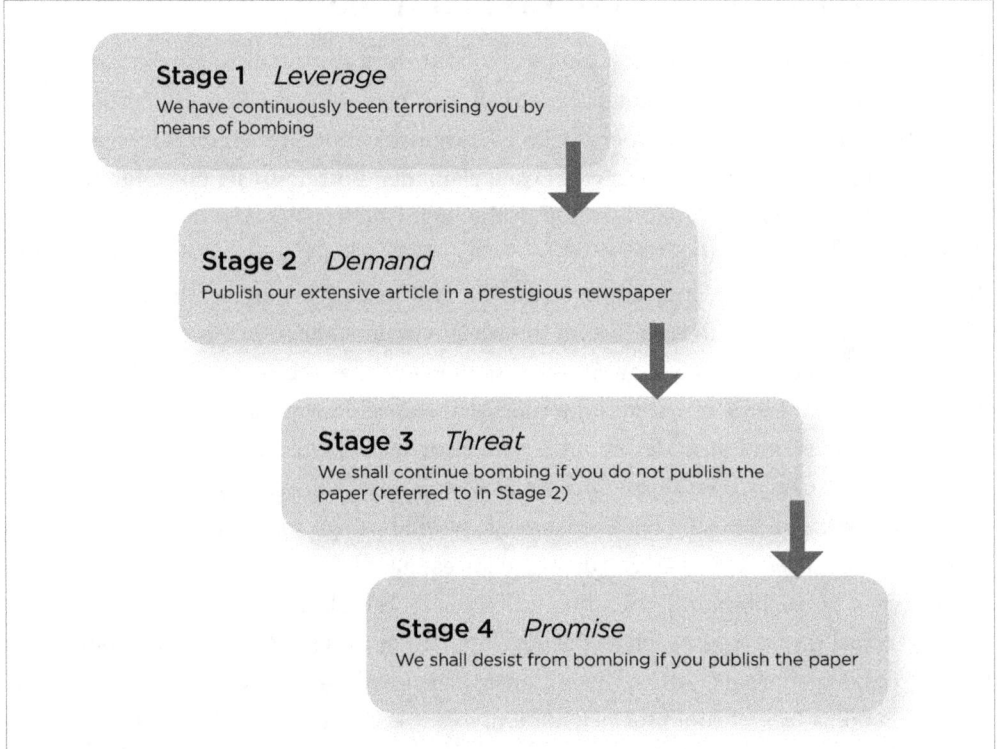

FIGURE 13.1 The developmental stages of written textual threats

The element of violence is typically inherent across these stages and may manifest in various forms, such as verbal abuse or suggestion of a physical threat to a loved one. In most cases, the topics of literature chosen in a threat text include the themes of hopelessness, violent behaviour, fantasies, suicide, profanity, intimidation, obsessive desires, weapons, description of the assault on the person or property, deadlines by when threats will be executed, racism, behaviours for which the victim needs to be punished, and the author as the victim (Gales, 2015a:4). These topics manifest linguistically. Grammatical features that are likely to be included in the threat text include adverbials of time, verbs of harm, second person pronoun, and first person pronoun (Gales, 2015a:4-5). Leveraging, for example, may entail dehumanising the receivers by means of name-calling, or insult through language, evolving into more serious threatening acts in the third stage. The promise could be the withholding of the violence, for instance. Studying ransom notes linguistically may reveal the specific threat to be fulfilled by the author if ransom demands are not met (Olsson, 2008:141-142), as the particular threat may not be stated literally, or may not be made explicitly clear.

Demands are typically expressed by verbs that imply or specify future action required, and also specify participants and their roles (Gibbons, 2003:268). The promise, often employing cause-and-effect clauses, expresses future action: what will be done or not done by the threatener, depending on whether or not demands are met. A perpetrator may typically use pronouns or proper nouns specifying who is involved: in carrying out the threat (promise), "I"; and to whom the threat is applicable, "you", or "Mr Y", or "Mrs Y". Alongside the nouns or pronouns lie the verbs, for example, modal verbs to commit ("will" and "shall"), and verbs of harm to convey the carrying out of an action ("harm", "kill" or "damage").

Olsson (2008:141-142) recognises the lack of negotiation as a characteristic of ransom notes. Studying ransom notes typically reveals promises to be fulfilled by the author if ransom demands are not met, with little or no room for negotiation. Gibbons (2003:263) again points out that, unlike ransom notes, bribes and blackmailing entail a proposition in the form of an answer to a presented problem and may allow for negotiation of terms. In this sense, one may consider the letter by the Unabomber as a form of blackmail, since it offers a solution to the problem of continued terrorist bombing (this aspect is elaborated upon in the next section of this chapter).

Cause-and-effect clauses, for example, "If you can get [the article] published according to our requirements we *will* permanently desist from terrorist activities" (our emphasis) may be characteristic (Olsson & Luchjenbroers, 2013) but is not always included. If such a clause is included, the linguist needs to scrutinise its linguistic elements to fully apprehend the author's terms of commitment. Depending on the linguistic realisation of such a clause, it may suggest different levels of commitment. Consider the following possible clauses:

(1) If you can get it published according to our requirements we will permanently desist from terrorist activities.
(2) If you can get it published according to our requirements we could/may/might desist from terrorist activities.
(3) If you can get it published according to our requirements, good things may come to you.
(4) Get it published, or else …

Sentences (1) and (2) supposedly convey a more urgent threat or promise with higher stance, whereas sentences (3) and (4) do not indicate clear reward, which may beg the question whether there is any intention of rewarding if the demand were to be met. As such, these examples reflect a lower stance. Olsson and Luchjenbroers (2013) suggest that the omission of an If-clause suggests severe danger to the threatened party, with the threatener potentially having no intention of fulfilling a promise, such as returning a hostage, even if ransom requirements are met. It is therefore paramount that linguists analyse these notes as soon as possible to help identify the (potential) author(s), and whether there would be any sense in adhering to the ransom instructions. The linguist's purpose is to determine the extent to which the promise of that threat is real. In other words, the linguist must scrutinise the linguistic features to unearth clues as to whether or not the author plans to fulfil the promise. Upon analysing the text, it may become evident, based on linguistic clues, that there is little commitment to fulfilling the promise.

"Threat stance" supposedly portrays the "level of commitment to an act" (Gales, 2011:27). Gales (2010, 2011, 2015a, 2015b) identifies a range of lexical and grammatical stance markers that typically occur in written textual threats. These markers assist in determining the intentions of the author. An author's intentionality and commitment can be seen through linguistic choices, language use either being conditional or, contrastingly, determined and definite. She argues that analysing stance enables the linguist to discern the degree of urgency with which the text should be dealt. Potentially, the text could be a hoax; or, in the case of an authentic threat, the plausibility of the threat being realised needs to be evaluated (Gales, 2010:1). She proposes that this be done in terms of socially, behaviourally and linguistically marked factors (that is, while some features remain irregular or marked when used in the social context, others become socially acceptable or unmarked) (2015a:2). Linguistic markers extend throughout the text, "possessing detailed, commanding forms that strengthen the threatener's role or apparent commitment to the act" (Gales, 2011:28). The more detailed the threat, the higher the threat level; and, by contrast, the threat is less dangerous when it veers to being vague, indecisive and noncommittal (Rugala & Fitzgerald, 2003).

The message may typically be formulated as a conditional rather than an actual promise, as is the case in the Unabomber example. Conditionals are, by definition, indirect; and, depending on the details provided in the antecedent and consequence, may suggest more or less commitment, as illustrated in sentences (1) to (4), with (3) and (4) exerting less commitment than (1) or (2).

Based on the principle of linguistic markedness, Gales (2015) suggests inspecting protruding grammatical markers, including those providing evidence of the behaviour and attitude of the author of the threat text. Such behaviours are said to include "spontaneity, deception, decision, emotional expression and intimacy" expressed through "verbal habits"

(Gales, 2015a:5). These habits are essentially linguistic markers and may include adverbs which indicate an author's dedication or obligation to carry out the action, and verbs that convey harmful intentions (Gales, 2015a:1, 6). Conditional language, with vague referral to time, place and victim in mind, renders it doubtful as to whether the threatened act can or will actually be carried (Gales, 2011:28 and 2015a:5-6). By contrast, Gales (2011:28) asserts that the threat is measured as a high-level threat when there is detailed description as to who is the target, the time the act will take place, verifiable facts, commitment, and how the target will be reached. The seriousness of a threat escalates as the plausibility increases and as the details included are more detail-specific, giving evidence of at least moderate preparation by the perpetrator. Gales (2011:27, 43) concludes that authors who construct written threatening texts use a variety of rhetorical strategies to convey interpersonal meaning, taking stances that both strengthen *and* weaken their displayed level of commitment. Threateners express various interpersonal meanings which may relate to the author's underlying intent for extending the threat. These may include reasons such as to instil fear, to negotiate interpersonal relations, and to justify acts of retribution (Gales, 2011:44). She notes that, counter to the notion of high-level threats typically containing commanding and strengthening language, threateners also use expressions of justification that weaken their role and perceived level of commitment. Ignoring this aspect of threatening language may be dangerous and justifies further research to understand how stance "*actually* manifests and functions in this oftentimes dangerous genre" (Gales, 2011:44). To this end, we will now explore the application of SAT to written threats.

Following from the line of our preceding argument, we conclude that the degree of directness or indirectness of threat or promise is of particular importance when evaluating stance. We posit that these "verbal habits" (Gales, 2015a:5) are complex linguistic entities influenced by context and can be related to Austin (1962) and Searle (1975)'s notion of speech acts. Consequently, the directness or indirectness of said habits or acts may be successfully described in terms of SAT principles. To follow on from this, we now engage in a discussion of speech acts as an additional means of refining the evaluation of the language of written textual threats as a means of exploring author stance and commitment.

The act of threatening

Departing from Tiersma (1986), we propose that applying principles of Speech Act Theory to naturally occurring threatening texts can assist in clarifying what it is that threateners do with their language, how they do this and, potentially, why. Of particular interest to us is the use of conditionals and indirect speech acts in threats as indicative of author commitment. Threats are not specifically addressed by Austin (1962), with Searle (1975) considering what has been called "elementary threats" only (cf. Salgueiro, 2010; Chojimah, 2016). Conditional promises have been perceived as warranting little regard (Grant, 1949:363-364;

Salgueiro, 2010:217). We consider that a more detailed account of the use of direct and indirect speech acts may aid the characterisation of interpersonal stance as indicative of an author's commitment to an expressed threat. To this end, we consider the application of SAT with reference to a letter written by the Unabomber. As our starting point, we consider limitations of the theory.

Austin (1962) proposed the notion of utterances as spoken acts, formulating Speech Act Theory. Searle (1971:1) describes a speech act as the literal act that one carries out through speaking, for example, the movement that one's body makes to utter words. Along with the physical act is the act of speaking of specific places, people, or things, and the verbal act of "making statements, asking questions, issuing commands, giving reports, greeting, and warning" (Searle, 1971:1). Through these acts, the speaker has a goal, one intended to receive a particular response from the hearer. Therefore, the speaker constructs this speech act to receive the reaction that he or she desires.

This theory focuses on analysing the speech act in totality, as opposed to sentences, and so avoids oversimplification of the meaning of a sentence, and the noting of an underlying, hidden meaning (Oishi, 2006:2). The concept of meaning entails the speaker utilising linguistic conventions (i.e. Grice's cooperative principles: 1957; 2004; 2008[1]) to perform a linguistic act, and attributing a specific intention with that act to the hearer (Oishi, 2006:1). The act refers to the idea that meaning exists in the relations between what is said and linguistic conventions (i.e. words or sentences) used to express meaning.

Three levels of meaning are distinguished, namely locution, illocution and perlocution, as will be discussed. The notion of illocutionary point (Searle & Vanderveken, 1985) is the characteristic aim of each type of speech act. Searle's (1975) taxonomy is then used to distinguish illocutionary acts (cf. Kravchenko, 2017:141-142; Levinson, 1983:240; Yule, 1996:53-54), comprising assertives, directives, commissives, expressives and declaratives.

Austin (1962) and Searle (1975)'s notion of speech acts has been widely applied to general conversation (Moeschler, 2002:2), instant messaging and chat (Twitchell & Nunamaker, 2004:1), biblical analysis (Poythress, 2008; Young, 1989) and has been applied as an approach to language philosophy (Tiersma, 1986:189). SAT has been used to analyse people's communication, specifically in relation to indirect speech acts in social processes

---

[1] Grice formulated the notion of the cooperative principle, in order to help explain how a hearer distinguishes between a literal and figurative meaning of an utterance, and accordingly chooses the appropriate interpretation within a context. The cooperative principle assumes that participants in a conversation generally cooperate to make shared meaning. 'Çonversational implicature' (Grice, 1975: 45-46) is based on four maxims that constitute the rules of everyday conversation – i.e. how to cooperate. These maxims help to eliminate irrelevant meaning, and to infer relevant meaning that may not be immediately clear. The maxims are: quality (truth value), quantity (sufficient information), manner (clarity) and relevance (related to the conversation). Cf. e.g. Tiersma (1986: 209-211) for a summary and application.

(Asher & Lascarides, 2001; Cooren, 2000; Holtgraves, 1986:306; Jacobsen 2010; and Kravchenko, 2017), conditionals (Young, 1989), and threats (Salgueiro, 2010). However, apart from Tiersma (1986), it has not generally been applied within the forensic linguistic context. To our knowledge, SAT has not yet been applied to an authentic example of a written threat text to evaluate its potential usefulness in forensic linguistic investigation, specifically to elaborate the notion of stance and author commitment, as put forward by Gales (2011). We posit that, when applied in recognition of its limits, SAT is potentially useful for analysing written acts of threat in a forensic linguistic arena.

Austin and Searle's work has been criticised and refined extensively by, amongst others, Allwood (1977); Bach and Harnish (1979); Cooren (2000); Habermas (1984, 1991); Kravchenko (2017); Levinson (1983); Oishi (2006); Poythress (2008); and Sadock (1974). We acknowledge this critique and address some issues here.

Allwood (1977) has criticised the theory of speech acts for lacking clarity, specifically pertaining to the use of the term "act" and in understanding the term "illocution". "Act", Allwood notes, conveys the notion of temporally distinct activities, as opposed to simultaneous aspects of a single action. However, note Searle's (1979:29) comment: "Often, we do more than one of these [kinds of acts] at once in the same utterance". This suggests that an act is not necessarily a singular entity but rather a complex phenomenon. Allwood (1977:29) sees the opaqueness of the term "illocution" as residing in the extent to which "illocutionary forces are conventional, intentional or tied to achieved effects, overt behaviour or context". Illocution is indeed complex, as Searle (1979:25) acknowledges when he refers to indirect speech acts as "cases in which one illocutionary act is performed indirectly by way of performing another". Kravchenko (2017) argues that not only indirect speech acts are complex in terms of illocution, as postulated by Searle (1969), but that direct speech acts also may comprise a compound structure of both direct and of indirect speech acts (cf. also Sadock, 2004:4). Furthermore, a single sentence may not necessarily constitute a single act – a particular complexity that appears to be oversimplified in Searle (1969:22-23; cf. Poythress, 2008). Thus, language use is complex and therefore illocution is complex.

SAT has been criticised (e.g. Emike, 2013; Poythress, 2008) for lacking in answers to some questions about contextual dynamics in language use across socio-cultural backgrounds. This is indeed a limitation that also applies to this discussion, which pertains only to English written textual threats, considered within a general Western culture where threats are presumably conveyed in a similar way. Similar applications are needed (cf. Miranda, 2013, in relation to advertising communication) to evaluate the potential usefulness of SAT across languages and cultures.

Yoshitake (2004) critiques the speaker-centeredness of SAT, arguing that the meaning of acts is negotiated or conceptualised. For Yoshitake, SAT downplays the integrated dialogical nature of communication and specifically the listener's derived meaning and potential multiple interpretations. We contend that verbal threats that are of forensic linguistic interest tend toward the more violent extreme of the threat continuum and become, by definition, speaker-centred. Threateners place themselves in a position of power and try to determine the communication. Little, if any, negotiation of meaning takes place. In the context of forensic linguistic analysis of written textual threats, we believe that the supposed speaker-centred model is therefore appropriate. We also stress that SAT was developed for the purpose of considering a speech act in its totality and mainly at sentence level (Searle, 1969:18). This too is appropriate, seeing as written textual threats are often monologues, as in the case of the Unabomber letter considered here.

We are cautious, however, of assuming the meaning of "exactness" of the sentence formulation claimed by Searle (1969:18) and do not interpret it to mean a perfect, precise and absolute formulation without variation. Individuals' linguistic executions vary to the extent that the notion of an idiolect is acceptable: individual utterances differ, both from one person to the next, but also for one person from one speech situation to the next. Therefore, the notion of an exact or precise utterance is not particularly useful in this context; but we accept that speech acts may be formulated in ways that are conventionally indisputable as embodying a certain act, such as "I now pronounce you husband and wife" or "You are now husband and wife". Both formulations express the same act, though formulated differently.

In view of the general nature of felicity conditions and macro-classes[2] (Allwood, 1977:10), SAT may lend itself to application as a component of a greater framework toward characterising the exact factors constituting the action of threatening as being of interest for forensic linguistic purposes. Such an analysis may be useful to identify the exact combination of general conditions and characteristic features of the natural language of threat acts. Thus, we consider SAT for application, within its limits, for the purpose of describing what is done with words when verbal threats are issued. We consider the actions conveyed through speech acts by threateners as indicating those who are in a position of power and hence strongly influence meaning. We do not contend that SAT can provide all the answers but intend the following discussion as an addition to work by researchers like Tiersma (1986), Gales (2010; 2011; 2015a, 2015b), Olsson (2008), Gibbons (2003), Shuy (2014), and Grant (2008).

Rather than rely on a single methodology to address questions of forensic linguistic interest, linguists should incorporate multiple sources of evidence to inform their findings. Assuming

---

[2] "Felicity conditions" refer to what Austin (1962) and Searle (1975) describe as the basic necessary conditions for communication to be successful. All participants must commit knowingly and willingly, while acknowledging social roles and acting according to conventions of the given communicative scenario. Macro-classes refer to Searle (1975)'s classification of the five categories of possible speech acts, viz.: declaratives, commissives, expressives, directives and representatives.

that one means of analysis is sufficient to address intricate language problems would be reckless and irresponsible. Instead, we aim to demonstrate additional means available to linguists to conduct analyses systematically toward a more comprehensive understanding of how the language of threats is used. We are of the opinion that analysing written textual threats from an SAT perspective contributes to a more comprehensive understanding of the idiosyncratic factors denoted in this communicative act. SAT should not be applied over-optimistically, as if it were the one and only key to understanding textual meaning. Rather, it should be considered as a means of exploring one more dimension of communication.

The Unabomber's threat text

In this section, various aspects of a letter written by Ted Kaczynski, the Unabomber (hereafter "TK" or "the Unabomber"; see the Appendix to this chapter), are explored in terms of the features already discussed. We discern elements of blackmail – as opposed to hate mail – before looking into the speech acts presented in the letter; how these acts convey intent and commitment; and the influence of direct and indirect aspects of the proposed linguistic acts.

An example of blackmail

The bomber proposes a bargain: to stop the bombing, an article must be published according to certain specifications. Declining would result in continued bombing; accepting would supposedly end the bombing. In this instance, however, there appears to be little room for negotiation: "If you can get [the article] published according to our requirements we *will* permanently desist from terrorist activities" [our emphasis].

The antecedent verb phrase, "can get it published", suggests some doubt as to the ability of the receiver to fulfil the demand; but this is followed by a strong commissive verb, "will", in the consequence. The stages of acceptance, rejection and delay follow the identification of the problem and proposal of the solution. In the infamous Unabomber case, the author posed a life-threatening problem – the bombings would continue – unless "their" proposal was accepted: if his manifesto were published, he would stop bombing public places. In this case, federal agents accepted the proposal and published the manifesto in the hope of getting information on the blackmailing bomber. As stakes were high (terroristic violence), and the so-called cost of the bargain comparably cheap (publication of a controversial text), the Federal Bureau of Investigation (FBI) engaged the demand, hoping that some information about the author(s) might come to them after publication. Based on a tip by a family member who had read the article and recognised some salient phrases, the FBI were able to track down a suspect. Following further comparison of the manifesto with other drafts found in possession of the suspect, the FBI was able to tie the suspect to the manifesto, identifying TK as the blackmailer and the bomber.

Speech acts in the Unabomber's letter

Representatives are words used to describe the speaker's opinion, usually to convince the hearer that something is the truth. In so doing, representatives commit the speaker to what they state: to something being or to the truth of the expressed proposition (Hancher, 1979:3; Searle, 1976:10). For TK, this meant opposing industrialisation and advancing a nature-centred form of anarchism – a view he shared with society to convince them of the evils of industrialisation: "The people who are pushing all this growth and progress garbage deserve to be severely punished".

Directives are the "attempts by the speaker to get the hearer to do something" (Hancher, 1979:2) and run on a continuum varying from "suggestions" to "commands" (Searle, 976:11). In the case of written textual threats – such as TK's demanded for his manifesto to be published – it is the attempt of the author to control the reader's behaviour. Olsson and Luchjenbroers (2013:163) specify this demand, which is usually a direct directive speech act, as a salient feature of threat. TK implores various directives, as in "It must be published in the New York Times", directly specifying conditions of the act of publishing the article.

Commissives are commitments to fulfil the speaker's future intentions, tying the speaker to a future course of action (Searle, 1976:11). In the Unabomber letter, we find "we will permanently desist from terrorist activities". This is a commitment or promise given by the Unabomber signifying an intention to carry out an action. Whether the commitment is sincere or not is irrelevant to the classification of the illocutionary act (also see section 5.2.1).

Expressive statements declare the speaker's feelings, showing their reaction to reality (Hancher, 1979:3) and exposes their psychological state, showing "the truth of the expressed proposition" (Searle, 1976:12). Unlike representatives and directives, they do not "represent or coerce reality" (Hancher, 1979:3), but rather accept and react to the state of the situation. Words like "disappoints" and "angers" are examples of the emotions expressed by the Unabomber, as is this statement: "Anyhow we are getting tired of making bombs. It's no fun having to spend all your evenings and weekends preparing dangerous mixures" (original spelling).

Declarations signal change, declaring something into being that was previously non-existent. Through successfully declaring something, the declaration "brings about the correspondence between the propositional content and reality" (Searle, 1976:13), therefore immediately making a change in the world (Hancher, 1979:3). These are often used when the threatener is stating the type of leverage that they have over the reader, which will convince the reader to adhere to the directives that are in the threat text: "Clearly we are in a position to do a great deal of damage" declares that the circumstance of the reality has been changed.

Hancher (1979:6-7) proposes an additional micro-class, combining commissives with directives. He says, "The response to [commissive directives] sought is itself illocutionary in nature" (1979:6). The type of speech class is termed "conditionals", as these conditions mean that, if the hearer performs a particular act, the speaker will reward the hearer with an act which the speaker committed to doing. Threats may typically be classified as commissive directives; or, as in most cases, a threat text contains a demand – i.e. a directive – which should be adhered to. If that demand is fulfilled, the reward for compliance to the demand will be the promised act – i.e. commissive – to be carried out by the speaker. The promised reward is classified as a commissive, regardless of the sincerity of the act. Salgueiro (2010) further distinguishes between commissive conditional threats or promises (CCT/P) aimed at committing the speaker to do something, and directive conditional threats or promises (DCCT/P) that aim to get the receiver to do something. We adopt this distinction to inform our discussion of threat acts.

We now consider the speech acts constituting threat in terms of locution, illocution and perlocution, as evident in the letter sent by TK as the Unabomber to the *New York Times* on 26 April 1995 (see the Appendix to this chapter). This is an example of authentic threatening discourse. Some lines are extracted here for ease of reference:

[1] We have a long article, between 29,000 and 37,000 words, that we want to have published.
[2] If you can get it published according to our requirements we will permanently desist from terrorist activities.
[3] It must be published in the *New York Times*, *Time* or *Newsweek*, or in some other widely read, nationally distributed periodical.

Locution refers to the syntactic or literal meaning of an utterance – the "mere uttering" (Searle, 1979:1). Content is basically propositional. In [1], TK makes known that he is in possession ("I have" as opposed to "I wrote") of a long article which he wants published. In [2], the assertion is a directive conditional threat; and [3] takes the locutionary form of a directive, stipulating requirements for publication. The utterance signifies this basic content of assertion in the form of a request, the primary illocution being to inform, i.e. representative.

The intended message of the speaker is called the illocutionary act – what the words do, or are intended to do, expressing some illocutionary force performed through an utterance. The concept of "intention" is a complex structure and may be conveyed by tone of voice or in context, to be correctly understood (or not) by the hearer. The illocutionary force remains valid, regardless of whether or not the hearer interprets it correctly – contrary to the suggestion of Habermas (1984; 1991), that the illocutionary force fails in such cases; though this may lead to miscommunication. This intention shapes the hearer's hypothesis about what the speaker's intention is and what the hearer's expected reaction is. It also aims to produce this reaction from the hearer (Grice, 1957, 2004, 2008; Kravchenko, 2017:136).

Basically, "we achieve what we try to do by getting our audience to recognise what we try to do" (Searle, 1969:47). An illocutionary act is "the minimal unit of linguistic communication" (Hancher, 1979:1) or a central component of language use (Hancher, 1979:1), representing engagement in a "rule-governed form of behaviour" (Searle, 1969:47).

Searle (1971:11) classifies the illocutionary act of a threat as doing something to the reader that will not please the reader. In [1], the illocutionary force is to inform the reader that the sender not only has the article, but has authored it, though this is not explicitly confirmed in the text. This may, in addition, suggest to the reader that the author is a well-versed person and someone to be, or who desires to be, respected. In [2] TK threatens to continue bombing unless this article is published. The illocutionary force is both the author committing to a possible future action, depending on whether demands are met, as well as ordering the receiver to publish a controversial article. Furthermore, it has the intended effect of evoking fear within the reader, convincing the reader that "they" are serious about their demand and thereby convincing the reader to accept the bargain and follow orders. A reading of [2] as a request as to whether the reader is physically capable of getting the article published is unlikely in this context and is therefore ignored for the moment. We consider this potential reading again in relation to the cooperative maxims described by Grice (1957; 2004; 2008).

Accepting the bargain and adhering to stipulated requirements would embody a felicitous or desired perlocution. A perlocutionary act is the result of words; the effect that the utterance has on the receiver; the "causing of any contingent consequence" (Hancher, 1979:1). "A uttered X with the intention of inducing a belief by means of recognition of this intention" (Grice, 1957:19). The effect may manifest as a verbal or cognitive response – also known as a "reflexive communication intention" (Bach & Harnish, 1979:13) and may be expected, desired, felicitous or unexpected (or undesired), infelicitous. Example [3] explicitly expresses the desired response to the threat: publishing the article in one of the major daily/weekly publications mentioned. TK supposedly includes this line with the intended illocutionary force of constraining the possible journals for publication to prestigious ones, ensuring his work will be recognised as valuable and respected. Sentence [3] is thus not merely an order, directing the future action of the receiver, but also a means of manipulating the greater audience's doing and opinion of "their" work. We therefore will now consider the notion of the author's intent in direct association with commitment to the offer.

Intent and commitment

Gibbons (2003) suggests that threats with a lower level of commitment may be expressed using modal verbs such as "may" or "might". One might also expect agentless passives to suggest less commitment to a threat. However, identifying these syntactic features alone does not bring the linguist much closer to explaining what threateners do with their language by employing these features. Applying rules of SAT may aid the linguist in the quest toward authorship attribution.

SAT is a rule-governed theory, as mentioned previously. Searle (1971:3) distinguishes between "regulative" and "constitutive" rules. The former regulate existing actions, stipulating regulative rules ("manners", following Searle, 1971:3) that demonstrate how one should behave in particular environments, e.g. the promise must be made in good faith. The latter bring about behaviour, with constitutive rules controlling how an act is constructed to constitute a speech act (i.e. how to threaten; Kreckel, 1981; Searle, 1969:37). For threats, this means that there must be an utterance that counts as placing the receiver in a vulnerable position; and that obliges the actor to carry out the proposal (Tiersma, 1986).

Interactors in a speech situation rely on the pragmatic meaning that is conventionally associated with a linguistic expression and the notion that every utterance has an illocutionary force embedded in its surface form (Ariel, 2012:30).

Though the Unabomber's intentions appear to be clearly stipulated, it should also be clear that the illocutionary force of threatening is multilayered, with meaning communicated directly or indirectly. Threatening is not so much an expression or manifestation of intent, as it is an act committing the threatener to certain future actions. This act is supposedly supplemented with a state of mind in which the threatener commits to the particular proposal; and the threatener must intend for this perception to be created in the receiver of the threat (cf. Tiersma, 1986). This then brings threateners to their responsibility to fulfil the promise. Through making a promise, the author binds himself to a responsibility to intend to fulfil the promise made. In this case, the conventional interpretation of [2] suggests that TK commits to no further bombing once the article has been published in a major daily/weekly. However, there is no linguistic evidence to suggest whether the author truthfully means to adhere to this promise. Whether or not the intention of fulfilling the promise is sincere, the promise is stated. Therefore, the speech act was committed, whether sincere or not (Hancher, 1979:6; Searle, 1971:14). This is because the regulative rules have been upheld – there is nothing wrong with the threat or the offer of a bargain. Alternatively, if the constitutive rules are broken, no threat will have been extended (Tiersma, 1986:196).

According to Tiersma (1986:200-201), "the prototypical way to commit oneself to a proposed bargain is by uttering the formula "I hereby offer you that p", where p indicates the proposition, as opposed to, "I hereby intend to carry out my part of the bargain". Intending is not an illocutionary act (rather a mental state), but offering is, and it is this act that binds the speaker. Thus, in uttering the formula, "So we offer a bargain", TK unambiguously engages the speech act of offering, indicated by "hereby". In so doing, TK assents to the terms of the bargain stated, in which case the performative verb is stated explicitly. As the formula is unambiguous, it counts as an act of commitment by the speaker.

Furthermore, TK then offers sentences [4] to [7], apparently to address openly the issue of his own commitment to the promise inherent in extending the bargain, albeit in the form of a threat:

> [4] How do you know that we will keep our promise to desist from terrorism if our conditions are met?
> [5] It will be to our advantage to keep our promise.
> [6] We want to win acceptance for certain ideas.
> [7] If we break our promise people will lose respect for us and so will be less likely to accept the ideas.

This, of course, reads two ways: "We will keep our promise to desist bombing if the article is published"; or "We will keep our promise to continue bombing if the article is not published". The general illocutionary forces of [4] to [7] is to increase the chances of the article being published by creating a sentiment of trust within the reader. The desired perlocution is the reader believing that the threateners will keep their end of the bargain and therefore the reader(s) will get the article published. In other words, the illocutionary force is that of directive conditional threat. TK tries to get the reader to recognise and believe the threat in its entirety. Statements [4] to [7] effectively support [2] and [3] to convince the threatened that the felicity condition of sincerity is being upheld. Theodore Kaczynski aims to achieve this through the use of direct representative statements in [5] and [6], followed by a conditional representative in [7] to qualify the two preceding statements.

In uttering these formulae, Theodore Kaczynski achieves what Tiersma (1986:226) terms "illocutionary intent". Illocutionary intent is distinct from the mental phenomena of intent and commitment, relating to the threateners' state of mind being positively attuned to the bargain, and indicates that he or she sincerely intends to carry out the proposal (Tiersma, 1986:224). For an offer or threat to constitute the speech act of threatening, the threatener must produce in the receiver the illocutionary effect of that offer or threat. The illocutionary intent pertains to the threatener getting the hearer to recognise or believe that an offer or threat is being extended by an uttered formula, and that by uttering these words that count as offer or threat, the speaker is committing to the bargain.

The mental state of the threatener in itself is outside the scope of a linguist's investigation, but the illocutionary intent is a key point of investigation to discern author commitment and the urgency of threat. The illocutionary force of a promising speech act (e.g. [2]), remains, regardless of whether the author actually has the intention of adhering to the promise. Tiersma (1986:226) notes:

> Sincerity is an element of an offer only to the extent that the offeror ought to be sincere in the moral sense, but it is not an essential condition for an offer ... Intending to carry out the proposal is a regulative rule but is not a constitutive rule of the speech acts of offering, accepting, or promising.

The linguist is therefore limited to identifying textual clues representing this mental state, as provided by [4] to [7]. The deliberate inclusion of linguistic evidence expressing honest and sincere intentions in this letter suggests the author's high commitment – sincerity and commitment to the promise – to keep the promise inherent in the threat. The linguist is not, however, in a position to comment definitively as to the mental state of the author. As Gales (2015b:171) suggests, threateners' words and their actions do not correlate one-to-one. The threatener may, for example, suffer from a severe form of depression and may be in an unstable set of mind unless medicated. It is thus beyond the scope of the forensic linguistic analysis to attest to this unconditionally. However, in combination with psychological analysis, linguists may contribute to a greater understanding of the threat being imposed. Speech acts remain effective, regardless of whether or not they are sincere: the threat is conveyed; the audience is manipulated; the article is published. Linguistic evidence in this case does then suggest sincerity and a high level of commitment.

Direct and indirect speech acts

Everyday communication entails the content of utterances and illocutionary force being expressed directly and indirectly; and it depends heavily on context for interpretation. Direct and indirect speech acts describe whether the speaker's locution and illocution are directly correlated, or whether there is a subtler message within the locution that may be implied. A direct speech act is the simplest form of a speech act, where the utterance or writing of a sentence, the locution, "means exactly and literally what he says" (Searle, 1975:59). In this case, the speaker relies on the hearer's general knowledge of the rules of speech. This insight controls the type of words spoken, and the speaker's expectations of a particular response, the meaning of which will be inferred from the hearer's response expressed through words arranged in accordance with the grammatical rules of the language (Searle, 1975:59). Indirect speech acts carry two illocutionary forces (Asher & Lascarides, 2001; Searle, 1969). They generally entail one meaning at a syntactical level and a different, implied, meaning by the speaker. Situational factors may typically influence whether the speaker chooses one meaning or the other. Although the priority, following Grice's interpretation, is usually the implied meaning (Grice, 1975, 2004; and Zabbal, 2008)' over and above the literal meaning, speakers tend to answer to both the literal and intended illocutionary force, in that order (Clark, 1979:431-432).

A direct correlation between locution and illocution is most often used in giving instructions in order to eliminate any confusion and to receive the expected response without hesitation. This allows the meaning of direct speech acts to be "undeniable and explicit" (Holtgraves, 1986:36). Since threateners do not exclusively employ direct speech acts, the question arises as to their reasons for using indirect speech acts. Out of courtesy, do threateners then employ indirect speech acts, such as [2] and [7], in an attempt to be considered socially polite? Probably not. Viewed in terms of Speech Act Theory, the conditional in [2] is considered an implicit performatives with the dual intention of doing more than conveying the condition (Young, 1989:39). However, it is most likely the most explicit way of formulating the content of a threat, without adding a performative verb, e.g. "I hereby threaten you", which may be considered socially awkward. The illocutionary point is quite direct, even if the directive is manifested grammatically as indirect conditional.

Threateners may rather employ such conditionals specifically to do something in addition to stating a condition, such as to persuade the threatened, make strong assertions, manipulate the receiver, give an exhortation, or to justify themselves. Indirect formulation of threats is more common than direct formulations but, with the performative verb being implicit, still counts as putting the author under obligation to keep his end of the bargain. Following Young (1989:45), for an indirect speech act to function as manipulation, the following conditions hold: the hearer performs a future act; the hearer is able to perform the act; it is not obvious that the hearer is willing to perform the act; the speaker wants the hearer to perform the act; and the speaker considers his utterance as a way of forcing the hearer to perform the desired act. In cases such as in [2] where a command is stipulated in the consequent, the truth value of the antecedent depends on the response to the utterance. To demonstrate, [2] may be rephrased as [2a]:

> [2a] We will permanently desist from terrorist activities, if you can get [the article] published according to our requirements.

In this case, publishing the article is the requirement for making the antecedent true – that is, to stop the terrorist bombings. The illocutionary force in the commissive-directive [2] is manipulation, entailing getting someone to do something they may not necessarily want to do, would not do under normal circumstances, or may think is wrong. The author of the threat intends an act such as the following: "I hereby endow a threat onto you by committing myself to further bombing if the article is not published. I hereby also commit myself to stop bombing in the case that you accept my bargain. I therefore hereby manipulate you to publish an article of a controversial nature which you may otherwise not have published". Prestigious newspapers may not have been likely to publish the Unabomber's manifesto had it not been for the threat. So [2] also conveys this notion: "I thus force you to engage in behaviour other than what you may have engaged under normal circumstances".

In the representative [7], the illocutionary force is persuasion, exhortation and justification with the performative potentially being, "I believe that", or "I hereby express my belief that". In order for a conditional to be used as an argument to persuade, all parties must agree that: either the antecedent "if" clause is true, or that the consequent "then" clause is false (Young, 1989:41). In the case of [7] then, the assumption is that the antecedent and the consequent would be true: TK will be disrespected if he does not uphold his end of the bargain. He wants to be respected and will therefore keep the promise. Therefore, the speech acts included are an assertion purposed to get the audience to believe that something is true, as well as a request aimed at getting the audience to do something. Exhorting and justification entails urging a hearer to do something recognised as proper (Young, 1989:45). In [7], the threateners themselves ("we") are supposedly urged to keep the promise (i.e. this is the proper thing to do) if they are to be respected by the community. By implication, it would also be the proper thing to do for the receiver to accept the bargain. Young (1989:45) notes that exhortation "differs from manipulation in the preparatory and necessary conditions; it is not obvious to the speaker that the hearer would do the act without being encouraged, and it counts as an attempt to urge the hearer to perform the act". In the representative act [7], the threateners appear to provide their own encouragement for keeping their promise. They also execute the additional illocutionary force of encouraging the reader as it may not be obvious to the threateners that the readers will do the desired act of publishing the article without being urged to do so: "Based on my belief that my audience will disrespect me if I break my promise, I hereby persuade you to trust me and in doing so I convince you to get the article published. For these reasons I hereby commit to keeping my promise".

Final consideration

The ultimate question of this paper to what extent the linguist may deduce an author's level of expressed commitment to the threat. We consider SAT as useful to aid this. Threats may be conveyed in various grammatical forms, though the conditions for an author to commit a bargain may be uniform. It is not so much a question of whether this commitment is stated directly or indirectly, but whether it is made explicitly in a conventional way, or implicitly. Following the application of Speech Act Theory in consideration of the letter sent by Theodore Kaczynski to the *New York Times*, it is clear that context and external historical circumstances play a substantial role in making clear the meaning of both direct and indirect utterances in terms of relevance, manner, quantity and quality. In cases where the literal language does not convey illocutionary force explicitly, threats may be conveyed quite clearly by utterances with idiomatic or an inferred sense. Meaning is then understood either through eliminating inappropriate interpretation, or through inference within context. Gricean (Grice, 1975, 2004; Zabbal, 2008) maxims of the cooperative principle, for example, are useful in attaining clarity in terms of the illocutionary force, as well as the illocutionary intent of threat acts. As such, these pragmatic tools appear to be valuable to aid the achievement of a comprehensible understanding of interpersonal stance and author commitment in written textual threats. By applying these tools, linguists can arrive at a more comprehensive understanding of what it is that threateners do with their language, how they do it and to what purpose they do so. Though limited to one text, we believe that this demonstration offers support for the application of SAT, within its limits, to address the question of authorship commitment, and therefore the urgency of threat, in forensic linguistic investigation.

Conclusion

This paper offers a theoretical contribution toward a framework for analysing threats, focusing on characterising the genre of threat text from a pragmatic point of view. In this paper, we considered the extent to which Speech Act Theory may be useful in forensic linguistic investigations of written textual threats to evaluate author commitment to the threat and, by association to evaluate the urgency of the threat. We defined the notion of threat as a statement uttered in a given social context in which the threatener exerts their power over another by means of language that promises harm to the subjected or threatened party, with the intent of producing a specific effect, e.g. payment of a ransom by the receiver.

We identified general salient features of written textual threats, such as that texts develop in four interlinked stages and contain an element in one or more of these stages. The inclusion of a cause-and-effect clause is central to the linguist's investigation, with the omission of such a clause suggesting a complete lack of commitment. There may or may not be room for negotiation: regardless of the extent to which negotiation is allowed, threateners place themselves in a position of power, expressing interpersonal stance. They achieve this by means of speech acts, as we demonstrated with reference to authentic natural threatening discourse as presented in the Unabomber letter. Based on this demonstration, we propose that Speech Act Theory does contribute to a more comprehensive analysis of interpersonal stance in terms of author commitment and intent. The notion of illocutionary intent is, furthermore, considered a useful tool to explain what it is that threateners do with their words and how they do it. We posit that verbal habits or speech acts are complex linguistic entities influenced by context. This context, in addition to the degree of directness or indirectness of threat, is of particular importance when evaluating stance. We therefore recommend that Speech Act Theory be more readily applied within its limits in forensic linguistic investigation of written textual threats.

References

Allwood, J. 1977. A critical look at speech act theory. In: P. Dahl (ed.), *Logic, pragmatics and grammar*. Lund: Studentlitteratur. pp. 53-99.

Ariel, M. 2012. Research paradigms in pragmatics. In: K. Allan & K.M. Jaszczolt (eds.), *The Cambridge handbook of pragmatics*. New York: Cambridge University Press. pp. 23-45. https://doi.org/10.1017/CBO9781139022453.003

Asher, N. & Lascarides, A. 2001. Indirect speech acts. *Synthese*, 128(1-2):183-228. https://doi.org/10.1023/A:1010340508140

Austin, J.L. 1962. *How to do things with words: The William James lectures delivered at Harvard University in 1955*. Cambridge MA: Harvard University Press. https://pure.mpg.de/rest/items/item_2271128/component/file_2271430/content [Retrieved 22 December 2018].

Bach, K. & Harnish, R.M. 1979. *Linguistic communication and speech acts*. Cambridge MA: MIT Press.

Biber, D. 2006. *University language: A corpus-based study of spoken and written registers*. Amsterdam: John Benjamins.

Chaski, C.E. 2013. Best practices and admissibility of forensic author identification. *Journal of Law and Policy*, 21(2):333-376. http://brooklynworks.brooklaw.edu/jlp/vol21/iss2/5

Chojimah, N. 2016. The act of promise and threat in translated verses of law in the Qurán. *Humaniora*, 28(2):152-163. https://doi.org/10.22146/jh.v28i2.16398

Clark, H.H. 1979. Responding to indirect speech acts. *Cognitive Psychology*, 11:430-477.

Cooren, F. 2000. Toward another ideal speech situation: A critique of Habermas' reinterpretation of speech act theory. *Quarterly Journal of Speech*, 86(3):295-317. https://doi.org/10.1080/00335630009384298

Davies, J.M. 2006. A discourse of threat? A textual analysis of the US report *Commission for assistance to a free Cuba*. Unpublished Master's thesis, Department of Sociology, University of Helsinki, Finland. http://ethesis.helsinki.fi/julkaisut/val/sosio/pg/davies/adiscour.pdf [Retrieved 19 December 2018].

Emike, A.J. 2013. Towards an extra-linguistic critique of J.L. Austin's speech act theory. *International Journal of Applied Linguistics & English Literature*, 2(5):241-248. http://dx.doi.org/10.7575/aiac.ijalel.v.2n.5p.241

Fitzgerald, J. 2006. *Forensic linguistic services at the Behavioral Analysis Unit-1: An FBI handbook detailing services offered at the BAU-1*. Quantico VA: FBI Academy and the National Center for the Analysis of Violent Crime.

Gales, T. 2010. Ideologies of violence: A corpus and discourse analytic approach to stance in threatening communications. Unpublished PhD thesis, University of California. Oakland CA. https://eric.ed.gov/?id=ED520035

Gales, T. 2011. Identifying interpersonal stance in threatening discourse: An appraisal analysis. *Discourse Studies,* 13(1):27-46. https://doi.org/10.1177/1461445610387735

Gales, T. 2015a Threatening stances: A corpus analysis of realized vs. non-realized threats. *Language and Law/Linguagem e Direito*, 2(2):1-25. http://ler.letras.up.pt/uploads/ficheiros/14124.pdf [Retrieved 27 February 2018].

Gales, T. 2015b. The stance of stalking: A corpus-based analysis of grammatical markers of stance in threatening communications. *Corpora*, special issue on Forensic Linguistics, 10(2):171-200.

Gibbons, J.P. 2003. *Forensic linguistics: An introduction to language in the justice system*. Oxford: Wiley-Blackwell.

Grant C.K. 1949. Promises. *Mind*, 58(231):359-366. http://www.jstor.org/stable/2250649

Grant, T. 2008. Approaching questions in forensic authorship analysis. In: J. Gibbons & M.T. Turell (eds.), *Dimensions of forensic linguistics*. Amsterdam: John Benjamins. pp. 215-229. https://doi.org/10.1075/aals.5.15gra.

Grice, H.P. 1957. Meaning. *The Philosophical Review*, 66(3):377-388. https://www.doi.org/10.2307/2182440

Grice, H.P. 1975. Logic and conversation. In: P. Cole & J.L. Morgan (eds.), *Syntax and semantics, Vol. 3, Speech acts*. New York: Academic Press. pp. 41-58. https://sites.ualberta.ca/~francisp/NewPhil448/GriceLogicConversation.pdf [Retrieved 12 February 2018].

Habermas, J. 1984. *The theory of communicative action, Vol. 1: Reason and the rationalization of society*, reprint edition, translated by T. McCarthy. Boston MA: Beacon Press.

Habermas, J. 1991. Comments on John Searle: "Meaning, communication and representation". In: E. LePore & R. Van Gulick (eds.), *John Searle and his critics*. Oxford: Blackwell. pp. 17-29.

Hancher, M. 1979. The classification of cooperative illocutionary acts. *Language in Society*, 8(1):1-14. https://doi.org/10.1017/S0047404500005911

Holtgraves, T. 1986. Language structure in social interaction: Perceptions of direct and indirect speech acts and interactants who use them. *Journal of Personality and Social Psychology*, 51(2):305-314. https://doi.org/10.1037/0022-3514.51.2.305

Jacobsen, R.R. 2010. The interpretation of *indirect speech acts* in relevance theory. *Journal of LIE*, 3:7-23.

Kravchenko, N. 2017. Illocution of direct speech acts via conventional implicature and semantic presupposition. *Lege Artis*, 2(1):128-168. https://doi.org/10.1515/lart-2017-0004

Kreckel, M. 1981. Where do constitutive rules come from? *Language and Communication*, 1(1):73-88. https://doi.org/10.1016/0271-5309(81)90007-0

Levinson, S.C. 1983. *Pragmatics*. Cambridge: Cambridge University Press.

Miranda, I.V. 2013. *The cooperative, relevance and politeness principles in jokes: Interpretation and complementariness*. Thesis submitted for degree in English Studies, University of La Rioja, Logroño, Spain. https://biblioteca.unirioja.es/tfe_e/TFE000347.pdf [Retrieved 19 December 2018].

Moeschler, J. 2002. Speech act theory and the analysis of conversations. In: D. Vanderveken & S. Kubo (eds.), *Essays in speech act theory*. Amsterdam: John Benjamins. pp. 239-261. https://doi.org/10.1075/pbns.77.15moe

Muschalik, J. 2018. *Threatening in English: A mixed method approach*. Amsterdam: John Benjamins.

Oishi, E. 2006. Austin's speech act theory and the speech situation. *Esercizi Filosofici*, 1(1):1-14. [Retrieved 19 August 2017] https://www2.units.it/eserfilo/art106/oishi106.pdf

Olsson, J. 2008. *Forensic linguistics: An introduction to language, crime and the law*. 2nd Edition. London/New York: Continuum.

Olsson, J. 2012. *Wordcrime: Solving crime through forensic linguistics*. London/New York: Continuum.

Olsson, J. & Luchjenbroers, J. 2013. *Forensic linguistics*, 3rd Edition. London/New York: Bloomsbury.

Oxford living dictionaries: English (OED). 2019. Oxford: Oxford University Press. https://en.oxforddictionaries.com

Poythress, V.S. 2008. Canon and speech act: Limitations in speech act theory, with implications for a putative theory of canonical speech acts. *Westminster Theological Journal*, 70:337-354.

Rugala, E. & Fitzgerald, J. 2003. Workplace violence: From threat to intervention. *Clinics in Occupational and Environmental Medicine*, 3(4):775-789.

Sadock, J.M. 1974. *Towards a linguistic theory of speech acts*. New York: Academic Press.

Sadock, J.M. 2004. Speech acts. In: L. Horn & G. Ward (eds.), *The handbook of pragmatics*. Malden MA: Blackwell. pp. 53-73.

Salgueiro, A.B. 2010. Promises, threats and the foundations of speech act theory. *Pragmatics*, 20(2):213-228. https://doi.org/10.1075/prag.20.2.05bla

Searle, J.R. 1969. *Speech acts: An essay in the philosophy of language*. Cambridge: Cambridge University Press. https://doi.org/10.1017/CBO9781139173438

Searle, J.R. 1971. What is a speech act? In: J.R. Searle (ed.), *The philosophy of language*. London: Oxford University Press. pp. 44-46.

Searle, J.R. 1975. Indirect speech acts. In: P. Cole & J.L. Morgan (eds.), *Syntax and semantics*, Vol. 3: *Speech acts*. New York: Academic Press.

Searle, J.R. 1976. A classification of illocutionary acts. *Language in Society*, 5(1):1-23. https://doi.org/10.1017/S0047404500006837

Searle, J.R. & Vanderveken, D. 1985. *Foundations of illocutionary logic*. Cambridge: Cambridge University Press.

Shuy, R.W. 2014. *The language of murder cases: Intentionality, predisposition, and voluntariness*. London/New York: Oxford University Press. https://doi.org/10.1093/acprof:oso/9780199354832.001.0001

Tiersma, P.M. 1986. The language of offer and acceptance: Speech acts and the question of intent. *California Law Review*, 74(1):189-232. https://doi.org/10.15779/Z383B2P

Twitchell, D.P. & Nunamaker, J.F. 2004. *Speech act profiling: A probabilistic method for analyzing persistent conversations and their participants*. Proceedings of the 37th annual Hawaii international conference on System Sciences, Hawaii, 5-8 January. https://doi.org/10.1109/HICSS.2004.1265283

Yoshitake, M. 2004. Critique of J.L. Austin's speech act theory: Decentralization of the speaker-centered meaning in communication. *Kyushu Communication Studies*, 2:27-43.

Young, R.A. 1989. A classification of conditional sentences based on speech act theory. *Grace Theological Journal*, 10(1):29-49.

Yule, G. 1996. *Pragmatics*. Oxford: Oxford University Press.

Zabbal, Y. 2008. Gricean conversational implicatures. Undergraduate Linguistics course material, Semantics I (CAS LX 502) Boston University. http://www.bu.edu/linguistics/UG/course/lx502/_docs/lx502-implicatures.pdf [Retrieved 12 February 2018].

APPENDIX

Text of Unabomber's Letter Received by the *New York Times* 26 April 1995

Source

The 'Lectric Law Library, https://www.upcounsel.com/lectl-text-of-unabombers-letter-received-by-NY-times-april-26-1995 1[Retrieved 5 January 2019]. The document is presented verbatim, with original spelling, emphasis and punctuation. Three passages were (historically) deleted from all such reproductions at the request of the FBI.

SIGN LANGUAGE AND HATE SPEECH

The potential pitfalls of iconic signs

Terrence R. Carney

Introduction

The naming of things is a powerful act. The one who names objects exercises a certain amount of influence. Bosmajian (1974) reminds his readers that to receive a name elevates an individual to the status of being human; to be without a name leaves one's identity questionable. Having a *good* name is so important to the individual that society has called for defamation laws to protect a person from name-calling. The power of naming is related to the defining of others. In following Edward Sapir, Bosmajian (1974) recalls that people's thoughts affect their language and their language affects their thoughts. There is a link between the way people see (and speak of) themselves and the way they view others. As Bosmajian (1974:5) puts it: "Our identities, who and what we are, how others see us, are greatly affected by the names we are called and the words with which we are labelled". Name-calling is not simply about giving someone a bad reputation; it relates directly to othering. The sender reminds the receiver that he or she is not like the sender and, as a result, inferior (see also Wolfson, 1997). It is here that a distinction can be made between affecting one's reputation and professional character on the one hand and demeaning one's self-worth and self-image on the other. The former deals with slander and libel and the latter addresses hate speech.

Though the term is considered by some to be imprecise and difficult to define (McGonagle, 2011; Parekh 2012), "hate speech" can be described as derogatory language directed mostly at minority groups (Bhatia, 2016; Wolfson, 1997). It includes a wide range of negative discourse (McGonagle, 2011) that ultimately leads to a break in peace (Trager & Dickerson, 1999) and damages core values like inclusiveness and dignity (Bhatia, 2016; Wolfson, 1997). Hate speech has historic ties with freedom of speech, freedom of religion and immigration (Walker, 1994). Contact between different peoples created a need to protect religious beliefs, cultural practices and linguistic rights and has led to the existence of in-groups and out-groups and, with it, a vocabulary. Parekh (2016:40) says hate speech "expresses, encourages, stirs up, or incites *hatred* against a group of individuals distinguished by a particular feature or set of features such as race, ethnicity, gender, religion, nationality, and sexual orientation". Parekh (2016:40-41) continues by identifying three features of hate speech:

(1) it is directed at an individual or group based on arbitrary and irrelevant features;
(2) it stigmatises the target group by ascribing undesirable qualities to that group; and
(3) due to its negative qualities, the target group is considered unwelcome and consequently a threat to the stability of society.

Ultimately, hate speech is communication that is offensive, hurtful and wounding (Trager & Dickerson, 1999), it causes emotional distress and leaves victims "threatened, humiliated and diminished" (Wolfson, 1997:47). It furthermore perpetuates stereotypes and mistrust.

The presence of social media has proven to be an ideal platform for the survival of hate speech. A case in point was when, much to her surprise, an estate agent from Durban became a household name in South Africa after she referred to black beachgoers as "monkeys" on Facebook (Evans, 2016). Penny Sparrow's Facebook post spread like wildfire. She made things worse when she tried to defend herself by saying that she was merely stating the facts (Wicks, 2016). Though not an isolated incident, it would become the archetype of hate speech on social media in South Africa. The public became increasingly aware of individuals spewing hatred through social media, affecting all cultures: a black man claiming he wanted to kill white and Indian people and rape their children (Pijoos, 2017); a white man who was unhappy with the Ministry of Sport and reverted to calling officials "a bunch of k*****s" (Davis, 2017); a Christian who was tired of "Muslim bastards" and their call to prayer (*News24*, 2017); a straight woman who called a gay editor a "faggot with a mouth" (*Mamba Online*, 2018); and a variety of people writing hateful things about the Chinese after illegal trade in donkey skins became public knowledge (Raborife, 2017). Matters got worse when individuals in more respected professions made themselves guilty of hate speech through social media: government officials (Velaphi Khumalo), university lecturers (Benny Morota), parliamentarians (Dianne Kohler Barnard) and even city mayors (Herman Mashaba) incited racial and xenophobic hatred (Davis, 2017; Etheridge, 2016).

Since 1994, many incidents like the examples mentioned have led to Parliament first promulgating the Promotion of Equality and Prevention of Unfair Discrimination Act in 2000 (the Equality Act), followed recently by the tabling by Cabinet of the Prevention and Combating of Hate Crimes and Hate Speech Bill (the Hate Speech Bill). The much-awaited Bill was first published for public comment in October 2016 and soon came under attack as being somewhat vague, containing broad definitions that might pose a threat to freedom in general and lead to the unreasonable incarceration of well-intentioned individuals (Griffin, 2017; Free Market Foundation, 2017; Wasserman, 2017). Furthermore, the Bill seems rather redundant in light of the Equality Act and the Constitution, which already deal with discriminatory concerns like hate speech (Dube, 2017; Griffin, 2017;

Wasserman, 2017). The Bill was subsequently revised and a second version was published in the *Government Gazette* of 29 March 2018.

When studying the social media examples cited above, as well as case law dealing with hate speech, it appears that identity signifiers lie at the heart of it. The following, amongst others, are mostly at the core of transgressions:

- race (*Donaldo v Haripersad*; *M v Ferreira*; *Khoza v Saeed*; *Magubane v Smith*; *ANC v Sparrow*; *Smith v Mgoqi*; *Herselman v Geleba*);
- religion (*Jamiat-Ul-Ulama of Transvaal v Johncom Media Investments Ltd*; *Islamic Unity Convention v Independent Broadcasting Authority*);
- gender (*Sonke Gender Justice Network v Malema*); and
- sexual orientation (*South African Human Rights Commission v Qwulane*).

Having legislation in place to prevent and act upon instances of hate speech (and other means of discrimination) is a necessity in each country, especially within nations that have suffered under an oppressive government where identity politics now remains an important issue. However, to what extent does legislation like the Equality Act and the Hate Speech Bill succeed in being a successful tool in combating these transgressions? Hate speech is often only considered in its verbal form. It is usually something that is said, sung or written down. But what about other forms of hate speech? For instance, how would courts deal with the use of symbols or accusations of discrimination in visual-spatial languages?

In an introductory sign language course, I became aware of lexis that I – as a hearing, nonsigning person – immediately thought of as politically incorrect (un-PC). Though the instructor insisted that these terms were acceptable within the specified Deaf community, it did make me wonder how many signs could be understood as offensive or even hateful. Initially, I looked up a number of these signs in the *Dictionary of South African Signs* (Penn, Ogilvy-Foreman, Simmons & Anderson-Forbes, 1992-1994) to confirm whether they were listed and whether the dictionary mentioned anything about them being derogatory. They were indeed lemmatised[1] and contained no warning labels. Considering the seriousness of hate speech and the qualifying criteria provided for in legislation, what would a signing Deaf person's position be if accused? Three related questions come to mind:

- To what extent do iconic signs qualify as hate speech?
- In what way do iconic signs qualify as hate speech when observed by hearing nonsigners?
- How sufficient are the definitions and criteria in the Equality Act and the Hate Speech Bill to address hate speech transgressions in sign language?

For the following discussion, this chapter is divided into three main sections. To start, the focus will fall on gestures, iconicity and socially unacceptable signs. Subsequently, an overview will be provided of what the Equality Act and the Hate Speech Bill say about hate

---

[1] A 'lemma' being the headword/main entry in a dictionary.

speech. The chapter will then proceed to discuss the questions previously mentioned in relation to the legislation.

Lexis in sign language

Gesturing

Most hearing people use silent or co-speech gestures that have been conventionalised by their culture at some time (Baker, Van den Bogaerde, Pfau & Schermer, 2016:10; Perniss, Özyürek & Morgan, 2015). It is generally a visual adumbration in the communication process, which may happen unwittingly (Perniss et al., 2015:6), for example, using your index finger to point at something when saying "Look over there". In South Africa, when you want the bill at a restaurant, you can catch your waiter's eye and gesture as if you are either writing in the air or writing on the palm of your hand. When indicating to someone at a distance from you that you will phone them, you place your hand next to your ear, with thumb and little finger extended to mimic the receiver of a phone. One of the universal signs for "good" is a clenched fist with a thumb raised upwards, whereas drinking is usually a hand in the shape of a vessel brought towards the mouth and then tipped (sometimes repetitively). In addition, when quoting someone while talking, people tend to draw inverted commas in the air (sometimes only with one hand).

Of course, as with spoken language, gestures are present in sign language, but they do not necessarily qualify as signs. For a gesture to qualify as a sign, it has to adhere to the four parameters of sign language – and always in relation to the signing space (see Fourie Blair, 2013:116-119; Mesthrie, Swann, Deumert & Leap, 2000:408-409):

- handshape
- location
- movement, and
- orientation

Handshape is used to give form to a sign. There are many different handshapes, like a Flat Hand, a B Hand, a Bent Flat Hand, and so on. Location is measured against the hand or position of the hands in relation to the body: hands are close to or far from the body, or they are kept in the middle, or on the periphery of the signing space. The third parameter is the type of movement for which the hand is used to articulate meaning. Orientation determines the position of the hand palm: when signing, the palm faces different directions, either away from the signer, or up and down, or facing the signer. All signs obey the four parameters, though gestures do not. For example, the South African Sign Language (SASL) verb "know" (Figure 14.1)[2] is a bent flat hand (handshape) with the palm facing downward (orientation), fingers touching (movement) the side of the head (location), repetitively (Baker et al., 2016:70).

FIGURE 14.1 *Know* in South African Sign Language
(Reproduced with permission)

Gesturing to someone that you will phone him or her (as described) does not have to adhere to movement or location in the same way a sign does. The speaker usually determines how far away he or she wants to place the hand from the ear and there is no fixed rule as to the orientation of the palm. Gesturing is often about the message conveyed and not so much the syntax that governs it. The signing space, however, consists of the area starting above the head and reaching the middle of the body; signs are made on, or close to, the body and seldom outside this space (Baker et al., 2016:2-3).

Arbitrary and iconic signs

In the same way as in spoken languages, sign language distinguishes between arbitrary and iconic signs. Arbitrary signs show no obvious relation between the sign and its meaning. The noun in SASL representing the gloss "name" (Figure 14.2) bears no clear resemblance to the concept of naming.

---

[2] All the illustrations of signs published in this chapter are used with the permission of Mr G. Maluleka of the Unisa Sound, Video and Photography Unit.

FIGURE 14.2 *Name* in South African Sign Language
(Reproduced with permission)

Iconic signs, on the other hand, show an apparent relation between form and meaning (Baker et al., 2016:37; Meir, 2010:874; Russo, 2004:167). A good example of iconicity in spoken language are the features onomatopoeia, phonesthesia and ideophone (Meir, 2010:866; Ortega, Sümer & Özyürek, 2014:1114; Perniss, Thompson & Vigliocco, 2010:2-3; Russo, 2004:165-166, 168). Words ranging from "meow" to "knock" and "buzz" are all examples of sound having a bearing on meaning. In addition to depicting the characteristics of an entity or action, Ortega et al. (2014:1114) point out that iconic signs may also indicate the motion patterns and the spatial relations between objects, and they can represent either the entity or action in part or entirely. Perniss et al. (2010:8) argue that both spoken and sign language users are aware of iconicity and make use of it deliberately. However, the occurrence of iconicity is much more prevalent in sign language than in spoken languages, mostly because they convey concepts through a spatial-visual modality (Meir, 2010:866, 871; Ortega et al., 2014:1115; Perniss et al., 2010:4). Tolar, Lederberg, Gokhale and Tomasello (2007:225) state that iconic signs are so prevalent because "individuals can interpret them without requiring a prior explicit connection between them and their referents". Some signs are only partially iconic, which means that not all of the components of form correspond with the components of meaning (Meir, 2010:873-874). Iconic signs are therefore either transparent or non-transparent.

Transparent iconic signs represent the visual aspects of an entity or action in such a way that its meaning becomes easily deducible, even for hearing nonsigners (Baker et al., 2016:37; Lieberth & Gamble, 1991:89; Tolar et al., 2007:226). An experiment by Lieberth and Gamble (1991) found that not only do sign-naive people understand and remember many transparent iconic signs, they also have success in identifying them. Examples in SASL include the glosses "baby" (holding it in your arms, Figure 14.3a), "hot" (wiping sweat from your forehead, Figure 14.3b) and "sleep" (Figure 14.3c).

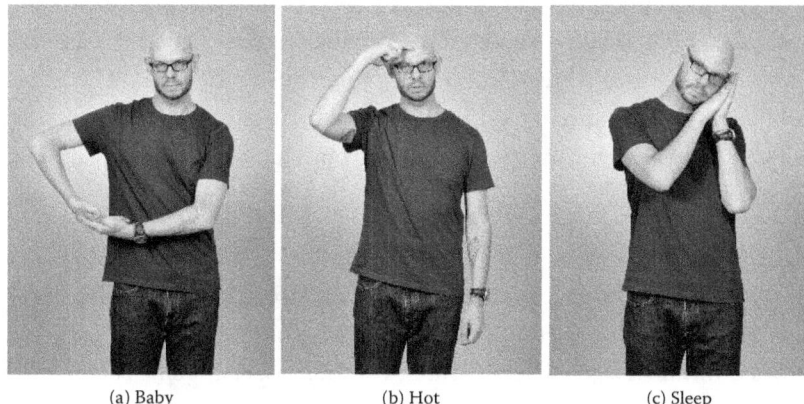

(a) Baby   (b) Hot   (c) Sleep

FIGURE 14.3 Transparent iconic signs in South African Sign Language
(Reproduced with permission)

Even though some signs may have been quite transparent when they were first introduced, they have become less transparent over time and therefore the relation between the sign and the feature of the action or entity is no longer that clear (Meir, 2010:866; Perniss et al., 2010:5). Examples in SASL include "washing" (of clothes, Figure 14.4a), which mimics the rubbing of cloth between two hands; and "coffee", which mimics the grinding of coffee beans (Figure 14.4b).

(a) Washing   (b) Coffee

FIGURE 14.4 Non-transparent iconic signs in South African Sign Language
(Reproduced with permission)

Just as signs are influenced by a variety of demographic factors like race, ethnicity, age, region and schooling, iconic signs are also determined by culture (Lieberth & Gamble, 1991; McKee & McKee, 2011). Similar to spoken language, differences in culture and subculture lead to sign variety (Aarons & Akach, 1998; Penn, Lewis & Greenstein, 1984:7-8; Woll & Ladd, 2003:160). Even if someone knows the form of a certain sign, that is no guarantee that he or she will understand its meaning (Russo, 2004:171-172). The sign for "cat" in American Sign Language (ASL) is indicated by using one hand to pull at a single whisker, whereas British Sign Language (BSL) uses both hands to indicate all the cat's whiskers (see Perniss et al., 2010:5).

Researchers have proven that Deaf children who speak sign language as their mother tongue do not find iconic signs easier to acquire than arbitrary signs (Lieberth & Gamble, 1991:90; Meir, 2010:867; Ortega et al., 2014:1115-1116; Tolar et al., 2007:226). They follow the same process for most signs when learning vocabulary. That being said, both Deaf and hearing older children and adults learn iconic signs much more quickly and are able to retain them in long term memory because they can relate the sign to the visual characteristics of the original referent (Lieberth & Gamble, 1991:90; Tolar et al., 2007:234). Many of these iconic signs are related to what Padden, Hwang, Lepic and Seegers (2015) call instrument and handling strategies. They found that iconic signs for objects are often connected to the way an instrument is shaped and used. The handling strategy involves the grasping of an imaginary tool and moving the hand(s) in a manner similar to how they would move when the object is used; whereas the instrument strategy usually shows the shape and dimension of the object in a motion typical of that tool in use (Padden et al., 2015:82-83). Identity signifiers are indicated by both action- and feature-based iconicity. Some identities relate to dynamic physical attributes (e.g. certain jobs, handicaps), whereas others depend on static physical features (wearing a Roman collar, or a bindi on the forehead).

Politically incorrect signs

Sign language is no different to spoken language when it comes to socially unacceptable or politically incorrect language. As Sutton-Spence and Woll (1999:242) point out, a younger generation may take offence to older signs, though the older generation may find no fault in the words they use. An example of this is the un-PC gloss "persons with disability" in BSL (Figure 14.5), which focuses on walking impairment.

FIGURE 14.5 *Person(s) with disability* in British Sign Language
(Reproduced with permission)

This is not to be confused with coarse or taboo language or even insults. Taboo language may include references to sex or religion and may leave conversational partners uncomfortable or embarrassed. Coarse language includes words like "bitch" or "fucker" and is used as an interjection to express emotional states. Insults are meant to degrade someone, usually by pointing at certain physical features and making fun of them, for instance, calling someone "four eyes" when they wear glasses. Though all of these may be socially unacceptable and may no doubt form part of hate speech, politically incorrect language is most relevant here. The *Oxford English Dictionary* (2018) defines political incorrectness as "discriminatory" and the opposite of social appropriateness. Sutton-Spence and Woll (1999:249) describe politically correct (PC) signs as "those that have been changed especially because it is feared that the [former] sign will offend someone", causing insult without meaning to. Due to pejorative connotations, sign language communities have started to change signs that may be viewed as un-PC. This may be related to increasing social contact on linguistic and cultural levels, as well as changes taking place due to socio-economic and socio-political needs of a younger generation (see Aarons & Akach, 1998; McKee & McKee, 2011). Examples in BSL include new signs for the glosses "Jew" and "India". Instead of using the iconic sign depicting a hooked nose or beard to gloss "Jew", the menorah is used instead (Sutton-Spence & Woll, 1999:250-251). For India, an arbitrary sign replaces the imagined bindi (red dot on the forehead) (Mickelburgh & Syal, 2004). Reasons for these changes came about in different ways. Explicit changes in BSL, for instance, include interventions applied by a television programme for the Deaf (Mickelburgh & Syal, 2004). Several older signs were dropped by the TV station because they were deemed inappropriate (Mickleburgh & Syal, 2004).

The proposed changes were initially met with resistance by some members in the Deaf community as interference in Deaf language and culture (*Sydney Morning Herald*, 2004). However, the results of a survey across the United Kingdom in 2012 has since confirmed that users of BSL have replaced several signs (like "China", "gay", "Jew" and "India") to reflect social changes and attitudes within British society (*Guardian*, 2012; Silverman, 2012).

Many signs that are potentially un-PC are still customary in sign languages across the world and in some varieties of SASL (Mickelburgh & Syal, 2004). Dutch (NGT), Flemish (VGT), ASL and Afrikaans sign language (AGT) use a depiction of a bindi on the forehead to gloss "Hindu"/"India".[3] ASL uses eye shape to gloss "Chinese" and "Japanese". NGT, ASL, VGT and Austrian Sign Language (ÖGS) use an iconic depiction of a beard to gloss "Jew".[4] Dutch sign language previously glossed "Jew" by referring to a hooked nose, but now uses a beard depiction as well (Baker et al., 2016:295). Along with an iconic representation of side curls (the payot), the beard depiction is considered less awkward. Nevertheless, these signs remain exclusively masculine and therefore continue to be problematic. AGT and VGT still refer to Jewishness through the stereotypical hooked nose (Figure 14.6).

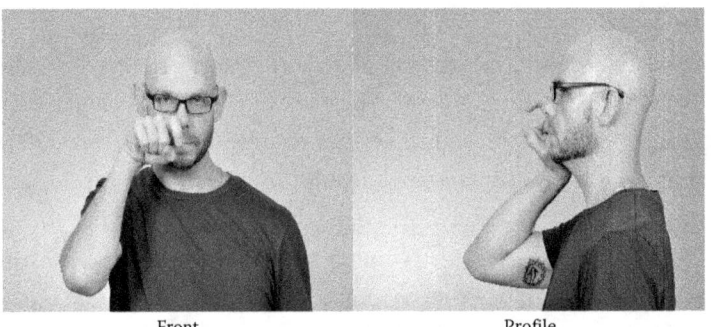

Front   Profile

FIGURE 14.6 *Jew* in Afrikaans and Flemish Sign Language
(Reproduced with permission)

Other contentious signs include iconic depictions of the hijab to gloss "Morocco" (NGT); iconic hand-over-mouth ululating to gloss "Native American" (VGT) (Figure 14.7); non-transparent iconic references to the African nose to gloss "Africa" (ASL); and an iconic flick of the wrist to denote gay people ("homo" – NGT). To gloss "walking frame", speakers of NGT use both hands to place the imagined instrument in front of them to denote walking, while bobbing their heads to indicate old age. Some users of SASL articulate "persons with

---

[3] Dutch examples are taken from the *Basiswoordenboek Nederlandse Gebarentaal* (Schermer & Koolhof, 2009); Flemish examples from *Vlaamse Gebarentaal Woordenboek* (Van Herreweeghe, Slembrouck & Vermeerbergen, 2004); ASL examples from Signing Savvy's *Sign Language Dictionary* (2018); and the SASL examples from the *Dictionary of Southern African Signs* (Penn et al., 1993;1994).

[4] Austrian examples are taken from Zentrum für Gebärdensprache und Hörbehindertenkommunikation's *Leda Sila* (2017).

disability" by contracting the arms into crooked positions, recalling a disabled person's mangled body.

FIGURE 14.7 *Native American* in Flemish Sign Sign Language
(Reproduced with permission)

These and other iconic identity signifiers that correspond with prohibited grounds of South African legislation could be experienced by others as hateful or harmful.

The Equality Act and Hate Speech Bill

Most countries have laws prohibiting hate speech in one way or another (Trager & Dickerson, 1999; Walker, 1994). South Africa is no exception. Legislation addressing hate speech in South Africa should be read together with Section 16 of the Constitution, which provides for the freedom of speech. However, freedom of expression is not extended to propaganda for war, incitement of imminent violence, or the advocacy of hatred based on race, ethnicity, gender or religion, which would cause harm. In addition, the Equality Act is meant to give effect to the spirit of the South African Constitution, to promote equality, and to correct what the apartheid regime has damaged through its discriminatory policies (Section 4(2)). The Act (Section 6) is also very clear in that neither the state nor any person may discriminate unfairly against any other person. Section 10 of the Act declares in no uncertain terms what South African citizens should refrain from doing if they want to steer clear of hate speech. Subject to a proviso in Section 12, no person may publish, propagate, advocate or communicate words based on one or more of the prohibited grounds listed in the Act against any person that could reasonably be construed to demonstrate a clear intention to be hurtful, harmful or incite harm, and promote or propagate hatred.

A court furthermore has the authority to refer a case to the Director of Public Prosecutions to institute criminal proceedings against an individual. Guilty parties have had to pay penalties or do community service as penance for their crime (Geldenhuys, 2017:25; Sethusa, 2014; SAPA, 2014).[5]

In their critique of the Act's hate speech provisions, Marais and Pretorius (2015:907) argue that the term "words" in Section 10(1) ("advocate or communicate words") should be replaced by the term "expression" and should, by extension, include the concept "symbolic expression" to cover more examples of hate speech. In their view, "expression" must then include vandalism of state symbols like the national flag (Marais & Pretorius, 2015:907).[6] However, the shortcomings of the Act do not stop here. The Act does not define what it signifies by the terms "publish", "propagate", "advocate" or "communicate". This means that these terms could be understood to include all manner of language output, regardless of the medium or channel of communication – public or private; signs produced through sign language are then no exception.

The prohibited grounds, mentioned in Section 1(xxii) of the Act, are quite exhaustive and include the following:

> (a) race, gender, sex, pregnancy, marital status, ethnic or social origin, colour, sexual orientation, age, disability, religion, conscience, belief, culture, language and birth; or
> (b) any other ground where discrimination based on that other ground –
>   (i) causes or perpetuates systemic disadvantage;
>   (ii) undermines human dignity; or
>   (iii) adversely affects the equal enjoyment of a person's rights and freedoms in a serious manner that is comparable to discrimination on a ground in paragraph (a).

Of equal importance is Section 13, which deals with the burden of proof. It is the respondent's duty to prove that unfair discrimination did not take place as alleged. In other words, the respondent has to prove that his or her words did not contravene any of the prohibited grounds and that there was no clear intention to be either hurtful or harmful. If, however, it can be proved that discrimination did take place, then the respondent needs to demonstrate that the discrimination was fair. The responsibility clearly lies with the speaker/signer and not the listener/looker. Another important aspect is the fact that hurt or harm does not need to be present for speech to be seen as hate speech, as long as the potential to be hurtful or harmful is present.

---

[5] Vicki Momberg became the first person in South Africa to receive a prison sentence for hate speech. However, the fairness and harshness of the sentence and her treatment by the presiding officer has been criticised (Saunderson-Meyer, 2018).

[6] In a similar vein, the Nelson Mandela Foundation (2018) has approached the Equality Court with a request to have the public display of the old South African flag declared as a form of hate speech.

For instance, this means that if someone takes offence to the use of an iconic sign that glosses "Jew", it becomes the signer's responsibility to argue that he or she was not being intentionally hurtful or harmful and that the sign is the only one to denote Jewishness within that particular sign language dialect. However, this could be a tough argument to sell, seeing as this is not only a matter of *intention*, but also of the *potential* to be hurtful and or harmful (see also Botha and Govindjee, 2014:149-150; Teichner, 2003:354). Add to this any effect the iconic sign might have on the accuser's human dignity, and it becomes increasingly difficult for a signer to prove his or her innocence. There is also the issue of perpetuating a stereotype, which might cause trouble further down the line.

Unfortunately, the fact that a word or sign should only be proven to be potentially damaging creates enough space for individuals to pursue personal vendettas, leaving the accused parties with the burden of proving their innocence. "Potential" as a criterion of hate speech also undermines the spirit and goal of the Act.

The goals of the Hate Speech Bill are similar to those of the Equality Act and mention human dignity, equality and, especially, non-racialism. The second version of the Bill defines "communication" as any "display; written, illustrated, visual or other descriptive matter; oral statement; representation or reference; or an electronic communication".[7] Almost identical to the Equality Act's description, "Hate speech" is defined by the Bill in Section 4(1) as follows:

> (a) Any person who intentionally publishes, propagates or advocates anything or communicates to one or more persons in a manner that could reasonably be construed to demonstrate a clear intention to –
> (i) be harmful or incite harm; or
> (ii) promote or propagate hatred.

To qualify as an offence of hate speech, the intended communication has to be based on one or more of the following grounds: age; albinism; birth; colour; culture; disability; ethnicity or social origin; gender or gender identity; HIV status; language; nationality, migrant or refugee status; race; religion; and sex, which includes intersex or sexual orientation. Subsections (b) and (c) extend the definition of hate speech to explicitly include electronic forms of communication and the display and distribution of any material that corresponds with its definition in Subsection (a). Interestingly, Section 4(1) of the Bill makes it clear that hate speech is not something that only occurs between a sender and an intended receiver: it also applies to a communication that is accessible by any member of the public. Potentially, this means that person A can direct his or her message at person B, but the reaction of anyone else who decodes this message will also be considered valid. This is

---

[7] Interestingly, the first version of the Bill also included the word "gesture" in its definition of "communication", which could have been used to address visual-spatial transgressions.

already visible in *Rustenburg Platinum Mine v SAEWA obo Bester and Others*, in which the Constitutional Court not only considered the reaction of the intended receiver of the contested message, but also the reactions of the people who were present where the verbal exchange took place.

At first, the Bill's definition of "communication" seems inclusive and broad enough to include every possible type of communication. However, the definition fails to explain precisely what communication is; instead it lists types of communication without elaborating on what each type means. For instance, where would the use or abuse of a state symbol like a flag be categorised? Visual communication? Display? Representation? What about sign language? Should a court classify it under "visual communication", "representation", "demonstration" (which is not included in the list) or "descriptive matter"? What exactly is meant by "electronic communication"? Does it simply refer to the channel of communication, or would it include language elements like emojis? Maybe emojis would be classified under "illustrated", "display", "descriptive matter" or "representation". What about braille? Does it qualify as "written communication"? The same level of vagueness is present in the use, in Subsection 4(1)(c), of the words "any material". How is "any material" different to the list of items included in the definition of "communication"?

Criticism is not restricted to the Bill; the Equality Act has not been spared either. The Act has been criticised for similar reasons – being too vague and too broad (see Marais, 2015:471; Marais & Pretorius, 2015; Teichner, 2003). Even its complex legalese has been analysed and found challenging (Nienaber, 2002). However, the Act too provides enough to include sign language in what qualifies as a communication exchange. In the end, it all comes down to a signifier and its signified; the use of a sign (in the semiotic sense) to communicate a concept. This incorporates both aural-oral and visual-spatial language.

Discussion

This section will briefly consider how each of the questions posed at the start of the chapter engage with the criteria in the cited legislation:

To what extent do iconic signs qualify as hate speech?[8]

Considering that sign language is a legitimate language like any other, there should be no exceptions. If a hearing speaker could be guilty of hate speech based on the words he or she uses, then a signing Deaf person could be, too. Considering also the criteria in both the Act and the Bill that clearly provide for visual communication, signs that communicate

---

[8] A search on the Juta Law Online Publications database for reported cases dealing with sign language related to hate speech delivered no results.

meaning could get a signer into trouble. Like words, signs are the containers for conceptual meaning. If that meaning is construed as being hateful, harmful, or aids in propagating (and perpetuating) hatred amongst people, then that specific sign and the context in which it was used should be scrutinised. If a signer is aware that a specific sign could be offensive to others, and he or she knows there are other signs to communicate the same concept and yet he or she continues to use this sign, then the user's sign choice creates the potential to propagate and perpetuate hatred.

In the first instance of the *Afriforum v Malema* case, Justice Bertelsmann said (par. 10, and further), that the true yardstick of hate speech is neither the historical significance nor the context of a phrase like "kill the boer", but rather "the effect of the words, objectively considered upon those directly affected and targeted thereby". This also means that a group of speakers cannot claim that a certain word or sign is acceptable just because they use it. Claiming that an iconic sign (like hand-over-mouth ululation to gloss "Native American") is suitable due to a lack of a more appropriate sign or due to token frequency, would be a weak argument. The *Herselman v Geleba* case is proof that the Equality Court is unsympathetic to references of culture and linguistic expression (as defence strategy), even when these are nuanced enough to make a difference in the verdict. When the appellant tried to argue that his use of the word *bobbejaan* was not meant in a racist manner, but rather used within a common Afrikaans expression indicating that someone was being silly, the court dismissed this view and sided with the original plaintiff.

Logically, this is not restricted to iconic signs only. Arbitrary signs that have developed a politically incorrect denotation or reference may cause the same damage. However, iconic identity signifiers are easier for Deaf and hearing people to infer, especially when they are based on physical attributes. Dehumanising someone or making that person feel inferior is what the Act and the Bill are trying to combat, regardless of the medium of communication (see also Teichner, 2003:355, 357).

Iconic signs as observed by hearing nonsigners

In what way do iconic signs qualify as hate speech when observed by hearing nonsigners? This depends primarily on whether the nonsigning person is able to interpret the contested transparent iconic sign. As the literature review has shown, hearing individuals can identify and understand certain transparent signs even if they do not understand sign language. However, this situation could also create many misunderstandings. An onlooker may think he or she understands the sign language observed, but unless they ask to confirm what the signer meant by a specific sign, a hearing nonsigning person might never really know. It is somewhat unlikely for unrelated nonsigning hearing people to observe signing

Deaf people so attentively that they will notice any un-PC language used by the signers in their conversation.

Yet, imagine two signing Deaf people, Johann and Thabo, sitting in a park. They are not used to seeing members of the Jewish community in their neighbourhood. When an Orthodox Jewish family walks by, Johann points to them and uses the hooked nose sign to say: "Look! Jews!" The very iconic nature of this sign and the fact that Johann pointed to the family to draw Thabo's attention, makes the sign reasonably obvious to both the family and any onlookers whose attention was caught by Johann's signing. If the hearing nonsigner is able to infer the meaning of the iconic sign, then a case could be made against Johann and it will be his responsibility to prove that his intentions were not discriminatory.

Of course, it is a different case entirely when one signing Deaf person uses an un-PC sign in conversation with another Deaf person. If the receiver experiences the sign as hateful (either an arbitrary or iconic sign), then a less complicated hate speech case may present itself.

Effectiveness of the Equality Act and the Hate Speech Bill

How sufficient are the definitions and criteria in the Equality Act and the Hate Speech Bill to address hate speech transgressions in sign language? As pointed out earlier, important words in the Act are either not defined, or they are defined in the Bill through words that need further explanation. As a result, both pieces of legislation are vague and broad, and consequently might provide many loopholes. Nevertheless, words and phrases in both the Act and the Bill that stand out and may be of concern here, are: causing hurt, promotion of hatred, undermining human dignity, perpetuating disadvantages and ridiculing a person or groups of persons. This speaks to the reason for the hate speech legislation. Hate speech goes beyond mere insult and concerns three main factors:

(1) it identifies and targets a traditionally oppressed group of people;[9]
(2) it attributes inferiority to that group; and
(3) the verbal (or visual) exchange employs hateful and degrading content directed at the target group (Janse van Rensburg, 2013:1, 3).

This corresponds with what Justice Lamont said during the *Afriforum v Malema* case of 2011 (par. 102), that the contested words "dehumanised" the group at which they were aimed. Whether or not intentions are deliberate, some language outputs may debase the addressee, or be potentially damaging to him or her (Teichner, 2003:354).

When one objectively summarises the Act and the Bill, it becomes clear that both pieces of legislation try to prevent the above from happening. In doing so, the Act and the Bill

---

[9] Of course, hate speech is by no means exclusive. Members of the in-group are also victims of hate speech and other forms of discrimination.

provide criteria and a list of qualifying grounds that must be used by a presiding officer in a test to determine if hate speech is applicable. Though not perfect, it is safe to say that the current and suggested legislation provide enough substance to gauge the contested output, verbal and visual alike. The real question should be whether an individual has truly been debased by another's communication. The present criteria (being hurtful or harmful, for instance) and the prohibited grounds (gender, religion, refugee status, etc.) are clear enough to include different forms of human communication, like spoken and signed language, and writing systems such as braille.

Conclusion

Both McGonagle (2011) and Parekh (2012) argue that antidiscrimination legislation seldom succeeds in changing the deep-rooted cause(s) of hate speech. Though the intention of these laws is to combat discrimination and to encourage citizens to take part actively in public life, legislation can easily become a blunt instrument or a means to suppress ideas and freedom. The ideal would be to address the causes that lead to hate speech, preferably through education. An approach would be for official institutions like religious congregations, the media, government, and so on to change their vocabulary deliberately and to involve the community in doing so. This is already visible in the world of mental health in which words with negative connotations (such as "crazy" and "asylum") are actively replaced with positive synonyms. Another example is the "Find New Words" campaign in which rural communities contribute new LGBTI+ identifying words to replace pejoratives like *isitabane* and *moffie* (Ntsabo, 2018).

Sign language is not new to changing vocabularies. Because sign language is seldom written down, there is a greater fluidity in adapting its vocabulary (Aarons & Akach, 1998:2, 24). This means that sign language can adapt and change more readily than spoken language. Signs are amended to fit both socio-political changes and the needs that arise because of them (McKee & McKee, 2011:511-512). When it comes to identity signifiers, the latest rule of thumb is to borrow the appropriate signs from the cultures that are being depicted. For instance, the official sign used in South African Sign Language for "Africa" has been adopted by other countries to refer to the continent and its people and features. It is not the purpose of this chapter to prescribe to the Deaf community; nevertheless, it would make sense for current standardisation and dictionary projects in South Africa to include initiatives that address older identity signifiers and explore why they are problematic.

As for the current legislation, more could be done to address its vagueness. The Equality Act should be revised to include clear definitions for "publish", "propagate", "advocate" and "communicate". Although the Hate Speech Bill does much better to define what types of communication qualify as hate speech, each of the types could do with examples or a brief elaboration. The Bill could also improve its definition of "communication" by saying what communication is. Both the Act and the Bill try to cover a wide spectrum of communication and its means of dissemination, but the true nature of its vagueness will only become known once courts start to deal with non-standard issues, like the use of sign language, braille, national symbols like flags, and audio files that do not qualify as oral statements. More thought should also be given to the way presiding officers interpret these statutes. Courts should consider a semiotic approach, in which the disputed communication is viewed from the perspective of a signifier–signified relationship. Alternatively, a contested communication can be scrutinised through cognitive semantics, in which the contested visual or lexical item(s) are viewed as a container of conceptual meaning. These approaches may save presiding officers from becoming entangled in wordy definitions of "hate speech" and "communication".

That being said, a reasonable person's understanding of what constitutes hate speech, depending upon the given criteria (like the prohibited grounds), makes it reasonably clear: using discriminatory language, regardless of its spoken or visual form, is unacceptable. Of course, if pragmatics has taught us anything, we should know that speakers do not keep to the rules and guidelines of language, be they grammar- or convention-based. Directing unacceptable identity signifiers (words or signs) at someone else, knowingly or ignorantly, will immediately place a legal burden squarely on the transgressor's shoulders. Hopefully, the context of the exchange may count in his or her favour.

Acknowledgement

I would like to thank Ms Karina van Aarde for her willingness to assist me with queries regarding South African Sign Language.

References

Aarons, D. & Akach, P. 1998. South African sign language – one language or many? A sociolinguistic question. *Stellenbosch Papers in Linguistics*, 31:1-28.

Baker, A.; Van den Bogaerde, B.; Pfau, R. & Schermer, T. 2016. *The linguistics of sign language*. Amsterdam: John Benjamins Publishing Company.

Bhatia, G. 2016. *Offend, shock, or disturb: Free speech under the Indian Constitution*. New Delhi: Oxford University Press.

Bosmajian, H. 1974. *The language of oppression*. Washington DC: Public Affairs Press.

Botha, J. & Govindjee, A. 2014. Regulating cases of "extreme hate speech" in South Africa: A suggested framework for a legislated criminal sanction. *South African Journal of Criminal Justice*, 27(2):117-155.

Davis, R. 2017. Pandora's box: South Africa and the (mis)use of social media. *Daily Maverick*. https://www.dailymaverick.co.za/article/2017-04-05-pandoras-box-south-africa-and-the-misuse-of-social-media [Retrieved 6 April 2017].

Dube, P. 2017. Rescuing the "hate speech bill". *News24*. https://www.news24.com/Columnists/GuestColumn/rescuing-the-hate-speech-bill-20170307 [Retrieved 17 January 2018].

Etheridge, J. 2016. Dianne Kohler Barnard absent as lawyers arrive in court for hate speech case. *Mail & Guardian*. https://mg.co.za/article/2016-09-13-dianne-kohler-barnard-absent-as-lawyers-arrive-in-court-for-hate-speech-case [Retrieved 6 April 2017].

Evans, J. 2016. Penny Sparrow back in court on criminal charges for racist comments. *City Press*. https://city-press.news24.com/News/penny-sparrow-back-in-court-on-criminal-charges-for-racist-comments-20160912 [Retrieved 6 April 2016].

Fourie Blair, H. 2013. Woordeboeke en Dowe gebruikers: Huidige probleme en die behoefte aan beter oplossings. *Lexikos*, 23:113-134.

Free Market Foundation. 2017. *Media release: New hate speech bill turns petty insults into a crime with 3 years in jail*. http://www.freemarketfoundation.com/article-view/media-release-new-hate-speech-bill-turns-petty-insults-into-a-crime-with-3-years-in-jail [Retrieved 17 January 2018].

Geldenhuys, K. 2017. Hate speech – a tricky toffee. *Servamus*, 1:23-27. https://journals.co.za/content/servamus/110/1/EJC199509

Griffin, R. 2017. *Why the Hate Speech Bill should be withdrawn*. Helen Suzman Foundation. http://hsf.org.za/resource-centre/hsf-briefs/why-the-hate-speech-bill-should-be-withdrawn [Retrieved 17 January 2018].

Guardian. 2012. Signs of the times: Deaf community minds its language. https://www.theguardian.com/society/2012/oct/07/british-sign-language-changing [Retrieved 16 October 2018].

Janse van Rensburg, L. 2013. *The violence of language: Contemporary hate speech and the suitability of legal measures regulating hate speech in South Africa*. LLM thesis, Rhodes University, Grahamstown.

Lieberth, A.K. & Gamble, M.E.B. 1991. The role of iconicity in sign language learning by hearing adults. *Journal of Communication Disorders*, 24(2):89-99. https://www.ncbi.nlm.nih.gov/pubmed/2066475

Mamba Online. 2018. Taking action against anti-LGBT online hate speech. https://www.mambaonline.com/2018/04/10/taking-action-lgbt-hate-speech [Retrieved 18 May 2018].

Marais M. 2015. Does the Constitution call for the criminalisation of hate speech? *Southern African Public Law*, 30(2):456-483.

Marais M.E. & Pretorius J.L. 2015. A contextual analysis of the hate speech provisions of the Equality Act. *Potchefstroom Electronic Law Journal*, 18(4):902-942. http://dx.doi.org/10.4314/pelj.v18i4.05

McGonagle, T. 2011. *Minority rights, freedom of expression and of the media: Dynamics and dilemmas*. Cambridge: Intersentia.

McKee, R. & McKee, D. 2011. Old signs, new signs, whose signs? Sociolinguistic variation in the NZSL lexicon. *Sign Language Studies*, 11(4):485-527. https://eric.ed.gov/?id=EJ940517

Meir, I. 2010. Iconicity and metaphor: Constraints on metaphorical extension of iconic forms. *Language*, 86(4):865-896. https://doi.org/10.1353/lan.2010.0044

Mesthrie, R.; Swann, J.; Deumert, A. & Leap, W.L. 2000. *Introducing sociolinguistics*. Edinburgh: Edinburgh University Press.

Mickelburgh, R. & Syal, R. 2004. Limp wrists and slant eyes must go as political correctness demands new signs for the deaf. *The Telegraph*, 21 March. https://www.telegraph.co.uk/news/uknews/1457400/Limp-wrists-and-slant-eyes-must-go-as-political-correctness-demands-new-signs-for-the-deaf.html [Retrieved 16 October 2018].

Nelson Mandela Foundation. 2018. *Media statement: The Nelson Mandela Foundation approaches the Equality Court to declare gratuitous displays of old South African flag as hate speech*, 28 February. https://www.nelsonmandela.org/news/entry/media-statement-nelson-mandela-foundation-approaches-the-equality-court-to-declare-gratuitous-displays-of-old-south-africa-flag-as-hate-speech [Retrieved 14 March 2018].

News24. 2017. "Am I famous yet?" asks Langebaan man who called for mosque to "burn". https://www.news24.com/SouthAfrica/News/am-i-famous-yet-asks-langebaan-man-who-called-for-mosque-to-burn-20170103 [Retrieved 6 April 2017].

Nienaber, A.G. 2002. Two cheers for equality: A critical appraisal of Act 4 of 2000 from a plain language viewpoint. *Journal for Juridical Science*, 27(1):1-13. http://dx.doi.org/10.4314/jjs.v27i1.27101

Ntsabo, M. 2018. Finding new affirming LGBTIQ+ words in indigenous languages. *Mamba Online*. https://www.mambaonline.com/2018/06/29/finding-new-lgbt-words-in-indigenous-languages [Retrieved 18 October 2018].

Ortega, G.; Sümer, B. & Özyürek, A. 2014. Type of iconicity matters: Bias for action-based signs in sign language acquisition. In: P. Bello, M. Guarini, M. McShane & B. Scassellati (eds.), *Proceedings of the 36th annual meeting of the Cognitive Science Society, Austin, TX*. Austin TX: Cognitive Science Society. pp. 1114-1119.

Oxford English Dictionary. 2018. "Politically incorrect". Oxford: Oxford University Press. http://www.oed.com/view/Entry/146889 [Retrieved 12 January 2018].

Padden, C.; Hwang, S.; Lepic, R. & Seegers, S. 2015. Tools for language: Patterned iconicity in sign language nouns and verbs. *Topics in Cognitive Science*, 7:81-94.

Parekh, B. 2012. Is there a case for banning hate speech? In: M. Herz & P. Molnar (eds.), *The content and context of hate speech: Rethinking regulation and responses*. Cambridge: Cambridge University Press. pp. 37-56.

Penn, C.; Lewis, R. & Greenstein, A. 1984. Sign language in South Africa: Some research and clinical issues. *The South African Journal of Communication Disorders*, 31:6-11. https://hdl.handle.net/10520/AJA03798046_539

Penn, C.; Ogilvy-Foreman, D.; Simmons, D. & Anderson-Forbes, M. 1992-1994. *Dictionary of Southern African Signs for Communicating with the Deaf*. Pretoria: Human Sciences Research Council with the South African National Council for the Deaf.

Perniss, P.; Özyürek, A. & Morgan, G. 2015. The influence of the visual modality on language structure and conventionalization: Insights from sign language and gesture. *Topics in Cognitive Science*, 7(1):2-11.

Perniss, P.; Thompson, R.L. & Vigliocco, G. 2010. Iconicity as a general property of language: Evidence from spoken and signed languages. *Frontiers in Psychology*, 1:227. https://doi.org/10.3389/fpsyg.2010.00227

Pijoos, I. 2017. Charge man who claims to use "gun to rob and kill Indians and whites". *News24*. https://www.news24.com/SouthAfrica/News/charge-man-who-claims-to-use-gun-to-rob-and-kill-indians-and-whites-20170311 [Retrieved 6 April 2017].

Raborife, M. 2017. Chinese Association lays charges over xenophobic Facebook comments. *News24*. https://www.news24.com/SouthAfrica/News/chinese-association-lays-charges-over-xenophobic-facebook-comments-20170207 [Retrieved 6 April 2017].

Russo, T. 2004. Iconicity and productivity in sign language discourse: An analysis of three LIS discourse registers. *Sign Language Studies*, 4(2):164-197.

SAPA (South African Press Association). 2014. Sentencing due in Van Deventer case. *IOL*. https://www.iol.co.za/news/crime-courts/sentencing-due-in-van-deventer-case-1794504 [Retrieved 17 January 2018].

Saunderson-Meyer, W. 2018. Vicki Momberg case was about vengeance, not justice. *IOL*. https://www.iol.co.za/ios/opinion/vicki-momberg-case-was-about-vengeance-not-justice-14164476 [Retrieved 18 May 2018].

Schermer, T. & Koolhof, C. 2009. *Van Dale Basiswoordenboek Nederlandse Gebarentaal*. Utrecht: Van Dale Uitgevers.

Sethusa, P. 2014. Racist sentenced to 720 hours mortuary time. *The Citizen*. https://citizen.co.za/news/south-africa/162079/sentenced-to-720-hours-mortuary-time [Retrieved 17 January 2018].

Signing Savvy. 2018. *Sign language dictionary*. https://www.signingsavvy.com/search [Retrieved 24 January 2018].

Silverman, R. 2012. Sign language users drop politically incorrect signs. *The Telegraph*. https://www.telegraph.co.uk/news/uknews/9594543/Sign-language-users-drop-politically-incorrect-signs.html [Retrieved 16 October 2018].

South Africa. 2016. Prevention and Combating of Hate Crimes and Hate Speech Bill, 2016. *Government Gazette*, Vol. 6 No. 40367 of 24 October 2016.

South Africa. 2018. Prevention and Combating of Hate Crimes and Hate Speech Bill, 2018. *Government Gazette*, No. 41543 of 29 March 2018.

Sutton-Spence, R. & Woll, B. 1999. *The linguistics of British sign language*. Cambridge: Cambridge University Press.

Sydney Morning Herald. 2004. Deaf signs ruled offensive. https://www.smh.com.au/world/deaf-signs-ruled-offensive-20040324-gdilmi.html [Retrieved 16 October 2018].

Teichner, S. 2003. The hate speech provisions of the Promotion of Equality and Prevention of Unfair Discrimination Act 4 of 2000: The good, the bad and the ugly. *South African Journal on Human Rights*, 19(3):349-381. https://hdl.handle.net/10520/EJC53107

Tolar, T.D.; Lederberg, A.R.; Gokhale, S. & Tomasello, M. 2007. The development of the ability to recognise the meaning of iconic signs. *Journal of Deaf Studies and Deaf Education*, 13(2):225-240. https://doi.org/10.1093/deafed/enm045

Trager, R. & Dickerson, D.L. 1999. *Freedom of expression in the 21st Century*. Thousand Oaks CA: Pine Forge Press.

Van Herreweeghe, M.; Slembrouck, S. & Vermeerbergen, M. 2004. *Digitaal Vlaamse Gebarentaal Vertaalwoordenboek*. http://gebaren.ugent.be [Retrieved 24 January 2018].

Walker, S. 1994. *Hate speech: The history of an American controversy*. Lincoln NE: University of Nebraska Press.

Wasserman, Z. 2017. Hate crimes and hate speech bill: The good, the bad – and the unspeakable. *Sonke Gender Justice*. http://genderjustice.org.za/article/hate-crimes-hate-speech-bill-good-bad-unspeakable [Retrieved 17 January 2018].

Wicks, J. 2016. "It's just the facts" – Penny Sparrow breaks her silence. *News24*. https://www.news24.com/SouthAfrica/News/its-just-the-facts-penny-sparrow-breaks-her-silence-20160104 [Retrieved 6 April 2017].

Wolfson, N. 1997. *Hate speech, sex speech, free speech*. Westport CT: Praeger Publishers.

Woll, B. & Ladd, P. 2003. Deaf communities. In: M. Marschark & P.E. Spencer (eds.), *Oxford Handbook of Deaf studies, language, and education*. New York: Oxford University Press. pp. 151-163.

Zentrum für Gebärdensprache und Hörbehindertenkommunikation. 2018. *Leda Sila*. http://ledasila.aau.at [Retrieved 24 January 2018].

Legislation

Promotion of Equality and Prevention of Unfair Discrimination Act, No. 4 of 2000.

Cases

Afriforum v Malema (18172/2010) [2010] ZAGPPHC 39.

Afriforum v Malema (20968/2010) [2011] ZAEQC 2.

ANC v Sparrow (01/16) [2016] ZAEQC 1.

Donaldo v Haripersad (29/05) [2007] ZAEQC 3.

Herselman v Geleba (231/2009) [2011] ZAEQC 1.

Islamic Unity Convention v Independent Broadcasting Authority (CCT36/01) [2002] ZACC 3; 2002 (4) SA 294; 2002 (5) BCLR 433.

Jamiat-Ul-Ulama of Transvaal v Johncom Media Investments Ltd 1127/06 [2006] ZAGPHC 12.

Khoza v Saeed (07/05) [2006] ZAEQC 2.

M v Ferreira (01/03) [2004] ZAEQC 1.

Magubane v Smith (01/2006) [2006] ZAEQC 5.

Rustenburg Platinum Mine v SAWEA obo Bester and Others (CCT127/17) [2018] ZACC 13.

Smith v Mgoqi (60/2007) [2007] ZAEQC 2.

Sonke Gender Justice Network v Malema 2010 (7) BCLR 729 (EqC) [2010] ZAEQC 2; 02/2009.

South African Human Rights Commission v Qwulane (EQ44/2009; EQ13/2012) [2017] ZAGPJHC 2018.

A CASE OF CRYING WOLF?

A linguistic approach to evaluating hate speech allegations as linguistic acts of violence

Karien van den Berg

Introduction

Globally, hate speech proliferation is a rising concern. The pressing need for measures to address the problem and invest in finding a solution attracts various stakeholders, including governments, empirical researchers and social media companies such as Twitter and Facebook. The anonymity and flexibility of social media fuel the problem. If perpetrators of hate speech are to be tracked down and prosecuted, they must be identifiable. Ideally this could be done automatically. However, despite a growing body of studies aiming to provide programmes for automatic hate speech identification, these systems are still immature and provide inaccurate results (Davidson, Warmsley, Macy & Weber, 2017; Gao, Kuppersmith & Huan, 2017; Zhang & Luo, 2018). Zhang and Luo (2018) note that the reasons behind problems of identifying hate speech (not only in social media, but also in everyday situations) are still poorly understood and therefore difficult to address. Even once automatic identification of hate speech in cyberspace becomes a viable countermeasure, trawling social media cites to pick up hateful words and phrases will not address the problem comprehensively as the problem is not only web-based. Since 2010, when the first case of hate speech was tried in local courts, South Africans have become accustomed to frequent media reports on judicial cases of alleged hate speech. In such cases, automatic detection may be of little value as the question may then rather be one of whether, or to what extent, an utterance constitutes hate speech. Globally, the trend for addressing this concern appears to be through litigation restricting hate speech, rather than a minimal regulation approach advocating dialogue to deal with offensive speech (Haraszti, 2012: xiii).

Defining hate speech, and operationalising such a definition as an evaluative measure, is a principled but notoriously difficult step required to combat the issue. Law is intrinsically a linguistic entity and it therefore stands to reason that linguistic theory may offer tools to assist the appropriate realisation of legal definitions. This chapter offers a starting point for addressing the need for an objective yardstick (Barrie 2013), based on a comprehensive scientific approach (Chaski, 2005), to combat the problem of hate speech as a linguistic act of violence. The notion of hate speech is problematised in view of international legal definitions. Context is established as an important determiner of hate speech; and it is argued that a speaker's intent – rather than impact on the hearer alone – is central in an investigation of speech crimes. Consideration is given to how the linguistic notion of intent may support legal interpretation and, in so doing, a working definition of hate speech may be established, while verifying the linguist's potential value in forensic evaluation of hateful expressions. Finally, a South African case study (*AfriForum and Another vs Julius Sello Malema and Others*, 2010) demonstrates how a working definition may be operationalised through linguistic theory. It is argued that linguistic theoretical tools, such as those drawn from Speech Act Theory (SAT), for example (Austin 1962; Searle 1975, 1979) and cooperative principles (Grice, 1957, 1975), are valuable in exploring characteristics of linguistic crimes with violent intent and, in so doing, can aid legal enquiry.

Problematising the restriction of hate speech

There is no distinct universal interpretation of what constitutes hate speech, for example, as opposed to offensive, yet non-hateful speech. Likewise, no universally applicable agreement for guiding the restriction of hate speech has been explicitly formulated. The right to freedom of expression is resolutely secured by the Universal Declaration of Human Rights (UDHR) (UN General Assembly, 1948, 217 A (III)), international treaties, regional human rights instruments, and domestic human rights laws (e.g. Canada, 1982; Council of Europe, 1950; Organisation of African Unity, 1981; Howie, 2018; Republic of South Africa, 1996; Triggs, 2011). Western countries that prioritise civil and political rights, in particular, uphold freedom of speech as "essential for any society", an "indispensable condition for full development of the person" and a "foundation stone for every free and democratic society", O'Flaherty (2010) notes in the Human Rights Committee, Draft General Comment No. 34. The question as to whether the right to freedom of speech includes the right to express violent, hateful or offensive opinions, or whether such expressions should be restricted, as infringing the right to equality, is widely debated (see, for example, Baez, 2013; Elbahtimy, 2014; Mendel, 2010, 2012).[1]

Hornsby and Langton (1998) raised the question of what one restricts when restricting hate speech; and what one protects when protecting free speech. To what limit can one allow offensive speech without infringing the right to be free from hate speech? This issue remains topical in the current context, as is evidenced by recent contention around the formulation of The Prevention and Combating of Hate Crimes and Hate Speech Bill (South Africa, 2018). Such concerns are not isolated. Various researchers (Brown, 2017; Butler, 1997; Özarslan, 2014) have pointed out that laws regulating hate speech are often

---

[1] The 2013 module published by the Freedom of Expression Institute (FXI, 2013:13) provides a comprehensive discussion of the debate on hate speech versus free speech in the South African context. Also see Becker, 1995; Heyman, 1996; Leidholt, 1995; MacKinnon, 1993, 1995.

ineffective in combating hate speech: they fail to reduce violence and hatred; they restrict freedom of speech; they punish the victims rather than the disseminator, while damaging democracy and legitimacy; and they harm autonomy.

One may argue that ultimately protecting the right to freedom of speech necessarily comes at the cost of the right to equality and dignity, and vice versa. Since it is not an absolute right, freedom of expression may be limited to protect superseding public and private interests (Mendel, 2010). Nevertheless, the right to freedom of expression limits the nature of speech that may be banned under hate speech (Mendel, 2010:1), despite the intention that these two laws be interpreted as complementary rights rather than conflicting ones (Pesinis, 2015:14-15). The outcome of the South African trial for the case between *AfriForum and Another vs Julius Sello Malema and Others* (2010), for example, was distinctly controversial owing to the severe limitation placed on the accused's right to freedom of expression. In the South Gauteng High Court in Johannesburg, sitting as the Equality Court, Judge Colin Lamont (Lamont, 2011) ruled that the song, *Dubula ibhunu* ("shoot the Boer"), constitutes hate speech and interdicting Mr Malema and the ANC from singing it. In this case, the judge ruled the song to be derogatory and dehumanising toward the Afrikaans minority in South Africa.

Furthermore, different international legal regimes vary in the scope and balancing of the right to freedom of expression on the one hand, and the right to freedom from discrimination on the other. Notably, in international law, all three regional human rights treaties protect the right to freedom of expression: the European Convention on Human Rights (ECHR) (Council of Europe, 1950), was adopted 4 November 1950 and entered into force 3 September 1953; the American Convention on Human Rights (ACHR) (Organisation of American States, OAS 1969), was adopted 22 November 1969 and entered into force 18 July 1978); and the African Charter on Human and Peoples Rights (ACHPR) (Organisation of African Unity, OAU 1981), was adopted 26 June 1981 and entered into force 21 October 1986. Only the latter, however, specifies the banning of hate speech in Article 13(5). This variation creates problems for interpreting international human rights standards and leads to confusion as to what constitutes hate speech (Mendel, 2010:4, 2012; Pesinis, 2015). Factors such as the following contribute to diverging interpretations (Elbahtimy, 2014:6-8): the emotional component within the right; complexities around proving incitement; tension between the rights of speakers and listeners; and tension between individual and group rights. Legal scholars (cf. Benesch, 2012; Bertoni & Rivera, 2012; Coliver, 1992; Matsuda, 1989; Sherry, 1991) aiming to define the legal concept of hate speech, therefore fail to establish general consensus on the notion.

Even in cases where laws are well formulated, operationalising the definition remains problematic (Amnesty International Index (AII) 2012; Mendel, 2010:10; Pálmadóttir & Kalenikov, 2018). In fairly clear terms, the International Covenant on Civil and Political

Rights (ICCPR) (UN General Assembly 1966: Article 20, par 2) prohibits "any advocacy of national, racial or religious hatred that constitutes incitement to discrimination, hostility or violence". Yet an evaluation of what transpires as "advocacy" and as "incitement" is complex and troublesome. Statements are not necessarily explicitly hateful, making hate speech difficult to recognise. Even when hatred is explicit, an utterance may not constitute violent speech. Hatred, according to Mendel (2010:8), is a state of mind – a mere opinion – protected absolutely by international law, as opposed to criminal acts of violence and discrimination. Thus, the identification of hate speech cannot depend on the presence of hate as a subjective and emotive element.

It is a fine and opaque line between hate speech and speech that is offensive but not hateful. Difficulties in reconciling the right to protection against incitement and the right to freedom of expression extend to the point where, Elbahtimy (2014:15-15) says, recent talks on the international rule against hate speech "have reached an impasse" and the evolution of this norm "appears to be almost frozen in time". Without a universally accepted conception of it, the model of hate speech remains malleable (Haraszti 2012; Massaro, 1991:213-14; Mendel, 2010, 2012; Pálmadóttir & Kalenikova, 2018), which is problematic for implementation of laws regulating expressions of hate and violence (AI, 2012; Elbahtimy, 2014), leaving legal practitioners without a general measure for alleged speech crimes.

General characteristics of statements that qualify as being punishable have been gleaned from international law, case-law principles, and academic writing on hate speech (e.g. AI, 2012; Elbahtimy, 2014; Mendel, 2010, 2012; Pálmadóttir & Kalenikova, 2018; Pesinis, 2015; Sorial, 2014). As hate speech is also a social, historical, political, philosophical and linguistic notion, Brown (2017:422) warns against focusing too narrowly on the legal notion of hate speech alone, since the notion may be defined with legal responses in mind and lead to an over-interpretation of – in this case – common expressions of dislike, or insulting expressions, as hate speech. Scholarly definitions (e.g. Nockelby, 1994; 2000) of hate speech focus on the element of violent intent, rather than the experience of violence alone. In its most basic form, Haraszti (2012:xiii) says that hate speech comprises "actual instigations to actual hate crimes". Matsuda (1989:2320) suggests that hate speech is "the structural subordination of a group based on an idea of racial inferiority". Likewise, Langton (1993, 1998), MacKinnon (1993) and Schwartzman (2002) support an equality-based justification of regulating speech that subordinates, marginalises, or harms individuals belonging to an oppressed group. Smolla (1992:152) regards the term "hate speech" as a generic term for "speech attacks based on race, ethnicity, religion and sexual orientation or preference". Matsuda, Lawrence, Delgado and Crenshaw (1993:1) describe hate speech as "words used as weapons" with the intention "to ambush, terrorise, wound, humiliate and degrade".

Following these definitions, the elements of intent (to enact hatred) and incitement (to raise or encourage hatred or violence), along with a causal link to effected results that constitute a criminal offence, must be established to achieve hate speech. "Advocacy", as termed in the ICCPR definition, is to be understood as an intent requirement, meaning that only utterances with the intent of stirring hatred are prohibited. Legally, establishing "incitement" is often based on evaluating a statement at the hand of its impact – i.e. the receiver's experience – in consideration of causation and context (Elbahtimy, 2014; Pesinis, 2015:13; Sorial, 2014). Causation and impact standards are generally weak, though (Mendel 2010:7), contributing to more subjective and inconsistent rulings. International rules vary as to the nature of impact that is proscribed, from being limited to inciting violence and other illegal acts (ACHR Article 13[5]), inciting discrimination and hatred (ICCPR Article 20[2]), to the banning of all ideas based on superiority (International Convention on the Elimination of all Forms of Racial Discrimination (CERD) Article 4[a]). Sometimes effects or consequences have to be established in a tangible way, but in other cases it is enough to show that expressing hate is likely to have a harmful result. To complicate matters even further, ascertaining these elements depends on the context of the communicative act, with the status of the speaker, the reach and goals of the utterance, the content of the words, and the social, economic and political climate being influential (Article 19, 2015; Carney, 2014; Pesinis, 2015; Sorial, 2014; Van den Berg, 2012).

In relation to *AfriForum and Another vs Julius Sello Malema and Others* (2010), for example, it was suggested that the true measure of hate speech resides in the realised effect of a speech act, regardless of context (Barrie, 2013). The above cited definitions, and linguistic theory even more so, however, suggest that the context of language use is essential to interpreting meaning. Meaning that is embedded in language is never realised in a vacuum (Halliday, Kirkwood, McIntosh & Stevens, 1964:18). An utterance is both a representation and product of the situational context in which actual circumstances are recognised (Massaro 1991:213-214). The meaning of language is grounded in experience and our physical embodiment representative of the world (Croft & Cruise, 2004; Ellis, Romer & O'Donnell, 2018; Langacker, 2000; Robinson & Ellis, 2008:489-546). Language could also relay the full context without reference to the physical situational setting (Hasan, 2005). Context, then, is "an instance of the social and cultural systems" that underpin a communicative event (Lukin, 2013:527). The linguistic choices people make in phrasing an utterance are governed by, but also attributable to, the immediate social and situational environment or register (e.g. Hasan, 1985:52; Halliday, 2003:210, 2009:181; Lukin, 2013). Thus, as language use is necessarily context dependent, extracting language from its context leaves an utterance void of meaning. Accordingly, Lukin, Moore, Herke, and Wegener (2011:190) describe an utterance as language shaping; and language being shaped by those who use it for specific activities; and the modes through which the interaction takes place.

In relation to this, an utterance of hate speech would be an example of a person shaping language to cause harm; the language then shapes a situation to affect the intended harm to another. Considering accusations of hate speech outside of a context other than the receiver or viewer's perception, is to ignore the shared referential circumstances in which the function that determines the form of an utterance is expressed. Ignoring the context in effect reduces an utterance to form only, while function is central to deciding what constitutes hate speech. Thus, reducing an interpretation of meaning to only the perception of meaning inferred is to reduce meaning in totality. From a linguistic point of view, as from a legal perspective, a speaker's contextualised intent is therefore central to a discussion of hate speech. Naturally, allegations of hate speech must then be evaluated in terms of contextualising the impact in relation to contextualised intent. A true yardstick of whether a statement constitutes hate speech may then depend on the "intentional incitement" of violence (Van den Berg, 2012). Therefore, investigating hate speech in a given context should entail considering the speaker's intention in view of the effect, rather than the effect alone.

Hence, when addressing alleged accounts of hate speech, the interpretation of "intentional incitement" is paramount in distinguishing whether a statement is classified in the typology of hate speech as proposed by the lobby group Article 19 (2015:19), reflecting international legal standards, under the category of "must be restricted", "may be restricted", or "must be protected". The notion of intent will be explored further on. The most difficult category to operationalise in the "Hate Speech Pyramid" presented by Article 19 (2015:121-123) is the one pertaining to what may be restricted in relation to protecting the rights or reputations of others, national security, public order, health or morals. Establishing benchmark cases for the upper and lower threshold of this category will depend on how the notions of "intent" and "incitement" are understood. Consideration is therefore given later in this chapter to these notions as per the South African Bill on Prevention and Combating of Hate Crimes and Hate Speech (South Africa, 2018) and limited to one case study.

Based on the preceding argument, it is apparent that intentional harm or violence is an intrinsic characteristic of hate speech. As such, it is an act of linguistic violence rather than speech alone. Following this characterisation, a taxonomy of hate speech is posited below to inform the remainder of this discussion:

1. Hate speech is an act that propagates, instigates or intends hate (i.e. a linguistic act of violence), mainly toward groups or individuals based on ethnicity, race, nationality, gender, religion, sexual orientation, etc.;
2. Hate speech, in any form of discourse, does not have a meaning other than one expressing hate toward a particular individual or group;
3. Messages containing hate speech will most likely elicit acts of violence.

According to this taxonomy, hate speech is a linguistic act in a specific reality that is intentionally violent or likely to have a violent consequence toward individuals, groups, based on racial, age, gender or other discrimination. The notion of intentional incitement, however, remains opaque and is concretised in context of the speech act in the next section.

The notion of intent

Everyday words sometimes get a different meaning when used in a specific environment. Legal jargon contains various examples of this. There are differences to be noted in the notion of "intent" as applied in an everyday context, in the legal environment, and in linguistic terms. These diverse interpretations may lead to confusion when linguistic evidence is presented. Therefore, this section explores the legal and linguistic concepts, aiming to reconcile the meanings to establish a rich conceptualisation that can inform an operational definition and guide linguistic analysis.

Legal intent

The legal notion of "intent" renders a more nuanced meaning than the colloquial understanding of the term as a noun indicating the thing(s) that you plan to do or achieve. In South African law, intent may occur in three forms: *dolus directus; dolus indirectus*; and *dolus eventualis*, relating to the extent to which a perpetrator either knowingly committed a crime, or had foresight of potentially committing a crime, and continued with the planned act regardless of this foresight (Kwanje, 2016). *Dolus directus*, or direct intent, is to be understood in line with its everyday grammatical meaning, conveying an informed and deliberate aim to break the law or, in this case, to cause violent harm. *Dolus indirectus* refers to indirect intent, where the perpetrators' main aim is not necessarily to break the law, though it may well be a foreseeable consequence of their actions. If a person decides to derail a train in order to stop it from reaching its destination, the intention is not to kill people. However, by choosing a less risky part of the train's course at which to derail the train, the perpetrators could be said to have displayed their "unintention" to cause death, while also displaying their knowledge that derailing a train may well lead to the deaths of passengers and bystanders. If passengers were then killed in the crash resulting from a derailment, perpetrators would be guilty of *dolus eventualis*, or legal intention. *Dolus eventualis* is similar to *dolus indirectus*, but with a focus on recklessness on the perpetrator's behalf. It may be likened to the criminal law equivalent of "gross negligence". An example may be where drag-racing under the influence of drugs resulted in the death of children. Establishing intent is thus important in determining whether or not, or to what extent, certain acts may be classified as criminal.

However, the legal notion of "intent" concerns a psychological phenomenon constituting the will to do something while knowing that it is unlawful. In view of hate speech crimes, how then may one assess the intent of what someone says, if undoing it may be as easy as saying, "That is not what I meant"? The legal test for intention is subjective, as the court must determine the state of mind of the perpetrator while committing the crime. The main question is not so much whether perpetrators should have foreseen certain consequences, but how they perceived the situation, what knowledge they had pertaining to the act being unlawful, and whether they did foresee those consequences and acted nonetheless. It is beyond the scope of a linguist to infer the presumed mental state of a perpetrator at the time of a crime. The linguist does not aim to evaluate this mental state, as the psychologist may do. Rather, the linguist focuses on linguistic intent, or what Tiersma (1986:226, following J.L. Austin, 1962) calls "illocutionary intent". The latter refers to the speaker's commitment to what is put forward as proposed meaning, expressed by an utterance. Investigating the meaning or intent of an utterance revolves around pragmatics: "the study of linguistics acts and the contexts in which they are performed" (Stalnaker, 1972:383; also see Kravchenko, 2017). As such, Speech Act Theory – a central subdomain of pragmatics – offers a linguistic frame of reference to describe violent speech acts.

Illocutionary intent

Austin's (1962) Speech Act Theory (SAT) is a theory of meaning based on the assumption that a speaker does something through a performative utterance, i.e. language is a mode of action (Malinowski, 1935); and that the nature of this act is strongly influenced by the intention of the speaker. Oishi (2006:2) writes:

> Through a description of the success/failure of the speech act purported, which is explained as a violation/observation of the felicity conditions, Austin formulated a method to describe [an utterance] in terms of the speech situation where it is uttered: by means of associated linguistic conventions, the speaker, with an associated intention, actually performs an act to the hearer, which induces a certain response from the hearer.

Speech Act Theory presents principles for classifying meaning, aiming to explain the phenomenon of words meaning more than, or something other than, what they appear to mean. The theory could therefore help to achieve a systematic description of a speaker's meaning when considering alleged hate speech.

Certain felicity conditions – referring to socially conventionalised rules of conduct – strongly suggest the acceptable way of interacting in a given situation, which may affect the way an utterance is formulated, interpreted and applied. An illocutionary act is "an act done as conforming to convention" (Austin, 1975:105). An utterance is thus seen as form-meaning mapping, dictated by social conventions regarding how a certain speech act should be conducted. It is not the words themselves that are important, but how an utterance is put to use in context (Austin, 1975:5; Carney, 2014; Van den Berg, 2012). Factors such as tone of voice, for example, may render an utterance to be face threatening, or as face saving, in terms of politeness strategies. Sbisà (2009:229) argues that the meaning of an utterance in the way that it is used, and its force, should be distinguished. SAT offers a means of circumscribing these differences.

One can "do" things with words on three levels: the locutionary, the illocutionary and the perlocutionary. Locution refers to the literal meaning of the words that form the utterance. Illocution refers to the intended meaning, with illocutionary point suggestion the aim – i.e. the intended action –of the utterance. Perlocution pertains to the uptake and effect of the utterance, which may be felicitous (intended or desired) or infelicitous (unintended or undesired). Speech acts may be classified as direct (e.g. bold and on-record) or indirect (off-record). To discern speech actions as either direct or indirect, the actions may be classified according to Searle's (1975) five macro-class categories: "Assertives" (making statements; describing the state of affairs in the world); "directives" (guiding another person's actions); "commissives" (indicating a speaker's commitment to a future action); "expressives" (revealing a speaker's emotional relation to the proposition); and "declaratives" (changing reality according to the suggestion of the statement). Thus, meaning can be inferred on three levels of locution, illocution and perlocution, in terms of the five categories of speech acts. Speech acts may be classified in terms of at least one of these classes; but any speech act may fall into more than one category.

This classification is done in view of the felicity conditions specified by Austin (1962:14-15) that govern the formulation of utterances. Any speech act is realised, given a set of felicity conditions dictated by the register of the speech situation. Theoretically, as long as all parties subscribe and meet these conditions by formulating an utterance in a linguistic way that is, conventionally, deemed appropriate to realise the intended meaning (in terms of providing sufficient relevant, unambiguous and truthful information, given the situation), successful communication takes place. Likewise, certain felicity conditions then enable or facilitate the realisation of hate speech.

Classifying utterances according to this framework aids a more objective evaluation of the extent to which the impact of an utterance may be valid in a given context. An objective evaluation of the relevance of the perlocutionary force can only be made by considering aspects that shape utterances and contribute to making meaning in context. This necessarily includes the author's intention – i.e. illocutionary force. In SAT terms, The South African High Court's comment with reference to *AfriForum and Another vs Julius Sello Malema and Others* (2010) (Barrie, 2013), suggests a focus on the perlocution, regardless of the illocutionary point in context, to identify hate speech. This entails impartially accepting perlocutionary force (i.e. the actual effect of an utterance) as the determining element in hate speech classification. This would mean that hate speech is measured based on a hearer's perception that something hateful was said about them. Such an argument is flawed, as the hearer's interpretation must be validated in the context of the illocutionary intent. Van den Berg (2012) and Carney (2014) support this argument, indicating that the hearer's perceptions are almost always subjective and therefore untrustworthy as a measure for hate speech.

As noted, not all communicative events are made intentionally clear. Identifying instances of hate speech is often difficult when such acts are committed indirectly. However, to ensure effective negotiation of meaning, speakers would need to comply with felicity conditions. If the speaker deliberately formulates an utterance indirectly, the speaker supposedly assumes that the hearer will infer the intended (indirect and possibly unclear) meaning without difficulty, in view of the felicity conditions pertaining to the parties involved (Grice, 1957:387).

Cooperative communication requires that a speaker provides enough honest information for the intended audience to interpret the speaker's intended meaning correctly and unambiguously. The intended meaning may be unclear to others, but for illocutionary intent to be realised, the speaker must bring the hearer (or receiver, or viewer) to recognise that a particular meaning is being conveyed. Otherwise the impact of the utterance is lost. If an utterance is deliberately not made clear, to the extent that a likely meaning cannot be attributed to it in consideration of the felicity conditions, the intention expressed would supposedly not be a sincere attempt at realising an effect. An intention effectively to cause harm to the extent of committing a criminal offence would require adherence to conditions that would render an utterance as effective violence. One may expect that, in legitimate cases of hate speech (i.e. speech that may or must be restricted), intent may be expressed more clearly – though sometimes indirectly – to effect the inflicting or stirring of violence.

Miscommunication happens when a hearer or viewer selects an interpretation other than the illocutionary point (Grice, 1957, 1975). The illocutionary act remains performed, regardless of whether or not the desired perlocutionary act is realised, but it does lose its impact. If a speaker were to propagate hate, but the hearer's reaction is infelicitous (i.e. no hate is interpreted), the act fails. Likewise, when a speaker does not mean to convey hatred, but is accused of effecting hate, the perlocution is infelicitous. Since speakers may simply deny their intentions, and hearers may simply claim having experienced harm, neither illocution nor perlocution alone can be sufficient to identify a linguistic act of violence. It is the alignment of the two, in consideration of contextual factors, that needs to be evaluated. Following are two examples to illustrate these complexities inherent in distinguishing punishable hate speech from protected offensive speech. They also demonstrate the effect of context on hearers' interpretation.

The first is an example of a situation where cultural differences contributed to a disalignment in the illocutionary force and perlocutionary effect. A recent advertisement by the international clothing company, H&M, caused an uproar on social media. The advertisement showed a black boy model wearing a green hooded sweatshirt displaying a printed message: "Coolest monkey in the jungle". The advertisement drew public accusations of racism across social media, with some international celebrities breaking ties with the company. The mother of the model child, however, condemned the critical responses, indicating that no racism was intended and that those who complained should stop crying wolf.

The primary aim of an advertisement is to attract consumers to purchase displayed products. Thus, one would have to consider under what circumstance a company might go to the extent of knowingly distributing a message intentionally aimed at spreading racist hate slogans. Such an act would not abide by standard felicity conditions, but it is possible. In the case of the "monkey" sweatshirt, the company may well be guilty of racial insensitivity in certain contexts, considering the extent of the supposedly unintentional impact the advertisement had. Referring to someone as "a monkey" has different connotations in different languages (cf. Carney, 2014), which the Swiss company did not take into consideration. Racial and cultural insensitivity, however, may not necessarily qualify as hate speech, following the definitions provided earlier.

The next example shows how, though a speaker may not intend hate speech, some hearers may (mis)interpret an utterance purposefully to advance their own agenda. For example, the broadcasting of a popular South African song, "De la Rey, De la Rey", during rugby matches at the Blue Bulls home ground, Loftus Versveld, elicited substantial media debate (without legal enquiry) in 2007 (Van den Berg, 2012). Some fans complained that the song was offensive and played deliberately as a sort of anthem to exclude non-white Afrikaans fans from the collective group of supporters. A ban was briefly instated following the complaints; but it was then lifted on account of the song not deliberately inciting violence, nor containing specific offensive references to other non-white South Africans. However, at the time, the Minister of Arts and Culture extended a warning that the song had the potential of being abused by a small group of right-wing political supporters, who might consider the song a call to arms, according to the *Sunday Times* editor, Mondli Makhanya (*Sunday Times*, 26 February 2007).

On account of such instances, Pálmadóttir and Kalenikova (2018) caution that speakers carry a responsibility when formulating an utterance, because "often a small seed sown may incite a person to commit atrocious deeds or to exercise injustice in some way or form". In identifying violent linguistic acts, however, the speaker cannot be held solely accountable for the perlocutionary effect of their utterances, because a hearer may hijack an utterance and apply it for an unintended (and therefore invalid) purpose. This is possible because, following Verscheueren (2009:19-20; also cf. Verscheueren & Brisard, 2009), language use entails making communicative choices in speaking and interpretation. The range of choices available is not fixed, but dynamic (Hymes, 1977:75; Vercheueren, 2009). Speakers operate under constraints of possible choices (i.e. adhering to felicity conditions) and have to make one that best meets their needs and that of the situational context. Hearers – adhering to felicity conditions – make the best selection to serve basic communicative needs that arise from the particular context (and may therefore be quite specific) (Grice, 1957:387; Verschueren, 2009:20). In other words, the most plausible linguistic intention or illocution is the most likely conventional meaning to be made of the form in use. This is not to say that instances of hate speech are necessarily the most conventionalised interpretation in a situation; but describing the likelihood of possible interpretations may serve as a reference point for scaling offensive utterances.

A conviction of hate speech thus cannot be reliant on the experience of the hearer alone; the speaker alone cannot be held accountable for the effect that words have. A linguistic account of an alleged violent speech act within a specific context can present an objective measurement for the identification of hate speech. In the event of a legal inquiry, linguists may typically not be asked to reach a verdict as to whether or not H&M, the Blue Bulls management, or the performing artist should be prosecuted for hate speech (cf. Chaski, 2013). Mainly, linguists may describe the linguistic acts performed in view of the customary felicity conditions applicable in the communicative event so as to establish the extent to which the illocutionary force and the perlocution align plausibly. A linguistic description then provides evidence to inform the final decision made by legal practitioners. When considering alleged utterances of hate speech, the linguist may be primarily concerned with questions such as: "What linguistic form gives rise to violence, hatred, harm to others, based on age, race, or gender?" More specifically, to assess the legitimacy of hate speech accusations, the linguist would consider: "Does the linguistic form of the utterance preclude any conventional meaning other than one of hatred, violence and harm; or that may incite violence, hatred and/or harm onto a person/persons based on age, gender, ethnicity, religion, etc?" A possible working method is illustrated with relation to a case study in the following section.

Hate speech in South Africa

South African law limits the right to freedom of expression to ideas and thoughts that do not propagate war, incite violence, or advocate hatred based on race, ethnicity, gender or religion and do not encourage harmful actions (S16 (1) of the Constitution of the Republic of South Africa Act, No. 106 of 1996 (South Africa, 1996); Van Wyk, 2002). Until very recently, no legal definition of hate speech had been formulated for the South African context, leaving the concept open to flexible interpretation by legal practitioners. The

Prevention and Combating of Hate Crimes and Hate Speech Bill of South Africa published in March 2018 (South Africa, 2018), officially proposes the criminalisation of hate speech for the first time. Some extreme forms of harmful speech – such as defamation and verbal domestic violence – have been addressed in South Africa for some time. The Prevention and Combating of Hate Crimes and Hate Speech Bill broadens the scope of verbal offences that are restricted in South Africa to include those intentionally expressing hateful behaviour or inciting hateful behaviour and is formulated thus:

Offence of hate speech	
4.(1) (a) Any person who intentionally publishes, propagates or advocates anything or communicates to one or more persons in a manner that could reasonably be construed to demonstrate a clear intention to – (i) be harmful or to incite harm; or (ii) promote or propagate hatred, based on one or more of the following grounds: (aa) age; (bb) albinism; (cc) birth; (dd) colour; (ee) culture; (ff) disability; (gg) ethnic or social origin; (hh) gender or gender identity; (ii) HIV status; (jj) language; (kk) nationality, migrant or refugee status; (ll) race; (mm) religion; (nn) sex, which includes intersex; or (oo) sexual orientation, is guilty of an offence of hate speech.	4.(1) (b) Any person who intentionally distributes or makes available an electronic communication which that person knows constitutes hate speech as contemplated in paragraph (a), through an electronic communications system which is – (i) accessible by any member of the public; or (ii) accessible by, or directed at, a specific person who can be considered to be a victim of hate speech, is guilty of an offence. 4.(1) (c) Any person who intentionally, in any manner whatsoever, displays any material or makes available any material which is capable of being communicated and which that person knows constitutes hate speech as contemplated in paragraph (a), which is accessible by, or directed at, a specific person who can be considered to be a victim of hate speech, is guilty of an offence.

However, the passing of this bill has been met with resistance on the grounds of the formulation overextending the definition of hate speech. Van Staden (2018), a Free Market Foundation Legal Researcher (*The Blog. Hate-speech bill: A threat to democracy in South Africa*[2]), said that it includes common insults and restricts offensive speech, which should not be regulated, to the extent that the bill "effectively abolishes freedom of expression, entirely, in South Africa". This is not a novel argument from those who oppose hate speech regulation (Brown, 2017:420; Post, 2009).

---

[2] Reference to popular media in this chapter is intentional and suggests public voices which contribute to the social context of the speech event. Whilst it is not assumed in this chapter that the views of individual reporters are necessarily representative of the general public, these voices are public and so are relevant to the argument.

In addition, and characteristic of legal definitions (cf. Brown, 2017; Özarslan, 2014), operationalising in real life the construct extended in the Bill is problematic. This definition echoes the key elements of hate speech as specified in international law, emphasising the notion of "incite": hate speech is publishing, propagating, advocating or communicating content that demonstrates a "clear intention to – (i) be harmful or to incite harm; or (ii) promote or propagate hatred". "Intentionality" depends on a subjective standard of "demonstrating a clear intention to" and being "in a manner that could reasonably be construed" as being hateful; communication which a person knows is hateful and may result in harm or encourages harm (4[1ai]), and/or gives rise to hatred (4[1aii]). Neither international law, nor South African law therefore provide clear guidelines for operationalising the definition and evaluating allegations of linguistic violence validly. This section now aims at achieving a working definition of hate speech by establishing a base line methodology, informed by linguistic theory, for describing alleged criminal utterances.

The case of Dubula ibhunu

During the *Dubula ibhunu* trial in 2010, the defence argued for a historical interpretation of the following speech act as a heritage tribute:

Ayasaba amagwala	They are scared the cowards
Awudubule (i)bhunu	Do shoot the/a boer (farmer)
Ziyarobha le zintsha	They rob us, these dogs
Ayasab' amagwala	The cowards are scared
dubula dubula	Shoot shoot
awe mama ndiyekele	Mother leave me be
awe mama iyeah	Oh mother
Ziyarapa lezinja	These dogs are raping/rape us

Considering such a case, the linguist may approach the question of whether the text constitutes hate speech, by trying to motivate that, in fact, it does not constitute hate speech, as per the argument put forward. A null-hypothesis may be formulated as follows:

> H1: Uttering *Dubula ibhunu* is an act of hate inciting violence to a group of persons based on ethnicity. As such, it cannot be interpreted prototypically as a non-violent heritage tribute.
> H0: Uttering *Dubula ibhunu* is not an act of hate and does not incite violence toward a group of persons based on ethnicity. As such it can be interpreted as a non-violent heritage tribute.

Thus, if one may succeed in arguing reasonably that the most likely conventional illocutionary intent of the utterance is not one of inciting violence, hatred, or harm onto a person(s) based on age, gender, ethnicity, religion, etc, one may support such a claim: *Dubula ibhunu* is viewed as an utterance that is unlikely to disseminate hatred. The aim of this analysis is to characterise those linguistic conventions applicable to the specific circumstances in which these words were performed as a speech act, with a particular conventional effect as a result (Oishi, 2006:14). To achieve this, the question is asked: "Does the linguistic form of the utterance preclude any conventional meaning other than one of hatred, violence and harm, that may incite violence, hatred and/or harm onto a person/persons based on age, gender, ethnicity, religion etc?"

The research question may be operationalised in terms of sub-questions, based on the taxonomy of hate speech formulated earlier in this chapter:

1. Does the text propagate or instigate hate, mainly toward groups or individuals specified in The Prevention and Combating of Hate Crimes and Hate Speech Bill of South Africa?
2. Does it have a meaning other than an offensive one expressing hate toward a particular individual or group specified in The Prevention and Combating of Hate Crimes and Hate Speech Bill of South Africa?
3. Based on the answers to these questions, how likely is the utterance to realise a perlocutionary act of violence toward any of the groups specified in The Prevention and Combating of Hate Crimes and Hate Speech Bill of South Africa, or in those averse to the target audience?

These questions may be answered based on an analysis of the speech acts. The analysis proceeds as follows:

(a) Characterise the locutionary act portrayed by the utterance;
(b) Establish the illocutionary force of the utterance, related to the speaker's probable intent toward members of groups specified in The Prevention and Combating of Hate Crimes and Hate Speech Bill of South Africa;
(c) Consider the most likely perlocutionary act of the utterance in hearers/viewers, specifically for groups specified in The Prevention and Combating of Hate Crimes and Hate Speech Bill of South Africa, and those who are averse to this target audience, given the situational context.

Locutionary act

Locutionary level enquiry explores the direct expression of the utterance. At locutionary level, the act speaks of violence, oppression, rape and murder. It contains declarative statements, describing "the boer[s]" in derogatory terms such as "scared", "cowards", "dogs" and those who rob and rape [us]. Speakers also extend commissive acts, instructing the shooting of these "boer[s]". This term *boers* may be broadly interpreted to refer to "farmers", but in the South African context, it is predominantly used to refer to Afrikaans-speaking white people, or white farmers. They are identified as the opposing "other" and subjected to the utterance. Representative statements express feelings of disgust by means of derogatory references that can be summarised as: "these cowards are scared"; "these dogs rape" (and rob). Directives pointedly instruct vengeance and the message is: "Shoot, shoot, shoot them with a gun"; "Shoot the *boer*"; and a request to the speaker's "Mother" to "let him shoot the *boer*". The mother is told not to interfere with the commitment to shooting the *"boer"*. During trial, it was argued that Afrikaners are identified as the enemy to be shot (*AfriForum and Another vs Julius Sello Malema and Others* (20968/2010).

The locutionary utterance can be contextualised in terms of field or subject matter of a text (i.e. what the text is about and aims to do); mode, meaning how a text is constructed (i.e. features of written/spoken language); and tenor which refers to all parties involved in the discourse, as well as the relationship between the author and audience (Hasan, 1985; Halliday 2003, 2009). The field of discourse is a song or chant expressing violence (rape, shooting, robbery). This refrain is directly associated with South Africa's apartheid history. Peter Mokaba first performed the utterance in 1993 at a Chris Hani memorial rally. Brkic (2010), a reporter writing for the *Daily Maverick*, writes: "On that day Mokaba, the then president of the ANC Youth League, galvanised his organisation's deep anger at Hani's murder by right wing whites into something concrete: a song that perfectly (and terrifyingly) expressed the anger". The song originated as a violent cry for revolt against inequality and oppression under the apartheid regime. Two decades since the abolishment of apartheid, the field of reference is one of a democratic "rainbow" nation. Apartheid is no longer a formal reality but racism remains, as the direct meaning of the song proclaims.

Considering who is involved in the performance of the utterance greatly contributes to the situational context and felicity conditions that apply. Tenor identifies different parties and a two-fold target audience: participants in the utterance, and subjects of the utterance. Prior to the 2010 trial, Mr Malema allegedly made the utterance while addressing various public meetings, including: at Polokwane during his birthday celebration; at the University of Johannesburg; during a Human Rights Day celebration at Mafikeng, addressing the public; and on another occasion in Rustenburg. Tenor therefore includes all who attended these occasions, with the majority presumably being ANC members taking part in the utterance. The broader audience, though, includes the former apartheid regime, white South Africans in general and *boers* in particular. The latter are not included as participants of the utterance; they are directly subjected to the act.

Contextualisation also requires considering the use to which an utterance is put, or its mode. In uttering these words, language is put to use as a vehicle for expressing an emotion, an identity and a desire or goal. The locution of this desire is expressed as one of violence and hate against farmers or *boers*. Language serves as the ignition and catalyst to incur harm to *boers*.

In this sense, the utterance is literally a command or encouragement to commit violence against *boers* and a commitment to the cause: "Let me shoot". The speech act is specified linguistically, as in "I order you to shoot the boer"; and, in so doing, the speaker activates associated conventions and establishes the speech situation that exists between himself or herself and the hearers (Oishi, 2006:8). The speaker is indicating to the hearer that he or she means to perform the specified act. In this scenario, the conventionality of the speech act is realised as (a) a command to shoot; and (b) an act of violence to *amabhunu*, who are specified as the target of the shooting. Supposing then that standard felicity conditions are being adhered to, a hearer may assume: the utterance is meant sincerely; that there is sufficient information for the intention to be clear, given the linguistic and social context; that the utterance is not ambiguous in terms of what is expected of the hearer; and that the utterance is relevant to the present situation.

Media reports (e.g. *Daily Maverick* of 29 March 2010) around the time of the trial suggested opposing intentional interpretations, however. ANC Secretary-General, Gwede Mantashe, allegedly argued that this literal and apparent interpretation would be a vulgarised one. He proposed the reference to *amabhunu* to be a reference not to whites, but to the system of apartheid, suggesting that the utterance should now be interpreted in light of this historical reference. In response, Ernst Roets, AfriForum Youth Chairperson, allegedly responded: "There is no way in which you can dismiss the song as something that simply has to be viewed in a political context and that doesn't have any real consequences".

Conflicting arguments warrant linguistic analysis beyond the locutionary level. The speaker's intention is potentially contentious, as it is easy to claim that one meant something other than what was perceived. The linguist may explore the probability that the non-violent interpretation of the song would be a likely one – given the contextualisation – by fitting the utterance to the given felicity conditions and evaluating it in terms of adherence to the cooperative principles. In so doing, one could describe the interpretation most relevant to the conversation or the speaker's actions; or to alternatives that could fit the purpose of the speaker (Grice, 1957:387).

Illocutionary force

For H0 to be supported, one would have to find that the illocutionary force inherent in *Dubula ibhunu* is that of a representative constituting an expression of the personal or group opinion or attitude of: (a) resistance to apartheid; and (b) celebration of the fall of apartheid. Furthermore, derogatory terms would have to be interpreted as non-derogatory and direct instructions to force would no longer bear a violent intent. Such an understanding would have to be encouraged by current felicity conditions.

In terms of illocutionary categories, directives ("Shoot!") also serve as commissive actions ("I shall shoot!", "Let me shoot!" or "You must shoot!"), by which performers tie themselves to future actions, resolving to execute the action proposed to the identified party or parties. The illocutionary force extended is one promising and eliciting violence toward a specified group. Words used typically have negative and hurtful connotations – "dogs" and "cowards", "rape", "shoot", "kill" and "boer" – as linguists may confirm by means of corpus analytic methods. Whether or not the intention of fulfilling the threat is sincere, the threat remains extended and is likely to effect harm in the given context. A hateful illocutionary force is executed (Hancher, 1979:6; Searle, 1969:14) which is unlikely to be understood in different terms. In a case like this, where the locution is directly hateful and words and phrases typically have negative connotations, it is highly unlikely that felicity conditions would encourage an illocutionary intent other than a vengeful one.

For the non-violent hypothesis to be supported would require that felicity conditions promote a connotative meaning in stark contrast to the locution. As suggested before, the context does not facilitate a "softer" interpretation other than the one expressed at locutionary level. The utterance was performed at various public gatherings not necessarily related to celebrations of the fall of apartheid, apart from the Human Rights Day celebration at Mafikeng; nor was the utterance made in response to specific political events representative of the apartheid regime. In addition, the continued violent farm attacks and murders on South African farms may be noted in this regard.

Social conventions support an utterance in whatever way makes it felicitous, i.e. conducive to shared meaning. In this case, those who assumed the violent interpretation posited in H1 (e.g. Roets of AfriForum) did not share the same linguistic conventions of performing an act of celebration (of the fall of apartheid), or of historical remembrance. The felicity conditions and conventionality of the speech situation required for a non-violent interpretation to uphold H0 is therefore spoilt (Austin, 1962:18) or considered as a misexecution (Oishi, 006:8). Reasons for this may be expressed in terms of Grice (1975)'s cooperative principles.

Too little information (Grice, 1957) is presented – other than explicitly violent content – to yield an understanding of the expression as a representative speech act unifying individuals of all racial groups against apartheid as prototypical. Furthermore, derogatory references such as "dogs" and "cowards" would then need to be considered as meaningless and without the intent of insulting members of a specific group. The relevance of the utterance in its current form then becomes questionable, as the derogatory references would have no intentional meaning. Those uttering the speech act and those who hear it would supposedly need to flout all maxims of cooperative principles to achieve a shared meaning that is distinctly different to the meaning attributed to the utterance through the socio-political history in the country. For H0 to be supported, the actuality of the speech situation would thus need to be unaccomplished deliberately, or consciously failed, by participants and subjects of the utterance. In order for *Dubula ibhunu* to be atypically offensive to (some) white South Africans would require a radical transposition of illocutionary intent from being an intentionally hateful and derogatory command to violence, to an anthem of unity for all. H0 is thus supported only when cooperative principles are violated and felicity conditions are not adhered to – i.e. unfelicitous – as a rule. H0 is supported only when the illocutionary intent fails.

Illocutionary speech acts may fail when: conventions to perform the act do not exist; existing procedures cannot be applied to a particular case; or because the speaker makes a mistake, for example, causing the performance not to conform to conventional procedure (Oishi, 2006:9; Schwartzman, 2002:423, 427). Non-performance is required for illocutionary acts to fail, as opposed to perlocutionary acts that fail when misinterpretation occurs. As Butler (1997) suggests, illocutionary forces are unlikely to fail because they depend on conventionality. Illocutionary acts fail only when conventions are not what speakers assume them to be. If non-performance is not invoked, then abuse of the procedure must be instated as the norm for interpretation, for example, based on insincerity (Austin, 1962:15-16; Oishi, 2006:9). Accepting a non-violent intention then implies accepting the abuse of felicity conditions and requires acknowledging that the conventional intention of any speaker performing the utterance in question is insincere in doing so. ("I order you to shoot the Boer, *but I don't mean* …; I call them dogs/cowards, *but* …"). In other words, those who utter the formula conventionally should have no intent of exercising the speech act purported in the linguistic form, despite uttering distinct encouragement to violence within a context that is exceptionally sensitive to racism.

Conventionality may change, but such changes are generally slow and gradual. The fact that an utterance is highly contentious suggests that such a change has not (yet, at least) taken effect. Based on a description of the illocutionary force, it appears as if H0 is unlikely to be upheld. Like the description of the locutionary act, the illocutionary act seems to align with that proposed in H1. Felicity conditions support the literal act and intended force as violent, with no other intention than one of causing harm. The final consideration then is the perlocutionary act or effect that the utterance elicits.

Perlocutionary effect

The linguist may consider the extent to which the perlocutionary effect aligns with the conventions of the speech situation. The extent to which the perlocutionary effect and speakers' intent line up may then be considered in terms of legal intent.

If a speaker extends an act of hate speech, but the hearer, for some reason, remains unoffended by the utterance, the act failed. No harm will have been done. In such a case, the speech act is unlikely to attract legal attention. However, if the perlocutionary act is successful, those who participate in the utterance may act violently; and those who are subjected to the utterance will be harmed. In such cases, forensic enquiry becomes relevant.

The main concern, in terms of the perlocutionary effect for the purpose of this discussion, is whether the utterance in question has the (main) effect of propagating hate or instigating violence. This entails considering whether members of specified social and cultural groups (other than the performing artist or composer) could feel anything other than resentment and hate when receiving this utterance, and whether the likely effect of this song is one that violently offends or elicits violence toward an individual or group, based on age, gender, ethnicity, etc. Also, it means considering whether those members who participate in the utterance may be likely to act in accordingly violent ways.

As for *Dubula ibhunu*, Matsuda (1989:36) argues that racist hate speech is speech that is harmful "because it is a mechanism of subordination, reinforcing a historical vertical relationship". One may argue that uttering *Dubula ibhunu* evokes the perlocutionary act of subordination and of reinforcing a historical vertical (now inverted) relationship; and, in so doing, it is harmful, not because the words themselves are harmful, but because of how, and the context in which they are put to use. The meaning of an utterance depends greatly on power structures in the immediate context of the utterance, as embodied in the conventions and rituals (Schwartzman, 2002:430). The utterance in question then appears to contain a message of racial inferiority toward a minority group, based on ethnicity, while being persecutory, hateful and degrading (Schwartzman, 2002:36; 43).

The possibility that the hearer may be crying wolf over hate speech must be recognised (cf. Verschueren, 2009:20). As indicated in the previous section, however, miscommunication may render a hearer's interpretation unfounded. A contextualised consideration of the utterance in question suggests that non-performance is required (violating felicity conditions to render the illocutionary intent unperformed), given the context for misunderstanding (inappropriate perlocutionary effect) to be relevant. As non-performance is highly unlikely given the communicative setting, this evaluation purports that expressing *Dubula ibhunu* amounts to an act of linguistic violence. Hereby this discussion supports the court's ruling of *Dubula ibhunu* as hate speech.

Final consideration

Miscommunication is a common occurrence, but supposedly the majority of alleged hate speech incidents that do become the object of legal investigation may be less the result of general misinterpretation. Linguists may then explore the notion of illocutionary intent according to non-performance requirements associated with felicity conditions of a speech act to aid a classification of the alleged word crime. Acts of hate speech are not necessarily black or white: hate speech manifests in multiple shades of grey, with some utterances being more explicit and violent than others. A linguistic analysis may be compatibly interpreted with the legal analysis of intent. If illocutionary intent is explicitly violent and hateful toward specified individuals or groups on the grounds stipulated in the Prevention and Combating of Hate Crimes and Hate Speech Bill, and that intended violence is realised by the victim (i.e. the speech act is successful), an account of *dolus directus* may be relevant. In cases where the illocutionary intent is plausibly not hateful or does not contain an explicit expression of violence or harm toward certain individuals or groups, but results in violence and explicit harm to said individuals or groups when uttered under relevant felicity conditions, regardless of this knowledge, a case of *dolus indirectus* could possibly apply. *Dolus eventualis* might apply in similar cases, but in the sense of gross negligence. For these legal labels to be fairly applied to alleged speech crimes, linguists and legal practitioners need to collaborate closely to establish a just classification.

Conclusion

The law being inextricably a linguistic entity, it seems senseless not to depart from linguistic foundations to explore criminal linguistic acts. In light of the recent publication of the Prevention and Combating of Hate Crimes and Hate Speech Bill of South Africa and the continuous stream of hate speech allegations, the value of linguistic evidence toward achieving a valid and objective measurement for evaluating such allegations is addressed in this chapter. As a starting point, this chapter problematises the concept of hate speech, unpacking it in terms of international (and South African) law. In so doing, a taxonomy of hate speech is informed. Emphasis is placed on the fact that communicative events never take place in a vacuum, and the determining effect of contextual features in communicative events is stressed. Hate speech proliferation cannot be considered outside of context. Specific attention is also paid to clarifying the problematic notion of intent. It is argued that this element is central to an evaluation of hate speech, both from a legal and a linguistic perspective, and that impact alone is insufficient to attain a balanced consideration of violent linguistic acts. The taxonomy of hate speech crimes is then operationalised and informs a systematic working method put forward for linguists to approach an evaluative description of hate speech crimes. Principles of Speech Act Theory and Gricean communicative cooperation are applied as descriptive tools, demonstrated in relation to *Dubula ibhunu*, with reference to the case of *AfriForum and Another vs Julius Sello Malema and Others* (2010). Based on a methodical linguistic analysis to meet national and international requirements of admissibility of evidence, the court's ruling on this case is supported.

Drawing from this discussion, legal practitioners will benefit from cooperation with linguists who can add important value to legal enquiry in situations where intricate language problems are at hand (cf. Carney, 2014; Van den Berg, 2012). Courts should not punish speech simply because it is vulgar or offensive, according to the South African constitution (South Africa 1996) and others (Brown, 2017; Solla, 1993). Linguistic theory offers a "scientific method of observation, description, hypothesis testing, and prediction"

(Chaski, 2005:506) which may guide a court's evaluation of alleged instances of hate speech. Various tools are available to the linguist (see Carney, 2014; Kotzé, 2007; Van den Berg & Surmon, this volume) to achieve a rich analysis. This chapter offers a limited glimpse of the use of these instruments, but hopefully it helps pave the way to greater understanding of how legal practitioners and linguists may work together in addressing word crimes.

References

AfriForum and Another v Malema & Others. 2010. (20968/2010) ZAEQC 2; SA 240 (EqC); South Gauteng High, sitting as the Equality Court, Johannesburg: Gauteng. 12 September 2011.

Amnesty International (AI). 2012. *Amnesty International Annual Report 2012: Nigeria*, 24 May 2012. http://www.refworld.org/docid/4fbe391ec.html [Retrieved 6 November 2018].

Article 19. 2015. "Hate speech" explained: A toolkit. London: Free Word Centre. https://www.article19.org/data/files/medialibrary/38231/'Hate-Speech'-Explained---A-Toolkit-%282015-Edition%29.pdf [Retrieved 22 December 2018].

Austin, J.L. 1962. *How to do things with words*. 2nd Edition, by J.O. Urmson & M. Sbisà (eds.). Oxford: Oxford University Press.

Baez, B. 2013. *Affirmative action, hate speech, and tenure: Narratives about race, law and the academy*. London: Routledge.

Barrie, G.N. 2013. The divergent constitutional approach to hate speech in South Africa and the United States. *Journal of South African Law*, 4:697-707.

Becker, M. 1995. The legitimacy of judicial review in speech cases. In: L. Lederer & R. Delgado (eds.), *The price we pay: The case against racist speech, hate propaganda, and pornography*. New York: Hill & Wang. pp. 208-215.

Benesch, S. 2012. Dangerous speech: A proposal to prevent group violence. *New York: World Institute Paper*. https://worldpolicy.org/wp-content/uploads/2016/01/Dangerous-SpeechGuidelines-BeneschJanuary-2012.pdf [Retrieved 22 December 2018].

Bertoni, E. & Rivera, J. 2012. The American convention on human rights: Regulation of hate speech and similar expression. In: M. Herz & P. Molner (eds.) *The content and context of hate speech: Rethinking regulation and responses*. Cambridge: Cambridge University Press. pp. 499-513. https://doi.org/10.1017/CBO9781139042871.032

Brkic, B. 2010. "Kill the Boer": A brief history. *Daily Maverick*, 29 March. https://www.dailymaverick.co.za/article/2010-03-29-kill-the-boer-a-brief-history/#.Wyynr6czbIU [Retrieved 23 December 2018].

Brown, A. 2017. What is hate speech? Part 1: The myth of hate. *Law and Philosophy*, 36(4):419-468. https://doi.org/10.1007/s10982-017-9297-1

Butler, J. 1997. *Excitable speech: A politics of the performative*. New York: Routledge.

Carney, T. 2014. Being (im)polite: A forensic linguistic approach to interpreting a hate speech case. *Language Matters*, 45(3):325-341. https://doi.org/10.1080/10228195.2014.959545

Chaski, C.E. 2006. Forensic linguistics, authorship attribution, and admissibility. In: C.H. Wecht & J.T. Rago (eds.), *Forensic science and law: Investigative applications in criminal, civil and family justice*. Boca Raton FL: CRC Press. pp. 505-521.

Chaski, C.E. 2013. Best practices and admissibility of forensic author identification. *Journal of Law and Policy*, 21(2):333-376. http://brooklynworks.brooklaw.edu/jlp/vol21/iss2/5.

Coliver, S. 1992. Hate speech laws: Do they work? In: S. Coliver (ed.), *Striking a balance: Hate speech, freedom of expression and non-discrimination*. London: Article 19 and Human Rights Centre, University of Essex. pp. 363-374.

Council of Europe. 1950. *Summary of Treaty No. 005, Convention for the Protection of Human Rights and Fundamental Freedoms*. https://www.coe.int/en/web/conventions/full-list/-/conventions/treaty/005

Croft, W. & Cruise, A. 2004. *Cognitive linguistics*. Cambridge: Cambridge University Press.

Davidson, T.; Warmsley, D.; Macy, M. & Weber, I. 2017. Automated hate speech detection and the problem of offensive language. *Proceedings of the Eleventh International Conference on Web and Social Media* (ICWSM), Montréal, Québec, Canada, 15-18 May. Sponsored by the Association for the Advancement of Artificial Intelligence. https://arxiv.org/1703.04009 [Retrieved 23 January 2018].

Elbahtimy, M. 2014. *The right to be free from the harm of hate speech in international human rights law*. CGHR Working Paper 7. Cambridge: University of Cambridge Centre of Governance and Human Rights.

Ellis, N.; Römer, U. & O'Donnell, M.B. 2016. *Usage-based approaches to language acquisition and processing: Cognitive and corpus investigations of construction grammar*. Hoboken NJ: Wiley.

European Court of Human Rights. 2014. *European Convention on Human Rights, as amended by Protocols Nos. 11 and 14, etc.* https://www.icj.org/wp-content/uploads/2014/06/ECHR.pdf [Retrieved 22 December 2018].

Freedom of Expression Institute (FXI). 2013. *Hate speech and freedom of expression in South Africa*. Freedom of Expression Institute Module Series. Braamfontein: Freedom of Expression Institute (FXI) https://www.fxi.org.za/docs-resources/Hate_Speech_and_Freedom_of_Expression_in_SA.pdf [Retrieved 23 December 2018].

Gao, L.; Kuppersmith, A. & Huan, R. 2017. *Recognizing explicit and implicit hate speech using a weakly supervised two-path bootstrapping approach*. Proceedings of the 8th International Joint Conference on Natural Language Processing (IJCNLP), Taipei, Taiwan, 27 November-1 December. pp. 774-782. http://aclweb.org/anthology/I17-1078 [Retrieved 24 December 2018].

Grice, H.P. 1957. Meaning. *The Philosophical Review*, 66(3):377-388. https://www.doi.org/10.2307/2182440

Grice, H.P. 1975. Logic and conversation. In: M. Ezcurdia & R.J. Stainton (eds.), *The semantics – pragmatics boundary in philosophy*. London: Broadview Press. pp. 47-59.

Halliday, M.A.K. 2003. Systemic grammar and the concept of a "science of language". In: J.J. Webster (ed.), *On language and linguistics*, Volume 3: *The collected works of M.A.K. Halliday*. London: Continuum. pp. 199-212.

Halliday, M.A.K. 2009. Methods, techniques, problems. In: M.A.K. Halliday & J.J. Webster (eds.), *Continuum companion to systemic functional linguistics*. London: Continuum. pp. 59-86.

Halliday, M.A.K.; Kirkwood, A.; McIntosh, K. & Strevens, P.D. 1964. *The linguistic sciences and language teaching*. London: Longmans.

Hancher, M. 1979. The classification of cooperative illocutionary acts. *Language in Society*, 8(1):1-14. https://doi.org/10.1017/S0047404500005911

Haraszti, M. 2012. Foreword: Hate speech and the coming death of the international standard before it was born (complaints of a watchdog). In: M. Herz & P. Molnar (eds.), *The content and context of hate speech: Rethinking regulation and responses*. Cambridge: Cambridge University Press. pp. xiii-xviii. https://doi.org/10.1017/CBO9781139042871.001

Hasan, R. 1985. Part B. In: M.A.K. Halliday & R. Hasan (eds.), *Language, context, and text: Aspects of language in a social-semiotic perspective*. Geelong, Vic. Australia: Deakin University Press. pp. 52-118.

Hasan, R. 2005. Code, register and social dialect. In: J.J. Webster (ed.), *Language, society and consciousness: The collected works of Ruqaiya Hasan*, Vol. 1, London: Equinox. pp. 160-193.

Herz, M. & Molner, P (eds.). 2012. *The content and context of hate speech: Rethinking regulation and responses.* Cambridge: Cambridge University Press.

Heyman, S.J (ed.). 1996. *Hate speech and the constitution.* Vol. 1 & 2. New York: Garland.

Hornsby, J. & Langton, R. 1998. Free speech and illocution. *Legal Theory*, 4:21-37.

Howie, E. 2018. Protecting the human right to freedom of expression in international law. *International Journal of SpeechLanguage Pathology*, 20(1):12-15. https://doi.org/10.1080/17549507.2018.1392612

Hymes, D. 1977. *Foundations in sociolinguistics: An ethnographic approach.* London: Tavistock.

Kotzé, E.F. 2007. Die vangnet van die woord: Forensies-linguistiese getuienis in 'n lastersaak. *Southern African Linguistics and Applied Language Studies*, 25(3):385-399. https://doi.org/10.2989/16073610709486470

Kravchenko, N. 2017. Illocution of direct speech acts via conventional implicature and semantic presupposition. *Lege Artis*, 2(1):128-168. https://doi.org/10.1515/lart-2017-0004

Kwanje, S.N. 2016. Distinguishing between intention and negligence in South African criminal law. Mini-dissertation for MLL degree, North-West University, Potchefstroom, South Africa.

Langacker, R.W. 2000. A dynamic usage-based model. In: M. Barlow & S. Kemmer (eds.), *Usage-based models of language.* Stanford CA: CSLI Publications. pp. 1-63.

Langton, R. 1993. Speech acts and unspeakable acts. *Philosophy and Public Affairs*, 22(4):293-330.

Langton, R. 1998. Subordination, silence, and pornography's authority. In: R. Post (ed.), *Censorship and silencing: Practices of cultural regulation.* Los Angeles CA: Getty Research Institute for the History of Art and the Humanities. pp. 261-283.

Leidholt, D. 1995. Pornography in the workplace: Sexual harassment litigation under Title VII. In: L. Leder & R. Delgado (eds.), *The price we pay: The case against racist speech, hate propaganda, and pornography.* New York: Hill & Wang. pp. 216-232.

Lukin, A. 2013. What do texts do? The context-construing work of news. *Text & Talk – An Interdisciplinary Journal of Language Discourse Communication Studies*, 33(4-5):523-551. https://doi.org/10.1515/text-2013-0024

Lukin, A.; Moore, A.R.; Herke, M.; Wegener, R. & Wu, C. 2008. Halliday's model of register revisited and explored. *Linguistics and the Human Sciences*, 4(2):187-213. https://doi.org/10.1558/lhs.v4i2.187

MacKinnon, C.A. 1993. *Only words.* Cambridge MA: Harvard University Press.

MacKinnon, C.A. 1995. Speech, equality, and harm: The case against pornography. In: L. Leder & R. Delgado (eds.), *The price we pay: The case against racist speech, hate propaganda, and pornography.* New York: Hill & Wang. pp. 301-314.

Makhanya, M. 2007. We must delve deeper into new wave of Afrikaner siege mentality. *Sunday Times*, 26 February.

Malinowski, B. 1923. The problem of meaning in primitive languages. In: C.K. Ogden & I.A. Richards (eds.), *The meaning of meaning.* New York: Harcourt Brace.

Massaro, T.M. 1991. Equality and freedom of expression: The hate speech dilemma. *William & Mary Law Review*, 32(2):211-265. http://scholarship.law.wm.edu/wmlr/vol32/iss2/3 [Retrieved 3 May 2016].

Matsuda, M.J. 1989. Public response to racist speech: Considering the victim's story. *Michigan Law Review*, 87(8):2320-2381.

Matsuda, M.J.; Lawrence, C.R.; Delgado, R. & Crenshaw, K.W. (eds.). 1993. *Words that wound: Critical race theory, assaultive speech, and the First Amendment*. Boulder CO: Westview. pp. 1-17.

Mendel, T. 2010. *Hate speech rules under international law*. http://www.law-democracy.org/wp-content/uploads/2010/07/10.02.hate-speech.Macedonia-book.pdf [Retrieved 16 February 2012].

Mendel, T. 2012. Does international law provide for consistent rules on hate speech? In: M. Herz & P. Molner (eds.), *The content and context of hate speech: Rethinking regulation and responses*, Cambridge: Cambridge University Press. pp. 417-429. https://doi.org/10.1017/CBO9781139042871.029

Nockleby, J.T. 1994. Hate speech in context: The case of verbal threats. *Buffalo Law Review*, 42(3):653-713. https://heinonline.org/HOL/Page?handle=hein.journals/buflr42&div=22&g_sent=1&casa_token=&collection=journals [Retrieved 23 January 2019].

Nockleby, J.T. 2000. Hate Speech. In: L.W. Levy, K.L. Karst, et al., (eds.), *Encyclopedia of the American Constitution*, 2nd Edition. New York: Macmillan. pp. 1277-1279.

O'Flaherty, M. 2012. Freedom of Expression: Article 19 of the International Covenant on Civil and Political Rights and the Human Rights Committee's General Comment No 34. *Human Rights Law Review*, 12(4):627-654. http://hrlibrary.umn.edu/gencomm/hrcom34.html [Retrieved 23 January 2019].

Oishi, E. 2006. Austin's speech act theory and the speech situation. *Esercizi Filosofici*, 1(1):1-14. https://www2.units.it/eserfilo/art106/oishi106.pdf [Retrieved 19 August 2017].

Organization of African Unity (OAU). 1981. *African charter on human and peoples' rights ("Banjul Charter")*. CAB/LEG/67/3 rev. 5, 21 I.L.M. 58 (1982). http://www.refworld.org/docid/3ae6b3630.html [Retrieved 6 November 2018].

Organization of American States (OAS). 1969. *American convention on human rights, "Pact of San Jose, Costa Rica"*. http://www.refworld.org/docid/3ae6b36510.html [Retrieved 6 November 2018].

Özarslan, Z. 2014. Introducing two new terms into the literature of hate speech: "Hate discourse" and "Hate speech act". Application of speech act theory into hate speech studies in the era of Web 2.0", İletişim, 20:53-75. http://iletisimdergisi.gsu.edu.tr/download/article-file/82871 [Retrieved 28 December 2018].

Pálmadóttir, J.A. & Kalenikova, I. 2018. *Hate speech; an overview and recommendations for combating it*. The Icelandic Human Rights Centre. http://www.humanrights.is/en/moya/news/hate-speecHan-overview-and-recommendations-for-combating-it [Retrieved 6 November 2018].

Pesinis, A. 2015. The regulation of "hate speech"; the meaning of "incitement" under the case-law of the European Court of Human Rights and the jurisdictions of the European Union, the United Kingdom and Greece. Unpublished LLM thesis, Budapest, Hungary: Central European University. www.etd.ceu.hu/2016/pesinis_antonios.pdf [Retrieved 28 December 2018].

Post, R. 2009. Hate speech. In: I. Hare & J. Weinstein (eds.), *Extreme speech and democracy*. Oxford: Oxford Academic Press. pp. 123-138. https://doi.org/10.1093/acprof:oso/9780199548781.003.0008

Robinson, P. & Ellis, N.C (eds.). 2008. *Handbook of cognitive linguistics and second language acquisition*. London: Routledge. https://www.academia.edu/6633691/HANDBOOK_OF_COGNITIVE_LINGUISTICS_AND_SECOND_LANGUAGE_ACQUISTION [Retrieved 28 December 2018].

Sbisà, M. 2009. Speech act theory. In: J. Verschueren & J. Östman (eds.), *Key notions for pragmatics*, Amsterdam: John Benjamins. pp. 229-244

Schwartzman, L.H. 2002. Hate speech, illocution, and social context: A critique of Judith Butler. *Journal of Social Philosophy*, 33(3):421-441. https://doi.org/10.1111/0047-2786.00151

Searle, J.R. 1969. *Speech acts: An essay in the philosophy of language*. Cambridge: Cambridge University Press. https://doi.org/10.1017/CBO9781139173438

Searle, J.R. 1975. A taxonomy of illocutionary acts. In: K. Gunderson (ed.), *Language, mind, and knowledge*. Minneapolis MN: University of Minnesota Press. pp. 344-369.

Searle, J.R. 1979. *Expression and meaning: Studies in the theory of speech acts*. Cambridge: Cambridge University Press.

Sherry, S. 1991. Speaking of virtue: A republican approach to university regulation on hate speech. *Minnesota Law Review*, 75:933-944.

Smolla, R. 1993. *Free speech in an open society*. New York: Vintage.

Sorial, S. 2014. Free speech, hate speech and the problem of (manufactured) authority. *Canadian Journal of Law and Society*, 29(1):59-75. https://doi.org/10.1017/cls.2013.43

South Africa. 1996. The Constitution of the Republic of South Africa, Act 106 of 1996. https://www.gov.za/documents/constitution-republic-soutHafrica-1996 [Retrieved 30 November 2018].

South Africa. 2018. Prevention and Combating of Hate Crimes and Hate Speech Bill. *Government Gazette*. (No. 41543). https://www.parliament.gov.za/storage/app/media/Docs/bill/9febb155-8582-4a15-bf12-5961db2828c2.pdf [Retrieved 28 December 2018].

Stalnaker, R.C. 1972. Pragmatics. In: G. Harman & D. Davidson (eds.), *Semantics of natural language*. Dordrecht: Reidel. pp. 380-397.

Tiersma, P.M. 1986. The language of offer and acceptance: Speech acts and the question of intent. *California Law Review*, 74(1):189-232.

Triggs, G. 2011. *International law: Contemporary principles and practices*, 2nd Edition. Sydney: LexisNexis Butterworths.

UN General Assembly. 1948. *Universal Declaration of Human Rights*. 217 A (III). http://www.refworld.org/docid/3ae6b3712c.html [Retrieved 6 November 2018].

UN General Assembly. 1966. *International Covenant on Civil and Political Rights*. United Nations, Treaty Series. http://www.refworld.org/docid/3ae6b3aa0.html [Retrieved 6 November 2018].

UN Human Rights Committee (HRC). 2011. *General comment No. 34, Article 19, Freedoms of opinion and expression*. CCPR/C/GC/34. http://www.refworld.org/docid/4ed34b562.html [Retrieved 6 November 2018].

Van den Berg (née Hattingh), K. 2012. The pragmatics of popular songs: Hate speech or patriotism? Paper presented at the Annual Joint Conference for SAALA/LSSA/SAALT. Bloemfontein, South Africa 25-20 June.

Van Staden, M. 2018. The Blog. Hate-speech bill: A threat to democracy in South Africa. *Huffington Post*, 3 May. https://www.huffingtonpost.co.za/martin-van-staden/hate-speech-bill-a-threat-to-democracy-in-south-africa_a_23374035 [Retrieved 19 June 2018].

Van Wyk, C. 2002. *The constitutional treatment of hate speech in South Africa*. 16th Congress of the International Academy of Comparative Law, Brisbane, 14-20 July 2002. http://www.stopracism.ca/content/hate-speechsouthafrica [Retrieved 4 June 2016].

Verschueren, J. & Brisard, F. 2009. Adaptability. In: J. Verschueren & J. Östman (eds.), *Key notions for pragmatics*. Amsterdam: John Benjamins. pp. 28-47.

Verschueren, J. 2009. Introduction: The pragmatic perspective. In: J. Verschueren & J. Östman (eds.), *Key notions for pragmatics*. Amsterdam: John Benjamins. pp. 1-27.

Wines, M. 2007. Song wakens injured pride of Afrikaners. *New York Times*. 27 February https://www.nytimes.com/2007/02/27/world/africa/27safrica.html [Retrieved 21 June 2018].

Zhang, Z. & Luo, L. 2018. *Hate speech detection: A solved problem? The challenging case of long tail on Twitter. Semantic Web* (in press). https://doi.org/10.3233/SW-180338

ABOUT THE CONTRIBUTORS

Mercy Akrofi Ansah is a Senior Research Fellow at the Institute of African Studies, University of Ghana. Her research interests include: the documentation and description of the grammar of minority languages; biographical studies; and the use of language in multilingual settings. In line with her primary interest in documenting and describing less-studied languages, she described the grammar of Leteh, a South-Guan language of Ghana, in her doctoral thesis (University of Manchester, UK), and has also published on this grammar in local and international journals. Her recent research and publications focus on language use in education with respect to minority languages; on language barriers in Ghanaian law courts and the role of the court interpreter; and on language barriers in the health sector, amongst others. She combines research and teaching at the Institute of African Studies, University of Ghana.

Celia Brown-Blake is a Senior Lecturer in Law at The University of the West Indies at Mona, Jamaica, and an attorney-at-law. With a Master of Laws and a PhD in Linguistics, she specialises in research on the impact of linguistic factors on the administration of justice where speakers of Caribbean vernacular languages, sometimes called "creole" languages, are involved. A key focus of her research has been the role that language rights may play in improving the situation of vernacular speakers in the English-dominant legal systems of the Common wealth Caribbean. She has published on the language communication difficulties arising between speakers of Jamaican and speakers of English in the criminal justice system in the UK and in Jamaica. In 2017 she was an international visiting scholar at Stanford Humanities Centre in the US where she developed and made presentations on the work that appears in this volume.

Terrence R. Carney is a Senior Lecturer at the University of South Africa where he teaches Afrikaans linguistics. His interest in forensic linguistics focuses mainly on semantic investigations into legal language. Apart from this, he also has a keen interest in language and gender studies.

Prince Ofei Darko is a Lecturer in African Studies at the African University College of Communications in Accra, Ghana. He holds a BA in Political Science with Classical History and Civilisation and an MPhil (African Studies) from the University of Ghana. He teaches the following undergraduate courses: Survey of African History I and II; African Diaspora Studies; and African Cultural Institutions. His research interest is social policy and social protection; child vulnerability and household insecurity; and human capital development of children. In researching these, he primarily uses qualitative methods underpinned by the view that people have varied experiences of vulnerability and related phenomena, hence the need for them to understand their own reality.

Annelise de Vries is a researcher in labour relations at the Solidarity Research Institution (SRI). She also holds the position of Director on the Afrikaans Language Board (ATR). Previous positions include: Language Planning Expert at AfriForum; Media Liaison Officer at AfriForum; and Lecturer in Afrikaans and Language Literacy at Aros, a private higher education institution. She is currently studying for a PhD in Forensic Linguistics at the University of Johannesburg. Her research interests include: language rights and activism; language in legal documents and in courts; and language policy in the higher education sphere.

Zakeera Docrat holds a BA Honours Degree (cum laude) in African Languages, an LLB and an MA (cum laude) in African Languages from Rhodes University. She is the recipient of several awards and fellowships: the 2018 Women in Science Award; the Albertina Sisulu Doctoral Fellowship; the African Languages Association of Southern Africa's "Most Outstanding Master's Thesis" for 2018; and is one of the 2018 *Mail & Guardian*'s 200 Young South Africans in the "Justice and Law" category. Her research is in the area of forensic linguistics (Language and Law) in which she has published widely. She is currently a full-time doctoral student in the Department of African Languages at Rhodes University, under the auspices of the NRF SARChI Chair in the Intellectualisation of African Languages, Multilingualism and Education.

Patson Kufakunesu is a lecturer in the Department of Linguistics of the University of Zimbabwe. He holds a BA, BA Special Honours, and MA in Applied Linguistics from the University of Zimbabwe. He also holds a Graduate Certificate in Education from the University of Zimbabwe and a Doctor of Literature and Philosophy from the University of South Africa. He teaches Academic and Professional Communication, Sociolinguistics, Applied Sociolinguistics, and Language Planning and Policy. His research interests lie in minority language studies, academic and corporate communication, sociolinguistics and discourse studies.

Ceyhan Sirma Kurt is a PhD candidate currently researching in the field of legal interpreting at Royal Melbourne Institute of Technology (RMIT University, Australia). Her study focuses on interpreter-mediated police investigative interviews, with special emphasis on the impact of an interpreter in cognitive police interviews and the effect of different interpreting modes. She is a NAATI-certified translator and interpreter in the language pair English-Turkish. She has been practising as a professional translator for more than 20 years and as an interpreter for more than 10 years in a wide range of community interpreting settings, mainly in court and police. She is also an English as an Additional Language (EAL) teacher and for many years has taught in EAL and English for Academic Purposes programmes for both local and international students in Melbourne. She is also an examiner on a number of language testing panels. She is interested in developing and delivering specialist training programmes, for both interpreters working in legal settings, and for the police.

Noleen Leach is the co-founder and Interim Co-ordinator of the Unit for Applied Law at the Cape Peninsula University of Technology (CPUT), and an attorney-at-law. She holds an honours degree in Education and a doctorate in Law from the University of the Western Cape. She is the project leader for Paralegal Curriculum Development at CPUT, and designer of the first degree in Paralegal Studies to be offered in South Africa. She is a recipient of the 2015 Doctoral Dissertation Proposal Fellowship from the international Social Science Research Council. Her research interests span Law, Language and Education, with the focus on access to justice, the transformation of the legal profession, and multilingualism in higher education.

Eliseu Mabasso is an Assistant Professor at Eduardo Mondlane University (UEM) in Maputo, Mozambique. He holds a PhD in Applied Linguistics for which he wrote a thesis entitled "Linguistic and Discursive Strategies in Police Interviewing: The Case of Police Stations in Maputo". He also holds an MLitt in the same field from the University of Sydney, Australia. He is particularly interested in police investigative interviewing and in cross-language and cross-cultural communication. He is known for being the first national to put together a course in Language and Law at UEM, probably the only such course offered in that country. With the Royal Melbourne Institute of Technology (RMIT University), Australia, he is currently engaged in a joint project to produce a plain language legal dictionary. He has published in local and international journals and chapters in books. He is co-author of a book on contrastive analysis of idioms in English, Portuguese and Shangaan, and also of two English language learners' books for Oxford University Press. Mabasso is currently Deputy Dean for undergraduates at the Faculty of Arts and Social Sciences, UEM.

Joseph MacFarlane is a current PhD candidate at the School of Global, Urban and Social Studies at RMIT University, Melbourne. His research focuses on the discretionary use of interpreters in the justice system and how the failure to recognise and cater for language difference reflects wider societal linguistic inequity and also creates an environment in which miscarriages of justice may arise. His masters' research focused on how managerialist concerns that emphasise the efficient and cost-effective processing of criminal cases serve to undermine the possibility of both procedural fairness for linguistically vulnerable people, and accurate outcomes in criminal cases. He has worked with RMIT University's Innocence Initiative, investigating claims of factual innocence.

Stanley Madonsela is an Associate Professor in the Department of African Languages at the University of South Africa. His involvement in language policy and planning led to his appointment as the Deputy Chairperson of the Gauteng Provincial Language Committee (GPLC). He is Academic Editor of the *Southern African Journal for Folklore Studies*, a journal accredited by the Department of Higher Education and Training (DHET). He has produced a number of research publications in various fields, including language policy and planning, sociolinguistics, and translation studies. He is actively involved in several collaborative research processes, such as The South African Centre for Digital Language Resources (SADiLaR) which supports research and development in the domains of language technologies and language related studies in the humanities and social sciences. His other research interests include semantics, and forensic linguistics.

Lirieka Meintjes-van der Walt holds the degrees B Juris, LLB (University of Port Elizabeth), LLM (Rhodes) and D Juris (Rijksunivesteit Leiden). Since 2005, she has been Adjunct Professor of Law at University of Fort Hare where she is currently Project Leader of the Law, Science and Justice Research niche area. Meintjes-Van der Walt practised at the Bar until she joined the academic staff of Rhodes University in 1994, where she was subsequently elected Deputy Dean of Law. In 2001, she received the Vice-Chancellor's Award for Distinguished Research at Rhodes. She has published prolifically in national and international peer-reviewed journals and books, and is the author of *Expert evidence in the criminal justice process: A comparative approach* (2001); and *DNA in the courtroom: Principles and practice* (2010), regarded as a seminal work on DNA evidence by the Supreme Court of Appeal in South Africa. She is the academic editor of the volume *Introduction to South African law: Fresh perspectives* (3rd edition forthcoming in 2019). She was rated an "Established Researcher" by the National Research Foundation and is an elected member of the Academy of Science of South Africa.

Theodore Rodrigues holds an MA in Applied Language Studies from North West University and is currently busy with his PhD in Linguistics at University of the Western Cape. His main fields of research include translation studies, reading comprehension, multilingual education, sociolinguistics, forensic linguistics and multimodal meaning-making in higher education. He has published a number of accredited articles and book chapters focusing on translation and applied language studies. He has also delivered a number of papers at national and international conferences.

Andy Roh is a current PhD candidate at the Royal Melbourne Institute of Technology (RMIT University), Australia. His research focuses on critically analysing Australian multicultural policy and its disconnect with the practices of the justice system, and aims to critique the symbolic rhetoric of multicultural policy as holding little substantive value for practical provision of high-quality interpreting support within legal contexts. Roh is a NAATI-certified interpreter in the language pair Korean-English and has worked in a wide range of community interpreting contexts. He has extensive experience working specifically within a justice context, interpreting during court proceedings and police interviews.

Michelle Surmon is a master's student in English at the School of Languages, North West University. Her research interests fall within forensic linguistics. In her master's dissertation, she is investigating the language of threatening texts, such as ransom notes, bribery, blackmail, fraudulent papers and hate mail. She is currently exploring the possibility of measuring the legitimacy of a threat text through compiling a framework of characteristic features key to a threat text and applying this framework to the text in question. She has also researched comedy and how language is used to create humour. She attended the International Association of Forensic Linguistics conference hosted in South Africa in 2017. She is an interpreter at North West University, translating both from Afrikaans to English, and English to Afrikaans.

Paul Svongoro is a Senior Lecturer in the Department of Linguistics of the University of Zimbabwe. He holds a PhD in Translation and Interpretation from the University of the Witwatersrand, South Africa; and an MA in Applied Linguistics and a BA (Honours) in Linguistics from the University of Zimbabwe. His interests are: corpus-based translation studies; court interpretation; the interface between language and the law; and academic and corporate communication. He has conducted consultancy projects in translation, transcription, text editing and proofreading. He has published in peer-reviewed journals such as *Per Linguam, Southern African Linguistics and Applied Language Studies* and *The South African Journal of African Languages*. He is currently working on developing programmes and teaching materials for corporate communication, liaison interpretation, and academic writing for students in Sub-Saharan Africa.

Karien van den Berg is a Senior Lecturer in English at the School of Languages, North-West University. Her research interests are in English Second Language (ESL) writing in general, with focus on: linguistic elements related to writing in terms of accuracy, fluency and complexity; investigation of the assessment of writing in relation to language testing and validation; forensic linguistic aspects of stylistic and statistical analyses of written text; vocabulary assessment; text messaging and ESL writing; trademark disputes; authorship attribution; and threat assessment. She held an exchange scholarship in teaching and studying English linguistics at University of Rostock, Germany, and has received international certificates in Applied Linguistics (Penn State University, US) and Language Assessment (Lancaster University, UK; and the European Association for Language Testing and Assessment, Spain). She has presented papers at multiple national and international conferences and published articles on various aspects of assessing written texts. She is a member of the South African Linguistics and Applied Linguistics Society; and of the South African Association for Language Teachers, on whose Executive Committee she served for six years. In addition, she supervises postgraduate research.

Kim Wallmach is the Director of Stellenbosch University's Language Centre in South Africa. She holds a PhD in Translation Studies from the University of the Witwatersrand, as well as an MA in Translation Studies and a BA with French and German as majors at the same institution. She has over twenty-five years' experience in higher education in the fields of language, translation, and interpreting. Her research interests include interpreting studies, liaison, court and conference interpreting, corpus-based translation and interpreting studies, multilingualism and blended learning.

www.ingramcontent.com/pod-product-compliance
Lightning Source LLC
Chambersburg PA
CBHW082058230426
43670CB00017B/2885